50 YEARS OF SOCIAL
ISSUES IN SINGAPORE

World Scientific Series on Singapore's 50 Years of Nation-Building

(Continued at end of book)

World Scientific Series on
Singapore: 50 Years of Nation-Building

SG
50

Foreword by Tharman Shanmugaratnam

Deputy Prime Minister of Singapore & Minister for Finance

50 Years of Social Issues in Singapore

Editor

David Chan

Singapore Management University, Singapore

World Scientific

NEW JERSEY · LONDON · SINGAPORE · BEIJING · SHANGHAI · HONG KONG · TAIPEI · CHENNAI

Published by

World Scientific Publishing Co. Pte. Ltd.

5 Toh Tuck Link, Singapore 596224

USA office: 27 Warren Street, Suite 401-402, Hackensack, NJ 07601

UK office: 57 Shelton Street, Covent Garden, London WC2H 9HE

Library of Congress Cataloging-in-Publication Data

50 years of social issues in Singapore / [edited by] David Chan, Singapore Management University, Singapore.
     pages cm. -- (World Scientific series on 50 years of nation-building)
   Includes bibliographical references.
     ISBN 978-9814632607 (hardcover : alk. paper) -- ISBN 978-9814632614 (pbk. : alk. paper) --
ISBN 978-9814696913 (hardcover with slip case: alk. paper)
   1. Singapore--Social conditions. 2. Singapore--Social policy. I. Chan, David (Industrial psychologist), editor.
II. Yap, Mui Teng. Ageing in Singapore. Container of (work): III. Title: Fifty years of social issues in
Singapore.
   HN700.67.A8A15 2015
   306.095957--dc23

                                                    2015004082

British Library Cataloguing-in-Publication Data
A catalogue record for this book is available from the British Library.

In-house Editor: Rajni Gamage

Typeset by Stallion Press
Email: enquiries@stallionpress.com

To all who want a Singapore society that
they can call a democracy of deeds and voices.

Foreword

When David Chan told me about this book, I thought it was a most worthwhile endeavour.

The book brings together a distinguished team of thinkers and scholars, to examine and reflect on a range of critical social issues that have received wide public and policy attention in Singapore. It is also one of the few volumes which explicitly link the historical evolution of our society to our current situation and future possibilities.

The values and aspirations that we embraced as a people when we had nationhood thrust on us are as relevant for our future as they were in 1965. To be one united people, regardless of race, language or religion. To be a society that is fair and just, where we progress together.

But the context in which we now strive to build our future is vastly different from what it was 50 years ago. Building a fair, inclusive and vibrant society is continuous work, and requires fresh strategies.

We are still a small nation in a world of much larger nations, but the world has changed. We have to earn our place, not in the region but globally, with both the most advanced countries and dynamic emerging players in the same arena. Conflict and tensions based on religious and sectarian beliefs have become more globalised, and a defining challenge of the times.

Our own society too is vastly transformed. Standards of living for most Singaporeans have increased five- to sixfold since the 1960s, including for the poorer in our society. But as both social mobility and income growth become slower, the need to temper inequality and life's disparities has grown. And while the Singaporean identity is strong and palpable after 50 years, we are more diverse in our preferences, and with a greater pursuit of the quality of life beyond the material.

But building a fair and inclusive society has to go beyond government redistributive schemes and social policy interventions, urban planning and developing new skills and economic capabilities. It is at its heart about achieving a stronger social compact for the future, where personal and collective responsibilities reinforce each other. Where everyone takes responsibility, for the family, for learning and continually improving, and for saving for retirement, but where we can also count on each other. It is about how we relate to each other: the respect we extend to each other as citizens, for the effort that each puts into their lives and the contributions each makes, in their own ways.

We must also keep thinking hard about how we can sustain a good society, not just for today but for our children's generation. The 50-year horizon, seen in some of the writings in this book, is not too far-fetched. They also display a healthy scrutiny of government policies, with many suggestions for improvement. It is part of a culture of active public discussion on policies that bodes well for our future. I am sure it will be aided in time by serious debate amongst scholars themselves, and within civil society, with thorough and dispassionate evaluation of analyses, perspectives and arguments.

We are building on the transformations we have achieved in our first 50 years, as we embark on our next phase of development as a nation. We must do so with the combination of imagination and practicality that made Singapore what it is today. With hard heads, but warm hearts too, so that we all move up together.

Mr Tharman Shanmugaratnam
Deputy Prime Minister & Minister for Finance

About the Editor

Professor David Chan received his PhD in Industrial and Organizational Psychology from Michigan State University. He is Lee Kuan Yew Fellow, Professor of Psychology and Director of the Behavioural Sciences Institute at the Singapore Management University (SMU). He is also Adjunct Principal Scientist at Singapore's Agency for Science, Technology and Research (A*STAR) and Co-Director of the Centre for Technology and Social-Behavioural Insights which is a centre jointly established by A*STAR and SMU. He was formerly the Deputy Provost of SMU and Deputy Director of the Wharton-SMU Research Centre.

Professor Chan's research includes areas in longitudinal modeling, personnel selection, adaptation to changes at work and subjective well-being. His works have been published in psychology, management and methods journals. He has co-authored with Neal Schmitt the textbook *Personnel Selection* published by Sage and edited the books *Individual Adaptability to Changes at Work* published by Routledge and *Liveability in Singapore* published by World Scientific.

In 2000, Professor Chan was ranked 9th worldwide in the list of Top 100 most published researchers of the 1990's in the top journals of Industrial and Organizational Psychology. His works have been cited over 3,000 times in various disciplines. He has received several international scholarly awards including the Edwin Ghiselli Award for Innovative Research Design, the William Owen Scholarly Achievement Award, and the Distinguished Early Career Contributions Award from the Society for Industrial and Organizational Psychology, and the Dissertation Research Award from the American Psychological Association.

He has served as Senior Editor of the *Asia Pacific Journal of Management*, Associate Editor of the *Journal of Organizational Behavior*, Advisory Editor for *Oxford Bibliographies (Management)* published by Oxford University Press, member on editorial boards of several journals and reviewer for grant agencies in United States, Hong Kong and Singapore.

Professor Chan is Consultant to the Prime Minister's Office and several government organisations in Singapore; a member of the National Council on

Problem Gambling (NCPG), Public Hygiene Council, Governing Board for the Workplace Safety and Health Institute, International Panel of Experts for the Urban Redevelopment Authority, Research Advisory Panel for the National Population and Talent Division, and Resource Panel for the National Environment Agency; a Director on the Board of the Singapore Corporation of Rehabilitative Enterprises; and Chairman of the International Advisory Panel to the NCPG & National Addictions Management Service.

He also does volunteer work as Scientific Advisor to the National Volunteer and Philanthropy Centre. He is a recipient of the Outstanding Volunteer Award from the Ministry of Social and Family Development.

Professor Chan writes op-ed articles in *The Straits Times*' By Invitation Series, which is a regular newspaper column on social issues. He is the consultant to the *Channel NewsAsia*'s "Social Experiment", which is a five-part programme series that examines human behaviours and social phenomena using scientific experiments, as well as "Days of Disasters", which is a five-part documentary series that examines the lessons learned from previous disasters in Singapore.

Together with Nobel Laureate in Economics, Professor Daniel Kahneman, and Professor Ed Diener, Professor Chan served on an international committee which submitted to the United Nations a report on measures of national well-being across countries. He is an Elected Fellow of the American Psychological Association, the Association for Psychological Science, the International Association of Applied Psychology and the Society for Industrial and Organizational Psychology.

About the Contributors

Ang Bee Lian is Director of Social Welfare at the Ministry of Social and Family Development. Her role includes providing independent views and advice on the standards of social work practice and the professional development of practitioners in the social service sector. She has served as the Chief Executive Officer of the National Council of Social Service. She was a member of the 2010 Censorship Review Committee and she currently serves as a member of the Films Appeal Committee. In 2000, she received the Outstanding Social Worker Award in Singapore.

David Chan is Lee Kuan Yew Fellow, Professor of Psychology and Director of the Behavioural Sciences Institute at the Singapore Management University. He is also Adjunct Principal Scientist at Singapore's Agency for Science, Technology and Research (A*STAR). He has received numerous international awards on scholarly achievement and scientific contributions. His works have been cited more than 3,000 times in journals and books in various disciplines. He has served as Editor or board member on several journals. He is consultant and board member to various organisations. He is Elected Fellow of four international psychological associations.

Willie Cheng is a former managing partner of Accenture, a global management consulting and technology services firm. He is a board member of UOB Bank, Far East Hospitality Asset Management, SingHealth and Integrated Health Information Systems. He is also a board member of several non-profit organisations including the Singapore Institute of Directors, Caritas Humanitarian Aid & Relief Initiatives, Singapore, apVentures, Council for the Third Age, Catholic Foundation, SymAsia Foundation and The Courage Fund. He has written extensively on the non-profit sector and authored a book on doing good well.

John Elliott is Associate Professor of Psychology at the National University of Singapore. Prior to joining the university, he worked as a psychologist at the then Ministry of Social Affairs and subsequently at the Department of Psychology, University of Sheffield. He is a member of the Resource Panel to the Singapore Police Psychological Services Division and he chairs the Research Committee of the Singapore Children's Society. He is a former member of the Bioethics Advisory Committee and the National Medical Ethics Committee in Singapore.

Christopher Gee is Research Fellow at the Institute of Policy Studies where he works in the Demography and Family Research Cluster. His research interests are focused on population-related issues, in particular housing, retirement and healthcare matters. He had worked in investment banking, analysing the real estate sectors in the Asian region. He was rated the top Singapore analyst in the Institutional Investor surveys from 2005 to 2010. He is also currently an independent Non-Executive Director of CapitaRetail China Trust Management Ltd.

Shirlena Huang is Associate Professor of Geography and Vice-Dean (Graduate Studies) at the Faculty of Arts and Social Sciences, National University of Singapore. She is also the current Chair of the Gender and Geography Commission of the International Geography Union. Her research interests are focused on gender and migration issues and urbanisation and heritage conservation in Singapore. She has authored articles and edited volumes in the areas of gender politics in the Asia Pacific region, women as transnational domestic workers, and cultural politics and talent migration in East Asia.

Mohammad Khamsya Bin Khidzer received his Master's degree in Sociology from the National University of Singapore. His research interests are focused on social inequalities, education and migration issues. He has also worked on research projects on urban poverty. He is a volunteer with TWC2 (Transient Workers Count Too) and Beyond Social Services.

Gillian Koh is Senior Research Fellow at the Institute of Policy Studies where she works in the Politics and Governance Research Cluster. Her research interests are focused on party and electoral politics, the development of civil society, state-society relations and citizen engagement in Singapore. She has conducted public opinion surveys on issues such as Singaporeans' sense of rootedness, citizenship and identity in the country, the integration of foreigners, social resilience and voter attitudes. She has published articles on civil society and political identities.

Tommy Koh is Ambassador-At-Large at the Ministry of Foreign Affairs, Chairman of the Centre for International Law and Rector of Tembusu College at the National University of Singapore. He is the Co-Chairman of the China–Singapore Forum, the India–Singapore Strategic Dialogue and the Japan–Singapore Symposium. He was Singapore's Permanent Representative to the United Nations in New York and Ambassador to the United States. He was also the Chief Negotiator for the USA–Singapore Free Trade Agreement. He has served as the United Nation Secretary-General's Special Envoy to Russia, Estonia, Latvia and Lithuania.

Jeremy Lim is Partner and Head of Health and Life Sciences Practice, Asia Pacific, Oliver Wyman. He had held different senior executive positions in both private and public sector organisations, including in the Ministry of Health. A medical doctor by training, he holds a Master's degree in public health from the Johns Hopkins School of Public Health and a Master's degree in medicine (surgery) from the National University of Singapore. He is the author of a book on the Singapore healthcare system. He also writes regularly for newspapers in Singapore.

Liu Thai Ker is an architect-planner and has been a Director of RSP Architects Planners & Engineers Pte Ltd since 1992. He is Chairman of the Centre for Liveable Cities and also an Adjunct Professor at the National University of Singapore and Nanyang Technological University. He is also a planning advisor to over 30 cities in China. He was formerly the Chief Executive Officer of the Housing and Development Board and the Urban Redevelopment Authority. He led the major revision of the Singapore Concept Plan.

Mathew Mathews is a Senior Research Fellow at the Institute of Policy Studies where he leads the Society and Identity Research Cluster. His research interests are focused on social cohesion and harmony in the context of racial, religious and nationality differences. He has published articles on immigrant integration in Singapore and the management of diversity. He is President of the Alive Community Network, Research Advisor to the Ministry of Social and Family Development, and a member on the advisory boards for OnePeople.sg and Hua Mei Centre for Successful Ageing.

Sharifah Mohamed is a lecturer in Republic Polytechnic where she teaches social research. Prior to joining the polytechnic, she worked at the Lien Centre for Social Innovation where she managed projects and research in the areas of philanthropy, social entrepreneurship and social innovation. She has co-authored and co-edited articles on unmet social needs and the social ecosystem in Singapore.

Mohamad Maliki Bin Osman is a Member of Parliament at the East Coast Group Representation Constituency. He is currently the Minister of State for National Development and Defence and Mayor of the South East District. He has led several government Inter-Ministry committees to address issues on vulnerable families and the elderly. He is Advisor to several voluntary welfare organisations. He obtained his PhD in Social Work from the University of Illinois at Urbana-Champaign. He was Assistant Professor of Social Work at the National University of Singapore from 1998 to 2004.

Manav Saxena is a Senior Consultant in the Health and Life Sciences Practice, Asia Pacific, Oliver Wyman. Prior to joining Oliver Wyman, he worked with the Ministry of Health in the areas of planning, development and implementation of specialty clinical services in the acute care sector. He has also worked with the National University Hospital in Singapore and academic medical centres in the United States.

Debbie Soon is a Research Associate at the Institute of Policy Studies. Prior to joining the institute, she worked for the Corporate and Marketing Communications

Division at the Singapore Workforce Development Agency. Her research interests are in the study of political identities, ideologies, and political communication. Her published work includes co-authored chapters on civil society, migration and identity issues. She received her Master's degree from the University of Essex in Sociology, and her Bachelor's degree from the National University of Singapore in Political Science.

Tan Ern Ser is Head of the Social Lab at the Institute of Policy Studies and Associate Professor of Sociology at the National University of Singapore. His research interests include social stratification, politics and democracy, welfare policy and ethnic relations. He has served as a consultant for several national social surveys on issues related to values and attitudes, national orientations and social stratification in Singapore. He is a member of the Research Advisory Panel for the Housing & Development Board. He was appointed a Justice of the Peace in 2013.

Tan Tarn How is a Senior Research Fellow at the Institute of Policy Studies. His research interests are focused on arts and cultural policy and media and Internet policy. He has published articles on the creative industries in Singapore, China and Korea. He has also conducted research on the management and regulation of media in Singapore and the impact of the Internet and social media on society. He was formerly a journalist, teacher and television scriptwriter. He is also a playwright and arts activist.

Astrid S. Tuminez is Microsoft's Regional Director of Legal and Corporate Affairs (Southeast Asia) and Adjunct Professor at the Lee Kuan Yew School of Public Policy. She is an Advisor to the Global Economic Symposium and the ASEAN Institute on Disability and Public Policy. She is also a Director of the Bank of the Philippine Islands; Singapore American School; and ASKI Global, an NGO that promotes entrepreneurship among Asian migrant workers. She holds a Master's degree in Soviet Studies from Harvard University and a PhD in Political Science from MIT.

Wong Meng Ee is Assistant Professor at the National Institute of Education where he teaches special education. His research interests are focused on special education and issues in disabilities and inclusive education. He is a recipient of the President's Social Service Award (2002). He is President of the Retinitis Pigmentosa Society, board member of SG Enable, and member of the Steering Committee for the 8th ASEAN ParaGames 2015. He has represented Singapore in swimming at regional and international meets including the 2002 Commonwealth Games. He is visually impaired.

Reuben Wong is Director of Studies at the College of Alice & Peter Tan, Jean Monnet Chair (European Integration and Foreign Policy) and Associate Professor of Political Science at the National University of Singapore. His research interests are focused on EU foreign policy and the politics of disability rights. He serves on the Singapore Institute of International Affairs Council and the EU Centre in Singapore. He is a former diplomat and a Fulbright scholar (2009).

Yap Mui Teng is Senior Research Fellow at the Institute of Policy Studies where she leads the Demography and Family Research Cluster. She is also an Associate of the Changing Family in Asia Cluster at the Asia Research Institute at the National University of Singapore. Her research interests are focused on policy responses to low fertility, migration policies, and health and social policies in ageing societies. She has formerly worked as a statistician in the Ministry of Health and the then Singapore Family Planning and Population Board.

Brenda S. A. Yeoh is Provost's Chair Professor of Geography and Dean of the Faculty of Arts and Social Sciences at the National University of Singapore. She is also the research leader of the Asian Migration Cluster at the Asia Research Institute at the university. Her research interests include the politics of space in colonial and postcolonial cities. She has published in a wide range of migration research in Asia, including cosmopolitanism and talent, gender and care migration, national identity and citizenship issues, globalising universities and international student mobilities, and international marriage migrants.

Preface

Social issues such as ageing population, social mobility, racial and religious harmony, and community building are matters that have an important impact on the people in a society. A good understanding of the various social issues will facilitate effective policy-making and constructive public actions. This involves knowing the historical context or background of how the social issue has developed over time. It also involves a linkage of the past and present to predict or anticipate the future. It is important to examine the relationships linking the past, present and future and to do so from a longer-term perspective, especially when the social context of Singapore is changing rapidly.

Understanding how people think, feel and act in various changing situations has become a key driver of effectiveness in addressing social issues. Clearly, an adequate understanding of cognition, emotion and behaviour requires an analysis that is rooted in the social and behavioural sciences. But in order to effectively address social issues, intellectual and practical perspectives need to be bridged. This requires a scientist-practitioner translational approach that enables science and practice to inform each other. This scientific analysis and translational approach is evident in all the chapters in this volume.

Collectively, the chapters provide a comprehensive review and examination of various critical social issues at multiple levels of analysis including the individual, group and society. The emphasis is people-centric, and the focus is on the critical ideas underlying public debates of social issues and their policy and practical implications.

The book is organised into three parts. Part I examines issues of population and social fundamentals in Singapore such as ageing, marriage, urban planning, healthcare, and racial and religious harmony.

In Chapter 1, Yap Mui Teng and Christopher Gee examine the social issues and policy challenges of ageing in Singapore. The chapter provides an overview of Singapore's demographic trends since the nation's independence in 1965, discusses the social issues and policies that arose from the demographic changes, and examines the state of the elderly person in terms of financial security, health and social well-being. The chapter ends with a discussion of future policy challenges.

John Elliott, in Chapter 2, extends the discussion of ageing by highlighting the need for policies to adopt a less pessimistic view of ageing. The chapter emphasises the diversity among elderly persons and notes that many of them are actually or potentially productive, both socially and economically. It cautions against policies that categorise elderly as a separate dependent group and argues that an inclusive Singapore society needs to focus on merit and not age.

One important challenge of an ageing population concerns healthcare needs, but the social issues need to be understood in the context of Singapore's healthcare system. Chapter 3, by Jeremy Lim and Manav Saxena, examines the evolution of the socio-political philosophy underlying health services planning and financing in Singapore. The chapter highlights several areas of health and healthcare that require more policy and public attention.

In addition to increasing lifespan, the causes of an ageing population in Singapore are falling marriage and fertility rates, delayed age at first marriage and rising singlehood, which constitute the focus of Chapter 4 by Paulin Straughan. The chapter discusses the social issues concerning marriage and parenthood and the adequacy of the state's interventions.

To address the social and economic challenges of a rapidly ageing population, Singapore has responded with rapid foreigner intake and immigration. This has led to a rapid increase in the size and diversity of the Singapore total population, which in turn brought about issues related to social integration and urban planning. One aspect of diversity and social integration that deserves more attention is the implications of and on the multicultural policies in Singapore. Chapter 5 by Mathew Mathews and Mohammad Khamsya Bin Khidzer discuss these social issues and contexts relating to Singapore's efforts in preserving racial and religious harmony.

The problem of infrastructure support for the rapid and large increase in population size has made clear the importance of effective urban planning that is forward-looking. However, urban planning is much more than increasing physical capacity to accommodate more people. It is about enhancing the living conditions and increasing people's quality of life, and often involves influencing people's way of life. As Singapore moves forward with a more sophisticated urban planning that incorporates social and behavioural factors, it is important to understand the historical context of urban planning in Singapore which in fact has a large focus on the social dimension. Chapter 6, by Liu Thai Ker and Astrid S. Tuminez, provides a useful account of how social factors were considered, particularly in the development of public housing in Singapore. The chapter ends with some useful guiding principles for urban planners and policy-makers.

Part II analyses Singapore's social progress through issues of inclusivity such as social mobility, developing communities and marginal groups that deserve more attention.

In Chapter 7, Tan Ern Ser uses the analogy of a game to examine social mobility and its relationships with social class, inequality and the Singapore Dream. The chapter links the historical changes in social mobility to the current situation and provides several policy recommendations.

An inclusive society will need to pay attention to people in the lower strata of a socially stratified society, but also to many other groups of people who are in need of social services. In this regard, trained social workers have been playing important roles in building inclusivity, long before the term of inclusive society was used in policy discourse. In Chapter 8, Ang Bee Lian reviews the contributions of the social work profession in conceptualising, planning and delivering the variety of social services to individuals and families, including the efforts to strengthen social institutions and social welfare functions to adapt to changing social realities.

Chapter 9, by Reuben Wong and Wong Meng Ee, examines inclusivity in relation to persons with disabilities. The chapter provides a historical overview of Singapore's policy progress on issues related to disabilities and examines the specific areas of employment and accessibility. It notes the gradual shift in the disability paradigm in Singapore from a medical model to a social model that focuses on human rights and social well-being.

Another marginal group that deserves more attention is foreign domestic workers who play a crucial role for housekeeping and care for many families in Singapore. An inclusive society is at odds with one that ignores this marginal group or treats them badly. This is the subject of Chapter 10 by Shirlena Huang and Brenda S. A. Yeoh. The chapter provides a historical and social context of Singapore's reliance on foreign domestic workers. It ends with a call for more attention to be paid to how Singapore treats foreign domestic workers.

In Chapter 11, Mohamad Maliki Bin Osman shares his experiences and views on community building in Singapore. The chapter emphasises the need for community development to go beyond organising mass activities for people of different groups to intermingle. It notes the increasing complexity of social issues that require community engagement and intervention, which is often beyond what the government alone can do. It highlights the importance of understanding the local manifestations of social issues in specific community contexts, building trust, and developing mutual self-help and resilience in the community.

Civil society organisations play an important role in promoting inclusivity and social progress. Gillian Koh and Debbie Soon, in Chapter 12, describe the current landscape of the civil society in Singapore and relate it to the historical context of civic activism in the country. The chapter ends with a discussion of the emerging trends in civil society and possible future directions.

Part III focuses on core principles and social processes related to social justice, doing good, social media, and approaches to understanding and addressing social issues in Singapore. The chapters in this part highlight several general themes in social issues that cut across the specific areas discussed in the earlier chapters in Part I and II.

To begin with, Tommy Koh articulates in Chapter 13 his personal reflections on social justice in Singapore. He suggests that Singapore is both a socially just and socially unjust society. To explain his assessment, he highlights several issues such as gender, racial and religious equality, meeting basic needs, education, income and wealth inequality, wages, and the needy.

Many individual and community efforts to address social issues involve the ability and the willingness to do good in society. As explained by Willie Cheng and Sharifah Mohamed in Chapter 14, it is important to relate doing good in society to the dynamics of the social sector in Singapore. The chapter discusses the social ecosystem in Singapore, describes the history of the social sector and the major changes that have shaped the sector, and suggests several factors that could affect the sector's future.

A contemporary volume on social issues in Singapore is incomplete without a chapter discussing the relationship between social media and social issues. In Chapter 14, Tan Tarn How examines how social media influences the way that social issues are raised and discussed in Singapore, which in turn affects how these issues develop and the behaviours of the various stakeholders in the issues.

Finally, in Chapter 16, I share my views on what is important in understanding and addressing social issues in Singapore.

On behalf of our team of authors, we hope readers will find this book a useful resource for making sense of Singapore society. Most importantly, we hope readers will identify many of the critical, unresolved and emerging questions on various social issues that will guide public discussion and policy deliberations on what matter in Singapore.

Professor David Chan
Lee Kuan Yew Fellow
Director, Behavioural Sciences Institute
Singapore Management University

Contents

PART I

Population and Social Fundamentals

Chapter 1

Ageing in Singapore:
Social Issues and Policy Challenges

Yap Mui Teng and Christopher Gee[1]

Singapore's transition from a young, rapidly growing, high fertility population into a rapidly ageing one with prolonged low, below replacement fertility and low domestic population growth is one of the most significant social transformations the country has undergone over the last fifty years (Yap, 2010, p. 183).

In 1970, the total population of Singapore registered at two million. Since then, Singapore's population has nearly tripled in size to 5.4 million in 2014 (Department of Statistics [DOS], 2014). Underlying this population boom however, is a myriad of demographic developments that has fundamentally altered the small island state's population structure within a relatively short time span of 50 years. From a young nation-state in 1970 where the median age of its population was 19.5 years, the median age has now doubled to 39.3 years in 2014 (*ibid.*) which makes Singapore one of the fastest ageing countries in the world. This demographic shift is even more pronounced when compared to its ASEAN neighbours. Numerically, Singapore has the lowest number of elderly (defined as those aged 60 years and older), at about 814,000, compared to other countries such as Indonesia which had over two million elderly in 2012 (United Nations [UN], 2012). Yet amongst the 10 ASEAN countries, Singapore has the highest proportion of the population that is elderly, at 15.6%. Comparatively, the elderly in other ASEAN nations (with the exception of Thailand) make up less than 10% of the population, with Laos registering a mere 5.7%, making it the "youngest" of the 10 countries (*ibid.*).

---

[1]The authors would like to acknowledge the invaluable assistance of Ms Lynn Sim Hwee Joo in producing this chapter.

The issue of a rapidly ageing Singapore population has now reached an important turning point. According to DOS projections, the proportion of the aged will rise to 18.7% of the resident population in 2030 with nearly 900,000 persons in this age category. Simply put, roughly one in five of Singapore's population will be elderly in less than two decades. This presents significant social, economic and political implications to this small, highly urbanised and industrialised nation-state (Yap, 2010). This chapter will begin with an overview of Singapore's demographic trends since the nation's independence in 1965. Next, both the public and private spheres of ageing will be examined. The public sphere of ageing will cover the social issues arising out of this demographic shift in tandem with the policies that have been put in place thus far. The private sphere of ageing will examine the state of the elderly person in terms of financial security, health and social well-being. The chapter will end with a discussion of the possible policy challenges ahead.

Singapore's demography: Declining fertility, greater life expectancy and liberal immigration policy

As elsewhere, population ageing in Singapore is influenced by changes in fertility, mortality and migration. These processes have shaped the age-sex structure of Singapore's population, which has shifted from one of a typical pyramid in 1970 to what has been called a "beehive" shape in 2010 (see Figure 1.1).

The country experienced an extended baby boom in the post-World War II period, lasting from about 1947 to 1964. The total fertility rate (TFR, or average number of children a woman could expect to have over her lifetime at fertility levels prevalent in the particular year) reached an unprecedented TFR of 6.56 children per woman in 1957 while annual births averaged about 60,000 over the period 1956–65 (DOS, 2002). This high fertility trend tapered down in the mid-1960s following Singapore's independence. A strict family planning programme in the 1970s as well as improving social and economic circumstances saw the TFR fall to the replacement level of 2.1 in 1975 and 1976, with annual births falling to about 46,000 over the period 1966–76. By 1977, the TFR fell below the replacement level and continued to fall thereafter (Yap, 2010). From the mid-1980s, the government changed its anti-natalist stance to one that was decidedly pro-natalist to curb the declining fertility rate. The new population policy "Have three, or more if you can afford it" was officially launched on 1 March 1987. Subsequent measures to boost fertility rates, however, yielded little results and Singapore now ranks among countries with the "lowest-low" fertility levels of 1.3 children per woman or lower — along with Japan, Korea, Hong Kong, and the Southern, Central and Eastern European countries. The TFR among Singapore's resident population, comprising citizens and permanent residents, in 2013 (the latest year for which data are available) is only 1.19 children per woman, with births numbering only 39,720 (*ibid.*).

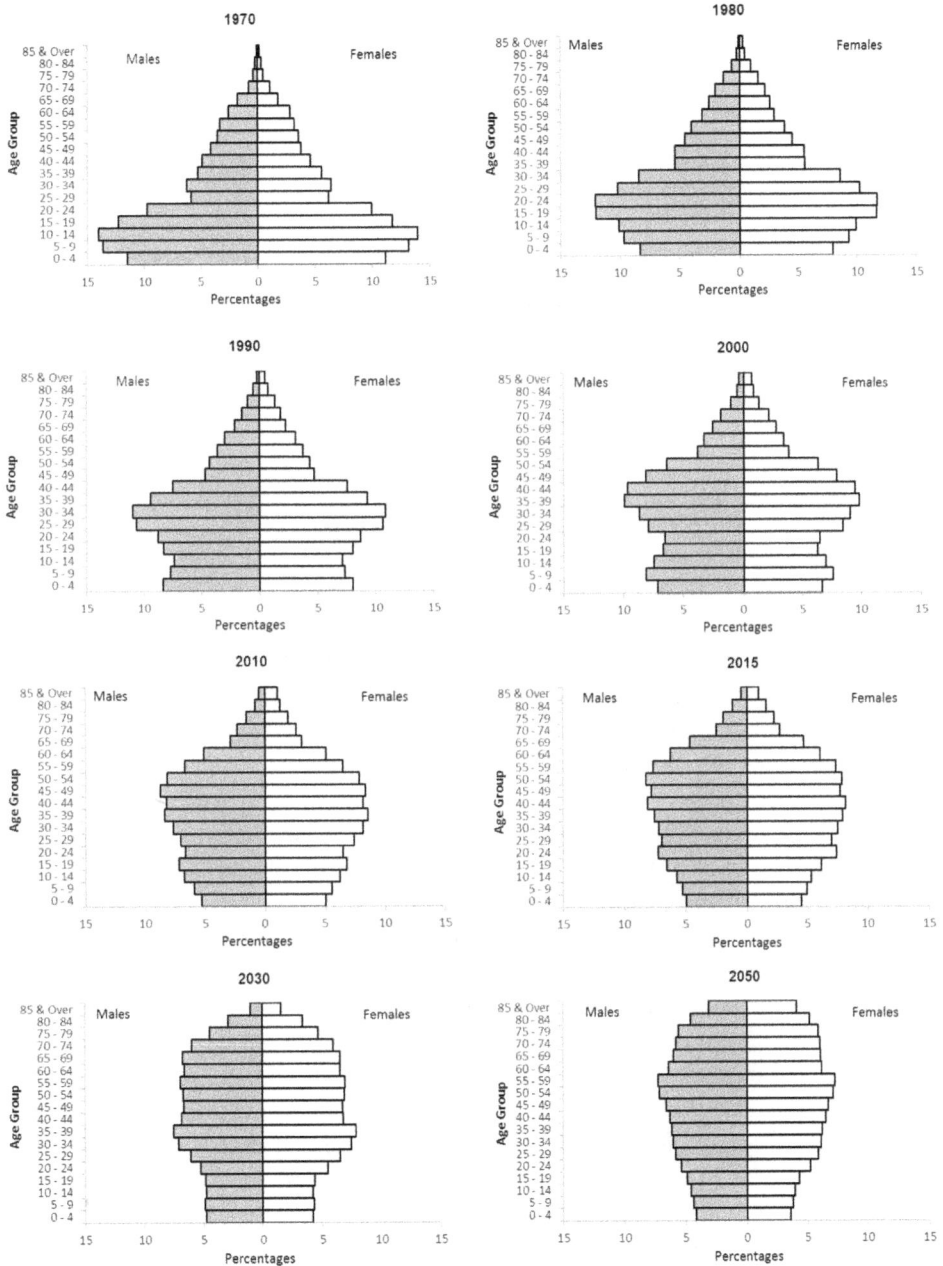

Fig. 1.1   Age-Sex Structure of the Singapore Resident Population, 1970–2050.

Source: DOS, Census 1970, 1980, 1990, 2000 and 2010 for historical data; Institute of Policy Studies (IPS) 2011, Population Projections 2005–2050, Scenario 2 for 2015, 2030 and 2050.

Table 1.1   Life Expectancy at Birth (Years).

	1970	1980	1990	2000	2010	2012	2013
Total	65.8	72.1	75.3	78.0	81.7	82.1	82.5
Males	64.1	69.8	73.1	76.0	79.2	79.8	80.2
Females	67.8	74.7	77.6	80.0	84.0	84.3	84.6

Source: DOS, Population Trends 2014.

Table 1.2   Age Composition of Resident Population (%), 1970–2014.

Age	1970	1980	1990	2000	2010	2014
0–14	39.1	27.6	23.0	21.9	17.4	15.7
15–64	57.5	67.5	71.0	70.9	73.7	73.1
65 and over	3.4	4.9	6.0	7.2	9.0	11.2
Total	100.0	100.0	100.0	100.0	100.0	100.0
Number ('000)	2,013.6	2,282.1	2,735.9	3,273.4	3,771.7	3,870.7

Source: DOS, Population Trends 2014.

Conversely, total life expectancy at birth rose from 65.8 years in 1970 to 82.5 in 2013 (see Table 1.1), an impressive gain of over 16 years. Women at 84.6 years outlive men at 80.2 years by 4.4 years, making Singapore the fourth and the fifth in the world for best life expectancy for women and men respectively (World Health Organization [WHO], 2014). Life expectancy at age 65 also rose from only 8.4 years to 20.6 years (22 years for females, 18.8 years for males) over the same period (Ministry of Health [MOH], 2014c). With smaller cohorts of babies born and longer lifespans, the proportion of the young aged 0–14 years has declined while the proportion of the elderly aged 65 and older has risen considerably (see Table 1.2).

In spite of a continued below-replacement level fertility, the number and proportion of the population in the middle-age band, 15–64 years, typically referred to as the working age population, has continued to grow. This was primarily due to a more relaxed immigration policy implemented by the government in the 1980s in response to the declining birth rates. The immigration policy was further liberalised in the 1990s to attract foreign talent with skills and qualifications to augment the existing workforce (Yap, 2010). To date, foreign workers make-up approximately 1.3 million or 38% of the total labour force (Ministry of Manpower [MOM], 2014a). Such foreigners are encouraged to become permanent residents (PRs) and eventually citizens. The number of new PRs rose steadily over the years and reached its peak at 79,167 in 2008 while new citizenships was at 20,513. Thereafter, the influx of new PRs has been moderated to below 30,000 from 2010 to 2013 while new citizenships remained relatively stable, hovering around 19,000 per year over the same period (The National Population and Talent Division [NPTD], DOS, Ministry of Home Affairs [MHA] & Immigrations & Checkpoint Authority [ICA], 2014, p. 13).

The elderly in Singapore

Current elderly

Preparation for an ageing population is a complex issue. A successful ageing policy takes into consideration not just the numerical aspects of ageing but also reflects an in-depth understanding of the elderly cohort in terms of their profiles and expectations. Different age cohorts brings with them distinct characteristics which in turn influence their outlook towards issues such as retirement, expectations of caregiving, etc. Other social determinants such as educational attainment, gender and ethnicity also play a part in influencing one's ageing trajectory. Singapore's current elderly generally have lower educational attainment compared to their younger cohorts (see Table 1.3). Due to the economic and social circumstances then, only 7.9% for those aged 65 years and over have tertiary qualifications compared to the younger age cohorts, where nearly one-third of those aged 50–54 years are tertiary educated. There is also a discrepancy between the male and female elderly in this area where 86.2% of female elderly reported below secondary qualifications compared to 71.3% of male elderly (DOS, 2011). These differences are likely to have an impact on their life-time employment, earnings and more importantly, their ability to adequately save for their retirement needs compared to their male counterparts (Yap & Kang, 2010).

Not only has the elderly proportion grown but the elderly, as a group, are themselves getting older with longer life expectancy. Those in the age cohort 75 years and over have become a larger proportion of the elderly population, from slightly over 27.5% in 1980, to 37.9% in 2014 (DOS, 2014). There are also proportionately more women than men and this increases with each older age cohort, signifying a feminisation of ageing trend which is consistent with demographic trends elsewhere in the world (see Table 1.4).

Almost all of Singapore's current elderly have ever married. This has implications for old-age support, in particular, the availability of family members as informal caregivers. On a positive note, the current elderly have access to greater caregiving

Table 1.3   Residents Aged 50 Years and over by Highest Qualifications Attained, Age Group, 2013.

	50–54 Years	55–59 Years	60–64 Years	65 Years & over
Below secondary	34.3%	43.5%	52.0%	73.9%
Secondary	27.5%	25.6%	24.5%	13.6%
Post-secondary (non-tertiary)	10.6%	10.1%	7.6%	4.6%
Diploma & prof. qualification	10.5%	8.5%	6.8%	3.6%
University	17.1%	12.3%	9.2%	4.3%
Total	100.0%	100.0%	100.0%	100.0%

Source: DOS, Population Trends 2014.

Table 1.4   Age Composition (%) and Sex Ratios.

Age Group	Total	Males	Females	Sex Ratio (males per 100 females)
65–69	37.3%	40.4%	34.9%	94.4
70–74	24.7%	25.5%	24.1%	86.2
75–79	17.7%	17.4%	17.9%	79.3
80–84	11.2%	10.1%	12.2%	67.5
85 and over	9.0%	6.7%	10.9%	49.8
Total	100.0%	100.0%	100.0%	—
Number	431,601	193,921	237,680	81.6

Source: DOS, Population Trends 2014.

and financial support from their children as nearly half have had five or more children. As shown in Table 1.5, the National Survey on Senior Citizens (NSSC) 2011 revealed that a significant number of them (44.3%) are also living with their family members in varying combinations while 12.2% live with their spouses (Ministry of Social and Family Development [MSF], 2013, p. 19). However, comparisons across different time frames revealed significant changes in the living arrangements of the elderly. More elderly are living alone rising from 3.1% in 1995 to 14.9% in 2011. Other types of living arrangements such as living with friends, siblings or unrelated individuals also surged to 28.6% in 2011 from a mere 5.6% in 1995. This rise is even more prominent for those aged 75 and above, with an overall increase of 37.7% in 2011 when compared to 1995 (*ibid.*, p. 22).

The NSSC 2011 showed that the majority of the elderly are still fairly independent. Specifically, 96% of them reported that they are ambulant and physically independent. This increased to 98% when those who are ambulant with a walking aid are included. In addition, the family is still a main source of support for the current elderly with 66.7% of the respondents citing income transfers from children as one of their main sources of income, which has not changed much from the 66% in 2005. As expected, those aged 75 and above received the highest level of support at 80.2%. The female elderly also tend to rely more on their children as 74.8% of them cited income transfers form their children compared to their male counterparts with 57.5% (MSF, 2011, p. 39).

Baby boomers

Despite the projected challenges anticipated with a rapidly ageing population, the picture seems less bleak when taking into consideration the profiles of the future elderly, namely, the baby boomers born immediately after World War II to 1964 and numbering approximately 900,000. According to Yap and Kang (2010), the baby boomers would have benefitted from the economic and social transformation that has characterised post-independence Singapore. Although there are some differences

Table 1.5   Living Arrangements of Those Aged 55 and above, 1995–2011.

	Total 55 and above	Age Group		
		55–64	65–74	75 and above
Living Arrangement 2011				
Total	100	100	100	100
Living alone	14.9	13.2	17.5	16.6
Living with spouse only	12.2	10.8	15.4	11.8
Living with spouse and children, no grandchildren	32.6	42.3	24.2	12.5
Living with spouse and grandchildren or great-grandchildren, no children	0.7	0.6	1	0.4
Living with spouse and children and grandchildren	6.5	6	8.1	5.8
Living with children and/or grandchildren, no spouse	4.5	3	5.4	8.3
Other living arrangements	28.6	24.1	28.4	44.7
Living Arrangement 1995				
Total	100	100	100	100
Living alone	3.1	2.7	2.9	4.4
Living with spouse only	5.2	4.2	7.3	4.5
Living with spouse and children, no grandchildren	37.1	51	25.8	14.2
Living with spouse and grandchildren or great-grandchildren, no children	—	—	—	—
Living with spouse and children and grandchildren	12.1	11.8	14	9.7
Living with children and/or grandchildren, no spouse	37	25.1	44.8	60.1
Other living arrangements	5.6	5.3	5.3	7

Source: NSSC 2011.

between the early and late baby boomers, those in this cohort, when compared to the current elderly, are generally better educated, hold higher skilled jobs and have greater real incomes. Gender differences remain but are narrowing. Additionally, the baby boomers differ from the currently elderly as more prefer independent living with their spouse. They are also less adverse to alternative living arrangements such as retirement villages and nursing homes. However, the sheer size of their numbers and better educational statuses could mean a greater political clout and a stronger influence over government policies on ageing.

Social issues arising from an ageing population

Much of the 1970s was devoted to assertive anti-natalist policies as a means to curb the burgeoning population that marked the first two decades following World War II. When it became clear that Singapore's population growth was stagnating

**Persons Aged 65 and over per 100
Youths 0–14 Years**

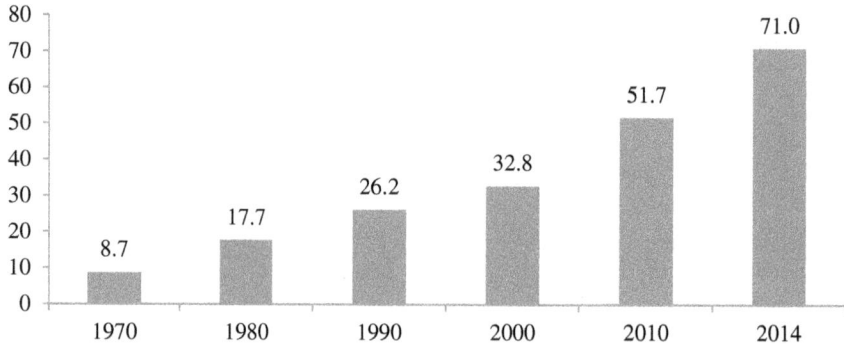

Fig. 1.2   Ageing Index, 1970–2014.

Source: Report on the State of the Elderly 2009 Release 1, MSF (2009) (based on Census 1970, 1980, 1990 and 2000) and DOS, Population Trends 2014.

in the early 1980s, the Committee on the Problems of the Aged was convened in 1984 to study the effects of population ageing in Singapore. Since then, the discussion on Singapore's major demographic shifts has steadily gained momentum. Policy-makers, demographers and academics alike delved deeper into the effects that an ageing society will have on healthcare, social security systems, future economic prosperity and political development. Demographers are interested in examining various summary indicators that describe and compare age structures of the population over time. The Ageing Index (see Figure 1.2) refers to the ratio of elderly aged 65 and over to the young aged 0–14 years. Whereas there were only 8.7 elderly per 100 youths in 1970, this figure has risen steadily to 71 in 2014. In other words, whereas there were more than 11 children to each elderly in 1970, this ratio has declined to fewer than two per elderly in 2014. This figure may be expected to decline further as low fertility continues. The Resident Old Age Support Ratio (see Figure 1.3) measures the number of working age population available (aged 20–64 years) to support each elderly (aged 65 years and over). This figure has also fallen by more than half from 13.5 per elderly in 1970, to 6 per elderly in 2014.

The rising Ageing Index and declining Old-Age Support Ratio will have a tremendous impact on the availability of support for the growing aged population. More specifically, it will have implications on the size of those in the working age population, the middle-age band that powers the economy and provides support to young and old. This segment is projected to decline to about 66% in 2030 (NPTD, 2013) from more than 70% currently as shown in Table 1.6 below.

Currently, the prolonged low, below-replacement fertility level has little impact on the population in the working ages due to the demographic bonus as the large

Resident Old-Age Support Ratio

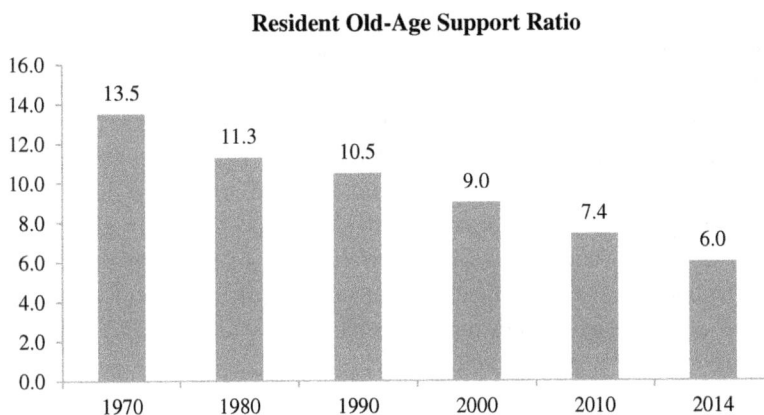

Fig. 1.3   Resident Old-Age Support Ratio.

Source: DOS, Chart on Resident Old-Age Support Ratio 2014.

Table 1.6   Age Composition of Resident Population, 1970–2014.

	1980	1990	2000	2008	2014
No. of resident population (000)	2,282.1	2,735.9	3,273.4	3,742.7	3,870.7
Age distribution (%)					
0–14 years	27.6	23.0	21.9	18.4	15.7
15–64 years	67.5	71.0	70.9	72.9	73.1
65 years & over	4.9	6.0	7.2	8.7	11.2
Total	100.0	100.0	100.0	100.0	100.0

Source: DOS, Population Trends 2014.

baby boom cohorts mature and move through the productive ages. However, the first wave of the baby boomers has hit age 65 in 2012 and subsequent cohorts will continue to swell the numbers of Singapore's elderly population. In 2012, there were 245,000 workers entering working age while another 123,000 exiting working age. This works out to roughly two citizens entering working age for every once citizen exiting. The picture will be significantly less rosy by 2030 as the projected numbers (assuming current birth rates and no immigration from 2013 onwards) show that only 171,000 citizens will enter working age versus 258,000 workers exiting (The National Population and Talent Division [NPTD], 2013, p. 11). Singapore's workforce is also maturing, where the median age of the workforce has increased from 39 years in 2003, to 42 year in 2013 (MOM, 2014a). This will rise further to 45 years by 2025 (NPTD, 2013, p. 10). With a smaller projected working age population, questions to be raised include whether the economy can continue to grow, or if productivity can be raised enough to offset the decline in the size of the workforce. Can an older workforce adopt new technology as quickly as a young one?

Immigration may help to ameliorate some of these effects. However, this is not an end all and be all solution. Projections prepared by the Institute of Policy Studies (IPS) suggest that the proportion in the working ages will not return to the present level even with a very high level of net immigration of about 100,000 annually from 2005 onwards if the TFR remains at the current ultra-low levels (Yap & Shantakumar, forthcoming). An unbridled influx of foreign labour also brings with it another set of complications. There are growing concerns that social cohesion may be affected by the presence of an extremely large pool of foreigners. The government has an uphill task of carefully calibrating its immigration policy to meet the manpower shortage while preserving the integrity of Singapore's social core, as well as orchestrating a comprehensive framework that will enable its elderly to continue to be active contributing members of society.

While increasing longevity is a cause for celebration, the possibility of the added years spent in poor health or financial inadequacy is a main source of worry for many elderly. Indeed the saying "one can die but cannot fall sick" has become a common catchphrase amongst the old in Singapore. Smaller family sizes also imply an increased burden on the younger population to provide for the elderly in their family, be it financially or physical care. As Singaporeans marry and start their families later, many fall into the "sandwiched generation" category, where they face the pressure of juggling between caring for their elderly parents and their young offspring. This can result in higher caregiver burden and adverse health consequences for the caregivers themselves (Chan *et al.*, 2013). With declining fertility rates and rising singlehood, more Singaporeans are also likely to approach old age with no children to provide for them.

At the national level, we are faced with the dual challenges of a projected increase in national health expenditure which is projected to triple to 12 million a year by 2020 (Saad, 2014, para. 1) and a shrinking tax paying population to finance the increase burden. Although Singapore, with its mandatory Central Provident Fund (CPF) scheme, is spared the funding problems of the pension schemes that have plagued their Western counterparts, the question remains as to whether savings accumulated under the current rules will be adequate in view of changing retirement expectations and increase in longevity. Demand for public health services and facilities will increase as the population ages. Already, public hospitals are showing signs of strain in terms of providing sufficient hospital beds. Part of the bed crunch problem is attributed to the growing elderly population as statistics show that public hospital admission for patients aged 65 and over has increased from 28.6% in 2006 to 33.4% in 2013. The average length of hospitalisation stay for this age cohort has also lengthened from 7.8 days in 2010 to 8.2 in 2013 (Gan, 2014a). The strain on health-care services and infrastructure will likely escalate in the future as studies show that longer life expectancy comes at a price of more years in disability (Khalid, 2012, para. 1).

The public sphere of ageing — The state's response

Old age is conventionally the lifecycle stage associated with retirement, withdrawal from the workforce as well as greater health and social care needs (Yap, 2010). Perhaps it should come as no surprise that terms such as the "silver tsunami" (Lee, 2006), or "tidal waves" (Khaw, 2009) started to emerge in the ageing discourse over the last two decades, painting a vivid pictorial depiction of a rapidly growing number of the elderly that could potentially overpower a dwindling younger populace. The development of an overarching national framework for ageing becomes all the more imperative as it sets the strategic direction for the umbrella of policies and initiatives that will help the elderly age successfully.

Development of a successful ageing agenda

As mentioned earlier, the Committee on the Problems of the Aged, chaired by the then Health Minister Howe Yoon Cheong, was set up to identify and tackle the "problems" that a greying population would bring. The committee tabled a report (MOH, 1984) which highlighted the concerns that an ageing population may result in an elderly population that could grow increasingly alienated from their family, the community and society as a whole. Escalating medical costs due to old-age-related frailty and diseases was another major concern.

Adding to the complexity of the ageing landscape, Singapore in the 1980s, was also on the cusp of rapid social changes. Urbanisation had resulted in the resettlement of large sections of the population from tightly-knitted clusters in *kampongs* and rural communities to high-rise housing units in new housing estates. The post-independence economic boom provided ample opportunities for more women, the conventional source of caregivers, to work instead of staying at home. Additionally, the confluence of an educational system that de-emphasised moral education, coupled with exposure to Westernised ideals that promoted "a more materialistic, self-orientated and individualistic way of life", led the committee to lament the possible erosion of Asian traditions and cultural concepts; the social glue integral to ensuring a strong support system for the elderly.

The main policy direction adopted by the 1982 committee then was one that is decidedly self-reliant and involves minimal intervention from the state. The elderly should be independent and continue living in the community for as long as possible; the family should be the first line of support; and where needed, they will be supported by services in the community. Institutionalisation should be a last resort (Yap & Kang, 2010, p. 174). This sparked the genesis of the "Many Helping Hands" approach for community care and has come to be the modus operandi of the government since. The policy comprised the following four elements:

1) Activity through continued employment and participation in family;
2) Financial independence with a regular income;

3) Organised community activities to involve the elderly and integrate them in the community. Voluntary community organisations can provide ancillary nursing and other healthcare services to supplement the effort of family members; and

4) Traditional family system to be strengthened through moral education and the inculcation of the virtues of filial piety, respect for the elderly in the family, and general reverence for old age.

Despite the public backlash that mired the 1982 Howe Report, primarily due to its recommendation of raising the CPF withdrawal age beyond 55 years, the basic principles of physical and financial independence in old age, integration of the elderly in the family, and community care over institutionalisation continue to feature prominently in the various committee's recommendation and continues to underpin the government's approach towards the elderly. Several committees on ageing were set up in the ensuing years: The Advisory Council on the Aged from 1988–1989, followed by the National Advisory Council on the Family and the Aged (NACFA) from 1989–1998.

When the Inter-Ministerial Committee on the Ageing Population (IMC) was set up in 1998 (and reconstituted in 2003), the approach taken has notably shifted from one of seeing the ageing population as a "problem" to one of challenges and opportunities. IMC proposed that the Successful Ageing framework be adopted where senior citizens are viewed as healthy, active, financially secure and independent people who are an integral part of their extended families and communities, maintaining a supportive and mutually interdependent relationship with them. The ultimate goal is to foster an inclusive, cohesive and economically vibrant society with strong intergenerational bonds (Balakrishnan, 2005). The Committee on Ageing Issues (CAI), set up in 2004, focused on "empowering seniors" through elder-friendly housing, a barrier-free society, holistic and affordable healthcare and eldercare, and active lifestyles and well-being.

State policies on ageing

To enable a more seamless "whole-of-government" approach, the Ministerial Committee on Ageing (MCA) comprising of government Ministers was convened in 2007 to oversee the implementation of policies and programmes on ageing under four strategic thrusts, namely:

- Improving employment and financial security;
- Enabling ageing-in-place;
- Providing holistic and affordable healthcare and eldercare;
- Promoting active ageing.

This section will examine the various policies and initiatives that have been implemented over the years under each of the strategic thrusts.

Improving employment and financial security

Ensuring that Singaporeans have adequate financial resources in old age has been a perennial objective in the agendas of all ageing committees. Financial security is undoubtedly a critical determinant of quality of life as it impacts on accessibility to the basic life necessities and healthcare services. Being financially secure refers to lifelong employability, prudent financial planning with CPF savings and support from the family.

Lifelong employability

To promote lifelong employability and increase in the employment rates of the elderly, the government has implemented various re-employment Acts over the years. It first introduced the Retirement Age Act in 1993, where the retirement age was extended from 55 years to 60 years and later pushed further to 62 years in 1999. However, it was only in 2012 that the Retirement and Re-employment Act (RRA) was introduced. Under the RRA, the statutory minimum retirement age is still 62, but employers are required to offer re-employment to eligible employees who turn 62, up to the age of 65. The Public Service Division recently announced that with effect from 1 January 2015, all eligible public service officers will be offered re-employment till age 67 upon turning 65.

To encourage employers to rehire mature workers, the government had at the beginning reduced the rates of employer contribution to their older workers' provident fund as the higher cost of employing such workers was seen as an obstacle to their continued employment (MOH, 1984, p. 22). Over the years however, in order to encourage more older workers to continue working, the government raised the total CPF contribution rates across the board for employees aged 50 and above in September 2012. More adjustments will be made on 1 January 2015, where CPF contribution rates by the employers will be raised by 2%, 1.5% and 1% for employees aged above 50 to 55 years, above 55 to 65 years and above 65 years respectively (CPF, 2014a).

Moves have also been made to encourage the low-wage older workers to continue to work with the implementation of the Workfare Income Supplement (WIS) scheme. The WIS has been enhanced recently to provide more cash income to the elderly and to put more money for contribution into their CPF accounts. To complement the WIS scheme, the Workfare Training Scheme, a three-year training programme, serves to encourage employers to send their older workers for retraining by making available a grant to subsidise costs. In 2013, the tripartite comprising of the Ministry of Manpower (MOM), the Singapore Workforce Development Agency (WDA) and the Singapore National Trades Union Congress (NTUC) jointly developed the WorkPro programme to facilitate the recruitment, training and retention of mature workers and back-to-work locals. WorkPro also aims to encourage employers to adopt more flexible work arrangements and job redesigns (Age Management Resource Portal, 2013).

% Resident Labour Force Participation Rate
(Aged 55 and over)

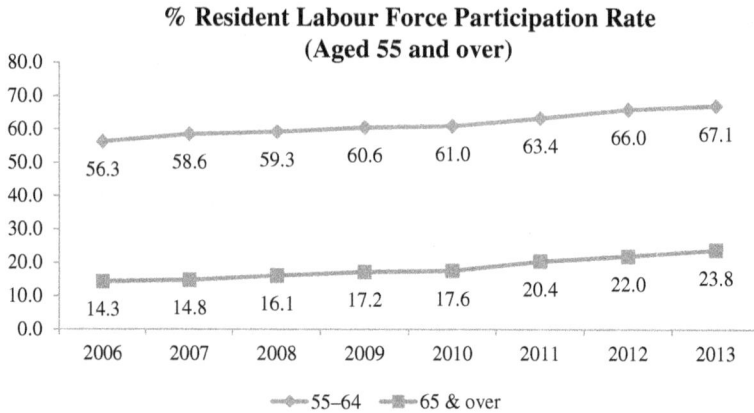

Fig. 1.4   % Resident Labour Force Participation Rate (Aged 55 and over).

Source: MOM, Labour Force Participation Rate 2006–2013.

The various initiatives and policy directives aimed at promoting lifelong employability seems to have taken effect. The labour force participation rate for mature workers has increased steadily from 56.3% in 2006 to 67.1% in 2013 for workers aged 55 to 64 years. The numbers also increased for workers aged 65 and over from 14.3% to 23.8% over the same period (see Figure 1.4).

Central Provident Fund

The Central Provident Fund (CPF) is another main formal source of old-age security in Singapore. Since its inception in 1955, the CPF has evolved from a scheme conceived simply as a source of retirement fund in its nascent stage, to include provision for home ownership, healthcare, family protection and investment (Yap, 2010). In January 1987, the government introduced the minimum sum scheme to help its CPF members set aside a sum of savings that will provide some basic form of subsistence during retirement. With effect from 2013, all CPF members aged 55 and with S$40,000 in their retirement account would be automatically enrolled in the CPF Lifelong Income For the Elderly (LIFE) annuity scheme. This will provide CPF members with a monthly payout from their retirement account for life starting from their drawdown age (DDA) instead of 20 years based on the original scheme.

Taking into consideration the longer life expectancies of Singaporeans, the DDA for the CPF LIFE payouts will be increased incrementally from 62 years to 65 years (CPF, 2014b). The minimum sum will also be raised progressively to factor in inflation, rising expectations and longer lifespans. By 1 July 2015, the minimum sum will be raised to S$161,000. However, there has been some expressed unhappiness over this increase, as this would mean a smaller withdrawal amount at age 55 (Tat, 2014, para. 5). The government has to tread a fine balance between respecting the autonomy of the individuals while putting in place sufficient safeguards to ensure Singaporeans have adequate funds to sustain them after retirement. Taking into consideration the ground sentiments, Prime Minister Lee Hsien Loong announced during the 2014 National Day Rally speech that an advisory panel will be set up to study the enhancements to the CPF scheme such as how the minimum sum should be adjusted to meet future retirement needs and how to enable CPF members to access a certain portion of their retirement funds but within a "reasonable" limit, while helping them understand the implications of such withdrawals (MOM, 2014b).

Enabling ageing-in-place

According to CAI, the concept of ageing-in-place refers to "growing old in the home, community and environment that one is familiar with, with minimal change or disruption to one's lives and activities. This is to promote social integration where the needs of seniors can be met within the community, rather than to segregate them as a distinct and separate group of the population" (CAI, 2006, p. 16). Sufficient support in terms of services and infrastructure needs to be put in place so as to enable the elderly to age comfortably within their community. One key thrust that the government has embarked on is the implementation of barrier-free access with features like ramps, railings and levelling steps in all public housing estates and highly frequented public areas. Significant progress has been made in this area, with all current public housing attaining barrier-free accessibility in 2012 (Siong, 2013, para. 1). The introduction of the Enhancement for Active Seniors (EASE) programme by the Housing & Development Board (HDB) extends the aim of achieving barrier-free access into the home environment too. Applicants for the EASE programme enjoy subsidies for home modification services such as installation of grab bars and slip resistant treatment to toilet and bathroom flooring (Gan, 2013).

To provide more integrated and seamless aged care services to the community, the Agency for Integrated Care (AIC) was formed in 2009 to serve as a one-stop solution for the various intermediate and long-term healthcare and social services needs of the elderly and their caregivers, providing referrals such as step-down care facilities and home care services. One of the key programmes it operates is the Singapore Programme for Integrated Care for the Elderly (SPICE). SPICE centres offer primary and preventive care, nursing and rehabilitative care, as well as social and leisure activities for elderly with high care needs, who would otherwise require admissions into nursing homes (AIC, n.d.). In addition, depending on the ambulatory and health status of an individual, a spectrum of care facilities have been put in place to encourage the elderly to stay within the community for as long as possible. Services range from Senior Activity Centres (SACs) that provide a platform for active elderly to interact and participate in social activities, to Senior

Care Centres (SCCs) and Day Rehabilitative Centres (DRCs) that offer care services for frail elderly requiring supervision for the former and rehabilitative services for the latter while their family members are at work. Even elderly with moderate to severe health conditions can avoid or delay institutionalisation with the Dementia Day Care and Hospice Day Care services (Singapore Silver Pages, n.d.). More assistance is also being given for the elderly who are homebound. This includes home medical and nursing services, home therapy and home help which takes the form of housekeeping assistance, meals delivery and befriending services. The government is ramping up the home care sector with the target of supporting 10,000 home healthcare clients and 7,500 social home care clients by 2020 (Gan, 2013).

Providing holistic and affordable healthcare and eldercare

To build a holistic yet affordable healthcare system is a monumental task by any other standards. To develop one in the face of a rapidly ageing population presents a whole new ball game altogether. Under the Health Masterplan 2020, the government has to adopt a multifaceted approach that serves to preserve the health status of the elderly for as long as possible, groom enough healthcare professionals and support staff to provide the necessary healthcare services, and build up sufficient care facilities that can meet the demands of the population with the aim of "enhancing the accessibility, quality and affordability of healthcare" for Singaporeans.

As part of the health awareness and prevention initiative, the Health Promotion Board has been actively involved in the dissemination of health knowledge to the masses through its Healthy Ageing Programme. It has also adopted a peer-to-peer approach by appointing trained seniors as change agents to guide their peers towards a healthier lifestyle. Under the national Integrated Screening Programme (ISP), screenings for common diseases and chronic conditions such as diabetes and high blood pressure are conducted at subsidised rates to provide up-to-date pulse checks on the general health of the elderly (Gan, 2013). To bolster the existing primary care services, the government has adopted a decentralised approach to offer basic health services within the community where possible. Private general practitioners and dentists are drawn in to provide care to the low-income elderly at subsidised rates under the Primary Care Partnership Scheme in 2010, now renamed as the Community Health Assist Scheme (CHAS). Further enhancements were made recently to the scheme such as raising the annual value of residence criterion for households without income from S$13,000 to S$21,000, removing the qualifying age from 40 and above, and expanding the list of diseases under the Chronic Disease Management Programme (MOH, 2014a). This will enable needy individuals, particularly the elderly, to be able to receive affordable healthcare services and to better manage their chronic health conditions near their homes. More new polyclinics will also be built, with two upcoming in 2017 and another four more by 2020 (Gan, 2014b).

MOH also implemented the Family Medicine Clinics (FMCs) and the Community Health Centres (CHCs) to allow greater accessibility and flexibility for Singaporeans to manage their chronic health conditions within their community (*ibid.*). Patients with referrals from hospitals and polyclinics can visit the FMC directly for follow-up health checks instead of doing it at the outpatient clinics in the hospitals. Instead of having to make a visit to one of the acute hospitals for specialised medical procedures such as diagnostic imaging services, digital diabetic eye screening and physiotherapy sessions, patients can now visit the CHCs, which provide supporting auxiliary facilities and do the follow-ups with their respective GPs in their neighborhood.

In terms of acute care services, the construction of several new acute and community hospitals are in the pipeline. With the opening of two new General Hospitals in Sengkang (Sengkang General Hospital) and Jurong (Ng Teng Fong General Hospital) and four new Community Hospitals in Yishun, Jurong, Outram and Sengkang, public acute hospital beds are projected to increase by 30% or approximately 1,900 beds, while community hospital beds will add another 1,800 beds to their existing ones (Gan, 2012). There are also plans to double the capacity of long-term care services, which includes nursing homes, home care, day care and rehabilitation facilities. Concurrently, the number of healthcare professional workforce such as doctors, nurses, dentists, pharmacists and allied health professionals will be bolstered by 50% (or about 20,000 more) by 2020 (*ibid.*) via increased intakes of local educational programmes for healthcare professionals.

A series of government-initiated medical savings cum insurance schemes were also rolled out over the years to help Singaporeans better finance their healthcare expenses (MOH, 2014b). A national medical savings scheme called Medisave was introduced in 1984 where individuals set aside part of their income into their Medisave accounts to defray future hospitalisation, day surgery or outpatient expenses for themselves or their immediate family members. However, Medisave is not a sufficient mechanism to cope with major or prolonged illnesses. MediShield, a catastrophic insurance scheme, was rolled out in 1990 to help Singaporeans deal with the hospitalisation-related expenses for these type of illnesses. It operates on a co-payment and deductible system and the premiums are payable by Medisave. The Medifund on the other hand, is an endowment fund set up in 1993 to serve as a basic safety net for needy Singaporeans who are still unable to pay for their subsidised bills after Medisave deductions and Medishield payouts. To further tighten the safety net, the ElderShield was rolled out in 2002 as a form of severe disability insurance scheme that provides a monthly cash payout to help pay the out-of-pocket expenses for the care of a severely disabled person.

Promoting active ageing

The Howe committee in 1984 recognises that the process of successful ageing begins first with a positive social construction of the elderly. The society at large must perceive that the elderly can continue to participate and contribute in "social, economic, cultural, spiritual and civic affairs, not just the ability to be physically active or to participate in the labour force" (WHO, 2002, p. 13). This is encapsulated under the concept of "Active Ageing", as defined by WHO, as "the process of optimizing opportunities for health, participation and security in order to enhance quality of life as people age" (*ibid.*). To promote active ageing, the Ministry of Social and Family Development (MSF) (formerly known as the Ministry of Community Development, Youth and Sports) began a series of public education programmes on active ageing since 1999, emphasising on themes such as leading an active lifestyle and being engaged with their families and the community (CAI, 2006). Since then, the active ageing landscape has flourished. The Council for Third Age was incepted in 2007 to promote active ageing in Singapore. It plays a catalytic role amongst government agencies, voluntary welfare organisations (VWOs), active ageing societies and educational institutions to develop active ageing programmes for the elderly and practitioners. To foster greater intergenerational understanding, C3A launched the Intergenerational Learning Programme (ILP) in 2011, pairing elderly participants with students who would teach them topics like information technology or photography. Various VWOs over the years have also developed engaging programmes catered specifically for the elderly such as the Active Ageing Academy by Fei Yue Community Services and the YAH! Community College by the Marine Parade Service Centre. The Wellness Programme, launched in 2008 by the People's Association, is another outreach programme for those aged 50 and above. It aims to enable the elderly to stay physically, mentally and socially active, and to go for regular health screenings. Since then, the programme has been rolled out to all 87 constituencies in Singapore and is validated by a 12-month impact study by Duke-NUS which reported an increase in the participation of physical activities and better social connectedness (Heng, 2014).

The private sphere of ageing

It has been three decades since the government first set up the Committee on the Problems of the Aged in 1984. Did the "problems" as identified by the Howe Committee where the elderly are socially disconnected, in frail health and the degeneration of societal norms come to pass? Are our elderly ageing successfully? Using the determinants identified during recent study by the IPS on Singaporean elderly which showed that "older adults value among other things physical health, financial independence and social connectedness" (IPS, 2014, p. 70) as a basis, we shall examine the ageing narratives of our old using data primarily drawn from the 2011 NSSC, the HDB 2008 survey, as well as the IPS 2014 survey.

Financial security

Based on the data from the NSSC 2011, more respondents reported that they are employed, from 28.2% in 2005 to 39% in 2011. This corroborated with the earlier findings that the labour force participation rate for the elderly has been increasing. More elderly are also citing employment as their main income source from 26.2% in 2005 to 38.9% in 2011. The higher employment rate amongst the elderly could be due in part to the higher educational qualifications of the younger elderly cohort and the pro-employment policies targeted at mature workers by the government. It is heartening to note that more elderly workers reported having "no issues/problems" in the workplace (58% in 2011 from 28.5% in 2005), signalling a more pro-elderly climate at the workplace. More importantly, most elderly (90%) support the idea of working after retirement as a source of added financial security and as a way to stay socially connected (IPS, 2014, p. 63).

Although the family still plays a pivotal role in providing financial support to the elderly (66.7% received income from their children), the proportion of elderly citing this source as their most important source of income has dropped for across all the age cohorts from 1995 to 2011 (see Table 1.7). These shifts could be due to the higher employment rate of the elderly, particularly for the younger cohorts, thus reducing the dependency on their children. It could also signal the changing mindsets of the elderly, with those in the younger age groups expecting less financial support from their children. Although women are still more dependent on their children for support compared to men, it is encouraging to note that more elderly women

Table 1.7   Main Sources of Income by Year and Age, 2011, 2005 and 1995.

Most Important Source of Financial Income	Age Group %		
	55 to 64 years	65 to 74 years	75 & above
1995			
Children	48.5	79.0	85.7
Personal savings	—	—	—
Paid employment	39.8	13.5	3.9
Income transfers from spouse	5.8	1.8	0.9
2005			
Children	31.9	55.8	63.7
Personal savings	11.0	15.0	10.7
Paid employment	38.9	12.7	3.7
Income transfers from spouse	—	—	—
2011			
Children	25.8	44.5	64.3
Personal savings	—	12.9	14.2
Paid employment	45.3	24.6	5.7
Income transfers from spouse	9.7	—	—

Source: NSSC 2011.

(46.6% in 2011 compared to 32% in 2005) have indicated savings as one of their main sources of income. Employment as a main source of income has also risen for women from 15.6% in 2005 to 30.6% in 2011.

Besides relying on family transfers and own savings, CPF also provides a basic safety net for elderly during their post-retirement years. Interestingly, there is a significant drop in the number of elderly who view CPF as one of their main sources of income, from 13.9% in 2005 to 6.7% in 2011. This could be due to more elderly opting to stay longer in the workforce to support themselves. It could also be a perception issue, as the elderly now expect a smaller withdrawal amount from their CPF when they reach the age of 55 due to changes in the minimum sum for their retirement account. However, CPF savings in the form of Medisave and Medishield still play a vital role in their healthcare financing. 37% will rely on their Medisave and Medishield accounts to pay for healthcare expenses while another 14% will utilise their family's Medisave account. In fact, the NSSC survey results from 2005 and 2011 showed that there was less reliance on children as more elderly paid for their own medical expenses.

Assets-wise, the NSSC 2011 survey revealed that the majority of the elderly (79.1%) list an owner-occupied home as one of their assets. The second most cited asset is their own savings or fixed deposits at 77.9%, followed by CPF savings at 59.1%. Owning a house is perhaps one of the most important assets one could hold as it provides different revenue alternatives such as renting out a room for income, downsizing to unlock the value of their property or opting for the lease buy-back scheme for HDB flat owners (HDB, 2010, p. 156). Although 74.2% of the elderly indicate that they are currently financially adequate, close to one in three elderly anticipate facing future financial inadequacy due to rising costs of living and medical expenses. Notably, family is still the number one source of support in the event of a financial shortfall where nearly half the elderly (47.2%) indicated that they would request more money from their children (MSF, 2011).

Health

Besides wealth, health is another critical component of successful ageing. Physical health has a significant impact at the individual and family level. Poor health affects an individual's ability to cope with the daily activities of life and his overall life satisfaction. The self-perceived health status of elderly is generally high as more than three out of four respondents rated their own health as good or very good. Not surprisingly, a higher proportion of those in the younger age cohorts reported a clean bill of health, from 45% for those aged 55–64, to 29.5% of those in the 65–74 age group and 19.4% of those aged 75 and older. Better-educated respondents are more likely to report a clean bill of health. It is also encouraging to note that nearly 67% of elderly aged 55 and older participate in regular sports with over 30% of elderly engaging in sports activities daily (MSF, 2013, p. 83).

As highlighted earlier, most respondents reported that they are ambulant and physically independent. However, there are some differences observed for age cohort, gender and ethnicity. Those aged 75 and above, female elderly and Malay elderly experience higher rates of requiring total physical assistance or are bedridden. 97% of the elderly indicate they could perform all six activities of daily living (ADLs) independently. Again, differences were observed for older age cohorts, with more females and Malays stating that they could not perform at least three ADLs compared to the other elderly.

In terms of health behaviours, most of the elderly respondents will seek treatment when they are ill. State subsidised medical services are the most popular choice, with half of the respondents (50.7%) stating that they will visit a government polyclinic while 39.1% will visit a general practitioner. Only 0.4% reported not seeking any form of treatment when ill. More elderly are also seeking treatment from Western-trained doctors for chronic conditions such as high blood pressure and diabetes when compared to the 2005 NSSC. All these suggest that most elderly have relatively easy access to medical services and will not hesitate to utilise the services when needed. However, the participation rates in regular health screening can be further improved as only slightly half (50.2%) of respondents reported that they do regular screenings. Notably, less of those with lower or no qualifications and living in one to two room flats take part in regular health screening.

Social well-being

Social well-being is perhaps one of the most difficult to measure and quantify. It goes beyond the mere physiological aspects of ageing and has profound implications of one's overall outlook towards life, feelings of belongingness and a general sense of a "purpose" in life. Areas commonly looked at include perception of life satisfaction, support received from their family, social participation and connectedness.

Life satisfaction

The HDB Sample Household Survey in 2008 found that life satisfaction amongst the elderly has remained consistently high across the years, from 89.1% in 1998, 93.3% in 2003, to 90.8% in 2008 (see Table 1.8). Interestingly, it is the current elderly (aged 65 and over), despite their less stellar socio-economic circumstances, who expressed a higher satisfaction with life compared to the future elderly (aged 55–64 years). Additionally, the elderly were more optimistic about their future in 2008 compared to 2005, the main reasons being having more financial security, being able to maintain good health and having a good relationship with their family (HDB, 2008, p. 177). The recent IPS study also showed that most of the elderly (80.8%) viewed ageing positively with the confidence that their needs will be taken care of as they age (IPS, 2014, p. 25).

Family support

There are concerns over the living arrangements of the elderly, especially with regard to the rising number of elderly living alone, as research indicates that this is a strong predictor for social isolation (Wu & Chan, 2012). However, other studies found that

Table 1.8   Overall Satisfaction with Life of Elderly and Future Elderly by Year.

Overall Satisfaction with Life %	1998		2003		2008		
	Elderly	All	Elderly	All	Elderly	Future Elderly	All
Very satisfied	9.8 ⎫	8.1 ⎫	9.2 ⎫	7.1 ⎫	10.9 ⎫	12.7 ⎫	10.3 ⎫
	⎬ 92.3	⎬ 89.1	⎬ 94.8	⎬ 93.3	⎬ 93.4	⎬ 90.0	⎬ 90.8
Satisfied	82.5 ⎭	81.0 ⎭	85.6 ⎭	86.2 ⎭	82.5 ⎭	77.3 ⎭	80.5 ⎭
Very dissatisfied	6.6	10.3	4.2	1.0	6.3	9.8	8.7
Dissatisfied	1.1	0.6	1.0	5.7	0.3	0.2	0.5
Total	100.0	100.0	100.0	100.0	100.0	100.0	100.0

Source: HDB Sample Household Survey 2008.

social isolation has to be viewed in context with other risk factors such as poor social networks, low economic status and being widowed (Chan *et al.*, 2011; Lai, 2014, para. 9). In another study, researchers found that it is the feelings of loneliness, rather than living alone, that has the greatest bearings on the psychological well-being and the functioning of the elderly (Lim and Kua, 2011, p. 9). The study also showed that an elderly could still feel lonely despite living with other family members, although living alone will exacerbate any feelings of loneliness that exist. Fortunately, Singaporean elderly living alone in fact report higher frequency of social contact than the rest of their peers. Their mental well-being and functioning as a whole are also comparable with the rest. It was posited that the general positive well-being of those who live alone here could be attributed to the success of befriending services set up by MSF, as well as government policies that encourage children to live in close proximity to their parents.

It is also interesting to note that there is a gradual, but discernible, trend that elderly in fact, prefer to *live close to* rather than *live with* their children. In the same vein, the proportions of elderly wanting to live near their children also decreased over the years from 75.7% in 1998 to 53.5% in 2008. More of the elderly in the younger cohorts also preferred living with their spouse and unmarried children than with their married children (HDB, 2010, p. 131). This suggests that more elderly may subscribe to the idea of "intimacy at a distance" where physical living arrangements may matter less than actual interactions with family members. The majority of the elderly (93%) reported regular contact with their family at least once a week or more. Those who do not stay with their children also reported frequent visits from their children (MSF, 2013, p. 23). 72.4% of them visit their parents at least once a week while 92.2% indicated at least once a month. Intergenerational ties also seem strong as 67% of respondents have meals with their grandchildren at least once a week (HDB, 2010, p. 135).

Social participation and connectedness

Studies have shown that volunteering is associated with greater health benefits such as reduction in depressive symptoms, better mental well-being and even greater longevity (Baycrest Centre for Geriatic Care, 2014; Schiwingel *et al.*, 2009). Despite CAI's target to increase the elderly volunteerism rate to 15% by 2030 (CAI, 2006, p. 62), the rate remains low at only 6% (MSF, 2013, p. 85). Similarly, the Perception and Attitudes towards Ageing and Seniors Survey 2013/14 revealed that although sentiments towards voluntary work are generally positive, only 43% indicated that they would consider volunteering over the next few years (IPS, 2014, p. 68). The low participation rate may be due in part to the demographic profiles of the current elderly, as studies indicate that volunteerism rates increase with improved education and income levels (Corporation for National & Community Service, December 2006, p. 7). Perhaps one way to encourage greater volunteerism amongst the elderly is to provide more flexible forms of volunteering. The term "episodic volunteering" refers to short-duration tasks that are more sensitive to the time constraints and responsibilities that typically inhibit people from taking on volunteering responsibilities (*ibid.*).

On a more positive note, the government's concerted efforts to promote active ageing with outreach programmes by various agencies such as the senior citizen clubs and community clubs under the purview of the People's Association, Senior Activity Centres run by VWOs and active ageing activities by C3A seemed to have taken effect, as participation rates of elderly in community activities have steadily increased, from 16.8% in 1998 to 46.9% in 2008. (HDB, 2010). The social networks for the elderly have also increased as more of them indicated that they have at least one to two close friends from 62% in 2005 to 72% in 2011. Most respondents (73.5%) also meet their friends at least once a week (MSF, 2013).

Overall, the elderly in Singapore are faring well in the various aspects of ageing. Family ties continue to be strong while notions of filial piety and obligations to the elderly remain relatively intact. The elderly, in times of need such as an illness, financial inadequacy or needing someone to talk to, can turn to their family as the primary source of support (MSF, 2013). While the elderly in the older age cohort rely more heavily on their family, this is mediated by strong family support as there are more children to spread the burden of care for this generation. The recent eight billion dollar pioneer generation package rolled out by the government for those born before 1949 will further ease their financial strain in terms of healthcare costs with greater healthcare benefits and subsidies for the rest of their lives (CPF, 2014c). Conversely, the family size for the elderly in the younger age group is shrinking but this group of younger elderly has better qualifications and is in a stronger financial position than their older counterparts. A gradual shift towards more self-reliance through employment and growing preference for independent living may also soften the social impact of smaller family sizes.

Policy challenges and opportunities

Fear of the traditional "Asian" values being eroded by Western ideologies seems to be unfounded as family support continues to be robust. However, with shrinking family sizes, the family as a social institution may no longer be able to cope with the physical caregiving responsibilities for the elderly, especially in dealing with diseases that are long drawn and increasingly debilitating. The state has moved in the right direction to enable the elderly to age in place with concrete plans to build up the supporting infrastructure and manpower but more needs to be done in terms of providing support to the family, such as greater respite care options. The state also has to keep abreast of the changing dynamism of family structures, notions of what constitutes familial obligations and the expectations of the future elderly. These "reinterpretations" in turn informs how current policies should be fine-tuned or changed.

For example, there is a need to re-examine what constitutes "caregiving" within the family. The number of families hiring foreign domestic helpers to provide care for the elderly is on the rise (Ang, 2010, p. B2; Duke Global Health Institute, 2013). As such, "caregiving" in the future may shift from the conventional concept of a family member as the caregiver to the elderly, to an external help who acts as a proxy to the family members by providing the main caregiving duties. Family members instead take on the subsidiary role of caregiving through the provision of financial, emotional and social support. This in turn implies a need for greater coordinated efforts to improve the skills set for this group of domestic helpers through a formal training and certification framework, particularly for cases where health condition of the elderly is complex (Ang, 2010). The private sector can also play a part in providing more innovative care options such as professionally trained live-in caregivers who are able to deliver care for elderly patients with serious illnesses such as cancer, stroke and dementia.

Another key area of concern for policy-makers is the feminisation of ageing. Across the various social determinants, gender is one of the most common differentiating factors for areas such as educational attainment, reliance on family for financial support and health statuses. As discussed earlier, women generally have lower educational attainment than men and this in turn, has an impact on their employment opportunities and financial adequacy for retirement. Elderly women are also more like than men to report poorer health and difficulty in carrying out ADLs. Widowhood is especially prevalent among the elderly females (42.3% for females versus 20.2% for males) due to the longer lifespans of women. More women may end up living alone and face a higher probability of social isolation and even depression (Lim & Ng, 2010; Chan *et al.*, 2011). Policy-makers, voluntary welfare organisations (VWOs) and healthcare practitioners alike must work together to identify elderly women who are at risk of being socially isolated or neglected. Similarly, attention needs to be paid to those elderly with low educational attainment and living in rental or one/two room flats as studies indicate that they are more likely to report poorer health and psychological well-being, are less financially secure and have a less positive perception of life (MSF, 2013; HDB, 2010).

Managing the perceptions and expectations of the future elderly will be another challenge for the government. The future old are better educated and more likely to be vocal in expressing their needs. Current surveys indicate that the younger elderly cohorts and those with higher educational attainment are generally more likely to disagree that the government has addressed the concerns of the elderly (MSF, 2013, p. 74). Their sheer numerical size could give them the ability to sway policies in their favour and intergenerational tensions may result. The government will have to tread carefully between meeting the demands and aspirations of these future elderly, while ensuring that the interests of the population at large are not compromised. The way the government engages this group of elderly will need to evolve as well, from a top-down approach to a more consultative one. The challenges that come in the wake of an ageing population are numerous but not insurmountable. Moreover, the future ageing landscape is not without its opportunities. The better anticipated ageing outcomes for the future old with their greater purchasing power could precipitate the advent of a booming silver economy. This will be a far cry from the original construct of the elderly in the 1984 report on "Problems of the Aged".

References

Active Ageing: A Policy Framework (2002, April). Retrieved 21 January 2015, from http://whqlibdoc.who.int/hq/2002/WHO_NMH_NPH_02.8.pdf?ua=1.

Age Management Resource Portal (2013). *WorkPro — Towards Progressive Workplaces.* Retrieved 9 October 2014, from http://www.reemployment.sg/web/Contents/Contents.aspx?ContId=330.

Agency for Integrated Care (AIC) (n.d.) *Singapore Programme for Integrated Care for the Elderly (SPICE).* Retrieved 13 October 2014, from http://aic.sg/page.aspx?id=782.

Ang, Y. (2010, May 19). Who's Really Caring for Singapore's Elderly? *The Straits Times.* Retrieved 14 January 2015, from http://newshub.nus.edu.sg/news/1005/PDF/CARING-st-19may-pB2.pdf.

Balakrishnan, V. (2005, June 4). *Successful Ageing.* Speech presented at The Chevrons, Singapore.

Baycrest Centre for Geriatric Care (2014, August 29). Evidence Mounting That Older Adults Who Volunteer Are Happier, Healthier. *ScienceDaily.* Retrieved 18 October 2014, from www.sciencedaily.com/releases/2014/08/140829135448.htm.

Central Provident Fund (CPF) (2014a, August 6). *Guide to CPF Contribution Rates from 1 January 2014.* Retrieved 15 October 2014, from http://mycpf.cpf.gov.sg/NR/rdonlyres/9557AE3D-D9C7-4DAB-A12C-E7E94DE8E50B/0/conrates_guide_2014.pdf.

Central Provident Fund (CPF) (2014b, August 19). *Minimum Sum.* Retrieved 15 October 2014, from http://mycpf. cpf.gov.sg/Members/Gen-Info/FAQ/MinimumSum.htm.

Central Provident Fund (CPF) (2014c, October). *Our Pioneer Generation — Overview.* Retrieved 16 October 2014, from http://www.cpf.gov.sg/pioneers/pgp_overview.asp.

Chan, A., Malhotra, C., Malhotra, R. & Østbye, T. (2011, June). Living Arrangements, Social Networks and Depressive Symptoms among Older Men and Women in Singapore. *International Journal of Geriatric Psychiatry*, 26(6), 630–639. DOI: 10.1002/gps.2574.

Chan, A., Malhotra, C., Malhotra, R., Rush, A. J. & Østbye, T. (2013, September 6). Health Impacts of Caregiving for Older Adults with Functional Limitations: Results from the Singapore Survey on Informal Caregiving. *Journal of Aging and Health,* 25(6), 998–1012. DOI: 10.1177/0898264313494801.

Corporation for National & Community Service (2006, December). Volunteer Growth in America: A Review of Trends since 1974. Washington, DC. Retrieved 5 March 2015, from http://www.nationalservice.gov/pdf/06_1203_volunteer_growth.pdf.

Committee on Ageing Issues (CAI) (2006, February 3). *Report on the Ageing Population, 5 Year Masterplan.* Retrieved 14 January 2015, from http://app. msf.gov. sg/Portals/0/Summary/research/CAI_report.pdf.

Department of Statistics (DOS) (2002). *Twenty-Five Years of Below Replacement Fertility.* Retrieved 14 January 2015, from http://www.singstat.gov.sg/pubn/papers/people/cp-fertility.pdf.

Department of Statistics (DOS) (2011, September). Statistics Singapore Newsletter. *The Elderly in Singapore.* Retrieved 14 October 2014, from http://www.singstat.gov.sg/publications/publications_and_papers/population_and_population_structure/ssnsep 11-pg1-9.pdf.

Department of Statistics (DOS) (2014, September 25). *Resident Old-Age Support Ratio.* Retrieved 8 October 2014, from http://www.singstat.gov.sg/statistics/visualising_data/chart/Old_Age_Support_Ratio.html.

Department of Statistics (DOS) (2014). *Population Trends 2014.* Retrieved 16 February 2015, from http://www.singstat.gov.sg/docs/default-score/default-document-library/publications / publications _ and _ papers / population _ and _ population _ structure / population2014.pdf.

Duke Global Health Institute (2013, June 10). *New Study Finds that Family Caregivers of Singapore Elderly Who Rely on Foreign Domestic Workers Fare Better.* Retrieved 14 October 2014, from https://globalhealth.duke.edu/media/news/study-finds-family-caregivers-singapore-elderly-who-rely-foreign-domestic-workers-fare.

Gan, K. Y. (2012, March 6). *MOH 2012 Committee of Supply Speech Healthcare 2020: Improving Accessibility, Quality and Affordability for Tomorrow's Challenges (Part 1 of 2).* Speech presented at the Parliament, Singapore.

Gan, K. Y. (2014a, January 20). In *Parliamentary Q&A 2014 — Bed Crunch.* Retrieved 18 September 2014, from http://www.moh.gov.sg/content/moh_web/home/press Room/Parliamentary_QA/2014/bed-crunch.html.

Gan, K. Y. (2014b, March 12). *Minister COS Speech 1: Together towards Better Health.* Speech presented at the Parliament, Singapore.

Heng, C. H. (2014, March 12). *Speech by Mr Heng Chee How, Senior Minister of State for Prime Minister's Office, at Committee of Supply 2014.* Speech presented at the Parliament, Singapore.

Housing & Development Board (HDB) (2010). *Public Housing in Singapore: Well-Being of Communities, Families and the Elderly HDB Sample: Household Survey 2008.* Retrieved 14 January 2015, from http://www.hdb.gov.sg/fi10/fi10297p.nsf/ImageView/Survey2008/$file/Monogram+2+Lores_R1.pdf.

Institute of Policy Studies (IPS) (2014, October). *Results from the Perception and Attitudes towards Ageing and Seniors Survey.* Retrieved 14 January 2015, from http://lkyspp. nus.edu.sg/ips/wp-content/uploads/sites/2/2014/10/wp22_151015.pdf.

Khalid, S. (2012, December 19). Singaporean 'Living in Good Health — and Bad'. *The Straits Times*. Retrieved 14 January 2015, from http://www.healthxchange.com.sg/news/Pages/Singaporean-Living-Longer-Good-Health.aspx.

Khaw, B. W. (2009, February 9). *Preparing for Silver Tsunami.* [Web log comment]. Retrieved 14 January 2015, from http://singaporepublichealth.wordpress.com/preparing-for-silver-tsunami/.

Lai, L. (2014, April 3). Study Highlights Need to Help 'Socially Isolated' Elderly Folk. *The Straits Times*. Retrieved 14 January 2015, from http://news.asiaone.com/news/singapore/study-highlights-need-help-socially-isolated-elderly-folk.

Lee, H. L. (2006, November 13). *Speech by Prime Minister Lee Hsien Loong.* Speech presented at the Parliament, Singapore.

Lim, L. & Kua, E. H. (2011). Living Alone, Loneliness, and Psychological Well-Being of Older Persons in Singapore. *Current Gerontology and Geriatrics Research*, 2(1), 33–40. DOI: 10.1155/2011/673181.

Lim, L. L. & Ng, T. P. (2010). Living Alone, Lack of a Confidant and Psychological Well-being of Elderly Women in Singapore: The Mediating Role of Loneliness. *Asia-Pacific Psychiatry*, 2, 33–40. DOI: 10.1111/j.1758-5872.2009.00049.x.

Ministry of Health (MOH) (1984, February). *Report of the Committee on the Problems of the Aged.* Singapore.

Ministry of Health (MOH) (2014a, January 1). *Community Health Assist Scheme.* Retrieved 12 October 2014, from http://www.moh.gov.sg/content/moh_web/home/costs_and_financing/schemes_subsidies/Community_Health_Assist_Scheme.html.

Ministry of Health (MOH) (2014b, January 1). *Financing Approach.* Retrieved 2 October 2014, from http://www.moh.gov.sg/content/moh_web/home/costs_and_financing/schemes_subsidies/financing_approach.html.

Ministry of Health (MOH) (2014c, October 1). *Population and Vital Statistics.* Retrieved 3 October 2014, from http://www.moh.gov.sg/content/moh_web/home/statistics/Health_Facts_Singapore/Population_And_Vital_Statistics.html.

Ministry of Manpower (MOM) (2014a, January). *Labour Force in Singapore, 2013.* Retrieved 10 October 2014, from http://stats.mom.gov.sg/Pages/Labour-Force-In-Singapore-2013.aspx.

Ministry of Manpower (MOM) (2014b, September 10). *Appointment of Central Provident Fund Advisory Panel.* Retrieved 6 October 2014, from http://www.mom.gov.sg/newsroom/Pages/PressReleasesDetail.aspx?listid=585.

Ministry of Social and Family Development (MSF) (2011). *State of the Elderly in Singapore 2008/2008, Release 1.* Retrieved 14 January 2015, from http://app.msf.gov.sg/Portals/0/Summary/research/State%20of%20the%20Elderly_Release%201.pdf.

Ministry of Social and Family Development (MSF) (April 2013). *The National Survey on Senior Citizens 2011.* Retrieved 14 January 2015, from http://app.msf.gov.sg/Portals/0/National%20Survey%20of%20Senior%20Citizens%202011_Complete_amended_use%20this%20CH.pdf.

National Population and Talent Division (NPTD) (2013). *A Sustainable Population for a Dynamic Singapore: Population White Paper.* Prime Minister's Office, Singapore.

National Population and Talent Division (NPTD), Department of Statistics (DOS), Ministry of Home Affairs (MHA) & Immigrations and Checkpoints Authority (ICA)

(September 2014). *2014 Population in Brief.* Retrieved 14 October 2014, from http://www.population.sg/population-in-brief/2014/files/population-in-brief-2014.pdf.

Saad, I. (2014, March 5). Healthcare Spending to Hit S$12b by 2020, Says Tharman. *Channel NewsAsia.* Retrieved 14 January 2015, from http://www.channelnewsasia.com/news/specialreports/budget2014/news/healthcare-spending-to/1021468.html.

Schwingel, A., Niti, M. M., Tang, C. & Ng, T. P. (2009). Continued Work Employment and Volunteerism and Mental Well-being of Older Adults: Singapore Longitudinal Ageing Studies. *Age and Ageing,* 38(5), 531–537. DOI: 10.1093/ageing/afp089.

Singapore Silver Pages (n.d.). *Eldercare Services.* Retrieved 13 October 2014, from https://www.silverpages.sg/eldercare_services.aspx?Fid=147&Title=Eldercare%20services#.VECsm0sttaY.

Siong, O. (2013, January 13). All Public Housing Estates Now Have Barrier-free Accessibility. *Channel NewsAsia.* Retrieved 21 January 2015, from http://www.channelnewsasia.com/news/all-public-housing-estates-now-have-barrier-free-accessibility-/515310.html.

Tat, H. W. (2014, June 6). CPF Issues Can Be Resolved. *The Straits Times.* Retrieved 21 January 2015, from http://www.straitstimes.com/news/opinion/more-opinion-stories/story/cpf-issues-can-be-resolved-20140606.

United Nations (UN) (2012, September). *Population Ageing and Development 2012.* Retrieved 30 September 2014, from http://www.un.org/esa/population/publications/2012PopAgeingDev_Chart/2012PopAgeingandDev_WallChart.pdf.

World Health Organization (WHO) (2002). *Active Ageing: A Policy Framework.* A contribution of the World Health Organization to the Second United Nations World Assembly on Ageing, Madrid, Spain, April 2002. Retrieved 3 March 2015, from http://who.int/hq/2002/WHO_NMH_NPH_02.8.pdf.

World Health Organization (WHO) (2014). *World Health Statistics.* Retrieved 3 October 2014, from http://www.who.int/mediacentre/news/releases/2014/world-health-statistics-2014/en/.

Wu, T. & Chang, A. (2012). Families, Friends, and the Neighborhood of Older Adults: Evidence from Public Housing in Singapore. *Journal of Aging Research,* 2012. DOI: 10.1155/2012/659806.

Yap, M. T. (2010). Ageing Population. In Terence Chong (ed.), *Management of Success: Singapore Revisited* (pp. 183–198). Singapore: Institute of Southeast Asian Studies.

Yap, M. T. & Kang, S. H. (2010). The Greying of Singapore's Population: Prospects and Challenges. In Dr W. Hofmeister, M. Sarmah & P. Rüppel (eds.), *Panorama Insights into Asian and European Affairs — Ageing and Politics: Consequences for Asia and Europe* (pp. 173–191). Singapore: Konrad-Adenauer-Stiftung.

Yap, M. T. & Shantakumar, G. (forthcoming). Demographic Trends and Social Security. In Gillian Koh (ed.), *Singapore Futures: Scenarios for the Next Generation.* Singapore: Institute of Policy Studies.

Chapter 2

The Psychology of Ageing: Social Implications for Singapore

John Elliott

Historically, people were considered to age rapidly and were retired early. Life expectancies were far shorter — in the US, life expectancy at birth was 47 years in 1900 (Barabba, 1975). Achievers were often young. Raffles was lieutenant-governor of Java at the age of 30 (Collis, 2009). Lee Kuan Yew became Prime Minister of Singapore, in 1959, at the age of 36.

This chapter is about the implications of the fact that life expectancy, with good mental and physical functioning, has virtually doubled in the last century. It argues that it is not useful to categorise the elderly as a separate dependent group, because they are so diverse and because so many are still productively active, both socially and economically. It explores the reasons why our views are still affected by a past legacy of thinking about the elderly as a "past-it" generation, deserving of respect but essentially dependent. The chapter concludes with the suggestion that, in the future, a well-integrated and fully inclusive society will judge and find a place for people on the basis of merit regardless of age.

The nature of changed life expectations

Around the world, life expectation is strongly predicted by per capita GDP. Overall life expectancy at birth in Singapore, for example, has increased from 66 in 1970 to 82 in 2010 (National Population and Talent Division [NPTD], 2013), and according to the World Health Organization (WHO, 2014a) rose further to 83 in 2013 (85 for women and 80 for men). This rise has gone hand in hand with an increase in per capita GDP from S$925 to S$46,241 over the period 1970–2010 (Index Mundi, n.d.), and with an obvious corresponding improvement in general health. It is worth noting, in passing, that the correlation between GDP and health is not universal.

Public health and life expectation actually improved in the US during the Great Depression of 1929–1933 (Tapia Granadosa & Diez Roux, 2009). These authors suggest that stress, social isolation, tobacco use, poor diet and pollution were lower during the depression, and that this could have explained the effect. Since Singapore has enjoyed tremendous improvements in public health and life expectancy as well as in economic growth in the last 50 years, the experience of the US in a depression eight decades ago might be thought irrelevant. However, it may not prove so if the consequences of economic affluence take a future toll in obesity and "lifestyle diseases".

Improvements in health and prosperity have meant that in contemporary developed societies almost everyone survives to a ripe old age. Survival curves, in which the proportion of the population surviving is plotted against age, remain above 90% until the mid-60s, and are still above 80% by age 80. An analogous curve would accurately describe a corresponding survival of function — the maintenance of healthy mental and physical functioning to a later average age than formerly. This simple fact has far reaching implications, which will be elaborated in this chapter.

It is important to understand what happens to healthy mental and physical functioning as we age. Research has shown that psychological functions do not decline gradually in the healthy elderly person. Instead, they plateau until a late age. The idea that abilities fall off gradually as we age probably has its basis in the well-recognised fact that athletic and sports skills, and physical fitness generally, peak while we are young. One does indeed decline soon after a physical peak somewhere in one's 20s or 30s. But while a similar gradual decline may also occur in certain cognitive processes, such as those comprising what is called fluid intelligence (e.g., speed of processing, reasoning skills with unfamiliar materials), such a decline is more than compensated for by gains in experience and the use of acquired knowledge and skills (sometimes referred to as crystallised intelligence). Moreover, when it comes to the wide variety of social skills including what has been called "situational judgment ability" (Chan & Schmitt, 2005) and the interrelated clusters of social abilities known as "emotional intelligence", "social intelligence" and "practical intelligence" (Lievens & Chan, 2010), there is no real evidence that it declines at all until very late in life. Therefore, the extension of life allowed by modern medicine allows an extension of active and productive life, and not just the pointless dragging out of an inevitable decline.

The idea of a slow and inevitable decline of mental and physical functioning as we age appears consistent with the common observation of older people physically or mentally affected by the diseases of old age, appearing frail, slow, forgetful or confused, sometimes to a point where they may be incapable of independent living. Most readers would be able to call to mind some friend or relative who did indeed suffer a slow decline in their abilities. Possibly too, they simply notice the greater visibility of elders in wheelchairs or being assisted by attendant maids. But the scientific evidence and the thesis of this chapter are not inconsistent with these common observations. The research literature suggests that diseases, and especially neurodegenerative diseases such as Parkinson's disease or various dementias, are not inevitable in the healthy elderly. The thesis in this chapter is that the extension of life in modern times means that the elders of the future — today's youth — will be much less affected by these diseases than old people we may see around us today.

Policy pessimism

Although things are starting to change, the improvement in life expectation, taken in isolation, has for quite some time been a concern among policy planners. For example,

> Recent data suggest that there are about ten people of working age per older person today, but that this will fall to only 3.5 persons economically active per elder person (Vasoo, Ngiam & Cheung, 2000, pp. 176–177).

Or more recently,

> A shrinking and ageing population would also mean a smaller, less energetic workforce, and a less vibrant and innovative economy. Companies may not find enough workers. Business activity would slow, and job and employment opportunities would shrink. It would become more difficult to match the higher aspirations of a better educated and mobile population. Young people would leave for more exciting and growing global cities. This would hollow out our population and workforce, and worsen our ratio of younger to older Singaporeans (NPTD, 2013, para 1.10).

This 2010 Op-Ed piece in *The New York Times* summarises the problem as seen from the US, and expresses a sceptical view of what can realistically be expected of the "old old",

> My hope is that I will not live as long as my mother and grandmother ... I, too, hope to go on being productive, writing long after the age when most people retire, in the twilight of the print culture that has nourished my life. Yet it is sobering for me — as it is for Americans in many businesses and professions that once seemed a sure thing — to see younger near contemporaries being downsized out of jobs long before they are emotionally or financially ready for retirement ... Furthermore, I am acutely aware — and this is the difference between hope and expectation — that my plans depend, above all, on whether I am lucky enough to retain a working brain. I haven't mentioned, because I don't like to think about it, that my paternal grandmother, who also lived into her 90s, died of Alzheimer's disease. The risk of dementia, of which Alzheimer's is the leading cause, doubles every five years after 65 (Jacoby, 2010).

See also Jacoby (2011) for a critique of tendencies to over-optimism in considering old age.

The pessimism arises, in part, because attitudes to and expectations of the elderly have not changed in line with the reality of actual changes, not only in life expectancy, but in terms of psychological functions that are maintained in those who are healthy but old. The concern is expressed through dire predictions about the burdens of a greying society, based on support ratios (of the supposedly unproductive elderly to the productive younger population). What are called "support ratios" are predicted to decline from 4.9 in 2015, to 2.1 in 2030 (NPTD, 2013, Chart 1.5). In other words, at present, for every person aged 65 or above there are nearly five adults of productive age in the population. However, by 2030, there would be barely more than two.

In reality, as noted by several authors (e.g., Chan *et al.*, 2014; Chan, forthcoming), support ratios presented in the NPTD Population White Paper may retain an unrealistically low bar (i.e., 65 years as cut-off age to compute the support ratio) for the age at which the elderly, as a group, can be characterised as necessarily unproductive. In fact, as I will argue later in this chapter, it may be problematic to try and characterise the elderly as a group at all. Interestingly, the NPTD chart just cited shows that the ratio *has already dropped* from 13.5 in 1970, to 5.9 in 2012; yet no one would argue that there has been a near threefold rise in problems arising from the increasing proportion of over-65s within that period.

The concerns generated by support ratios are probably also to some extent a legacy, in public attitudes, of a colonial belief in the need for early retirement in hot and, what were then, unhealthy tropical climates. Even until very recently, the productive years were taken to be those between 15 and 65. These figures can be adjusted at both ends. In a society stressing the importance of education and training, many nowadays do not become fully productive members of the workforce until much later than 15; conversely, many adults work beyond 65, and more would probably do so if they were allowed to remain in employment, judging by the concerns expressed in the newspapers over the need for retraining and employment opportunities for older citizens. In fact, if the old-age support ratio were recalculated treating the productive years as those from 25 to 74 inclusive, the ratio immediately more than doubles, and does not look nearly so troubling.

In recent years, it has been common to redesignate the elderly as a "silver" generation, or to try and distinguish the "young old" and the "old old", as Vasoo, Ngiam & Cheung (2000) and Jacoby (2010) did, with the "young old" still active but the "old old" needing support including assisted living. From the perspective of ensuring adequate infrastructure and social services, these designations could be seen as steps in the right direction or at least as responsible planning parameters. However, this chapter argues that more effort should be made to consider individual differences, and that simply offering a more refined categorisation of people by age is not really the answer to the supposed problems of the elderly. If there is to be categorisation at all, it should surely be by level of function and not by age.

Part of the concern is also that the support ratio appears even less favourable due to a failure to reach population replacement levels in societies where women have fewer children later in life. However, looking to sustainability in the long run, and the universality of the trend to lower reproductive rates as a function of GDP, a lowering of the reproductive potential of women might prove to be part of the solution, not part of the problem. Singapore itself is so manifestly a sought-after destination for foreigners that there should be no difficulty maintaining any desired population level by the judicious use of immigration policy. More importantly, the fertility rate among married women is actually around the replacement level of two. As of 2011, the average number of children born to women who are or have ever been married, who are aged 40–49 years, and who are Singapore citizens is 2.08 (NPTD, 2011). This suggests, and this is a point noted informally by many social scientists in Singapore, that the solution to the problem of not enough babies, if it is a problem, may be addressed more by encouraging marriage than by encouraging the already married to procreate more. However, this is an aspect of demographic change and planning beyond the scope of this chapter (for a review and analysis of marriage and procreation in Singapore, see Straughan, this volume).

Relevant findings

Examination of studies of psychological functioning in the elderly reveals four particularly relevant areas. There are others studies which provide similar conclusions, but these are the ones on which the thrust of this chapter depends.

Lessons from longitudinal studies

The first relevant area of research comes from longitudinal studies. As discussed earlier in this chapter, the healthy elderly show a marked ability to maintain psychological functioning until late in life. This ability in the elderly to maintain cognitive functioning at a high level, by compensating for certain kinds of underlying decline, has not always been clearly recognised. It has, however, become much more evident following research that tracked the maintenance of functioning over time. Studies have shown that a range of cognitive abilities hold up well in populations at all levels of ability, and not, as was once thought, only in the intellectually more able (Schaie & Strother, 1968; Anastasi, 1988; Schulz & Ewen, 1988; Whitbourne & Whitbourne, 2011).

These findings have been known for some time, but the implications are only more gradually becoming obvious. The perception of the elderly as a group afflicted by dementias and other debilitating diseases, with consequent prolonged slow deterioration, is not accurate as a view of what the last years of life need be *in the absence of disease.* Incontrovertibly, as some diseases are cured, others become more prominent, since we all die of something specific eventually. However the popular picture (and experience) of slow deterioration is greatly biased by the widespread existence of various forms of dementia. These neurological conditions are diseases, are the subject of sustained active research, and it is most unlikely that they will continue to represent such a considerable problem in future decades. The fact that an increasingly aged population will contain a greater proportion of people with dementia is providing fresh impetus to research aimed at combatting such conditions.

If one imagines a Singapore where dementia was no commoner than dengue, it would utterly transform our expectations of old age. But I do not think it unreasonable to plan on the assumption that the diseases of old brains will yield to sustained medical research and consequent treatment. Any pharmaceutical company discovering a cure, or an effective means of really postponing the onset of dementias or other diseases of the nervous system will, after all, be sitting on a gold mine. There is also a debate to be had about the ethics and risks of drug-induced enhancements to brain function, as opposed to preventive treatments for deterioration (see Elliott, 2012), but this is beyond the scope of this paper.

Compensatory mechanisms

Studies on compensatory mechanisms provide another area of research relevant to understanding elderly functioning. The findings show that there are mechanisms whereby older people are able to compensate for decline in certain basic cognitive functions, which does occur, while sustaining high level abilities, especially in familiar domains. So, while it is common knowledge, especially common among all older persons, that aspects of memory decline in later life, this particularly impacts efforts to learn new tasks and adapt to new situations with high information processing demands (for an overview of relevant memory studies, see Baddeley, 2002). Old people learn new things more slowly. But the benefit of familiar settings, the deployment of established expertise and experience, and the use of various kinds of mnemonic aids, will typically outweigh the handicap of declining memory or slower reactions until quite late in life. It is for this reason that a distinction is sometimes made between fluid intelligence (raw problem-solving potential minimally tied to specific tasks, and important in coping with novelty) and crystallised intelligence (developed intelligence which is more context dependent) (Stuart-Hamilton, 2000). These advantages of the older person have been known for decades and discussed by several authors (e.g., Elliott, 1994; Rabbit, 1993). They have not however, been much recognised by policy-makers until more recently.

Moreover, while psychological research has often focused on cognitive skills, similar effects are likely in social and personal life. Few would disagree that the everyday notions of maturity and wisdom — traditionally associated with ageing and respected in Asian cultures — are high-level abilities that develop over the lifespan. Older people are also sometimes stereotyped as more inflexible and less creative, although a contrary view — that it is young, idealistic, energetic and inexperienced young people who tend to be rigid thinkers — is plausible. Some would also argue that the apparently more conservative views of the old can be a rational response to the lessons of life, rather than prima facie evidence of inflexible thinking. A thorough and recent review of these and other social aspects of ageing is available in Charles and Carstensen (2010).

Cohort effects

Studies on cohort effects constitute the third area of research relevant to elderly functioning. We have tended to underestimate the potential of the elderly through overlooking cohort effects, that is, the advantages or disadvantages conferred on an entire generation by circumstances. The generation that survived World War II and the Japanese Occupation of Singapore did not have the advantages and benefits of health and education that later generations have increasingly enjoyed. They may have therefore reached a lesser average level of psychological competence and realised potential, just as they reached a lesser average physical stature. Loke, Lin and Deurenberg-Yap (2008) have provided data on growth trends of Singapore children spanning five decades, and while we have no comparable local data for improvements in psychological functioning, there is ample evidence to support it from elsewhere, most notably in the phenomenon known as the Flynn effect (see Lynn, 2013 or Williams, 2013), which refers to the tendency for assessed intelligence to increase with successive cohorts in recent decades. It is therefore highly plausible to suppose that children born now will realise considerably more potential, and realise it later in life, than those, such as the author, who represent the end of a generation of wartime children. The 80-year-old in 2080 should be, on average, a more competent and high functioning person than today's 80-year-olds, not just because they will be more healthy, but also because they will have benefitted from a general improvement in psychological function grounded in better education.

Societal expectations and opportunities

Finally, research indicates that older people are themselves affected by the expectations of the society they live in. When society expects its elders to be helpless, dependent or incapable of gainful employment, the elders tend to oblige. One of the mechanisms by which older persons end up being what society expects them to be is the tendency for older persons to internalise the stereotypes about themselves. These stereotypes can be positive or negative, but where they are negative, they appear to be associated with a range of adverse cognitive and physical effects (e.g., Levy, 2003, 2009). There is a literature devoted to self-perceptions of the elderly, and how these perceptions are affected by societal expectations; although as with many areas of ageing there is apparently little or no local research on the matter. But it is clear from studies elsewhere that discriminatory attitudes towards the elderly, sometimes under the label "ageism", can be the basis of self-perception stereotypes in the old (see Butler 2010). A kind of self-perpetuating cycle can be envisaged in which the old are perceived by younger generations as inadequate or in some sense "past it", and this perception affects the self-concept of the elderly, who therefore tend to comply with it. This process is not necessarily conscious. Many prejudices and stereotypes are not matters of conscious awareness; but they can be the more insidious for being unrecognised.

It may also be the case, in Singapore at least, that the idea of the deserving elder, one who has earned a rest by a lifetime of work, and who now deserves the chance to retire and enjoy life and be supported, is a part of the self-perceptions of older people. Especially where work is uncongenial, such ideas of an entitlement might have strong appeal. Indeed, it is important not to overlook the fact that by no means does everyone want to continue working into late life. Many would also want to argue that people should retire while still young enough and fit enough to enjoy their retirement. But the thesis in this chapter is not that everyone must work longer, but only that age should not be the criterion by which we — as a society — determine whether people can work or not.

The combined effect of the four points discussed above has been an under-estimation of the potential for many older persons to function as productive members of society, especially, but by no means exclusively, where cognitive abilities are concerned. However, the situation is complicated by at least two additional considerations. As mentioned, one of these is the difference between those who are motivated to continue productive work and those who would like to retire completely as soon as possible. The former group seeks to continue in work not only for the income, but because it gives them satisfaction or meaning in life, or because they wish to retain independence and influence. The latter group tend to be those doing unfulfilling, menial or physical work. Any solution to issues of employment and opportunity for older persons needs to recognise different motivations and the constraints on possibilities. One does not, by and large, maintain physical power and strength when old as well as one maintains social and cognitive skills.

Another consideration is the persistent tendency to regard older persons as less employable, being supposedly less adaptable, more expensive (i.e., more senior and less healthy) and liable to have family commitments. Actually, this sits oddly with the self-evident tendency for the self-employed, or those in public life, to continue to the limits of their ability, even when amply able, financially speaking, to sit back and retire. There are many manifestly competent older persons who can be found in the news every day.

Some limitations

The relatively optimistic picture being developed so far in this chapter may strike some readers as actually too optimistic. It may appear as if the author is overlooking some real difficulties arising if and when an old person reaches the end of life and may require a great deal of individual attention. This section will attempt to somewhat disarm this criticism.

We cannot, in the name of potential, ignore the actual. Anyone with experience in social services appreciates that there is a real problem with frail and lonely elders, often with chronic medical conditions. Many readers will know of old people who in various ways fit a stereotype of the debilitated old person who needs at best supervision, and at worst, outright full-time care. Others will have elderly relatives in need of care. Indeed, care is itself a potentially debilitating issue for old couples in situations where one partner is devoted to looking after the other, only to be left bereft after the decease of the dependent partner, as "death do us part". The situation is magnified in cases where children or other relatives are either non-existent, or unwilling or unable to help. The Maintenance of Parents Bill was enacted in 1995 precisely because of an increasing tendency for a minority of parents in need to be inadequately cared for by their offspring.

How then can we reconcile the discrepancy between optimistic pictures of sustained social and economic engagement among active ageing members of society, with the obvious cases where there is debilitation and a clear need for social, financial or medical support (sometimes all three)? I will call this the reconciliation issue.

My answer is that we need to focus on the circumstances of individuals, and reduce or abandon the idea that these circumstances define groups of individuals in some particular age band. Disability in the form of a medical or psychological condition, such as dementia, is not an inevitable accompaniment of ageing. Healthy ageing to a later age is likely to become more the norm. The medically and psychologically healthy can look after themselves. They are not individuals in need of assistance. Those who are less fortunate do require assistance, and a great deal of thought is currently going into providing it. But this is not different from the situation at any given age. Age, *as such*, is not very relevant. This will require a very considerable shift in our thinking, a cognitive challenge. At the moment, certain diseases or limitations are associated with the elderly, and in some cases, the conditions are, indeed, found in the elderly and not the young. But, at any age, we may be affected by diseases or limitations, just typically different ones at different ages. However, these conditions should be dealt with as such, and not taken to exemplify a general problem for an age group. I will provide the following three examples to clarify this approach.

The overall suicide rate for Singapore is 7.4 per 100,000 (WHO, 2014b). Some elders commit suicide, but so do some people at all ages from the teens onward. The numbers at various ages are provided by the Samaritans of Singapore (SOS, 2014). Lonely, unbalanced, depressed or hopeless people, at any age, are at risk of harming themselves. Age is not the key factor here. Research suggests that life satisfaction tends to be very stable even if quality of life may decline slightly in old age (e.g., Schilling, 2006).

As my second example, consider an elderly wife trapped in the home caring for an elderly husband with a medical condition. She does her duty but loses time out of her life, feels isolated, suffers financial loss, and in the end, the husband leaves her anyway, as "death do us part". But here too, age is not the key. A much younger housewife may feel trapped in a home caring for her children, the more so if one or more are in some way handicapped or have limited potential. She does her duty but loses time out of her life, sees less of her friends, falls behind in whatever career she may have had, and in the end the children leave home anyway and she is left with an empty nest, save for a husband who either still works, or, having retired, likely expects to be cared for exactly as before (a dilemma known for decades, see Gavron, 1966, for a popular account).

As my third and final example, consider Alzheimer's disease. This is undeniably a disease of older people, and it is presently incurable, though it may be possible to delay its onset somewhat by drugs, lifestyle over the lifespan, or both (e.g., Gatz, Prescott & Pedersen, 2006; the Alzheimer's Association website provides contemporary updates on research and interventions). But, comparable incurable diseases also strike at other ages, often similarly producing progressive physical or mental deterioration. One could mention motor neurone disease, or any of the many other progressive neurological conditions that can afflict children or younger people. The problems created by the existence of debilitating chronic conditions are not confined to the elderly.

The conclusion I would draw from the above examples is that we need to stop thinking about the elderly as a separate category of people in society, and start thinking about them as people like anyone else who may, sometimes, have conditions that create social, medical or financial problems. The critical step is to stop thinking of age as the yardstick by which everything else about a person is judged. If there are caretaking issues, social isolation issues, or intractable medical conditions that affect and impair people, they should be treated as matters for social policy generally. For example, should there be some kind of allowance or subsidy for those who care for others, rather than regarding it as an entirely private matter, even though it saves the taxpayer money? Should there be some kind of national effort to address the problems of loneliness at any age, rather than seeing it as a particular problem of the elderly? The thinking here is to avoid stereotyping, and to increase, wherever we can, a more inclusive approach. So the solution to the reconciliation problem is to address the problems of the elderly as individual problems, which in other guises affect many who are not elderly. They are problems of some elderly people, not "the problems of the elderly".

Social implications

Like many other policy areas in Singapore, policies related to elderly issues require a proper understanding of the competencies and motivations of the target persons (in this case, older persons), which can be provided by research in the social and behavioural sciences. The social implications for Singapore could be considerable. The generation who are now the focus of help hotlines for silver citizens and other such laudable initiatives, are not necessarily a model for how future old people will appear. Old people, defined by age, are going to be increasingly with us, numerous, and often active; and as such the social discourse, the topics in the public space, may change quite a bit. The old will generate economic activity as consumers, and they will also generate fresh debates on issues that affect them particularly. I will end this chapter by speculating on some possibilities for Singapore, which may appear unconventional to some but are, in my view, workable at least in principle.

Any line drawn between the retired and the working is arbitrary and policies that assume a clear line as such are likely to waste valuable human resources in Singapore. By drawing and adhering to a line, some employees will be retired when they are still full of useful potential, and others will stagger on watching the calendar as well as the clock, waiting to escape, as if for the expiry of a custodial sentence. This obvious point needs to be articulated because arbitrary retirement ages exist in Singapore. The solution could be to make retirement an entitlement that falls due at a certain age, which might vary with different kinds of work; but it would be better still to simply treat the employed as the self-employed treat themselves. If employees can work well, they should not be stopped. If they cannot work, their employment should be discontinued, or they should be moved to other positions where they can still usefully contribute. This in fact happens willy-nilly with the self-employed. This same idea is what Singapore needs, albeit implemented in a more orderly manner within a framework of employment. Age should not be either a qualification or a disqualification for employment. It is strictly irrelevant. It only *appears* relevant because it is a proxy for other considerations, primarily health, which are age-related. But health and competence are things "personal to holder" and are not best related to work by the use of arbitrary cut-off points.

The notion of payment by seniority results in a reluctance to employ seniors. Obviously, this can be remedied by a shift to payment by results and value, not by position and age. Automatic seniority increments for time served should be regarded as an anachronistic anomaly; although paying for the application of experience, if a real productive benefit, should not. It should also be possible to envision, and devise practically, as a matter of policy, a normal life trajectory of employee income in which income peaks nearer times of need (e.g., supporting family, paying for housing) and declines in later life. This is especially feasible if there is an integrated approach to the provision of medical safety nets in the older population, a development clearly already under way.

Singapore's social and physical infrastructure is increasingly more integrated and inclusive in ways that accommodate diverse needs of the heterogeneous population, including the needs of older people. A recent longitudinal study of ageing in Singapore suggested that, "... continued work involvement or volunteerism [among those over 55] provides opportunities for social interaction and engagement and may be associated with enhanced mental well-being" (Schwingel, Niti, Tang & Ng, 2009). There is increasing provision for cyclists. There is a recent roll-out of a public mobility scheme for elders using electric buggies, and the government offers a Seniors Mobility and Enabling Fund (SMF) to those over 55 meeting certain means-test criteria and assessed by a public assessor (AIC, 2014). Public transport is becoming more user-friendly for people with disabilities. Condominiums designed for easier access and with facilities needed by frail retirees are selling extremely well. Minute dwelling units for singles are apparently quite fashionable. This list could be extended. Appreciation of the diversity of the older folk means that they can be absorbed into many aspects of this list. For example, some elders cycle for recreation or to work. A newspaper story reported a two-day recreational excursion from Bukit Batok to Changi and back, for 22 cyclists aged from 84 to 51 years ("At 80, She's All Ready," *The Straits Times*, 2014).

Bold and innovative changes should not be restricted to infrastructure enhancements. For example, in social services for the elderly, one could think innovatively in the area of alternative care arrangements for the elderly. In a recent report by a group of authors of which I am a part (Chan *et al.*, 2014), we proposed that the government consider authorising the formation of a quasi-family unit where elderly Singaporeans are allowed to live together in the same housing unit and care for each other with legally binding rights and responsibilities.

Another future possibility has to do with end-of-life issues, which Singapore has hitherto somewhat played down. Examples of end-of-life issues include the ethics of assisted suicide and palliative care, and how we die. The lack of public policy discussion on these issues may be due to concerns with religious sensitivities, but it may also be because local sentiment tends strongly to the view that old people should be venerated and that anything other than the prolonging of life if at all possible is unfilial. Moreover, the challenges to medical ethics can be considerable in this area. Increasingly, however, issues such as these will, in my view, become topics for public discussion. Old people near the end of life tend to have definite views on such things as the balance to be struck between quality of life and extension of life, or whether it should be possible to seek legal release from a life no longer felt worth living or tolerable.

Many elders are single and live independently, some from choice, and some not. Some elderly persons require special provisions by way of transport, whereas others are still capable of running marathons. Some are healthy, and others not. So, it is inaccurate to see elderly persons as a homogeneous group with unique special needs. The fact is elderly Singaporeans are a diverse group who do not always have much in common despite their similar age. A stronger focus on the positive attributes and less on the negative ones both at the individual person and the policy levels might raise the quality of life of elderly persons. Increasingly, we are encouraged to speak of people as individuals with attributes, not as categorised by those attributes. It is nowadays better manners to speak of those with hearing or visual impairments, rather than of "the deaf" or "the blind"; to refer to children with Autistic Spectrum Disorder or with Spastic Cerebral Palsy, rather than "autistic children" or "spastics"; to refer to adults as "having dementia" rather than as "being demented". This is not merely what is sometimes derisively called political correctness. It is an effort to ensure that people are not defined or stereotyped by their disorders or limitations. Referring to the elderly as a single group defines them by their age, which is generally seen as a limitation. The thrust of this chapter is that people should not be defined by their age.

It is not that age is unimportant. We do need to know it in many situations, but not in all. Newspaper reporters habitually ask for and report the age of people they interview, whether age is relevant to the topic of interview or not. If challenged, reporters indicate that this is a house rule, and if pressed, may say something like "it makes for a more credible report". The press could lead the way in reducing this determination to treat age as important regardless of its actual relevance.

Awareness of the potential of old age, as well as of its genuine limitations, and of the extent of individual differences, should contribute to a revision of negative stereotypes of people who happen to be old. This awareness should also result in a far more positive expectation by current younger generations of their expectations for themselves when they, in turn, are old. Economically and socially productive citizens, potentially or actually, include adults of all ages. Given the advances in electronic communications, they can be and many are already highly interconnected, and interacting in a myriad ways with people and organisations for various economic and social purposes. Future generations will function in an even more interconnected society. They will likely be less defined by age or employment, and more by their activity profiles. This means the elderly will be less defined as a group, and to the extent they are so defined at all, may be increasingly seen as a net resource rather than a burden. The last 50 years have seen a complete transformation of the conditions of life for the older citizens of Singapore. Hopefully, the next 50 could see a transformation of Singapore societal attitudes to old age.

References

Agency for Integrated Care (AIC) (2014). *Seniors Mobility and Enabling Fund* (SMF). Ministry of Health, Silver Pages. Retrieved 26 October 2014, from https://www.silverpages.sg/money_matter_article.aspx?FID=389&CID=1319&View=All&Title=What%20is%20SMF?.

Alzheimer's Association website, www.alz.org.

Anastasi, A. (1988). *Psychological Testing* (6th ed.). NY: Macmillan.

At 80, She's All Ready to Ride 100km (2014, July 2014). *The Straits Times.* Retrieved 16 February 2015, from http://yourhealth.asiaone.com/content/80-shes-all-ready-ride-100km.

Baddeley, A. (2002). *Your Memory: A Users's Guide,* 2nd ed. London: Prion Books.

Barabba, V. P. (1975). *Historical Statistics of the United States, Colonial Times to 1970* (pp. 107–115). Part 1, Series B. Washington, DC: US Bureau of the Census.

Butler, R. N. (2010). *The Longevity Revolution: The Benefits and Challenges of Living a Long Life*. NY: Public Affairs.

Chan, D. (forthcoming). The Future of Singapore's Ageing Population: Ageing as Asset and Adaptation. In E. Quah (ed.), *Singapore 2065: Insights on the Economy and the Environment from 50 Singapore Icons*. Singapore: World Scientific.

Chan, D., Elliott, J., Koh, G., Kong, L., Nair, S., Tan, E. S., Wee, A. & Yeoh, B. (2014). Social Capital and Development. In M. Yap & C. Gee (eds.), *Population Outcomes: Singapore 2050*. IPS Exchange Series, 1 May 2014.

Chan, D. & Schmitt, N. (2005). Situational Judgment Tests. In A. Evers, O. Smit-Voskuijl & N. Anderson (eds.), *Handbook of Personnel Selection* (pp. 219–242). Oxford, UK: Blackwell Publishers, Inc.

Charles, S. T. & Carstensen, L. L. (2010). Social and Emotional Aging. *Annual Review of Psychology*, 61, 383–409.

Collis, M. (2009). *Raffles: The Definitive Biography*. Singapore: Marshall Cavendish Editions.

Elliott, J. M. (1994). Conceptualising Ageing: Issues in Psychological Research. In C. Bentelspracher & K. Minai (eds.), *Ageing in Japan and Singapore* (pp. 210–223) Singapore: NUS Department of Japanese Studies Monograph Series #3.

Elliott, J. M. (2012). On Not Reinventing the Wheel: Need We See the Governance of Research in Neuroscience as Somehow Special? *Asian Bioethics Review*, 4(4), 330–343.

Gatz, M., Prescott, C. A. & Pedersen, N. L. (2006). Lifestyle Risk and Delaying Factors. *Alzheimer Disease & Associated Disorders*, 20, Supplement 2, S84–S88.

Gavron, H. (1966). *The Captive Wife: Conflicts of Housebound Mothers*. London: Routledge & Kegan Paul.

Index Mundi (n.d.). *Singapore — GDP per Capita*. Retrieved 29 October 2014, from http://www.indexmundi.com/facts/singapore/gdp-per-capita.

Jacoby, S. (2010, December 30). Real Life among the Old Old. *The New York Times*. Retrieved 23 October 2014, from http://www.nytimes.com/2010/12/31/opinion/31 jacoby.html?pagewanted=all&_r=0.

Jacoby, S. (2011). *Never Say Die: The Myth and Marketing of the New Old Age*. NY: Vintage Books, Random House.

Levy, B. (2009). Stereotype Embodiment: A Psychosocial Approach to Aging. *Current Directions in Psychological Science*, 18(6), 332–336.

Levy, B. R. (2003). Mind Matters: Cognitive and Physical Effects of Aging Self-Stereotypes. *Journals of Gerontology, Series B: Psychological Sciences and Social Sciences*, 58(4), 203–211.

Lievens, F. & Chan, D. (2010). Practical Intelligence, Emotional Intelligence, and Social Intelligence. In J. L. Farr and N. T. Tippins (eds.), *Handbook of Employee Selection* (pp. 339–355). NY: Routledge.

Loke, K. Y., Lin, J. B. Y. & Deurenberg-Yap, M. (2008). The Past, the Present and the Shape of Things to Come. *Annals of the Academy of Medicine*, 37(5), 429–434.

Lynn, R. (2013). Who Discovered the Flynn Effect? A Review of Early Studies of the Secular Increase of Intelligence. *Intelligence*, 41, 765–769.

National Population and Talent Division (NPTD) (2011). *Population in Brief 2011.* Singapore: Prime Minister's Office.

National Population and Talent Division (NPTD) (2013). *A Sustainable Population for a Dynamic Singapore: Population White Paper.* Singapore: Prime Minister's Office.

Rabbit, P. M. A. (1993). Does It All Go Together When It Goes? The Nineteenth Bartlett Memorial Lecture. *Quarterly Journal of Experimental Psychology (A): Human Experimental Psychology,* 46(3), 385–434.

Schaie, K. W. & Strother, C. R. (1968). A Cross-sequential Study of Age Changes in Cognitive Behavior. *Psychological Bulletin,* 70(6), 671–680.

Schilling, O. (2006). Development of Life Satisfaction in Old Age: Another View on the 'Paradox'. *Social Indicators Research,* 75(2), 241–271.

Schulz, R. B. & Ewen, R. (1988). *Adult Development and Aging: Myths and Emerging Realities.* NY: Macmillan.

Schwingel, A., Niti, M. M., Tang, C. & Ng, T. (2009). Continued Work Employment and Volunteerism and Mental Well-being of Older Adults: Singapore Longitudinal Ageing Studies. *Age and Ageing,* 38(5), 531–537.

Samaritans of Singapore (SOS) (2014). *National Suicide Statistics.* Retrieved 26 October 2014, from https://www.sos.org.sg/images/facts-figures/National_Suicide_Statistics2014.pdf.

Stuart-Hamilton, I. (2000). *The Psychology of Ageing: An Introduction.* London & Philadelphia, PA: J. Kingsley.

Tapia Granadosa, J. A. & Diez Roux, A. V. (2009). Life and Death During the Great Depression. *Proceedings of the National Academy of Sciences of America,* 106, 17290–17295.

Vasoo, S., Ngiam, T. L. & Cheung, P. (2000). Singapore's Ageing Population: Social Challenges and Responses. In D. R. Phillips (ed.), *Ageing in the Asia-Pacific Region: Issues, Policies and Future Trends* (pp. 174–193). London: Routledge.

World Health Organization (WHO) (2014a). *Life Expectancy. Data by Country.* World Health Organization. Retrieved 20 October 2014, from http://apps.who.int/gho/data/node.main.688?lang=en.

World Health Organization (WHO) (2014b). *Suicide Rates. Data by Country.* World Health Organization. Retrieved 26 October 2014, from http://apps.who.int/gho/data/node.main.MHSUICIDE? lang=en.

Whitbourne, S. K. & Whitbourne, S. B. (2011). *Adult Development and Aging: Biopsychosocial Perspectives.* NY: Wiley.

Williams, R. (2013). Overview of the Flynn Effect. *Intelligence,* 41(6), 753–764.

Chapter 3

Social Challenges in Singapore's Healthcare System

Jeremy Lim and Manav Saxena

Singapore has traditionally eschewed the notion of the "welfare state", preferring to instead promote an ethos of self-reliance and the concept of "Many Helping Hands". However, in recent years, the changes in demographics and epidemiology (i.e., disease patterns) coupled with a more rambunctious political landscape and activist public, have compelled a fundamental re-examination of the balance between state and individual responsibility. This chapter will describe how the socio-political philosophy in health services planning and financing has evolved and also highlight areas where more focus will be needed.

The Singapore health system: Much vaunted but starting to creak

Singapore's healthcare system is much acclaimed globally. One of the highest accolades came in 2000 when the World Health Organization (WHO), reviewing ad ranking the world's health systems, proclaimed Singapore's system the 6th best in the world. Recently, World Health Statistics 2010 ranked Singapore 2nd lowest for Infant Mortality Rate while the latest statistics rank Singapore 4th highest for Life Expectancy at birth (World Health Statistics, 2010). Singapore enjoys a constant stream of visitors from around the world seeking to understand how Singapore can achieve such sterling health indicators while still spending relatively little on healthcare. Singapore spends 3.9% of its GDP on health which is less than half that of the UK (9.3%) and not even a quarter that of the United States of America (16.2%) (WHO, 2014). The dream of every health planner (and citizen) — high quality, low cost and universal access — seemed to have been found in Singapore.

Singapore's healthcare system is built on the political philosophy of "individual responsibility" coupled with "Many Helping Hands" and a state-provided "safety net". Underpinning this is a pragmatic acceptance that healthcare must be affordable to individuals and society, necessitating rationing and prioritising.

The Singapore government has consistently emphasised the erosive effects of handouts on work ethic. Singapore's founding Prime Minister Mr Lee Kuan Yew described subsidies on consumption (including healthcare) as akin to opium and heroin, proclaiming them ruinous as no country could afford to carry the consequent financial burden (Lee, 2008). Furthermore and critical to policy understanding was his stand that such subsidies also reduced the work ethic. The language softened over the years but the underlying principles of governance remained. One Health Minister publicly mused that "I prefer to slightly under-supply than to over-supply as this will put pressure on ourselves to intensify usage and minimize over-consumption" (Khaw, 2007). Healthcare in some respects was seen as a "bottomless pit" needing constant vigilance to ensure fiscal prudence, and politicians constantly reminding the public of the dangers of "welfarism" and the fiscal dangers of allowing healthcare spending to creep up to levels seen in Europe and especially America.

At the same time, Singapore was throwing its doors open to multinational corporates and experiencing first-hand the benefits of competition as company after company elected to base factories, research centres and regional offices in Singapore over other countries, preferring the stability, skilled workforce and pro-business policies of the PAP (People's Action Party) government. These perspectives naturally spilled over into healthcare planning and the role of the market was exhorted as being best able to provide Singaporeans with the accessible and quality healthcare sought after yet balancing financial realities.

Seen through these lenses, it is easier to understand the Singapore health system of the 1980s through to the first decade of this millennium. Where were the guiding parameters for health policy-makers? The White Paper of 1993 led by the current Prime Minister Lee Hsien Loong (when he was then the Minister for Trade and Industry) articulated these concepts succinctly:

> We owe it to ourselves individually to keep fit and healthy. The healthcare system needs to be structured to strengthen this sense of personal responsibility. It must give the individual maximum incentive to stay healthy, save for his medical expenses and avoid using more medical services than he absolutely needs (Ministry of Health [MOH], 1993).

The White Paper went on to explain the role of the government and markets, stating baldly:

> We must rely on competition and market forces to impel hospitals and clinics to run efficiently, improve services and offer patients better value for money. When hospitals are insulated from price signals and market forces, the potential for inefficiency and waste is enormous. However,

market forces alone will not suffice to hold down medical costs to the minimum. The health care system is an example of market failure. The Government has to intervene directly to structure and regulate the health care system, to prevent over-supply of medical services and dampen demand.

How were these translated into policy and practice? The examples are myriad and we will confine the illustrations to four policies.

First, consider the policy on subsidies. Subsidies were deliberately reserved for treatments that were "cost-effective and of proven value" with the government firmly declaring it will "not provide the latest and best of everything" (MOH website). Wealthy Singaporeans seeking treatments that were newer and had not yet passed the government's assessment of being "cost-effective" or "of proven value" would have to pay for these themselves rather than rely on the public purse. Subsidies were further conserved for only those most in need through Medifund, which is a means-tested government medical aid scheme for the truly indigent.

Related closely to subsidy policy was the use of co-payments. The fledging PAP government introduced co-payments in 1960 for outpatient services, partly to recover some costs but much more so to minimise the wastage of medicines. Mr Lee Kuan Yew described how patients would discard medicines from the government dispensaries (where they were free) and treasure instead the medicines from the private clinics which the patients had to pay for (Lee, 2000). Since then, co-payments had progressively been ratcheted up through the 1980s and 1990s, leading to today's reality where private spending accounts for approximately two-thirds of all healthcare spending, which is a reversal of the situation in the 1980s where government spending covered almost two-thirds.

The third policy example worth highlighting is Medisave. Medisave was enacted in 1983 and remains the only national level health savings account in the world. It is the policy manifestation of "personal responsibility" with a tweak to enable family members to tap on each other's Medisave monies aimed at reinforcing "family" as the building block of the Confucian society Singapore was building. There may have been some efforts at deliberately downplaying the government's role in aggregating resources and risk pooling. In the book *Lee Kuan Yew: Hard Truths to Keep Singapore Going*, Mr Lee described how he had paid special attention to Medisave in the early years of its implementation:

> 'So if Low Thia Khiang says now, let's set up a common pool, I think he'll lose votes in the next election. Are you prepared to put your money into a common pool, having slogged and built up your CPF nest egg? It's yours and if you don't use it, you can leave it to your children or your relatives or whoever you like. Why should you put it into a common pool and everybody draws out at your expense, which is what's happening in some Western countries? The system has collapsed' (Lee Kuan Yew, 2011, quoted in Ibrahim *et al.*, 2011).

In addition to the congruence with "personal responsibility" for healthcare, Medisave was also driven by a strong belief that co-payments, or having to spend one's own money, would lead patients to be more prudent in healthcare utilisation decisions.

But intervening only on the "demand" side of the equation would be incomplete, and hence corporatisation of the government hospitals (our fourth example) was also necessary. Patients behaving as consumers would need hospitals genuinely competing with each other for patients and staff. Even in subsequent clustering of the corporatised hospitals, two groups, Singapore Health Services and National Healthcare Group, were maintained to enable elements of competition to persist.

It is worth noting that despite the seeming callous attitude of the government and the apparent "selfish" and individualistic approach that it promulgated, the government philosophy is in reality biased towards community self-help. During the years of Medisave implementation, Singapore simultaneously advocated a "Many Helping Hands" philosophy. This approach promoted community organisations as the next level of support after individual and family. The inefficiency of having to maintain multiple organisations for the different racial and special interest groups was deemed a price worth paying to maintain the ethos of community and "total involvement". The key thrust was to move away from dependency on the government, as noted in the 60th anniversary commemorative publication of the Ministry of Community Development, Youth and Sports in 2007:

> This turned welfare around. True, the indigent and the disadvantaged still had to be looked after, but emphasis was given to getting the entire community to play a role in social development. The "Many Helping Hands" approach, the involvement of the private sector and the voluntary sector set the tone for total involvement (Ministry of Community Development, Youth and Sports [MCYS], 2007).

Today, three key principles guide health and social services in Singapore: self-reliance, having the family as the first line of support and the "Many Helping Hands" approach.

The "New Normal"

The principles discussed above have served Singapore well over these last five decades, keeping healthcare costs remarkably low and achieving impressive population health outcomes. Why then is there the chorus for change and the government so ready to acquiesce? There are arguably three main drivers for reform — ageing, changes in disease patterns together with medical advances and recognition that Singapore's rapid advances did not benefit all population groups.

Ageing

Singapore is one of the fastest ageing countries in the world. The numbers have been repeated ad nauseam and we shall confine ourselves to three statistics. First, the number of seniors, defined as those above the age of 65 years, will triple between now and 2030. Second, seniors consume four times the healthcare (measured in dollars) compared to their younger peers. Third, Singaporeans are not having enough babies. Total fertility rate (TFR) was 1.19 in 2013, far off from the replacement rate of 2.1.

Take the first two statistics together and it is clear that Singapore's healthcare infrastructure will struggle to cope and the situation will not improve in the short or even the medium term. The effects are already being seen with regular reports of long waiting times and temporary structures such as tents erected in hospitals to cope with demand.

Throw in the third statistic on TFR and two further implications emerge: the need for a large foreign workforce, at least in healthcare, and concerns about financial sustainability given rapidly worsening dependency ratios.

Changes in disease patterns

Colonial Singapore was rife with tropical diseases and leading causes of death were tuberculosis and pneumonia. Fast forward to today and the non-communicable or chronic diseases predominate. Medicine has also made tremendous strides in treating previously untreatable and uniformly fatal conditions. The treatment armamentarium has expanded widely but with commensurate increases in costs. The "treatment" for heart attacks was once aspirin, morphine for pain relief, bed rest and a darkened room. Today, there is a plethora of advanced stents, pharmaceuticals, an army of specialists and sub-specialists. Medical technologies are also diffusing more quickly and more intensely. Kidney dialysis was once the purview of the wealthy but today any Singaporean "heartlander" with kidney failure expects and receives very high quality dialysis at heavily subsidised rates. Healthcare has improved by leaps and bounds and is becoming more accessible to the man in the street. However, this has come at a price, and a price that the average citizen is increasingly hard-pressed to bear on her own. Even in America, "Unless you're Warren Buffett, your family is just one serious illness away from bankruptcy" (David Himmelstein, Harvard Medical School) (Arnst, 2009).

Finally, the epidemiologic transition from infectious to chronic diseases also forces fundamental changes in the medical paradigm. Where previously doctors enjoyed the luxury of "silver bullets" (e.g., the treatment for pneumonia was administering of the right antibiotic to cure the patient), today's diseases are chronic, meaning cure is not possible and we can only control diseases and ameliorate symptoms. The role of health promotion and proactive management of complications arising from these chronic diseases, such as a foot ulcer in a diabetic patient, becomes much more important, crucial even in today's medical realities.

Vulnerable populations

The Singapore story of progress in one generation, *From Third World to First*, as Mr Lee Kuan Yew eloquently depicts in his seminal writings is one any country would be proud of, but the rapidity of the progress ironically hurts most the generation on whose backs Singapore was built.

When Medisave was first introduced, Singaporeans were advised that — "Used prudently, account holders would find their Medisave funds adequate for their hospitalisation expenses" (Yeo, 1990). However, this optimistic projection made over two decades ago has not been borne out by reality. While nationally cumulative Medisave monies have crossed the S$61 billion (MOH website — "Healthcare Financing") mark and are still growing, drilling down to the level of individuals, Minister Gan Kim Yong let on in parliament recently that at the time of death, "[h]alf of CPF members aged 65 or older who passed on in 2012 had about [S]$2,700 or less. About one-third of them had less than [S]$1,000" (Gan, 2013). In an analysis of admissions to a large restructured hospital by the Department of Economics at the National University of Singapore, it was found that almost half the elderly had tapped on their children's Medisave accounts to pay for their hospitalisation expenses.

A histogram of the Singapore population's amount of monies in Medisave accounts with age groups on the x-axis would actually reveal very powerfully and very simply the reality. This has not been released into the public domain thus far but we can speculate on what the observations would be at this point: The elderly, those who consume the most healthcare, will likely also have the least Medisave monies in their personal accounts as a group. The reasons are intuitive: Firstly, the elderly have had less time to set aside Medisave savings as the scheme only started setting aside monies in 1984. A 70-year-old in 2014 who had retired at age 55 would have had only 16 years to accumulate Medisave funds. Secondly, the elderly are drawing down from their accounts with no regular replenishments from employment. The government, in good budgetary times, does provide for Medisave top-ups. For example, the 2013 Budget provided for S$200 top-ups to the Medisave accounts of all Singaporeans aged 45 years and above. However, these top-ups are ad hoc and by no means guaranteed year after year. The only regular top-ups to Medisave were through the GST Voucher scheme which provides for means-tested Medisave top-ups of between S$150 to S$450 (GST voucher website — "Medisave"). Thirdly, MediShield premiums for the elderly are much larger in proportion to their younger counterparts. The annual premium in 2013 for a basic MediShield plan for a 35-year-old is S$105 but this escalates to S$1,190 for an 86-year-old (MOH website — "MediShield Premiums"). The difference is even more significant for the so-called "Integrated Shield Plans" which are add-ons to the basic MediShield offered by private insurers. NTUC Income's Enhanced IncomeShield (Preferred) has premiums of S$341 per year for the 35-year-old. What about premiums for an 85-year-old? S$5,360! (NTUC Income website — "Enhance IncomeShield Health Insurance").

Economically, Medisave is inefficient as there is a substantial amount of money set aside specifically for healthcare which is not being utilised — S$60 billion is four years' worth of total healthcare spending. Secondly, Medisave is not an effective health savings account for the most vulnerable group, the elderly, who need to use it most. Clearly, the most efficient economic vehicles for low probability, high-risk events are insurance and risk-pooling. However, as we have discussed, individual responsibility and the mitigation of moral hazard arising from collective financing of healthcare are two central tenets of the healthcare financing ideology. What then?

These three factors have come together to place tremendous strain on the social compact. Changes outside health have also impacted this compact — our social protection model has been premised on employment and jobs to enable self-reliance and "personal responsibility". Singapore's economic model is increasingly emphasising entrepreneurship and innovation, but risk-taking must preclude risking essential services like healthcare. Failure in commerce cannot literally be a matter of life and death. Add in a stuttering global economic outlook and wage stagnation amongst the lower socio-economic classes, and it is clear the model which had served well in the first 50 years is in need of a make-over to prepare for the next 50.

One last but crucial point as Singapore looks to the next 50 years: As the young nation comes out of adolescence, it has to articulate what it means to be Singapore and Singaporean. On Total Defence Day commemorated on 15th February, the anniversary of the fall of Singapore to the Japanese in 1942, activities are held across schools which "serve to remind pupils that Singapore can be defended and is worth defending, and that Singaporeans themselves are responsible for the defence of Singapore" (SCDF website).

Why defend Singapore? Why stay here in difficult times when it is easier and safer to leave? Singapore has to be more than a land to make one's fortune or a convenient, comfortable place to live while times are good. It has to become also an emotional construct, an aspiration of nationhood that is "worth defending", worth living and worth dying for.

Reformulating the healthcare compact

What needs to be done? Credit must be given to the government for moving boldly and decisively policy-wise, to assuage concerns. It has initiated two schemes in 2014 — MediShield Life and the Pioneer Generation Package — and greatly expanded a third Community Health Assist Scheme (CHAS) as part of a wider

Primary Care Masterplan initiative, which collectively will help tremendously in addressing some of the issues raised previously.

MediShield Life, as its tagline "Better Protection. For All. For Life" connotes, will cover every Singaporean from birth for life, and offer much higher coverage. Once fully implemented, co-insurance rates are intended to fall from the current 10%–20% to 3%–10%. Annual claim limits will also be raised and the lifetime cap removed. Seniors who previously would have automatically been excluded upon reaching 90 years of age (when MediShield was first launched, age of exclusion was 65 years) and those with congenital or pre-existing illnesses will be enrolled into MediShield Life for life (MOH website — "MediShield Life"). Today, MediShield covers approximately 93% of the Singapore population and the inclusion of the remaining 7% may not seem monumental in terms of absolute numbers but as Minister Gan Kim Yong emphasised in explaining the reforms in parliament, "The idea of MediShield Life goes beyond healthcare and insurance. It is a reflection of the kind of society we want to build: A more inclusive society ... and a more caring society" (Gan, 2014).

How quickly the governing ethos has changed is perhaps well-illustrated by describing the response to previous calls to extend MediShield to children with congenital illnesses. In 2007, *The Straits Times* journalist Salma Khalik made an impassioned plea to include such children into MediShield, writing "MediShield is the national medical insurance scheme — and that should make it difficult to justify denying coverage to unborn babies." She decried the government excluding this group, arguing that MediShield unlike private insurers should not be run on commercial principles and that "A national insurance scheme should provide coverage for anyone who wants it" (Khalik, 2007).

The government, however, declared that while it had sympathy for this group of Singaporeans, its first priority was to avoid "financial insolvency for MediShield" and that "actuarial studies suggest that premiums will have to go up significantly if MediShield is to cover congenital illnesses" thus rendering MediShield unaffordable to many (MOH, 2007). This utilitarian proposition of the "greatest good for the greatest number" was justifiable and perhaps even appropriate previously but in 2014 was no longer defensible. Interestingly enough, in a nod to the heightened efforts towards inclusivity, the MediShield Life Review Committee recommended covering not just children with congenital illnesses but also treatments relating to HIV/AIDS (MediShield, Life Review Committee Report, 2014).

The Pioneer Generation Package (PGP) likewise directly addresses the healthcare concerns of a particular vulnerable group, the seniors or those in the pioneer generation, defined as Singaporeans born on 31 December 1949 or earlier. The limitations of the 3M (Medisave, MediShield, Medifund) framework for this group of Singaporeans have been detailed above and the PGP, through its higher coverage of both outpatient and inpatient healthcare charges as well as cash payouts for those with functional disabilities, seeks to ameliorate these concerns. Prime Minister

Lee Hsien Loong in announcing the PGP details declared the aim was to "make sure that our pioneer generation will be well-covered and would not need to worry about healthcare in their old age. I think we owe it to them" (Lee, 2013).

The sub-text of the announcements and the budget earmark model are also illuminative of the thinking of the government. Firstly, the PGP was framed as a one-off scheme designed to help a defined population of first generation Singaporeans who had "built" Singapore and whom Singapore owed a debt of gratitude to. The implication is that future generations of seniors would be hard-pressed to justify similar policy treatment. Secondly, the funding for the PGP was a one-time commitment of S$8 billion taken entirely out of the FY2014 government budget (Singapore Budget, 2014). Taken collectively, these signal in no uncertain terms that some fundamental tenets of Singapore's governing philosophy such as targeted subsidies and prudent fiscal spending without burdening future generations would continue to be sacrosanct even as others like "personal responsibility" evolved to "shared responsibility".

Many have criticised CHAS as simply being the rebranding of the former Primary Care Partnership Scheme. This would be unfair and it is important to consider CHAS in the wider context of the Primary Care Master Plan which Minister Gan Kim Yong announced in October 2011. The Plan recognised that the nature of diseases in Singapore had shifted from acute, episodic illnesses which were often treated in hospitals or acute medical settings to chronic diseases which require continuing, periodic care ideally in the community. Hence, the Plan's three thrusts: CHAS which provided GPs with the necessary financing mechanisms to effectively manage patients with chronic diseases such as diabetes proactively instead of reactively only when complications arose; Community Health Centres which enabled easier access to ancillary services such as digital retinal photography for diabetics or dietetics support for weight management; and Family Medicine Clinics (FMCs) which promoted new models of public-private partnerships and greater engagement between hospital specialists and private General Practitioners (GPs) and their staff working together in multi-disciplinary teams.

What would success of all these initiatives look like? Firstly, all Singaporeans should enjoy better peace of mind, and disconcerting surveys such as the 2012 Mindshare survey which highlighted that 72% of Singaporeans believing they "cannot afford to get sick these days due to high medical costs" (Hooi, 2012) should be wiped away by newer surveys reporting greater assurance and financial security from catastrophic healthcare costs. Secondly, the unique circumstances of the pioneers and their vulnerabilities should be addressed without committing the public purse to perpetual subsidies for senior healthcare in future generations. For younger Singaporeans today, the fundamental subsidies and "3M" framework would be sufficient for them. Thirdly, and this is critical to avoid the financial pressures from out-of-control healthcare spending seen in many other countries, a transformed model of care which emphasises good health, preventive healthcare and greatly expanded roles for community healthcare instead of expensive hospitalisations.

What more?

The government has made impressive strides in moving the health system towards a future state better prepared for ageing and an onslaught of chronic diseases. At the same time, healthcare financing has been revamped to strengthen societal bonds, increase risk pooling and protect vulnerable groups of Singapore, while at the same time taking care to not overburden public finances.

The operational challenges are formidable but confidence is high that Singapore's very strong and competent public sector will rise to the challenge. Can more be done beyond what has already been announced? Should more be done given the already very full plate?

Two issues perhaps remain outstanding and it would be worthwhile for policy-makers to consider them and how they can be addressed as part of the overall transformation.

Health and social services integration

Both the health and social sectors are in the midst of fundamental reforms to better meet the needs of Singaporeans. Whilst coming under two different ministries, they are in reality attached at the hip as health issues commonly give rise to social challenges and vice versa. A devastating diagnosis of cancer even after successful treatment often causes tremendous difficulties with employment and even something as simple as an unreplaced light bulb due to limited finances can be a hazard leading to a fall and a hip fracture. Poverty can lead to poor nutritional options and deterioration in diabetes control and the list goes on and on. There have been some attempts at integrating the effector arms of both ministries such as the merging of the Centre for Enabled Living and the Agency for Integrated Care but much more can be done. Data, for example, can be shared seamlessly across at the patient/client level so that health professionals and social services resource persons can work together more effectively. Budgets too in select instances can be harmonised and even combined to enable front line staff to work together to meet the whole-of-patient/client needs rather than force-fit into what each ministries' funding parameters are.

Putting a price to life

The challenge of quantifying "what price is life" remains regardless of how much the government pours into healthcare. Healthcare demand is infinite but resources are not. Andrew Dillon, former CEO of England's National Institute for Health and Clinical Excellence explains that "When treatments are very expensive, we have to use them where they give the most benefit to patients" (Dillon, 2007). *The New York Times* columnist David Leonhardt succinctly puts it, "There is no such thing as a free lunch. The choice isn't between rationing and not rationing. It's between rationing well and rationing badly" (Leonhardt, 2009).

In Singapore, the rhetoric of caring for all Singaporeans aside, very real questions remain for some slivers of the Singapore population. What happens to children with haemophilia? Current financing practice is to not cover prophylactic Factor VIII. Should public monies be used to do so, so that the children can enjoy some normalcy of life? Is it more cost-effective to pay for prophylaxis so that the arthropathies that result from bleeding into joints can be minimised and downstream costs reduced? Even less clear-cut would be children born with lysosomal storage disorders (LSD). Treatment costs can be as high as S$300,000 per year per child. Singapore is estimated to have 12 such affected patients and it is clear patients and their families cannot fund treatment costs on their own. Is S$3.6 million a year reasonable to spend out of the public purse for 12 patients? What does Singapore wanting to be a more inclusive, a more caring society mean for these 12 patients? The answers are not straightforward but the national conversation needs to be had. Duke-NUS oncologist Ong Sin Tiong wrote poignantly about his patient "Stephanie" in "How much would you pay for an additional year of life?" and outlined how advances in modern medicine had changed a hitherto death sentence to a treatable but expensive condition. He described how explaining the disease and prognosis was easy, but "more difficult was explaining that the [medicines] would cost over S$4,300 per month for the rest of her life". He urged that the stakeholders "all need to engage with each other to decide how society will support individuals like Stephanie", acknowledging that this was a "difficult conversation" that was all the more urgent because the stakes were so high (Ong, 2013).

Singapore has had the easy "national conversation" of what it would like Singapore to be; it needs to also have the more difficult one about what price Singapore was prepared to pay collectively to realise this vision for Singapore.

Singapore can rightly be proud of her outstanding achievements in healthcare these last five decades. The next 50 years will be equally challenging but in different ways. The health concerns of 1965 are largely addressed only to be replaced with a different and perhaps even more "wicked" set of issues. A future of both ageing and endemic chronic diseases will test the mettle of Singapore's health leaders to the fullest but without underestimating the enormity of the challenges, there is reason for optimism. Singapore transforms from a position of strength with a healthy fiscal position, probably the best-trained health workforce in Asia and a government prepared to make the tough but necessary changes to ready Singapore and Singaporeans for the future.

References

Arnst, C. (2009). Study Links Medical Costs and Personal Bankruptcy. *Business Week*. Retrieved 14 January 2015, from http://www.businessweek.com/bwdaily/dnflash/content/jun2009/db2009064_666715.htm.

Dillon, A. (2007). Cited from 'Anger over Blindness Drugs Ruling'. *BBC News*. Retrieved 14 January 2015, from http://news.bbc.co.uk/2/hi/health/6749351.stm.

Gan, K. Y. (2013, April 8). *Annual CPF Medisave Account Balances from Accounts of the Deceased.* Singapore Parliament Reports, Hansard.

Gan, K. Y. (2014, July 8). *Opening Speech for Parliamentary Debate on MediShield Life Review Committee Report.* Singapore Parliament Reports, Hansard.

GST Voucher. *Medisave.* Retrieved 14 January 2015, from http://www.gstvoucher.gov.sg/faqs.html#3.

Hooi, J. (2012, October 6). Singapore's Emigration Conundrum. *Business Times Singapore.* Retrieved 16 February 2015, from http://www.businesstimes.com/sg/premium/top-stories/singapores-emigration-conundrum-20121006.

Ibrahim, Z., Han, F. K., Lin, R., Chan, R., Chua, M. H., Lim, L. & Low, I. (2011). *Hard Truths to Keep Singapore Going.* Singapore: Straits Times Press.

Khalik, S. (2007, March 17). MediShield Must Remain Affordable. *The Straits Times.* Retrieved 14 January 2015, from https://www.moh.gov.sg/content/moh_web/home/pressRoom/Media_Forums/2007/MediShield_must_remain_affordable.html.

Khaw, B. W. (2007, September 25). *Building Hardware, Software and Heartware.* Speech at SGH Pathology Groundbreaking Ceremony.

Lee, H. L. (2013). National Day Rally Speech 2013. Retrieved 14 January 2015, from http://www.pmo.gov.sg/content/pmosite/mediacentre/speechesninterviews/primeminister/2013/August/prime-minister-lee-hsien-loongs-national-day-rally-2013--speech.html.

Lee, K. Y. (2000). *From Third World to First. The Singapore Story 1965–2000.* Singapore: Singapore Press Holdings.

Lee, K. Y. (2008). Cited in Barr, Michael Dominic's — Singapore: The Limits of a Technocratic Approach to Health Care. *Journal of Contemporary Asia,* 38(3), 395–416.

Leonhardt, D. (2009, June 17). Health Care Rationing Rhetoric Overlooks Reality. *The New York Times.* Retrieved 14 January 2015, from http://www.nytimes.com/2009/06/17/business/economy/17leonhardt.html?_r=0.

MediShield Life (2014). *MediShield Life Review Committee Report.* Retrieved from 14 January 2015, https://www.moh.gov.sg/content/moh_web/MediShield-life/mlrc-report.html.

Ministry of Community Development, Youth and Sports (MCYS) (2007). *Helping Hands Touching Lives: 60 Years Making a Difference.* Singapore: Ministry of Community Development, Youth and Sports.

Ministry of Health (MOH) (1993). *Affordable Healthcare 1993 White Paper.* Retrieved 14 January 2015, from https://www.moh.gov.sg/content/moh_web/home/Publications/Reports/1993/affordable_healthcare.html.

Ministry of Health (MOH) (2007, March 22). *Reply from MOH.* Retrieved 14 January 2015, from https://www.moh.gov.sg/content/moh_web/home/pressRoom/Media_Forums/2007/MediShield_must_remain_affordable.html.

Ministry of Health (MOH). *Healthcare Financing.* Retrieved 14 January 2015, https://www.moh.gov.sg/content/moh_web/home/statistics/Health_Facts_Singapore/Healthcare_Financing.html.

Ministry of Health (MOH). *MediShield Life.* Retrieved 14 January 2015, from https://www.moh.gov.sg/content/moh_web/MediShield-life.html.

Ministry of Health (MOH). *MediShield Premiums.* Retrieved 14 January 2015, from https://www.moh.gov.sg/content/moh_web/home/costs_and_financing/schemes_subsidies/MediShield/Premiums.html.

Ministry of Health (MOH) website, www.moh.gov.sg.

NTUC Income. *Enhanced IncomeShield Health Insurance*. Retrieved 14 January 2015, from https://www.income.com.sg/forms/brochure/EIS.pdf.

Ong, S. T. (2013). What Would You Pay for Another Year of Life? *Today*. Retrieved 14 January 2015, from http://www.todayonline.com/commentary/what-would-you-pay-another-year-life.

Singapore Budget (2014). *Pioneer Generation Package*. Retrieved 14 January 2015, from http://singaporebudget.gov.sg/data/budget_2014/download/FY2014_Budget_Statement.pdf.

Singapore Civil Defence Force (SCDF). Retrieved 14 January 2015, from http://www.scdf.gov.sg/content/scdf_internet/en/community-and-volunteers/community-preparedness/total-defence.html.

World Health Organization (WHO) (2014) *Global Health Expenditure Database*. Retrieved 14 January 2015, from http://apps.who.int/nha/database/QuickReports/Index/en.

World Health Statistics (2010). Progress on the Health-related Millennium Development Goals (MDGs). Retrieved 16 February 2015, from http://www.who.int/whosis/wostat/2010/en/.

Yeo, C. T. (1990, July 18). Singapore Parliament Reports, Hansard.

Chapter 4

Marriage and Parenthood in Singapore

Paulin Straughan

Perhaps the one singular concern that has dominated headlines in post-independence Singapore is the country's below replacement fertility since the late 1970s. For a small nation-state which relies on manpower as her only resource, this has caused alarm both for the government as well as for Singaporeans. The latest report on marriages and divorces (Department of Statistics [DOS], Statistics on Marriage and Divorces 2013, 2014) highlighted what has become the norm for the city-state — falling marriage and fertility rates, delayed age at first marriage, rising singlehood — all cumulating in indicators warning of a fast-ageing society. This chapter will look at the state's response to the population dilemma and critically discuss the adequacy of these interventions.

Singapore's pro-family policies

Singapore thrives as a very successful Asian economic powerhouse and given the compact geographical nature of the city-state, it is no surprise that economic forces have tremendous influence on the construct of everyday life, including perspectives on personal private spheres like marriage and procreation. Research on marriage and family in Singapore inadvertently showcase the significance of perceived opportunity cost of investment in family endeavours and work-life balance concerns (see Straughan *et al.*, 2008). More Singaporeans had to make personal choices between family formation and career investments as more economic opportunities availed. As a result, the transformation of the city-state from a third-world developing nation to a First World economic hub saw a corresponding shift in population trends.

In the immediate post-independence stage between 1965 and 1974, the main concern of the new government was population control. Given Singapore's limited land space and high unemployment, incentives were introduced to encourage smaller families. Induced abortion and sterilisation were liberalised and legalised (Saw, 2005). Family policies that favoured the two-child family model were mainstreamed. These included no paid maternity leave for mothers after their second child, increased accouchement fees (SFPPB, 1969) and amended primary school registration priority ("Registration for Primary One Classes", *The Straits Times*, 1976). In 1968, changes were made in public housing such that couples without children, or with only one or two children could now apply for flats (HDB, 1978). The anti-natalist phase was very successful, with the total fertility rate (TFR) falling from 4.62 in 1966 to 1.8 in 1980 at the end of the third five-year plan (Wong & Yeoh, 2003).

The inverse relationship between economic growth and population growth posed serious concerns for a small city-state that has manpower as her only resource. By the late 1970s, it was clear that the concern of the state had to shift from population control to population growth. The government responded through a series of family-related policies in an attempt to mitigate the effects. Broadly, these policies attempted to address the specific concerns triggered by demands of economic advancements.

Period of rapid economic growth and population decline, 1975–1985

During the early stages of nation building, the quality of our labour force was enhanced with more enjoying skills training and formal education. This period also saw a tremendous increase in the number of women who entered tertiary education, which is significant in the transformation of marriage and family formation in Singapore. In 1980, 18% of females aged 20 to 25 years old had graduated from secondary school in 1980, while this number had increased to 46% in 1995 (DOS, 1995). Endowed with higher formal education, getting married was no longer the only option for young women entering adulthood. Instead, like their male counterparts, they were eager to see returns to their investment in formal education, and career advancement became a more pressing life goal than finding a life partner.

Concurrently, in a fairly traditional Asian culture where patriarchy is the dominant ideology and husbands are still very much viewed as the rightful heads of households, it became more challenging for women with tertiary education to find suitable partners as the pool of eligible shrunk to a much smaller group of men with similar education. To exasperate matters, men continued to prefer marrying "down" and look towards less-educated peers as potential life partners (Lauer & Lauer, 2008). This mismatch in aspirations created two dominant groups of singles who were unlikely to see potential life partners in each other — highly educated females with tertiary qualifications and males with less than primary school education.

By the earlier 1980s, it was clear that the total fertility rate (TFR) had fallen to below-replacement level. For a small nation-state like Singapore, unchecked decline in TFR would ultimately result in a shrinking population. This period of Singapore's development also coincided with healthy economic growth and where employment opportunities were available for both men and women. As seen in Tables 4.1 and 4.2 below, the fall in marriage rates and TFR was most acute among women with tertiary education (DOS, 2014a).

As a result, the then Prime Minister Lee Kuan Yew initiated a carefully calibrated approach to population growth where differentiated policies were targeted at different segments of the population to encourage those with better means (defined most commonly as those with higher formal education) to expand family size. The rationale — that those with tertiary education should be endowed with better genes, so the union of two graduates should result in brighter children. This period, commonly referred to as the "Eugenics Phase" was very unpopular, particularly among the graduate community who were the target of the incentives.

Table 4.1(a) Proportion of Single Males among Resident Population by Age Group and Highest Qualification Attained in 2003.

Highest Qualification Attained	Below Secondary	Secondary	Post-Secondary (Non-tertiary)	Diploma & Professional Qualifications	University
Age Group					
25–29	66.8	64.8	63.7	75.1	69.8
30–34	42.3	34.1	30.9	33.1	28.7
35–39	27.3	19.8	20.4	14.1	14.1
40–44	22.1	13.0	11.3	10.7	8.5
45–49	15.8	9.7	12.4	7.2	4.5

Source: DOS, Population Trends 2014.

Table 4.1(b) Proportion of Single Males among Resident Population by Age Group and Highest Qualification Attained in 2013.

Highest Qualification Attained	Below Secondary	Secondary	Post-Secondary (Non-tertiary)	Diploma & Professional Qualifications	University
Age Group					
25–29	68.1	70.0	78.0	83.1	82.1
30–34	41.8	41.1	39.8	41.6	36.7
35–39	32.2	22.5	23.8	18.2	17.2
40–44	25.5	15.9	14.5	11.6	10.8
45–49	18.3	12.3	12.2	11.2	8.0

Source: DOS, Population Trends 2014.

Table 4.1(c)   Proportion of Single Females among Resident Population by Age Group
and Highest Qualification Attained in 2003.

Highest Qualification Attained	Below Secondary	Secondary	Post-Secondary (Non-tertiary)	Diploma & Professional Qualifications	University
Age Group					
25–29	22.5	34.0	44.8	50.8	56.3
30–34	13.8	17.2	24.4	22.8	24.4
35–39	10.5	14.5	18.5	21.0	20.2
40–44	9.9	14.1	17.4	21.1	19.3
45–49	8.5	14.8	18.8	23.6	20.6

Source: DOS, Population Trends 2014.

Table 4.1(d)   Proportion of Single Females among Resident Population by Age Group
and Highest Qualification Attained in 2013.

Highest Qualification Attained	Below Secondary	Secondary	Post-Secondary (Non-tertiary)	Diploma & Professional Qualifications	University
Age Group					
25–29	30.6	41.2	52.6	60.5	67.8
30–34	15.9	19.3	25.9	25.5	29.3
35–39	10.3	11.9	15.4	18.4	20.5
40–44	8.3	10.0	12.4	15.6	16.1
45–49	9.2	12.7	12.3	17.2	17.1

Source: DOS, Population Trends 2014.

Table 4.2   Average Number of Children Born to Resident
Ever-married Females Aged 40–49.

	Year	
Highest Qualification Attained	2003	2013
Below secondary	2.24	2.15
Secondary	2.05	2.01
Post-secondary (non-tertiary)	2.02	1.86
Diploma & professional qualifications	1.93	1.82
University	1.84	1.72

Source: DOS, Population Trends 2014.

The Social Development Unit (SDU) was established in 1984 to provide match-making services to single graduates in ministries, statutory boards and government-linked companies. In addition, there was enhanced child relief for specially educated women in terms of income tax returns to encourage them to re-enter and remain in the workforce. Child relief was raised to 5% of these highly educated women's income for the first child, to 10% for the second child, and to 15% for the third child.

Eligibility was also widened to include women with at least five "O" level passes (Saw, 2005). Further, the government deterred less-educated women from having large families by offering S$10000 sterilisation cash grants to women with no "O" levels below the age of 30 ("Cash and Cut", *The Sunday Times*, 1984). The grant was either deposited into their Central Provident Fund (CPF) to be withdrawn at 55 or to be used to purchase an apartment. In March 1985, accouchement fees were raised for Class C wards, which primarily served the less-educated women. Conversely, delivery fees remained the same for Class A wards, typically used by better-educated women ("Maternity Fees", *The Straits Times*, 1985).

Not surprisingly, the TFR continued to decline further below the replacement level to 1.64 in 1986.

Balancing work–family interweave, 1986–1999

By the mid-1980s, the TFR had fallen so low that it was clear every baby counted regardless of the social class background of the parents. Nonetheless, still concerned that those without financial means should not expand family size, the government shifted its emphasis to promote fertility by launching a new population policy titled "Have Three or More Children If You Can Afford It" in 1987 (Wong & Yeoh, 2003). The new campaign targeted married couples with messages such as "Children — Life Would Be Empty Without Them", "Life's Fun When You're a Dad and Mum". Furthermore, unmarried singles were urged to get married and start a family with campaign slogans such as "Make Room for Love in Your Life" and "Life Would Be Lonely without a Family".

To boost fertility rates, the government began relaxing some of the old anti-natalist policies. These included concessions to facilitate young couples to start a family by permitting down payment for HDB flats to be made in two stages, extending the Medisave to allow payment of delivery and hospital charges for the third child, as well as the introduction of paid unrecorded leave to working mothers to attend to their sick children ("Don't Worry about Discrimiantion", *The Straits Times*, 1987). To encourage married women with children to remain economically engaged, more was done to facilitate work-life integration. For example, female officers in the civil service with a child under six years old were given the option of taking up flexible work arrangements for a maximum of three years and childcare subsidies of S$150 were also granted to parents sending their young children to approved full-day childcare centres ("Sterilisation Leave Changes", *The Straits Times*, 1987). However, these policies did not work to boost fertility rates as the TFR continued falling to 1.60 in 2000.

Shifting the focus on the family, 2000 and beyond

Revisions to the pro-family policies shifted more dramatically to encourage more Singaporeans to start families by the introduction of fiscal incentives, popularly termed as the Baby Bonus Scheme. Cash grants were gifted; both directly upfront at the birth of baby and through a co-saving scheme (for details, see Straughan *et al.*, 2008). More enhancements were made to facilitate the dual roles for married women. These included levy subsidies for foreign domestic workers to help fill the gap at home when the mother returns to work, and revised public housing allocation policies to facilitate larger families (Ministry of Community Development, Youth and Sports [MCYS], 2003).

The policies were further enhanced in 2004 by the then new Prime Minister Lee Hsien Loong to cover three broad areas of creating family time, addressing work-life balance and expanding childcare options (Lee, 2004). For example, the Grandparent Caregiver Tax Relief aims to encourage grandparents as primary caregivers when the mother is engaged in paid work. Several public housing policies were also initiated to facilitate the three-generation extended family (see MCYS, 2004). It was also noted that mothers' educational qualification was no longer a criteria in the pro-family tax incentives. The fertility rate had slipped so low that it was no longer feasible to maintain selective pro-natalist policies, the ideological stance that was dominant in earlier phases.

To address this, a three-day paternity leave was introduced in 2000, more symbolic than substantial but nonetheless, an important signal to all that fathers have an important role to play in the lives of their newborn. Concurrently, unrecorded childcare leave was also made available for fathers. (A more elaborate analysis of the 2000 and 2008 schemes can be found in Straughan *et al.*, 2008.) In 2008, fine-tunes were made to the (now-labelled) Marriage and Parenthood (M&P) Package. Fiscal incentives through the Baby Bonus and tax incentives through the working mother child relief scheme were enhanced, with more privileges going to larger families. Extension of maternity leave and both paid and unpaid childcare leave, enhanced childcare and infant care subsidies all affirmed the importance that mothers should return to the workplace (Ministry of Manpower [MOM], 2008).

Yet, despite the generous M&P Package in 2008, the TFR continued its decline, falling to an unprecedented low of 1.15 in 2010. Although the TFR increased slightly to 1.29 in 2012, it may not be an accurate reflection of the 2008 M&P Package's efficacy given that 2012 is the year of the Dragon, which the Chinese regard to be an auspicious year for having babies (Saw, 1990).

An enhanced Marriage and Parenthood (M&P) Package was announced in 2013 to complement the existing pro-natalist policies. Overall, the aim of the package was to help offset the high perceived costs to parenthood. The enhancements facilitated housing for growing families, support for incurred medical costs (including cost of Assisted Reproductive Technologies), and childcare through promotion of better work-life balance, as well as further defrayed childcare costs (for details, see National Population and Talent Division [NPTD], Marriage and Parenthood Package, 2013). In spite of these generous incentives, the latest Population Trends 2014 report listed the TFR for 2013 at 1.9. The TFR declined across all ethnic groups, with the Chinese suffering the lowest TFR at 1.05. Of greater concern was the slowdown in marriage rates, with the number of marriages involving at least one citizen having decreased from 23,192 in 2012 to 21,842 in 2013. We also registered the slowest population growth in the last 10 years (DOS, 2014a).

Beyond 2014 — What else can be done to arrest population decline?

In general, the pro-family policies centred around incentives in housing allocation, tax benefits, as well as financial incentives for having children. In the recent enhancements (2008 and 2013), there was more emphasis on leave benefits and creating time-off for nurturing children. The governing principles have not changed much: family formation should not be done at the expense of engagement in paid work, and a significant part of the pro-family policies focus on encouraging married women to remain in the workforce as they venture into motherhood.

These policies come with a hefty price tag as the government struggles to entice more young Singaporeans to invest in family formation. The 2013 enhanced package was estimated to cost S$2.3 billion. In terms of scope and expansion of interventions, the latest enhancements to the Marriage and Parenthood Package (MPP) announced in 2013 are very comprehensive. In addition to the fiscal policies that cover baby bonuses, tax incentives, housing incentives, adjustment to Medisave coverage and co-funding of Assisted Reproductive Technologies, the MPP also extended parenting leave to include a more gender-neutral stance on childcare responsibilities (for details, see NPTD, 2013, Hey Baby website). So when the Marriages and Divorces 2013 Report (DOS, 2014b), and later, the Population Trends Report were released (DOS, 2014a), the decline in marriage and TFR made headlines ("Can the Taxman", *The Straits Times*, 2014).

While the effects of the 2013 enhancements to the MPP (if any) will take some time to register statistically, the observable returns to the pro-family incentives in place since the 1980s have been rather discouraging. While marriage rates and TFR may have dived even further without these pro-natalistic initiatives, it is nonetheless quite clear that the initiatives in place were not game changers. TFR continued to drop, from 1.62 in 1987 (when the first major pro-natalistic measures were introduced) to 1.19 in 2013. This begs the question: Why are the initiatives not able to counter the downward trend of falling TFR?

To address this, we can glean the dynamic complexity that governs marriage and procreation decisions from the recently concluded Marriage and Parenthood Study[3] (see NPTD, Marriage and Parenthood Study 2012, 2013). The survey of singles showed that marriage and family formation remains an important life goal. However, meeting the appropriate partner and having contesting life goals remain top reasons cited by singles to explain why they had yet to actualise their aspirations. Among women, most articulated the desire to remain economically engaged if they should embrace motherhood. Indicators of work-life balance suggested that more should be done to free employees for pursuits outside of paid work. The ideals of shared parenting responsibilities reflected shifting gender norms in Singapore. A notable finding showed that over 70% surveyed believed that they would have little problem conceiving even if they were over 35 years.

I will deconstruct these findings systematically to tease out the social and cultural barriers which have yet to be addressed by current pro-family policy initiatives, which may explain the limited effect these policies have on improving marriage and fertility trends.

Contesting life goals

The fact is, with modernisation comes tremendous opportunities in the realm of paid work that are, by and large, gender neutral. While marriage used to be perceived as a natural progression in the lifecycle of a young person (especially a young woman) and not getting married by a certain age was viewed as suspect, singlehood is now considered normal, especially for those aged 30 and younger. As the proportion of singles grows, being married before the age of 30 is fast becoming the "anomaly" as young Singaporeans invest in self-actualisation through formal education and career advancement. Although getting married and parenthood remain important life goals, investment in career is just as important. In capitalist economies that thrive on competition, the rewards (both tangible and intangible) for those with the tenacity to clock long hours and remain locked in overdrive in the office is tremendous.

While the government has tried to reposition the importance of parenthood, the gestation for rewards to be manifested for investment in family is long and the returns intrinsic. And when a young couple enters marriage and family formation, they very quickly realise that despite their personal beliefs, the institution of marriage is still very much governed by traditional gender norms. While we have made it easier for fathers to participate in child rearing, parenthood is still very much a mother's responsibility. Involved mothers very quickly find out that there are real costs to their career advancements when they step out to raise children. While we do not yet have specific data on Singapore, research elsewhere shows that there are real effects on salaries of women when they enter motherhood, and women gain as much as a 9% increase in salary for every year they delay child bearing (Miller, 2011).

The truth of the matter is, there will always be costs involved in family formation. And while the larger cost to society is often observable only much later (after years of persistent trends), the cost to the individual is immediate and very real. The opportunity costs invoked by women in a marriage are expected to be negated by intrinsic rewards of parenthood and the promise of a lifelong couplehood where gains (and costs) are shared as a single unit. However, the increase in incidence of marriage dissolution has also made many more cautious about suffering individual costs.

Increasingly, with women demanding that men play equal roles at home, there are perceived opportunity costs in marriage for men as well. While the perceived costs do not necessarily deter one from marriage, they do however put more pressure on selecting "the right partner" for marriage.

The challenge of spouse selection in modern society

The proportion who are single has increased significantly over the past 10 years (see Tables 1(a)–1(d)). Noteworthy is the proportion of 25–29-year-old females who are single. This is the age band for which we typically expect that women should be married and would have started building their families. Median age at first marriage is now at 30.1 years for males, and 27.8 years for females. As we are still very much a conservative Asian society where procreation is only sanctioned within the marital union, getting married is a precondition for parenthood. And when we marry later, it reduces the likelihood of growing large families.

Why, then, the delay in marriage? Broadly, there are three main reasons. First, the meaning of marriage has transformed, and along with it, the expectations of the ideal life partner. Modern marriages, as Cherlin (2004) and Coonzt (2004) argued, are deinstitutionalised and serve to fulfil personal satisfaction. This places a much higher stake on spouse selection as we strive to search for our "soul mate", someone who would add value to our lives. This is especially so for women in Singapore who are now economically independent and can afford to live their lives out as singles if they choose to do so. Rather than rush into the marital union which is expected to bind "till death do us part", most take a more cautionary approach in their search for a life partner.

Second, the hectic pace of a competitive economic power house has rendered leisure a luxury few can afford. This perceived stress from paid work is especially acute for young professionals who are just starting off in their careers. A highly competitive performance-based evaluation system and the ever competitive work place result in an over-investment in paid work with Singapore employees registering one of the highest number of hours worked in the world ("Average Singaporean", *AsiaOne Business News*, 2013). Many succumb to the pressure of having to clock long hours, even though they feel that they are less productive during the extended hours. This suggests a work culture that still relies on face-time to validate commitment at the work place. This consistent need to overwork has made it difficult for young singles to expand their social network, and engage in courtship. Since 2004, singles have consistently reported their inability to find a suitable partner as the top reason for not marrying (NPTD, Marriage and Parenthood Study 2012, 2013).

Third, in the face of multiple contests of one's time and attention, courtship and marriage are not accorded as much urgency. Giddens (1991) argued that compared to pre-modern societies where people's lives are largely ordered and scripted by societal norms such as one's social class location, family background or gender (Hogan & Astone, 1986), contemporary societies present a multiplicity of choice which suggests flexibility in options and progression of life goals. Whereas in traditional societies marriage is the gateway to adulthood, it is but one of many options which is presented to young adults in modern society. While most singles in Singapore continue to value marriage as a life goal, it is not necessarily the top-ranked aspiration but one of many (which include career advancement).

Myths on the biological clock

Another reason that accounts for the delay in marriage and procreation is simply the fact that we are now living longer. As life expectancy inches up due to advances in medical innovations and general improvement in living conditions, many simply do not see the urgency to get married and start a family so early. In particular, news headlines on celebrity couples who embrace parenthood in their 40s (way past the prescribed mid-to-late 20s as the ideal age bracket for natural procreation) and success stories of miracle births from artificial reproductive technologies (ART) continue to entrench the myth that medical innovations have debunked the limitations of the biological clock. That the enhanced pro-family policies now include subsidies for ART reflect how serious this misperception is, as more couples now need medical interventions because late marriage results in greater difficulties for natural conception.

Work-life balance — Or lack of

Now more than ever, it is critical that we address the implications of interweave between paid work and family commitment. The myth of dual-sphere ideology (see Lopata, 1993) must be debunked as we no longer have the full-time homemaker to weave the interface between the public world of paid work and the private world of the family. In Singapore, where human resources are limited and highly valued, the call to play meaningful roles in economic production is gender neutral. Overtime, women have adopted similar life goals as their male counterparts. They value formal education and skills enhancement, and see these as preconditions for career advancement. Like men, women delay marriage because they want to see returns to the pricy investment of higher formal education. Because they are now engaged in paid work, any distraction to full-time commitment to career advancement comes with a perceived opportunity cost.

Significant to this is the concern that family formation may come at a higher cost to women than men. As long as child rearing is still expected to be women's work, pro-family incentives will have limited appeal for these address short-term financial setbacks, but pale in comparison to long-term disadvantages in terms of step back at workplace. Because more women now share similar aspirations of career advancement as men, work-life balance is a key factor that would determine if couples opt to grow larger families.

Pro-family policies — Will they work?

Pro-family policies tend to focus on incentivising individuals to have children — to compensate for the opportunity cost involved in building families. However, we are cognisant that no government can afford to pay for women to have babies. There is limited reach to fiscal incentives — with rising affluence, these incentives will not draw those in upper middle and upper classes. Unless we can remove the structural barriers that continue to segregate family work from paid work, we may have to accept the fact that more will choose the path with extrinsic rewards.

The key to the issue lies in those who are delaying or not even considering marriage and family formation. The contesting goals of career advancement, lifestyle choices or perhaps the inability to find a suitable life partner will continue to be formidable barriers which public policy cannot mitigate. If we are serious about promoting investment in marriage and family, we have to be prepared for a radical transformation of our society and be prepared to exchange short-term material gains from riding economic growth cycles for long-term social stability that comes with a steady population growth. Structural barriers to work-life balance will have to give way to a cultural shift that repositions the importance of growing a family. To reduce over-investment in paid work, a new remuneration system that privileges a more balanced approach to work will have to replace the current one which encourages annual competition among peers. More radical measures like restricting hours worked may have to be invoked if we believe that personal choice no longer privileges family time.

All these measures will come at a cost to the state and will have serious implications on economic growth. But the question is — can we afford to conduct business as usual? So perhaps, as we continue to make it easier for those who want to get married and have kids to do so and grow a nurturing environment for supporting families, we must be prepared for the inevitable shift in demographics and be prepared that many may remain single, and the implications of an ageing population where family support will have to be augmented by strong social safety nets and infrastructural preparedness.

References

Average Singaporean Works 2,287 Hours a Year: Study (2013, September 2). *AsiaOne Business News*. Retrieved 3 February 2015, from http://business.asiaone.com/career/news/average-singaporean-works-2287-hours-year-study.

Can the Taxman Play Stork Too? (2014, February 4). *The Straits Times*. Retrieved 5 January 2015, from http://www.straitstimes.com/the-big-story/budget-2014/story/can-the-taxman-play-stork-too-20140204.

Cash and Cut to Save a Child (1984, June 3). *The Sunday Times*, p. 1. Retrieved 5 January 2015, from http://eresources.nlb.gov.sg/newspapers/Digitised/Article/straitstimes19840603-1.2.7.aspx.

Cherlin, A. J. (2004). The Deinstitutionalization of American Marriage. *Journal of Marriage and Family*, 66, 848–861.

Coontz, S. (2004). The World Historical Transformation of Marriage. *Journal of Marriage and Family*, 66(4), 974–979.

Department of Statistics (DOS) (1995). *General Household Survey, Singapore Census of Population 1980 and 1990*. Singapore: Department of Statistics.

Department of Statistics (DOS) (2014a). *Population Trends 2014*. Singapore: Department of Statistics.

Department of Statistics (DOS) (2014b). *Statistics on Marriage and Divorces 2013*. Singapore: Department of Statistics, Ministry of Trade & Industry.

Don't Worry about Discrimination, Cheow Tong Tells Working Mums (1987, March 7). *The Straits Times*, p. 1. Retrieved 5 January 2015, from http://eresources.nlb. gov.sg/newspapers/Digitised/Article/straitstimes19870307-1.2.6.aspx.

Giddens, A. (1991). *The Consequences of Modernity*. Cambridge: Polity Press.

Housing & Development Board (HDB) (1978). *HDB Annual Report*. Singapore: Housing & Development Board.

Hogan, D. P. & Astone, N. M. (1986). The Transition to Adulthood. *American Sociological Review*, 12, 109–130.

Lauer, R. & Lauer, J. (2008). *Marriage and Family: The Quest for Intimacy*. New York: McGraw-Hill Higher Education.

Lee, H. L. (2004). Our Future of Opportunity and Promise. *National Day Rally 2004*. Singapore: Singapore Press Holdings.

Lopata, H. Z. (1993). The Interweave of Public and Private: Women's Challenge to American Society. *Journal of Marriage and Family*, 55, 176–190.

Maternity Fees Go up Next Month (1985, February 8). *The Straits Times*, p. 19. Retrieved 5 January 2015, from http://eresources.nlb.gov.sg/newspapers/Digitised/Article/ straitstimes19850208-1.2.30.17.aspx.

Miller, A. (2011). The Effects of Motherhood Timing on Career Path. *Journal of Population Economics*, 24(3), 1071–1100.

Ministry of Community Development, Youth and Sports (MCYS) (2003). *Family Policy Directory: A Guide to Government Policies for the Family*. Singapore: Ministry of Community Development, Youth and Sports.

Ministry of Community Development, Youth and Sports (MCYS) (2004, October 5). Retrieved 11 July, 2014, from www.babybonus.gov.sg.

Ministry of Manpower (MOM) (2008). *2008 Workplace Measures to Support Marriage and Parenthood*. Singapore: Ministry of Manpower.

National Population and Talent Division (NPTD) (2013). *Marriage and Parenthood Package*. Retrieved 15 October, 2014, from Hey Baby website, http://www.heybaby.sg/ mppackage.html.

National Population and Talent Division (NPTD) (2013). *Marriage and Parenthood Study 2012*. Singapore: Singapore Press Holdings.

Registration for Primary One Classess Will Begin on July 26 (1976, July 18). *The Straits Times*, p. 6. Retrieved 5 January 2015, from http://eresources.nlb.gov.sg/ newspapers/Digitised/Article/straitstimes19760718-1.2.42.aspx.

Saw, S. H. (1990). *Changes in the Fertility Policy of Singapore*. Singapore: Institute of Policy Studies and Times Academic Press.

Saw, S. H. (2005). *Population Policies and Programmes in Singapore*. Singapore: ISEAS Publications.

SFPPB (1969). *Fourth Annual Report of the Singapore Family Planning and Population Board*. Singapore: Singapore Family Planning and Population Board.

Sterilisation Leave Changes (1987, April 4). *The Straits Times*, p. 11. Retrieved 5 January 2015, from http://eresources.nlb.gov.sg/newspapers/Digitised/Article/straitstimes 19870404-1.2.25.9.aspx.

Straughan, P., Chan, A. & Jones, G. (2008). *Ultra-low Fertility in Pacific Asia: Trends, Casues and Policy Issues*. London: Routledge.

Wong, T. & Yeoh, B. (2004). *Fertility and the Family: An Overview of the Pro-natalist Population Policies in Singapore*. Singapore: Asian Meta-Centre.

Chapter 5

Preserving Racial and Religious Harmony in Singapore

Mathew Mathews and
Mohammad Khamsya Bin Khidzer

This chapter discusses the social issues and contexts relating to Singapore's efforts in preserving racial and religious harmony.

A history of violence

While not necessarily unanimous, there are numerous accounts of conflict in Singapore's pre-independence history arising over issues related to the primordial differences of race and religion. However, two instances of ethno-religious violence in history have been consistently evoked by the Singapore government to exemplify the extent of destruction that could overwhelm the vulnerable nation lest we slip into complacency.

The first instance is the Maria Hertogh riots, named after a 13-year-old girl. In 1950, while Singapore and Malaysia were still under British rule, tensions culminated into riots when the High Court decided that a child (Maria Hertogh) who had been raised by her Muslim parents be returned to her biological parents, who were Dutch Catholics. Amid the growing fervour of anti-colonialism and increasingly pronounced antagonism between Muslims and Christians, the decision by the court served only to add fuel to the flames, leading to clashes between Muslims and those of European descent (Syed Khairudin, 2010). The Maria Hertogh riots left 18 people dead, with many more injured.

The second instance is the 1964 racial riots. Before Singapore separated from Malaysia, the intense communal politicking involving the United Malays National Organisation (UMNO) and the People's Action Party (PAP) on race-based issues took centre stage. Both political parties had been overindulgent in pursuing their respective political objectives, violating pre-agreed political boundaries which eventually led to the now well-known racial riots of 1964 which left 23 people dead and many more injured (Turnbull, 2009).

There were other riots which had ensued in Singapore's relatively nascent history, some even intraethnic in nature.[1] These other riots have also been couched in a similar cautionary tone, based on the narratives of vulnerability and fragility which often accompany discussions on racial and religious differences in Singapore. Not surprisingly, the state's treatment of history has been criticised by scholars who propounded that the incidents of violence, which were embedded in the political discourse, glossed over the layers of complexity that are inherent in history. The charge has been that the state uses these historical events to justify its policies so as to maintain hegemony (Loh, 1998; Narayanan, 2004).

This criticism notwithstanding, the violent incidents which had erupted at various junctures of Singapore's history coincided with issues of communal allegiances which remain salient up till this day. Only today, globalisation and the advent of technology have made individuals more cognisant of an array of identities, thus accelerating the potential for tension and conflict. Despite this, the Singapore government has managed to keep a tight grip on multicultural harmony, the constituents of which shall be elaborated later in this chapter.

When Singapore gained independence, its founding fathers were quick to articulate policies to safeguard racial and religious harmony. Forging social cohesion in a demographically diverse society was crucial partly because of the economic imperative to attract foreign investments in an otherwise resource-scarce economy. While Malaysia stuck to its stand to push for Malay rights and privilege, the Singapore government, then led by Mr Lee Kuan Yew, pursued a multiracial and multireligious policy which would emphasise equal rights and opportunities for all its citizens, regardless of race, language or religion. This was seen as a logical direction, given the still raw wounds inflicted during the racial conflict in 1964 and the fact that Singapore had inherited a very fractured society, one which led its leaders to adopt a continuously proactive, pre-emptive and interventionist orientation in managing the country. As Mr S Rajaratnam, then Minister of Culture who penned the Singaporean pledge stated: "In a multi-racial, multi-lingual and multi-cultural society like ours, the communal problem... must always remain one of the major problems which, if we do not resolve intelligently, could break our society" (S. Rajaratnam in Chin & Vasu, 2007, p. 2)

---

[1] Other less known riots in Singapore's history include the Hokkien-Teochew Riots in 1854 where the Chinese secret societies were involved (Yong, 2011b) and the Anti-Catholic Riots in 1851 where approximately 500 people were killed (Yong, 2011a).

The need to exercise vigilance led to the state implementing various disciplinary legal measures such as a tight control of press and public discourse to ensure that any form of excessive racial and religious sentiments which may be offensive to others are checked. Understandably, measures such as these have attracted unflattering labels by commentators, especially from the international media (Lee & Wilnat, 2009; Mauzy & Milne, 2002). Yet the Singapore government has often come out to rationalise these steps as pre-emptive actions, viewed as essential in order to maintain its version of peace and harmony. The state is also aware of the need to protect the rights of the minority groups — the Malays, Indians as well as other groups. The Malays are viewed as indigenous to Singapore and have special rights as enshrined in the constitution. In Article 152 of the Singapore constitution entitled "Minorities and special position of Malays", it is stated that:

> (1) It shall be the responsibility of the Government constantly to care for the interests of the racial and religious minorities in Singapore.
>
> (2) The Government shall exercise its functions in such manner as to recognise the special position of the Malays, who are the indigenous people of Singapore, and accordingly it shall be the responsibility of the Government to protect, safeguard, support, foster and promote their political, educational, religious, economic, social and cultural interests and the Malay language.

In 2009, when Nominated Member of Parliament Viswa Sadasivan in his maiden speech in parliament called for the government to reaffirm its commitment to the pledge, it elicited a very strong reaction from then Minister Mentor Lee Kuan Yew. The latter was concerned that such "highfalutin ideals" would mislead Singaporeans and added that the constitution never guaranteed full equality in the first place, with Malays holding a special position in Singapore society (Oon, 2009). Whether these special rights of the Malays in Singapore have been enforced or not is debatable but there is clearly some recognition of minority and indigenous rights. Corollary to this, policies and programmes have also been shaped to ensure that minority groups do not fall behind and that there is adequate minority representation in nation building processes and national institutions. The state also manages programmes for interracial and interreligious integration. This is deemed to be especially crucial in order to foster a harmonious society.

Multiculturalism, disciplinary legal instruments and other soft policies/programmes are three ways in which the state preserves racial and religious harmony in Singapore. They fall neatly into the Singapore government's pre-emptive and interventionist modus operandi which has in the past decades, worked in maintaining harmony in its simplest manifestation — social order. However, it would be naive to assert that harmony in Singapore is without problems. On the contrary, the Singapore brand of harmony has encountered its fair share of problems, alluding to the imperfections of the system. The rest of this chapter will discuss, in greater detail, the three ways in which the state preserves harmony, their shortcomings and suggestions for which Singapore can develop a more resilient brand of harmony for the decades ahead.

Multicultural policy in Singapore

Ever since its inception in 1965, the state has never believed that Singaporeans from different races and religious groups would be able to organically sustain a social environment based on comity and harmony. There is a strong belief that if left to their own devices, people will merely retreat into their homophilic shell, preferring to mingle only with those of a similar religion, race or language. Such a scenario creates and reproduces segregation of various kinds. This would explain the proactive, interventionist stand the Singapore government takes in engineering a particular brand of harmony and effectively maintaining social order. One of the ways in which the state engineers social harmony is to implement a multiracial and multireligious system, or what is currently known as multiculturalism (Tan, 2004).

Multiculturalism is premised on the acknowledgement of ethnic diversity and in ensuring the rights of individuals to retain their culture. Individuals in a multicultural system therefore enjoy full access to participation in a society built on constitutional principles and commonly shared values. By acknowledging the rights of individuals and groups and ensuring equitable access to society, advocates of multiculturalism maintain that it reduces social pressures based on disadvantages and inequality which benefits individuals and the larger society (Inglis, 1996).

Rather than the domination of a single national culture, multiculturalism acknowledges, embraces and even emphasises the importance of the diversity of ethnic cultural heritage and practices of the various groups to achieve a cohesive society (Owen, 2005; Pereira, 2008). The aim is to foster better understanding of one another's differences through promoting cultural exposure and cross-cultural interaction, so that members of society will be better able to negotiate cultural diversity and interact with one another (Owen, 2005). Further to this, Singaporeans, regardless of race, religion or language are expected to negotiate a fair system based on meritocracy. Multiculturalism in Singapore today also stresses the importance of maintaining common spaces for Singaporeans in addition to the private cultural spaces entitled for practice and expression. These common spaces would serve as a repository of common values and aspirations for all Singaporeans. Dubbed "unity in diversity", multiculturalism is visualised as four overlapping circles akin to a Venn diagram (C. Tan, 2012, p. 25). The overlapping areas are the common spaces where Singaporeans meet to study, work and communicate.

The state also pays close attention to the needs of minority groups in Singapore. Minority rights are protected utilising other state apparatus such as the Presidential Council of Minority Rights, established in 1970 (Lin, 2009). These are meant to be safeguards. The Presidential Council for Minority Rights works by scrutinising new bills passed by parliament and checking against the government implementing any laws which discriminate against any race, religion or community. The committee reports any biased provisions to parliament so that the Bill would be reconsidered. It will also investigate complaints and report any issues affecting the racial or religious community to the government.

Given the special place of the Malay Muslim minority in Singapore as aforementioned, they have been granted special allowances in accordance to their religious needs. Article 153 of the constitution provides that "the legislature shall by law, make provision for regulating Muslim religious affairs and for constituting a Council to advise the President of Singapore in matters relating to the Muslim religion". In addition, Muslims in Singapore are governed under the Administration of Muslim Law Act (AMLA), which was formed in 1966. The Act came into effect in 1968 and defined the powers and jurisdiction of three key Muslim institutions: 1) the Islamic Religious Council of Singapore, 2) the Syariah Court, and 3) the Registry of Muslim Marriages. These institutions fall under the purview of the Ministry of Culture, Community and Youth (MCCY) and the Minister-in-Charge of Muslim Affairs (Administration of Muslim Law Act, 1966).

The minority groups are also provided with ethnic-based platforms through which they can channel their grievances and get support. This innovative mode of delegated welfare through community self-help groups, including MENDAKI for the Malay community, SINDA for the Indian community and the Eurasian Association for the Eurasian community, was also meant to ensure that the minority groups never lagged behind and are given the necessary support in the form of culturally sensitive ethnic-based help the state feels to be advantageous to its minority citizens.

The Group Representative Constituency (GRC) was another mechanism to ensure minority representation in policy-making. The electoral system was established because the then Prime Minister Lee Kuan Yew felt that the younger Singaporeans did not seem to factor in considerations of ensuring racial balance when voting (Hussin, 2002, p. 664). The sentiment was echoed by the then Deputy Prime Minister Goh Chok Tong, who had observed the trend of Singaporeans voting along ethnic lines which would ultimately lead to a lack of representation of minority ethnic communities in parliament (*ibid.*, p. 665). In order to ensure that minorities are represented in politics, the state introduced the GRC system in 1988 which guaranteed minority representation in the political arena. While it can be read that the GRC system was meant to ensure ethnic representation in parliament and "entrench multiculturalism in the legislative process" (Tan, 2005, p. 417), such a policy is also viewed as detrimental to minority candidates because it promotes the perception that the minority politicians are only "riding the coat tails of their ethnic Chinese electoral colleagues in GRC seats" (Tan, 2005, p. 422).

Multiculturalism does not just manifest itself in state policy and practice. It also acts as an extremely effective tool which informs individuals of the orientation they would have to adopt in order to maintain the overarching objective of social harmony. Thus, while multiculturalism as a system acknowledges the importance of ethnic cultures, it also imposes limits to the extent in which these cultures can be expressed. Ultimately, in the context of a diverse society, the state prefers for its citizens to adopt a "moderate" stance in the expression of ethnic or religious identities. As former Prime Minister Goh Chok Tong expressed:

> 'To progress and strengthen racial harmony, every racial group must take middle of the road, moderate positions and reject extreme views. If Malay leaders take radical positions for their community, the backlash will be Chinese chauvinism. In the same way Tang Liang Hong in Cheng San GRC turned the Malays against himself and the WP' ("Let's Take the Middle Path to Maintain Racial Harmony", *The Straits Times*, 1997).

Racial or religious chauvinism are deemed to be the antitheses of a *correct* multicultural behaviour which is to not offend the sensibilities of the other race or religious groups. In the Tang Liang Hong affair, the state accused the Worker's Party politician as being an "anti-Christian Chinese chauvinist" when he had called for a greater emphasis on Chinese language and culture due to what he believed to be a case of cultural erosion in Singapore ("Tang Affair — All S'poreans Should Learn", *The Straits Times*, 1997). Moderation and sensitivity also extends to the realm of religion as evidenced by the state's repeated calls for sensitivity when proselytising. Religious groups have therefore either avoided a particular group altogether when evangelising or adopted innovative methods to do so (Mathew, 2008).

Legal apparatus and deterrence to conflict

Much has been made of the vagueness of "out of bounds" (OB) markers in the discussion of race and religion in Singapore. The OB markers represent a pre-emptive measure that the government deems necessary in order to avoid potentially damaging scenarios for the country. During the civil society conference organised by the Institute of Policy Studies in 2013, Foreign Affairs and Law Minister K. Shanmugam reiterated this position when he remarked:

> 'At a very philosophical level, you could say we should be able to talk about each other's racial and religious issues without having to really damage society... Often you will have a group of people who will debate it at that level, but then you will have probably a larger group, in any society, for whom this becomes very visceral and impacts on their perception of another race' (M. Tan, 2013).

The way in which OB markers have been articulated by various government actors has changed, as compared to an era when Singaporeans were strongly discouraged to discuss issues on race and religious difference in the past ("Nation Building a Hard Task: Lau", *The Straits Times*, 1979). However, fundamentally, the stand remains — there definitely needs to be some form of limit to what is being discussed when it involves race and religion.

In many closed-door conferences and seminars on race and religion the authors have organised or attended recently, the medley of activists, academics and students who participated have often expressed approval for the trajectory of greater openness to discussions on race and religion. Some organisers even remarked that such events, even if held behind closed doors, would have some years ago invited the unsolicited attentions of the Internal Security Department. The worry for the state, as the quote by Minister K. Shanmugam clearly shows, is that because race and religion are seen by people as being rooted in primordial origins, any form of criticism (even when constructive) might be misconstrued as insults thereby leading to conflict. There is therefore an apparent mistrust of the citizen body to be able to engage in dialogue and discourse without the situation deteriorating as the state expects.

While there have been criticism against the Singapore government for being overly cautious in not allowing its citizen body to engage in the aforementioned issues in an open manner, the government has continually refuted them, reminding Singaporeans that instruments put in place, even if they were as vague as OB markers, serve to protect the state of harmony in Singapore and it is the responsibility of the government to ensure that this harmony remains.

There are legal instruments which have been progressively put in place in order to preserve the state of racial and religious harmony in Singapore. As Tan (2008) examined in his paper on the management of religion in Singapore, these are either embedded in the constitution, thus being inextricably linked to the concept of multiculturalism as discussed earlier, or appear in the penal code.

1) The Constitution of Singapore guarantees the freedom of religion under Article 15 but it is not without limitations. Tan (2008, p. 62) explains that while the freedom of religious belief is protected, the actions motivated by such beliefs which may be contrary to Singapore's laws, are not (*ibid.*). Ultimately then, sovereignty, integrity and the unity of the nation take precedence and therefore anything in opposition to these objectives must be dealt with (*ibid.*, p. 63).

2) The Sedition Act, which was inherited by the colonial administration, considers words promoting feelings of ill-will and hostility between different races and classes of the population to be seditious. It also grants the government pre-emptive power by allowing them to detain any individual who may act "in any manner prejudicial to the security of Singapore... or to the maintenance of public order". This Act has been used against several individuals. In 2005, three people who made offensive remarks about Malays and Islam online were also charged under the same Act (Wong, 2005). In 2009, SingTel technical officer Ong Kian Cheong and his 46-year-old wife, UBS associate director Dorothy Chan Hien Leng, had been found guilty on four charges each of sedition (Quek, 2009). The couple, both Protestant Christians, mailed pamphlets to addresses picked out from the telephone directory — those of Muslims included. They "clearly did so with the intent of convincing the Muslim reader to convert to Christianity",

a district court found. The pamphlets also contained material deemed by the court to have promoted feelings of ill will and hostility.

3) The Internal Security Act allows for "preventive detention for a two year renewable period" as the government sees fit in order to prevent a person from acting in a certain manner which would be prejudicial to the security of the country, public order or essential services. It has been described as a draconian measure and has been famously used against the alleged Marxist conspirators in 1987, which the state explained to be necessary because of the existence of communist elements under the guise of the church, which would have destabilised the social and political system in Singapore then (Crossette, 1987). The ISA was also used against the Jemaah Islamiyah, when the state uncovered a terrorist plot organised by a group of Muslim terrorists ("JI Men Planned to Attack Singapore", *AsiaOne News*, 2012).

4) The Maintenance of Religious Harmony Act (MHRA) was established in 1989, allowing the Minister of Home Affairs to "make a restraining order" against any religious leaders or religious groups who are "deemed to have trespassed the rules of engagement in their religious, social or political causes". The MHRA also led to the formation of the Presidential Council for Religious Harmony which advises the President on matters relating to race and religion. The MHRA was developed amidst an environment of increasing religiosity, where there had already been insensitive incidents and aggressive proselytising. Through the MHRA, the government also made it clear that there was to be no mixing between religion and politics, especially as the state saw the potential of religious power and influence to sway political considerations:

'Churchmen, lay preachers, priests, monks, Muslim theologians, all those who claim divine sanction or holy insights, take off your clerical robes before you take on anything economic or political ... take it off. Come out as a citizen or join our political party and it is your right to belabour the Government. But if you use a church or religion and your pulpit for these purposes, there will be serious repercussions' (Lee Kuan Yew in Zakir, 2009).

There have been voices against what has been perceived as overregulation of society with some even regarding the state policies, in particular the ISA, as draconian. In April 2010, United Nations Special Rapporteur Githu Muigai released a report in which he criticised the multicultural policies undertaken by the Singapore government to maintain order in the state as being outmoded, calling for a revision of the existing laws. Among other things, the diplomat expressed concern with laws which cripple freedom of speech on issues such as race and religion. The Ministry of Foreign Affairs responded that while the UN representative's assessment was greatly appreciated, the Singapore government has to strike a fine balance between granting freedom of speech and maintaining harmony and it is up to the government to ascertain where the lines should be drawn because if anything went wrong, it is the Singapore government, not the UN, who will have to bear responsibility (Ministry of

Foreign Affairs [MFA], 2010). Such a defensive stand fits neatly into the pre-emptive orientation Singapore has adopted in order to avoid conflict.

The concept of multiculturalism and the set of legal instruments work in tandem, providing the ideological basis which informs Singaporeans of the correct multicultural orientation and providing the necessary instruments to prosecute individuals who have overstepped the boundaries and threaten Singapore's fragile social make-up. In shaping the structures to manage the multiracial and multireligious landscape, the state also managed to establish itself as the bearer of peace, order and harmony in Singapore.

Nudging intercultural interaction

Besides the multicultural policy and legal instruments which the state has put in place in order to ensure that Singapore society remains harmonious, the state has also started many programmes and worked closely with various community organisations which share the principles it espouses. This "softer" approach represents the state's belief in the need to seed intercultural interaction given its pessimistic view that such forms of interactions would not develop naturally. The state also believes in educating the citizenry to appreciate racial and religious harmony other than using overt disciplinary mechanisms — in short, to develop the "heartware" needed for Singaporeans to be more receptive towards diversity (Mathew & Hong, 2014b).

Education for diversity is fostered in the formative years of schooling where the character and citizenship syllabus aims to communicate to students the need for respect for "diversity for food and cultural festivals in Singapore; religious festivals and places of worship in Singapore; food practices and books of wisdom from the different socio-cultural groups". The syllabus also aims to provide an understanding of national identity through "respecting multi-culturalism" and "appreciating and embracing other cultures". Based on the syllabus guidelines, it is anticipated that students would have experiences participating in Racial Harmony Day and communicating with peers who are culturally different (Ministry of Education [MOE], 2014).

Within state institutions, the state builds platforms such as the Community Engagement Programme (CEP) to encourage intercultural understanding and interaction. This started in the aftermath of the London bombings in 2005, where Singaporean state leaders looked for strategies to build social resilience geared towards the preservation of unity at times of crisis. To achieve this, much emphasis is placed on building networks of trust in the wider society through strengthening "ties and understanding among people of different races and religions". The CEP initiative engages six government clusters — the Ministry of Culture, Community and Youth which looks at building such interracial and interreligious trust among religious and cultural groups; the Ministry of Education which sees to strengthening harmony in educational institutions; the Ministry of Manpower which strategises initiatives in the workplace; the Ministry of Community and Information among academics and media persons; the Ministry of Home Affairs among its uniformed services and the broader community; and the People's Association among constituency and grassroots groups. A cursory examination of the list of initiatives to strengthen interracial and interreligious understanding and interaction include seminars by experts explaining aspects of diversity, exhibitions to showcase cultural heritages of different communities, games which forge interaction between participants of different faiths and races, and the celebration of cultural and religious festivals (SG United, 2014).

While the CEP is a broader strategy to ensure community preparedness for crises which may undermine racial and religious trust, some of the organisations prominently involved in aiding the push for intercultural harmony are the Inter-Religious Organisation (IRO), the Inter-Racial and Religious Confidence Circle (IRCC) and OnePeople.sg.

The IRO is made up of representatives from different religious groups in Singapore. Founded prior to national independence, one of the main aims of the IRO is to inculcate "the spirit of friendship and cooperation among the leaders and followers of different religions in Singapore" ("Inter-Religious Organisation, Singapore", 2014). The way it does this is to organise lectures, dialogues and conduct prayers and meditation "for the well-being of mankind as often as possible and convenient" (IRO website). Lai (2008) explains that because the IRO is perceived as having the potential to be influential in society given its symbolic importance, the state has conveniently latched on to it, deploying the set of IRO religious leaders to bless state-related events such as the passing out parade of national servicemen in the Singapore Armed Forces. The relationship holds positive implications for the state since the multireligious and peaceful character of the organisation epitomises the government's aspirations for Singapore. Although the IRO has sometimes been criticised as being superficial in their treatment of interreligious harmony and lacking consistency in organising activities and events (other than praying and blessing), Lai (2008) believes that being the only formal interreligious organisation, it remains important in fostering interreligious understanding through education.

The IRCC movement, which currently comes under the purview of the Ministry of Culture, Community and Youth was first formed after the Jemaah Islamiyah arrests in 2002. It brings together religious and community leaders who have their activities in various neighbourhoods. Because of its close connection to the Community Engagement Programme, the most important function of these circles is to network leaders who will provide a concerted front in the event of a crisis which might undermine racial or religious trust. Besides engaging in tabletop exercises to prepare for such possibilities, the IRCC tries to engage religious and community groups at the neighbourhood level to engage in basic harmony building activities such as visits to places of worship.

Like the IRO, the IRCC is not immune from criticism either. There have been questions asked of the relevance of the IRCC, especially from younger Singaporeans who think that the older generation of Singaporeans are "too concerned with race and religious relations" by subscribing to contrived machinations such as the IRCCs ("Groups Urged to Connect with the Young", *The Straits Times*, 2004). Meanwhile, studies on the IRCC have also shown that while the IRCCs focus substantially on issues of commonalities, it seldom deals with potentially disconcerting issues which affect different religious groups (Mathew & Hong, 2014a).

Perhaps, even within such platforms the discussants submit themselves to some form of self-censorship for fear of crossing OB markers and being taken to task. Despite its various shortcomings, Mathew and Hong (2014a) point out that while such an arrangement can be easily criticised for not being organic and thus more likely to result in very cursory interactions, the overall benefit of such groupings are without question.

If the IRO and IRCC focus chiefly on building interracial and interreligious understanding through networking religious and community leadership, then OnePeople.sg, which has close links with the People's Association and self-help groups, aims to raise awareness on the issues concerning both race and religion in Singapore at the grassroots level. Its primary focus has been in providing intercultural educational programmes for youths (e.g., HarmonyWorks! Conference, Camp Teen, Race and Ethnicity Awareness Programme, Explorations in Ethnicity) as well as engaging the broader community through workshops that impart skills for multicultural living. Its annual Orange Ribbon Run, which in 2014 attracted 5,000 participants, is themed the "Race against Racism" and aims to raise social awareness of the need for Singaporeans to continue to fight against discrimination based on racial identities.

Another way in which the state nudges intercultural interaction is through the deliberate mixing of different ethnic groups in public institutions such as schools and especially public housing. The Ethnic Integration Policy (EIP) was implemented in 1989 to ensure that there would be no racial regrouping in public housing estates which would deprive Singaporeans of the opportunity for intercultural interaction. A survey report by the Housing & Development Board (HDB, 2010) showed that generally, interethnic interaction was widespread, with more than three quarters of residents interacting with neighbours of other ethnic groups or nationalities. This was a positive reflection of the EIP. But it was also found that among the 23% who did not engage in interethnic interaction, more of them belonged to the groups below the age of 35, or above the age of 65. The younger respondents who did not engage in interethnic interaction explained that they were too busy to interact, while the elderly mentioned language barriers as an impediment to interethnic interaction. The survey also found that incidence of interethnic interaction actually increased with length of residence.

The effectiveness of the EIP has also been evaluated by scholars. Ooi (2010) explained that the policy seems to have affected the minorities more than the Chinese majority. She observed that the members of the minority groups have invited their Chinese friends for special occasions although she did question if it was the EIP which was the determining factor for this behaviour. Meanwhile, the Chinese majority reacted slowly to calls to foster interethnic friendships. Ooi (2010) suggested that this was probably because it was difficult for Chinese individuals to make friends from other ethnic backgrounds due to there being only a small number of those from minority groups (Ooi, 2010). Other studies relating to neighbourhood integration and the EIP also point to underlying problems with the EIP, such as the lack of appeal for minority groups in the programmes organised by the grassroots organisations and the inconvenience created by the imposition of quotas for people wanting to move houses (Chih, 2002). Other studies also found that modern day living arrangements and patterns have made the neighbourhood less salient in the building of social connections and the choice site for integration efforts (Mathew, 2014).

Despite these issues, the state remains steadfast on the issue of the EIP, which it regards as among the best way to cultivate harmonious relations especially in an increasingly diverse society brought about by rapid immigration. In September 2013, Minister of State for National Development, Dr Maliki Osman, reaffirmed the government's commitment to the EIP and its objective of ensuring a good mix of different races in neighbourhoods, saying that it poses only minimal problems for some families who intend to move ("Ethnic Integration Policy in Public Housing Still Needed", *Channel NewsAsia*, 2013).

Can the trifecta hold?

The many policies that reinforce multiculturalism in Singapore are integral to the management of racial and religious harmony. However, this multipronged approach to preserving racial and religious harmony is not always effective. In his ethnographic work of cosmopolitan Philadelphia, Anderson (2004) documents the strain people experience when they live in their cosmopolitan worlds in the public sphere but retreat back to their monocultural world in their private lives. Occasional racial insensitivities are symptomatic of such strain. In the Singaporean case there have been a number of such racial and religious tension points which have received public attention over the last few years. A few are spelt out below:

1) Christian pastor Rony Tan of the Lighthouse Evangelism was summoned by the Internal Security Department officers in February 2010 over postings of video clips from his sermons which were deemed offensive towards Buddhists and Taoists in Singapore. He apologised on his website the day after the visit, promising to respect other faiths and not ridicule them in any way (Feng, 2010).

2) In 2011, Jason Neo, a member of the Young People's Action Party (YP), resigned from the political party following a controversy when he posted a photograph of Malay children sitting in a school bus on the online social networking site, Facebook, with the caption, "Bus Filled with Young Terrorist Trainees?" ("PAP Youth Member Quits over 'Racist' Online", *AsiaOne News*, 2011).

3) In 2012, former assistant director of membership at the National Trades Union Congress (NTUC), Amy Cheong, was dismissed from her post at the National Trade Union Congress after she posted comments online which disparaged the practices of Malays in Singapore. Her post sparked an uproar amongst netizens (Durai, 2012).

These incidents of racial and religious insensitivities were widely reported in the print and online media. Online, these reports drew various comments and reactions. Whenever a sensitive issue pertaining to race and religion is presented in the newspapers, it is always accompanied by a government representative disapproving of the actions the perpetrators were involved in. They would then reiterate the importance of the state in maintaining an otherwise fragile social system. The reactions of state-affiliated actors encompass all the approaches undertaken by the state in the maintenance of harmony — the emphasis of multiculturalism and its requisite orientation, the invocation of legal instruments and the reminders to engage in interethnic interaction. Despite having an elaborate system in place, some social commentators question the effectiveness of the Singapore model alleging that racial and religious harmony are at best a veneer. Below the surface, there are supposedly strong undercurrents that could destabilise society. Several questions have consistently been raised about different aspects of multicultural policy here.

First, commentators have taken issue with the racialisation that is an inherent part of state management of racial harmony. The CMIO model (i.e., classification of people into one of four ethnic groups: Chinese, Malay, Indian, Others), which was inherited from the colonial government, was and still is seen as an instrumental mechanism through which Singapore society is managed. The racial parameters comprising Chinese, Malay, Indian and Others worked to inform Singaporeans of their identities in a fairly diverse cultural landscape. Consequently, while the multicultural paradigm aids in the structuring and management of a fairly diverse society, it also serves to obscure structural as well as historical factors which have affected minority communities such as the Malays in Singapore as examined by scholars (Lily, 1998). This has contributed to the Malay malaise or what is alternatively known in the national discourse as the "problematic Malay" narrative (Suriani, 2004). The problems of the minority community are almost always attributed to attitudinal and/or cultural deficiencies.

The mechanism through which problems become racialised and individualised has been examined in depth by Chua (1998). According to Chua (1998), the very same multicultural policy, complemented by an emphasis on merit, works to depoliticise issues such as the educational and socio-economic backwardness of the Malays compared to the other races in Singapore. Scholars also pointed out that the racialised discourse and system only serves to worsen the perceptions of minority populations such as the Malays, spreading stereotypes and tension rather than maintaining harmony.

There have been calls by scholars to do away with ethno-racial categorisation (based on ethnic self-help groups) in favour of a class (Lily, 1998) or national (Tan, 2004) approach. Lily (1998) explains that the system of ethnic self-help groups, in which specific, government-linked institutions manage the problems of a particular ethnic group, results in the perpetuation of racial stereotypes. Tan (2004) goes on further to elaborate that "... the self-help group's approach to improving community's life chances, through the singular focus on the uplifting of educational economic performance, can be regarded as ethnic competition" (*ibid.*, p. 79). This would in turn lead ethnicity being reduced to a "badge of honour" in which ethnic commonality is privileged over a broader, more encompassing civic and national identity.

Gomez (2010) also sees ethnic based self-help groups to be divisive, suggesting instead that there be a national help group that administers assistance across all ethnic groups. The question of racialised treatment of national data was also broached in 2012, when PAP politician Dr Janil Puthucheary had asked if the state's practice of identifying top PSLE students by ethnic groups was still relevant given the increase in interethnic marriages ("Education Minister on Identifying Top Students by Ethnic Groups", *Channel NewsAsia*, 2012). The Education Minister responded during a parliamentary session that:

> '... in a multi-racial and multi-religious country like Singapore, it is important to give space to each community to celebrate its heritage ... top students will then be identified by the race classifications chosen by their parents.'

The response given suggests that even within the context of a diverse society with increasing incidences of intermarriage, race as a part of social identity still matters. *The Straits Times* deputy editor Zuraidah Ibrahim wrote an opinion piece on the issue explaining that while "race blind" data as an ideal seems a noble idea, it might obscure racial inequalities (Zuraidah, 2012). The argument is similar to that made by Gallagher (2003) in the American context when they argued that the government should aspire to be more transparent by providing more information and access to statistics that would give a clearer picture of social problems, be it regarding race or other pertinent issues.

In May 2012, the Prime Minister tackled the issue of ethnic based self-help groups, giving an unequivocal statement which stood for the continued relevance of such groups (Chan, 2012). Citing measurable progress for underachieving communities like the Singaporean Malays, Mr Lee claimed that groups such as MENDAKI, SINDA and CDAC have been successful and effective because "they understand the unique circumstances and concerns of respective communities ... can rally members of community to help one another out, whether as volunteers or as donors". Further, in a published interview, the Prime Minister reiterated his position when asked if interethnic organisation collaborations signalled the end of ethnic-based help groups (Yong, 2012). However, Mr Lee praised the joint efforts of the help groups, expressing that there were areas where it made sense for self-help groups to share resources such as in education. In the last few years for instance, students from all racial groups have been able to use the tuition centre resources of any self-help group, ensuring that no child is deprived of educational support because of the lower levels of resources of his/her community.

Second, while the state has tried to limit speech on issues related to race and religion since these are often sites of contention, there have been increasing calls for more candid discussion about these sensitive issues. At the Institute of Policy Studies flagship conference, Singapore Perspective 2014, sociologist Chua Beng Huat questioned the state's penchant for organising closed-door discussions to regulate racial and religiously sensitive discourse. Commenting on the Prime Minister's closed-door discussion with the leaders of the Muslim community over the issue of the *tudung* (a Malay word referring to the headscarf worn by Muslim women), he argued that since the banning of the *tudung* was partly couched as being problematic in that it would create divisions between Muslims and others in society, he believed that a national discussion was more appropriate (Mahbubani & Chua, 2015). Another problem with not debating on racial and religious issues in the public domain has to do with the choice of community representation when it comes to closed-door discussions. While the different racial and religious communities that constitute Singapore society have never been homogeneous, in the wake of globalisation, there has been a plethora of racial and religious identities with its concomitant positions. The risk of such closed-door resolutions are that it inevitably misses out on the plurality of positions which cannot be surfaced by established racial or religious leaders. Thus, national platforms are more useful to capture diverse viewpoints which may have traction in the wider population.

However, the state errs on the side of caution, not willing to commit to optimistic hypothetical scenarios that such public discussions will not generate interracial and interreligious tensions, which once stirred cannot be easily resolved. If there is any consolation and room for future optimism, it is that there are more Singaporeans who are able to transcend their particular identities and support fair positions. This is apparent when examining recent instances of racial and religious tension, where many Chinese Singaporeans came out in online and mainstream media platforms to support minority members when their rights were perceived to be infringed upon (Lai & Mathew, 2014). More inclusive national conversations on these sensitive issues can be a messy, protracted and even conflict-ridden process. But as Taleb (2012) would suggest, in order for an entity to be resilient and anti-fragile, it would first need to be exposed to trauma and then experience post-trauma growth. Perhaps, that is what Singapore should be looking towards in order to sustain long-term harmony.

For this to happen, the state might need to take a step back (which it recently seems to be doing) and allow the community to be more involved in the resolution and policing of elements that may harm racial and religious harmony. This may be necessary, given that a large proportion of the population still views the state as the ultimate arbitrator of any racial or religious infraction. According to the results of the IPS Survey of Race, Religion and Language, two-thirds of the nationally representative sample of respondents agreed that the responsible Singaporean should report matters to the authorities for a number of racial and religious infractions (Mathew, Mohammad Khamsya & Teo, 2014). While these results underscore the high trust that many Singaporeans accord to the state to maintaining harmony, it also highlights that the Singapore brand of harmony tends to breed conformity and timidity (Barr, 2010). The lack of open discussions or dialogues which are accessible to all has the tendency to reduce problems to being rule based and cause people to sweep their unhappiness or ignorance without confronting or being confronted with those views. In the interest of building a more resilient population, it will be important to allow the public to confront racial and religious insensitivities and develop the appropriate mechanisms to deal with them based on the spirit of respect and tolerance. In that way, when apologies are made by those who had caused racial and religious upset, it will be seen as sincere rather than a quick response because of fears of state action.

Third, commentators have called for a more principled approach when dealing with issues related to race and religious matters. Unlike what is visible in some multicultural societies where the rights of the individual to preserve his culture is constitutionally enshrined, Singapore's position tends to be more pragmatic as can be seen in debates on the wearing of the *tudung* for Muslim women in national schools and uniformed positions. The much promoted "moderate" stance which has been a feature of Singapore's multicultural orientation is unraveling since the country is beginning to experience a state of hyper-diversity — many groups, orientations and perspectives exist even within the familiar CMIO categories under the state-prescribed multicultural rubric, which makes more imperative the existence of clear transcultural principles. Moreover, unlike what is considered a clear position on secularism as seen for instance in France, the differentiation of the secular and sacred in Singapore is unclear. While religion is not to be used as the basis of policy-making, some quarters of society are opposed that considerations of the religious sensibilities of Muslims and Christians have influenced the state's position on issues related to homosexuality (Chong, 2014).

While a principled position is itself not always tenable, as has been the experience of France where the decisions to outlaw the burqa was questioned because it did not fit well with the French position on human rights, it certainly provides a set of clear guidelines for the debate on sensitive racial and religious matters. Lacking such a framework leaves policy-making on this front to be viewed as rather subjective and largely premised on the pragmatic considerations of the day.

Conclusion

Issues relating to racial and religious harmony will continue to be significant in the years to come. Religious identity and participation is high and important especially among some communities (Mathew, Mohammad Khamsya & Teo, 2014). The growth of a vocal and educated community who profess no religion and an equally influential Christian community would mean that some sparring will continue on matters related to public morality. Considering that Muslims and Christians share substantial similarity when it comes to moral positions and Buddhists, Taoists and those with no religion are probably more sympathetic to more liberal stances, one hopes that debates will not surface into a polarising "us" and "them" divide based on religious affiliation (Mathew, 2015). The age-old issue of ethnic and religious integration in Singapore still remains relevant today. As Singapore society tries to break down pre-existing barriers and categories such as the all too familiar CMIO model and tries to makes sense of diversity, the process of integration is renewed. However, the rate of integration for different segments of society will be different. While some groups will have more overlapping common spaces due to factors such as socio-economic status and fewer restrictions based on religious prohibitions extended to dietary habits, it is important that the groups which are slower to establish common spaces or have different views on certain issues not be excluded. How this is managed is crucial since relegating a particular group, such as Malay-Muslims, as unwilling to integrate does not bode well for harmonious relations between racial and religious groups.

Singapore's immigrant-friendly population policies also mean that there will be a constant stream of migrants. These migrants will bring with them their racial and religious identities that have been formed in societies elsewhere, where they might have experienced pronounced tension between groups, overt discrimination and communalism. Immigrants' motivation to keep the familiarity of their culture in an otherwise unfamiliar country would mean greater salience accorded to their primordial identities of race and religion vis-à-vis local-born Singaporeans who would react to be more cognisant of their national identity. Local-born Singaporeans who have grown up to practise their racial and religious culture in a context very different from immigrants will continue to be puzzled at the new arrivals' insistence to practise race and religion differently. Amidst these potential tensions, however, the fact that an overwhelming proportion of local-born and foreign-born new citizens view the maintenance of racial and religious harmony as the marker of Singaporean identity (Mathew & Hong, 2014b) provides much comfort as to the stability of the Singaporean project to reify the importance of this core tenet.

Singapore's aspiration in the coming years should not be to merely preserve current levels of the state of racial and religious harmony. While social policies are crucial in ensuring that racial and religious conflicts of yesteryears are never repeated on Singaporean shores, the decades ahead call for greater citizen involvement to develop a keen interest in understanding and appreciating diversity. In this way, multicultural living can be a pleasurable part of everyday life and not just a reality to be tolerated. We might then be close to the multicultural nirvana we so hope for Singapore.

References

Administration of Muslim Law Act (1966). Retrieved 16 February 2015, from http://statutes.agc.gov.sg/aol/searchdisplay/view.w3p;query=DocId%3A3e90fc65-b364-434b-b2dc-ced1d9608640%20%20Status%3Ainforce%20Depth%3A0;rec=0.

Anderson, E. (2004). The Cosmopolitan Canopy. *The ANNALS of the American Academy of Political and Social Science*, 595, 14–31.

Barr, M. D. (2010). Harmony, Conformity or Timidity? Singapore's Overachievement in the Quest for Harmony. In J. Tao, A. B. L. Cheung, M. Painter & C. Li (eds.), *Governance for Harmony in Asia and Beyond* (pp. 73–102). London: Routledge.

Chan, R. (2012, May 23). PM: Self-help Groups Vital for Mobility. *The Straits Times*. Retrieved 16 February 2015, from https://global-factiva-com.librpoxy1.nus.edu.sg/ha/default.aspx#./!?&_suid=14234754016170879301742833991.

Chih, H. S. (2002). The Limits to Government Intervention in Fostering an Ethnically Integrated Community — A Singapore Case Study. *Community Development Journal*, 37(3), 220–232.

Chin, Y. & Vasu, N. (2007). *The Ties that Bind and Blind: A Report on Inter-Racial and Inter-Religious Relations in Singapore*. Singapore: S. Rajaratnam School of International Studies.

Chong, T. (2014). *Christian Evangelicals and Public Morality in Singapore*. Singapore: ISEAS.

Chua, B. H. (1998). Culture, Multiracialism and National Identity in Singapore. In K. H. Chen (ed.), *Trajectories: Inter-Asia Cultural Studies* (pp. 186–205). London: Routledge.

Crossette, B. (1987, June 21). Singapore Is Holding 12 in 'Marxist Conspiracy'. *The New York Times*. Retrieved 16 February 2015, from http://www.nytimes.com/1989/06/21/world/singapore-is-holding-12-in-marxist-conspiracy.html.

Durai, J. (2012, October 8). NTUC Assistant Director Sacked for Racist Remarks. *The Straits Times*. Retrieved 15 January 2015, from http://www.straitstimes.com/breaking-news/singapore/story/ntuc-assistant-director-sacked-racist-remarks-2012 1008.

Education Minister on Identifying Top Students by Ethnic Groups (2012, January 16). *Channel NewsAsia*. Retrieved 15 January 2015, from http://ifonlysingaporeans.blog spot.sg/2012/01/education-minister-on-identifying-top.html.

Ethnic Integration Policy in Public Housing Still Needed (2013, September 16). *Channel NewsAsia*. Retrieved 15 January 2015, from http://www.channelnews asia.com/news/specialreports/parliament/news/ethnic-integration-policy/814926.html.

Feng, Y. (2010, February 9). ISD Calls up Pastor for Insensitive Comments. *The Straits Times*. Retrieved 15 January 2015, from http://news.asiaone.com/News/the+Straits+Times/Story/A1Story20100209-197516.html.

Gallagher, C. A. (2003). Color-blind Privilege: The Social and Political Functions of Erasing the Color Line in Post Race America. *Race, Gender & Class*, 10(4), 22–37.

Gomez, J. (2010). Politics and Ethnicity: Framing Racial Discrimination in Singapore. *The Copenhagen Journal of Asian Studies*, 28(2), 103–117.

Groups Urged to Connect with the Young (2004, April 5). *The Straits Times.* Retrieved 16 February 2015, from http://global-factiva-com.libproxy1.nus.edu.sg/ha/default.aspx#./!?&_suid=142347594935009873311978299171.

Housing & Development Board (HDB) (2010). *Public Housing in Singapore: Well-being of Communities, Families and the Elderly.*

Hussin, M. (2002). Constitutional-Electoral Reforms and Politics in Singapore. *Legislative Studies Quarterly*, 27(4), 659–672.

Inglis, C. (1996). *Multi-culturalism: New Policy Responses to Diversity.* Retrieved 16 February 2015, from http://www.unesco.org/most/pp4.htm.

Inter-Religious Organisation (IRO) website, http://iro.sg/.

Inter-Religious Organisation, Singapore (2014). Retrieved 19 March 2015, from http://eresources.nlb.gov.sg/infopedia/articles/SIP_2014-12-09_125938.html.

JI Men Planned to Attack Singapore (2012, May 9). *AsiaOne News Portal.* Retrieved 15 January 2015, from http://news.asiaone.com/News/Latest%2BNews/Singapore/Story/A1Story20120509-344836/2.html.

Lily, Z. R. (1998). *The Singapore Dilemma: The Political and Educational Marginality of the Malay Community.* New York: Oxford University Press.

Lai, A. E. (2008). The Inter-Religious Organization of Singapore. In A. E. Lai (ed.), *Religious Diversity in Singapore* (pp. 605–641). Singapore: ISEAS.

Lai, A. E. & Mathew, M. (2014). Navigating Disconnects and Divides in Singapore's Cultural Diversity. In M. Mathew & C. W. Fong (eds.), *Management of Diversity in Singapore* (forthcoming). Singapore: ISEAS Publishing.

Lee, T. & Wilnat, L. (2009). Media Management and Political Communication in Singapore. In L. Wilnat & A. Aw (eds.), *Political Communication in Asia* (pp. 93–111). New York: Routledge.

Let's Take the Middle Path to Maintain Racial Harmony (1997, January 7). *The Straits Times.* Retrieved 16 February 2015, from https://global-factiva-com.libproxy1.nus.edu.sg/ha/deafult.aspx#./!?&_suid=142347719263306578769388142973.

Lin, T. Y. (2009). The Presidential Council for Minority Rights. Retrieved 15 January 2015, http://eresources.nlb.gov.sg/infopedia/articles/SIP_1605_2009-10-31.html.

Loh, K. S. (1998). Within the Singapore Story: The Use and Narrative of History in Singapore. *Crossroads*, 12(2), 1–21.

Mahbubani, K. & Chua, B. H. (2015). Consensus Rather than Contest Will Shape Singapore's Future. In M. Mathew, C. Gee & W. F. Chiang (eds.), *Singapore Perspectives 2014* (pp. 53–76). Singapore: World Scientific.

Mathew, M. (2008). Negotiating Christianity with Other Religions: The Views of Christian Clergymen in Singapore. In A. E. Lai (ed.), *Religious Diversity in Singapore* (pp. 571–604). Singapore: ISEAS.

Mathew, M. (2014). Integration in the Singapore Heartlands. In M. T. Yap, G. Koh & D. Soon (eds.), *Migration and Integration in Singapore: Policies and Practice* (pp. 132–159). London: Routledge.

Mathew, M. & Hong, D. (2014a). Managing Risks amidst Diversity: The Case of the Inter-Racial and Religious Confidence Circles (IRCCs) in Singapore. In M. Mathew & W. F. Chiang (eds.), *Management of Diversity in Singapore* (forthcoming). Singapore.

Mathew, M. & Hong, D. (2014b). Social Intergration of Immigrants into Multiracial Singapore. In N. Vasu, S. Y. Yeap & W. L. Chan (eds.), *Immigration in Singapore* (pp. 93–114). Amsterdam: Amsterdam University Press.

Mathew, M. (2015). The State and Implication of Differences: Insights from the IPS Survey of Race, Religion and Language. In M. Mathew, C. Gee & W. F. Chiang (eds.), *Singapore Perspectives 2014* (pp. 107–142). Singapore: World Scientific.

Mathew, M., Mohammad Khamsya, K. & Teo, K. K. (2014, June). Religiosity and the Management of Religious Harmony. Institute of Policy Studies Working Papers no. 21.

Mauzy, D. K. & Milne, R. S. (2002). *Singapore Politics under the People's Action Party.* London: Routledge.

Ministry of Education (MOE) (2014). *Character and Citizenship Education — Primary.* Singapore: Ministry of Education.

Ministry of Foreign Affairs (MFA) (2010). MFA Press Statement: MFA's Response to the Press Statement of Mr Githu Muigai, UN Special Rapporteur on Contemporary Forms of Racism, Racial Discrimination, Xenophobia and Related Intolerance. Singapore: Ministry of Foreign Affairs.

Narayanan, G. (2004). The Political History of Ethnic Relations in Singapore. In A. E. Lai (ed.), *Beyond Rituals and Riots: Ethnic Pluralism and Social Cohesion in Singapore* (pp. 41–64). Singapore: Eastern University Press.

Nation Building a Hard Task: Lau (1979, November 4). *The Straits Times.* Retrieved 16 February 2015, from http://eresources.nlb.gov.sg/newspapers/Digitised/Article/straitstimes19791104.2.59.aspx.

Onepeople.sg website, http://www.onepeople.sg/.

Ooi, G. L. (2010). Good Governance — Sustainability and the City. In G. L. Ooi & B. Yuen (eds.), *World Cities Achieving Liveability and Vibrancy* (pp. 13–27). Singapore: World Scientific.

Oon, C. (2009, August 20). MM Rebuts NMP on Race. *The Straits Times.* Retrieved 16 February 2015, from http://news.asiaone.com/News/the+Straits+Times/Story/A1Story20090820-162121.html.

Owen, D. (2005). *American Identity, Citizenship, and Multi-culturalism.* Paper presented at the German-American Conference. Retrieved 15 January 2015, from http://www.civiced.org/pdfs/germanPaper0905/DianaOwen2005.pdf.

PAP Youth Member Quits over 'Racist' Online Posting (2011, November 18). *AsiaOne News Portal.* Retrieved 15 January 2015, http://news.asiaone.com/News/AsiaOne+News/Singapore/Story/A1Story20111118-311261.html#sthash.cyeJVf2i.dpuf.

Pereira, A. (2008). Does Multi-culturalism Recognize or 'Minoritise' Minorities? *Studies in Ethnicity and Nationalism*, 8(2), 349–356.

Quek, C. (2009, June 11). Seditious Tract Duo Jailed Eight Weeks. *The Straits Times.* Retrieved 10 August 2014, from https://global-factiva-com.libproxy1.nus.edu.sg/ha/default.aspx#./!?&_suid=14235410432650825946092605590 8.

SG United (2014). Community Engagement Prorammes Factsheet. In S. United (ed.). Singapore. Retrieved 10 August 2014, from http://www.singaporeunited.sg/

CEP/CEP%20Documents/Our%20News%20pdf%20Files/Factsheet%20detailing% 20the%20progress%20of%20the%20CEP.pdf.

Suriani, S. (2004). 'Problematic Singapore Malays' — The Making of a Portrayal. Paper presented at the International Symposium on Thinking Malayness. Retrieved 15 January 2015, from http://www.fas.nus.edu.sg/malay/publications/working_papers/Problematic%20Singapore%20Malays.pdf.

Syed Khairudin, A. (2010). Rethinking Riots in Colonial South East Asia. *South East Asia Research*, 18(1), 105–131.

Taleb, N. N. (2012). *Antifragile: Things Gain from Disorder*. United States: Random House.

Tan, C. (2012). Deep Culture Matters: Multiracialism in Singapore Schools. *International Journal of Educational Reform*, 21(1), 24–38.

Tan, E. (2008). Keeping God in Place: The Management of Religion in Singapore. In A. E. Lai (ed.), *Religious Diversity in Singapore* (pp. 55–82). Singapore: ISEAS.

Tan, E. K. (2005). Multiracialism Engineered: The Limits of Electoral and Spatial Integration in Singapore. *Ethnopolitics*, 4(4), 413–428.

Tan, E. K. B. (2004). We, the Citizens of Singapore: Multi-ethnicity, Its Evolution and Its Aberrations. In Lai Ah Eng (ed.), *Beyond Rituals and Riots: Ethnic Relations and Social Cohesion in Singapore* (pp. 65–97). Singapore: Eastern Universities Press.

Tan, M. (2013, November 12). Everything You Need to Know about Minister K. Shanmugam's Dialogue Session at the Civil Society Conference in 60 Seconds. *Mothership.sg*. Retrieved 15 January 2015, from http://mothership.sg/2013/11/minister-shanmugams-dialogue-session-civil-society-conference-60-seconds/.

Tang Affair — All S'poreans Should Learn (1997, January 13). *The Straits Times*. Microfilm Reel no. NL20155. Retrieved 24 July 2014, from the National Library Archives.

Turnbull, C. M. (2009). *A History of Modern Singapore, 1819–2005*. Singapore: NUS Press.

Wong, G. (2005, October 1). Singapore Prosecutes Bloggers with Colonial-era Sedition Law. *Associated Press*. Retrieved 16 February 2015, from http://www.singapore-window.org/sw05/051001ap.htm.

Yong, C. Y. (2011a). Anti-Catholic Riots (1851). Retrieved 15 January 2015, from http://eresources.nlb.gov.sg/infopedia/articles/SIP_100_2005-01-24.html.

Yong, C. Y. (2011b). Hokkien-Teochew Riots (1854). Retrieved 15 January 2015, from Singapore: http://eresources.nlb.gov.sg/infopedia/articles/SIP_104_2005-01-25.html.

Yong, J. A. (2012, October 29). Race-based Self-help Groups Still Have Important Role, Says PM Lee. *The Straits Times*. Retrieved 16 February 2015, from http://www.straitstimes.com/breaking-news/singapore/story/race-based-self-help-groups-still-have-important-role-says-pm-lee-2012.

Zakir, H. (2009). Religious Harmony: 20 Years of Keeping the Peace. *The Straits Times*. Retrieved 16 February 2015, from http://lkyspp.nus.edu.sg/ips/wp-content/uploads/sites/2/2013/06/ST_RELIGOUS-HARMONY-20-years-of-keeping-the-peace_240709.pdf.

Zuraidah, I. (2012, November 28). Hiding Ethnic Data Won't Solve Problems. *The Straits Times*. Retrieved 15 January 2015, from http://www.singapolitics.sg/views/hiding-ethnic-data-won%E2%80%99t-solve-problems.

Chapter 6

The Social Dimension of Urban Planning in Singapore

Liu Thai Ker and Astrid S. Tuminez[1]

The world has never before seen the rise of cities at their current pace. In fact, the World Bank calls urbanisation the "defining phenomenon of the 21st century", with half the world's population today living in cities and another two billion expected to move to cities in the next two decades (World Bank, 2012). 90% of this growth will come from the developing regions, particularly Asia and Africa.

As cities grow, competent urban planning becomes ever more critical. Urban planning involves not only technical processes, but also the art of creating communities and facilitating human interaction within deliberately and thoughtfully constructed spaces. As Singapore celebrates its 50th birthday in 2015, and without undue modesty, it may be useful to examine the social dimension of urban planning in this city-state, which has been widely acclaimed as a success. What lessons from the Singapore experience might be shared with those who are engaged in urban planning elsewhere? How can governments and the societies they serve best deploy their limited resources to plan and create urban centres that are liveable, resilient and dynamic? This chapter will seek to answer these questions by elucidating the social dimension of Singapore's urban planning, focusing particularly on the HDB (Housing & Development Board) and the public housing story.

The sections below will elaborate on the social dimension of HDB planning, execution and refinement; articulate the planner's ethos that underpinned the HDB story (as lived by Liu Thai Ker, the principal author and source of original materials

---

[1]The authors collaborated on this chapter using the principal author's (Liu Thai Ker) personal and historical perspectives from his tenure at the Housing & Development Board (HDB) as Chief Architect and CEO from 1969–1989 and the Urban Redevelopment Authority (URA) as Chief Planner from 1989–1992. The second author (Astrid Tuminez) helped to translate these perspectives into this chapter and provided additional inputs.

for this chapter); and highlight some insights from the HDB's past that might be useful for the future.

Social dimension of the HDB experience

Public housing flats (or HDB housing) are a defining feature of the Singapore urban landscape. Today, roughly 82% of Singaporeans live in HDBs, and over 90% of Singaporeans and permanent residents own their flats (or, for a smaller segment, houses). Unlike in many cities, where people equate public housing with architectural blight, poverty and crime, Singaporeans, over 90% of whom are eligible for public housing, regard HDBs as generally affordable and desirable, and definitely liveable. Public housing does not suffer the stigma of sub-standard quality, nor is it equated with only the lower socio-economic stratum of society. Outside Singapore, many international bodies and experts have also heralded HDB housing as an outstanding example of effective urban planning. Among its many plaudits, the HDB received in 2010 the UN Scroll of Honor Award, which recognises individuals and organisations that have been instrumental in improving living conditions in the world's urban centres. The citation for Singapore highlighted the HDB's success in "providing one of Asia's and the world's greenest, cleanest and most socially conscious public housing programmes" (HDB, 2010).

The decision to properly house all Singaporeans was made in 1960, guided by ambitious but pragmatic policies, as well as meticulous and precise planning that evolved further as people, circumstances and knowledge changed. The overarching goal has remained the same over the years: To provide Singaporeans with quality homes and living environments. This goal was audacious, given that in 1960, when the HDB was established, roughly 1.35 million of Singapore's 1.65 million residents lived in squatters. Singapore's urban dwelling landscape at that time could be described as dilapidated, dirty, crowded, unsanitary and unattractive. Ethnic enclaves were also common, with residential communities divided into Malay, Chinese, Indian and European neighbourhoods. Even among the Chinese, residents tended to congregate in separate localities by dialect groups.

The HDB estimated in the 1960s that Singapore needed 147,000 housing units, but, due to resource constraints, just over 110,000 units were built from 1960–1970. Public housing construction intensified in the 1970s onwards, effectively eliminating squatters and ethnic enclaves within a couple of decades. The HDB's overall track record is impressive, with 1,040,515 dwelling units finished as of 2013, public demand continuing to be high and a good level of social integration achieved.

The HDB's success has been due in part to high technical standards. But beyond the technical, and embedded at the HDB core, is a definite social aspect — one might call this the "software" behind the "hardware" of ubiquitous public housing flats. An analysis of five elements integral to the HDB story yields insights into the social dimension of urban planning in Singapore: 1) Physical spaces, 2) People, 3) Community organisations, 4) Liveability, and 5) Human scale.

Physical spaces

Land in Singapore is highly finite. The country is referred to as "the little red dot" because that is exactly how it looks when viewed on a map that includes large neighbours like Malaysia and Indonesia. Limited land requires precision planning. For example, the principal author recalls spending over a year and a half studying the optimal size of a new town. "Optimal" meant that the town would have all the essential amenities for a high degree of self-sufficiency. Based on research, the size of a new town was set at approximately 12 square kilometers (km^2) and projected to accommodate around 200,000 people (the total population then was only 2.2 million, see Figure 6.1).

Land use within a new town was generally made up of the following: residential (45%), educational (6.9%), institutional (2.1%), parks and gardens (7%), sports and recreation (1.5%), reserve sites (0.3%), transportation (13.3%), industry (8%) and utilities and others (8%). This fundamental approach to physical space had a social component at its core: To nurture meaningful communities and facilitate a good quality of life, instead of merely giving people a concrete roof over their heads. When one looks at the planned use of land in new towns, clearly the physical home was most important. Even then, it takes up only 45% of allocated space. But, simultaneously, that home would be surrounded with services and other types of support to make all the activities of work and life doable, possible and manageable. Detailed research was conducted whenever necessary, including a study to provide guidelines for the placement of gasoline stations so that their location, size, number and range of services and products could serve the needs of residents while not cannibalising other businesses in a neighbourhood. In HDB estates, emporium owners, shopkeepers, cinema operators, restaurant owners, small-scale supermarket managers and government clinic supervisors all had a chance to share their knowledge on what it would take to make their businesses sustainable. Their feedback helped planners and architects to improve their design continuously.

As shown in Figure 6.2, the new towns were further subdivided into neighbourhoods of approximately 50 hectares each, with a neighbourhood centre that

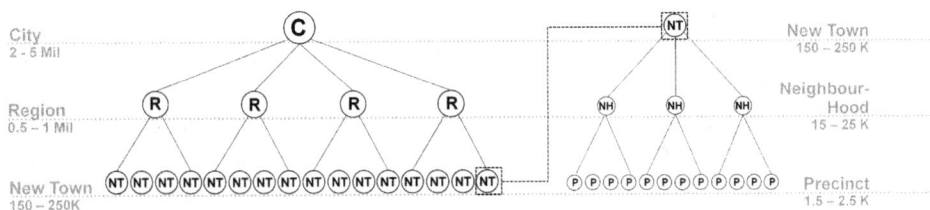

Fig. 6.1   Hierarchy of Urban Cells 1 — City to New Towns.

Fig. 6.2   Hierarchy of Urban Cells 2 — New Towns to Precincts.

was complemented by all relevant amenities. But neighbourhoods were still too large a community to facilitate close and meaningful social interaction between residents, and posed challenges for nurturing emotional identification or rootedness. The HDB sought to address this in the 1970s. New subdivisions of physical space were introduced, including what is well-known today as "precincts". A UK survey in the 1950s showing that people could not relate to their residential area if it was larger than 5–6 acres sparked the decision to create precincts. Consultations with a sociologist further indicated that 700–1000 flats would provide the suitable scale for a variety of housing types for a "basic community". Translated into HDB density, this became roughly 2.5–3.5 hectares of land. Precincts allowed sufficient proximity for social interaction and emotional identification; enough scale to accommodate different housing types (allowing for socio-economic diversity and preventing ghetto formation); and a self-contained space and community that could be protected by a green barrier when construction on adjoining precincts began (minimising public distraction and discomfort).

In each precinct, there was also a precinct centre — usually a green space with a playground, sandpit, exercise space and sitting areas where parents could sit and talk while their children played. The precinct centre was configured, first and foremost, for safety. Its location within the precinct allowed sufficient visibility to residents so that younger children could play under supervision, while older ones could enjoy unsupervised outdoor time. These spaces were designed to accommodate multiple uses by diverse age groups and, in general, to facilitate social interaction. Over time, green spaces and gardens were refined and broadly integrated into public housing and design. With so little land in Singapore, how could a planner afford to make gardens and thus "waste" precious space? The principal author recalls a conversation with a Member of Parliament from Toa Payoh, a professor, who pithily made the case: "If I quarreled with my wife in my flat, where could I go?" That conversation was just one of many data points that underscored the desirability and justifiability of green spaces in public housing.

In addition to green spaces, void decks were introduced to apartment blocks in the very early days. These were empty spaces at ground level that could be used for shelter from the rain or as venues for social functions such as weddings, birthday parties and even funerals. Void decks also served as a bridge to link groups that might otherwise not interact much with one another. But a void deck without any inhabitants might also cause some insecurity for people, particularly young women who might be coming home late at night. Consequently, wherever possible, plans were made to dedicate one end of a void deck to a crèche, while the other allocated as homes for older people, keeping the void space in the middle. By design, the elderly could see younger faces that cheered them up, while younger residents could look to the elderly as a form of security if and when they came home late at night.

The social component of apartment block design evolved over time based on feedback from research, surveys and comments from residents and other

Long Corridor

One Staircase Connecting Two Units

Segmented Corridor

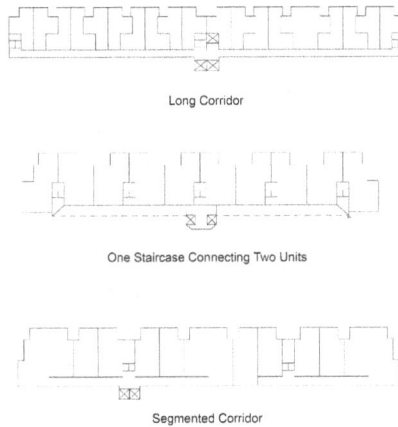

Fig. 6.3   Evolution of HDB Block Layout.

Source: Wong, A. K. & Yeh, S. H. K. (1985). Housing a Nation: 25 Years of Public Housing in Singapore. Housing & Development Board, Singapore.

stakeholders. As depicted in Figure 6.3, some of the earliest housing units had long corridors from one end of the building block to the other. These proved impersonal, poorly configured for privacy, and not entirely conducive to closer, neighbourly interaction. Later, an alternative block arrangement was introduced, with staircases connecting two units. The latter, however, also had a clear disadvantage. With only one neighbour sharing the staircase, life could be tough when the inevitable neighbourly quarrel happened. Eventually, a better version of the long corridor came about, by having the long corridor segmented to serve only six to eight apartments. These shorter corridors, slightly wider than the long ones, were dubbed "courtyard in the sky". Sociologists had suggested that the maximum number of neighbours an individual could comfortably cope with was about six to eight, hence the new configuration. "Courtyards in the sky" were a welcome innovation, giving residents outdoor space high up from the ground for a wide array of purposes: play, socialisation, family horticulture and others.

Other less obvious aspects of the HDB physical space and configuration also required thoughtful social analysis. For example, the decision to have only one entrance to a precinct was meant to facilitate eye contact, thus enhancing residents' sense of security from mutual recognition. By the same token, corner provision shops, initially implemented at the precinct level, were soon discontinued because residents did not feel comfortable with the amount of outside traffic that they generated.

People

When Singapore became independent, a number of commentaries predicted that the newly-independent nation would not survive. One journalist noted: "An independent Singapore was not regarded as viable three years ago. Nothing in the current situation suggests that it is more viable today" (Dennis Warner in the *Sydney Morning Herald*, as quoted in Lee, 2000, pp. 19–20). Singapore had many poor citizens whose standard of living needed to be raised, three major ethnic groups that needed to be integrated and sizeable informal urban settlements that had to be moved into modern housing. Integration had to be a key consideration in public housing. The first task was to resettle squatters and, in the process, address the sometimes difficult and daunting transition from an impermanent squatter style of living to a modern urban environment. The HDB carefully planned the resettlement mix, aiming to cap the resettlement household to about a third in each precinct, with the rest consisting of urban folks. This mix was designed to ensure that those being resettled would have a built-in empathetic community that shared the challenges of adjusting to a more modern urban lifestyle. At the same time, they and their children, in particular, could learn from new and more urbane neighbours how to adjust quickly and effectively to a new way of living.

In addition to resettlement, socio-economic gaps also had to be taken into account. For example, one building block might have a mix of one- and two-room flats, while another a mix of two- and three-room flats. It was inadvisable to mix one- and three-room or two- and five-room flats because larger socio-economic disparities could create divides or diminish natural social interaction and cohesion. In addition to the basic mix of flats, in the mid- to late-1970s, the Housing and Urban Development Company (HUDC) was set up to build more spacious apartments $(150–170\,m^2)$ to appeal to newly-minted professionals, whose incomes were too high for public housing but not high enough for the private option. A few years later, as Singapore's socio-economic condition improved, the need for HUDC flats diminished and the government stopped building them. The HDB's careful approach catered to varying needs and means among Singaporean families, while addressing social integration and, over time, allowing the socio-economic mix and housing type offerings in HDBs to become more diverse.

Ethnic integration was also a critical component of HDB design. In the early 1980s, the HDB noticed that, in some estates, ethnic enclaves were forming. This did not align with the longer-term aspiration of an ethnically integrated and more nationally cohesive society. HDB estate officers and sociologists studied ways to refine the upper and lower limits of ethnic distribution for HDB blocks and precincts, and recommended quite precise numbers. This systematic approach tried to approximate the ethnic mix in society overall and thus help each citizen feel secure wherever he or she might live, while ensuring that each person also had the chance to interact with Singaporeans of different ethnic backgrounds. Introduced in 1989, this Ethnic Integration Policy was well-received by the people. In many societies, ethnic sensitivities arise and manifest themselves in different ways. For Singapore, the approach has been to integrate openly and systematically, leveraging the system of public housing. This approach has facilitated social cohesion and community building, which are crucial for nationhood.

Community organisations

The Singapore government aspired not only to build hard shelter for Singaporeans, but also to create cohesive and participatory communities. Planning itself was a type of community effort, with the senior staff in HDB receiving feedback nearly every week from HDB area officers, academics and other specialists, and civil servants whose work overlapped with the HDB. At the ground level, various organisations contributed to creating and cementing the community spirit. The People's Association, formed in 1960, provided oversight for formal community centres, as well as future grassroots organisations such as Residents' Committees (RCs) and Citizens' Consultative Committees (CCCs). RCs, established in 1978, worked to ameliorate the impact of dislocation, improve HDB estates, organise resident activities and promote overall neighbourliness. In its early days, RCs undertook activities such as collecting residents' newspapers, selling them and using the funds collected for social activities. This may sound quaint and old-fashioned, but reflected civic initiative and participation. CCCs were first created in 1965 and have become the lead grassroots organisation in Singapore's constituencies (electoral divisions represented by single or multiple members in parliament). They promoted welfare activities, conveyed citizen feedback and recommendations to government, communicated government policy and actions, and promoted citizenship and community.

The organisations embedded in, and working with, HDB estates all reflected the spirit of the old *kampong* (a Malay word which means "village") or traditional communities in Singapore that preceded modern housing. The *kampongs*, for the most part, are gone, but they have found their modern equivalent in the precincts of HDB new towns. The precinct provides a conducive, long-term social platform for residents to nurture the *kampong* spirit. In fact, in recent years, there has been increasing evidence that such a spirit is emerging in a number of precincts. For example, residents have taken the initiative to plant flowers, fruits or vegetables, or decorate their void decks collectively and with pride.

Besides community organisations, area officers in new towns also played a significant role in building social cohesion. In addition to collecting rents, loan repayments, and service and conservancy charges, these officers also listened to residents and took the pulse of the community's state of mind. Residents relayed various concerns to them, including design flaws and construction defects, management woes, garbage collection, and even family, educational, financial and marital issues. Sometimes area officers became a social safety net resource, helping jobless residents get employed in the HDB and working out repayment plans from their wages. The RCs and CCCs, along with estate officers, became sources of indispensable and valuable feedback to senior HDB staff. Rich, accurate, timely and constant feedback flowed to planners, architects and other professionals, as well as officials. In turn, they undertook refinements and improvements that significantly enhanced customer satisfaction with public housing. In fact, HDB resident satisfaction was at 95% in the 1980s and 1990s.

Building and sustaining community in Singapore reflects real partnership between the government and citizens. In 1989, Town Councils were created to enhance local governance, self-sufficiency and self-determination. These councils included elected Members of Parliament (MPs) as well as residents, who participated in decision-making and local management related to their HDB estates. This participatory mechanism diluted the traditional authority and decision-making power of the HDB, but was a welcome change that reflected greater resident maturity and responsibility for the management, welfare and improvement of their housing estates. In theory, Town Councils represented a new phase in the evolution of leadership in Singapore — one that was heavily top-down but, over time, has integrated stronger and more expansive direct participation by citizens on issues that mattered most to them.

Liveability

Strangers visiting Singapore's HDB estates for the first time are struck by certain features often integrated into housing complexes including hawker centres and eating houses, cake shops, doctor's offices, and even libraries and mini-amphitheaters in some cases. Convenience and liveability are two characteristics that immediately come to mind. Planning for new towns aimed for high liveability. It began with basic facilities and accessibility. Each new town, for example, was typically framed by expressways on its four peripheral boundaries and included stations and routes for the MRT (Mass Rapid Transit) and buses (see Figure 6.4). Next came amenities

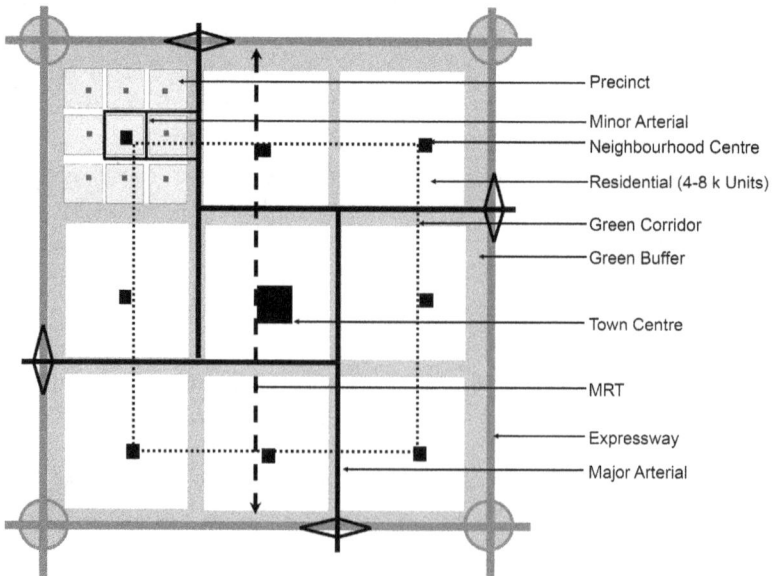

Fig. 6.4   HDB Cell Prototype.

such as restaurants, emporiums or small department stores, fresh food and dry goods markets, food courts, coffee shops, new town libraries, public plazas, amphitheatres, sports centres, petrol stations and others. Public services such as fire stations, police and polyclinics were also added.

Adequate primary and secondary schools were provided in every new town, and institutes of technical education (ITEs), polytechnics and even hospitals for every two to four new towns. HDB planners systematically studied details such as the optimal distance to schools. For example, primary schools and some kindergartens were situated closest to residences so that, in the later new towns, young kids could walk to and from school in 10 minutes, while parents could drop off their children and then easily continue their day shopping for the family's needs. Upper level schools, which typically served larger catchment areas, were located farther from residences. Schools were also situated with some distance from neighbourhood centres to reduce vehicular congestion at peak times when parents were dropping off their children.

In short, the integration of residential, commercial, recreational and civic spaces (see Figure 6.5), as well as ingresses and egresses into and out of new towns made the whole of these planned urban centres definitely much more valuable than their individual parts — hence, a high liveability score (see Figure 6.6).

To further integrate socio-economic groups, the government subsequently decided to sell land for private housing within HDB new towns. Initially, some thought that buyers from a higher socio-economic stratum would not want housing near the less glamorous public housing environment. Indeed, when only smaller one- to three-room flats were built, an early stigma arose, associating HDBs with poor people. But the worry and stigma, over time, proved groundless. Private housing sites close to HDB estates sold very well. It appeared that the affluent who could pay much more for private housing were also eager to avail of the amenities and services that surrounded HDB estates and made life convenient. The government's approach of economic viability for public housing was vindicated. Careful and intelligent calculation went into the construction of one- to three-room flats for the "poorest" — the poorest who could afford to pay rent at the level set by the government. Dead-end or welfare ghettos were avoided. New towns came with job opportunities, and became synergistic places for living, working, playing, learning and moving (for example, see Figure 6.7).

Human scale

The second author lived in Moscow, the capital of the former Soviet Union, in the mid- to late-1980s and then again in the early 1990s. The former USSR (Union of Soviet Socialist Republics) prided itself in its public housing programme. Indeed, it had its own version of new towns, mostly located outside the city centre. These new towns usually meant endless, faceless rows of massive concrete blocks that

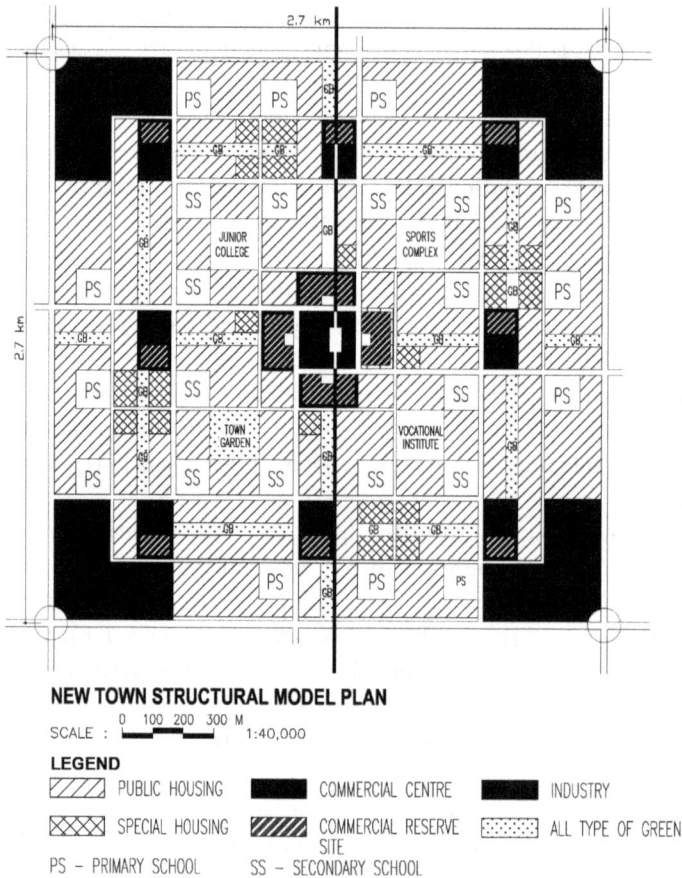

NEW TOWN STRUCTURAL MODEL PLAN

SCALE : 0 100 200 300 M 1:40,000

LEGEND

▨ PUBLIC HOUSING	■ COMMERCIAL CENTRE	■ INDUSTRY
▧ SPECIAL HOUSING	▨ COMMERCIAL RESERVE SITE	░ ALL TYPE OF GREEN
PS – PRIMARY SCHOOL	SS – SECONDARY SCHOOL	

Fig. 6.5   HDB Land Use Prototype.

Source: Housing & Development Board, Singapore, October 1999 (adapted to B/W from a coloured version).

intimidated viewers and residents with their sheer size. Craning one's neck while walking between buildings did not guarantee a glimpse of the sky. Singapore, which has a few super high-rise HDB blocks, has consciously sought to avoid the more impersonal and super-imposing quality of high-rises. In fact, planners deliberately factored the human scale into the planning and construction of public housing.

The principal author notes that a "chessboard" approach was used for Singapore's urban planning. Metaphorically speaking, HDB residential blocks were placed on the black squares of a chessboard, whereas the low-density shopping centres, schools, sports fields, and even gardens and parks were placed in the alternate white squares (see Figures 6.8 and 6.9). In this manner, planners could minimise the impact of high-rise residential blocks and achieve the illusion of a lower-density

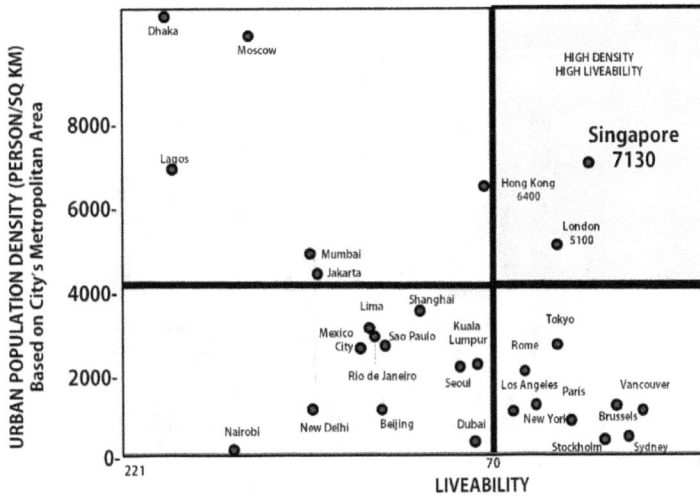

Fig. 6.6   Centre for Liveable Cities (CLC) Liveability Matrix.

Source: Centre for Liveable Cities, Singapore.

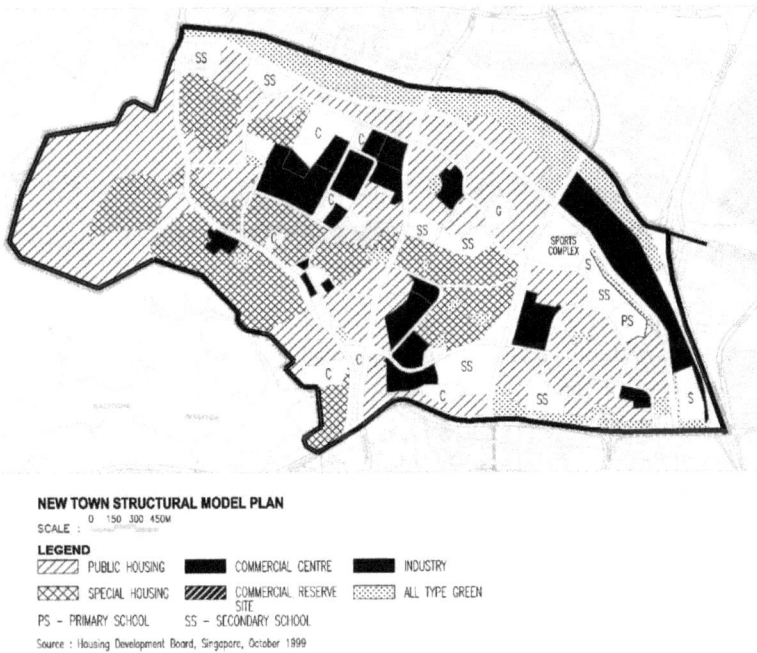

Fig. 6.7   Bishan New Town.

Source: Urban Development Authority (1947). Bishan Planning Area, Planning Report 1994.
Urban Development Authority, Singapore (adapted to B/W from a coloured version).

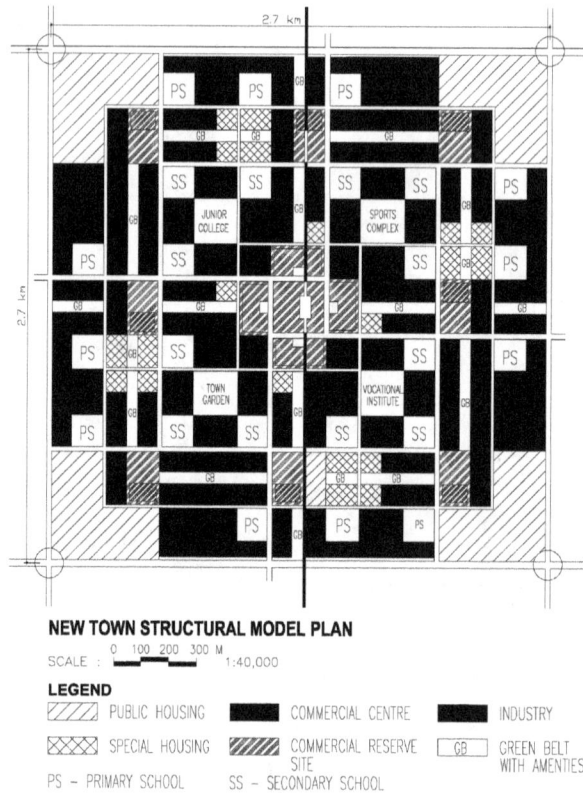

NEW TOWN STRUCTURAL MODEL PLAN

SCALE : 0 100 200 300 M 1:40,000

LEGEND

▨ PUBLIC HOUSING	▮ COMMERCIAL CENTRE	▮ INDUSTRY
▨ SPECIAL HOUSING	▨ COMMERCIAL RESERVE SITE	GB ▭ GREEN BELT WITH AMENTIES
PS – PRIMARY SCHOOL	SS – SECONDARY SCHOOL	

Fig. 6.8   New Town Prototype.

Source: Housing & Development Board (adapted from Figure 6.5).

environment. The overall result was having low-rise buildings interspersed between high-rise blocks, with parks and greenery punctuating the spaces between buildings.

The expression of human scale can be found in most new towns today, where high- and low-rise buildings are mixed, and the sky is visible. Traditionally, people were most familiar, and therefore comfortable, with buildings of one to three stories, and at most up to seven stories. But the HDB did not have the luxury of building too many of these because they did not meet public housing density requirements and would have impeded the vision of "Home Ownership for All". Instead, two- and three-story constructions were built for non-residential uses, including kindergartens, religious buildings and community centres. These were planned carefully and spread evenly as "scale indicators" that provided relief from the dominating scale of high-rises. In addition, these buildings, with their varied functional demands, were given a more individualistic architectural style and expression. They were built in many instances on street corners and served as markers of specific neighbourhoods.

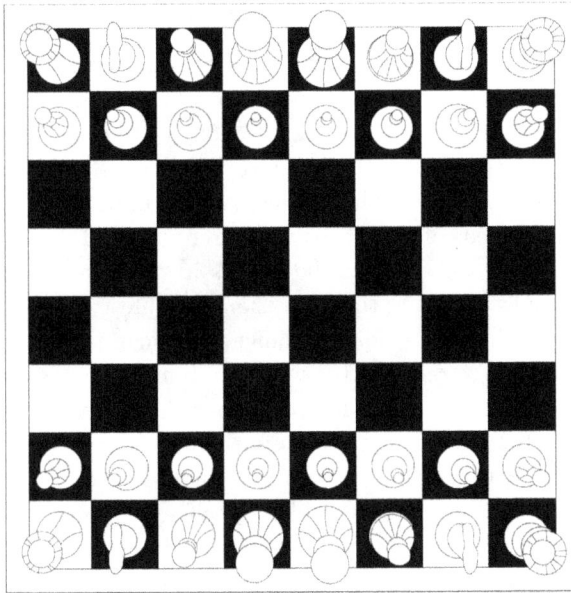

Fig. 6.9   Chessboard.

Continuity, neatness and order in new towns and HDB estates might lead observers to think that the visual environment in Singapore lacked variety and was too regimented. However, the human scale programmed into Singapore's urban planning has actually created variety and reduced the sensation of high density, even with the large masses of tall buildings in parts of the city. Compared with other styles such as that of Soviet public housing mentioned before, Singapore emerges as having more successfully integrated the human scale. Buildings are neat and tidy, yet diverse in size, scale, character and use; green spaces are plentiful; the sky is visible by design; and a mix of high- and low-density clusters can be found in new towns as well as in Singapore as a whole.

A planner's ethos

In the business of planning cities, professionals surely need solid technical expertise and arguably, healthy egos in order to frame and articulate a vision, persuade others to support it, and bring projects to fruition. In the case of Singapore, the principal author of this chapter led the teams that shaped much of the urban landscape and certainly the face of public housing. What ethos — values, aspirations and attitudes — did Singapore's leading planners bring to the work they did? Looking back at a journey of over 20 years, primarily in the 1970s and 1980s, leading the HDB and URA, the following four interrelated ethos emerged for the principal author.

The planner is a humble translator of ideas

A planner translates or interprets ideas, and systematically thinks of the steps needed to turn those ideas into concrete reality, while bearing in mind the context of constrained resources and resolving tensions among competing demands. One must resist the temptation to do something "clever" and let the ego get ahead of the purposes of a project. Instead, a planner must focus on fundamentals that endure. What are the critical needs of the city at its current stage of development, and how would foundations built today affect the city as it grows in the future? What are the resources on hand? What are the aspirations and lifestyles of the people? What steps are needed to bring about initial change? How can projects be economically viable? There is no need to reinvent the wheel. In Singapore, planners took existing examples and maximised the use of limited resources by creating prototypes based on the collective knowledge that was already there to harness. In cases where that knowledge was absent, they came up with new knowledge and innovation.

In the HDB case, for example, the idea of self-sufficiency for new towns came from studies that others had done, but these were reinterpreted and adapted to the Asian context through research and surveys. The actual execution of self-sufficiency into brick-and-mortar, size and scale, took into account the people, mentality, needs and culture of Singapore. Interestingly, the size of a community has stayed the same over time even as Singapore's population has more than doubled from just over two million in the late 1960s–early 1970s to 5.5 million today. At the same time, the concept of "self-sufficiency" has evolved. In the past, a population of 200,000 was deemed necessary for self-sufficiency. This number has gone down — in some cases today to 150,000 mainly due to smaller household sizes and the higher purchasing power of residents. In other words, fewer numbers of people could still sustain the same level of amenities in a viable new town.

Translating ideas also means looking for measures that entail low costs but deliver maximum effects. For example, making Singapore beautiful was a desirable idea that planners were able to execute without depleting scarce financial resources. They translated this idea into reality by picking the cheapest and fastest method for urban beautification: turfing and tree planting. Flowers came into the picture only occasionally at the start because they were more expensive and harder to maintain. The "clean and green" movement in Singapore thus began and thrived, with millions of trees, plants and shrubs planted throughout all types of neighbourhoods, raising citizens' collective pride in the country's growing green and pleasant physical environment.

Good urban planners, indeed, must know how to interpret and translate ideas. In the HDB, refinements, additions and modifications were always informed by ideas and knowledge from sociologists, estate officers, HDB staff and other professionals. Each time, these ideas were interpreted in relation to circumstances on the ground. In a conscious and deliberate process, the HDB consistently expanded its understanding and enhanced its practice of urban planning.

Humility and learning must be core to the trade

The principal author often said: "My best talent is my ability not to believe in my own talent". Having joined the HDB at the age of 31, it was impossible not to be humbled by the idea that one made plans on disposable paper, but the results would affect the daily lives of hundreds of thousands, even millions, for a long period of time. Moreover, the ultimate results of urban planning may not be known until two or three decades after projects are completed. A tremendous burden of accountability thus rests on the shoulders of those planning public housing, new towns or entire cities. Humility is important because it cultivates caution, deliberation and accountability. Moreover, it makes the mind open to learning and allows the community of professionals to foster an open and learning culture that is never self-content — one that always asks how planning and execution may be improved to benefit citizens and customers. In the 1970s and 1980s, planners in Singapore began with limited skills, experience and budgets. However, step by step — learning and keeping humble along the way — other skills were acquired and resources mustered. These were deployed and put to the test over and over again, in the service of creating good living environments for citizens. As time, experience and results accumulate, a planner feels more confident in his skills and contribution. That confidence and mastery of skills are earned and forged by testing. Good planners must not ask what would make them popular today, but ask: What will stand the test of time?

Trust is the foundation of effective leadership

Urban planning happens in a context of competing voices and demands. The early days were not easy for Singapore, when there were tense relations among squatters, landlords, landowners and government. Unemployment was high, and so was discontent. People were steeped in habits and mentalities that were not quite conducive to modernisation. The government had to take strong measures. One contentious area, for example, was government acquisition of fire sites for redevelopment. In 1961, Singapore's Legislative Assembly passed an amendment to the Land Acquisition Ordinance to allow the government to acquire the Bukit Ho Swee fire site for redevelopment and forbid unauthorised structures on the site. According to one study:

> The [Legislative Assembly] session centred on a motion proposed by Tan Kia Gan for an amendment to the Land Acquisition Ordinance. He asked the government to acquire the fire site for redevelopment and forbid unauthorised structures on the site. Tan also assessed the value of the land based on its inhabited state prior to the fire, which was much lower than as an unoccupied site. The motion was passed ... Although the state had previously acquired fire sites for re-development, the PAP's proposed motion gave it far greater power in acquiring fire sites henceforth ... In supporting Tan's motion, Lee Kuan Yew emphasised

that allowing the landowners to profit from the sale of their land would 'only be an inducement, a temptation, to arson by those who possess land with squatters on it'. According to the government land valuer, land without tenants was worth about three times more than land with tenants. The onus, Lee continued, was on landowners to prove that their land was vacant at the time of the fire, where-upon the minister for national development had the discretion to raise the amount of compensation made to them (Loh, 2013, pp. 173–4).

When tenants became homeless, the government had to find ways to resettle them. But in the process of resettlement, squatters who moved into high-rise dwellings lost their animals or farms, and yet had to pay rent to the HDB. To alleviate resettlers' challenges, the new housing estates offered them job opportunities in the community centres, wet markets, shophouses and factories. By using the law, together with the provision of alternative housing and livelihoods, the government helped bring an end to suspicious fires and also helped landlords relocate squatters. This is an example of using the law or coercive power to change behaviour on one hand, while simultaneously offering solutions or incentives to help the parties affected. This push and pull approach, a hallmark of the Singapore government's strategies, helped to gain public trust, which was a critical ingredient for advancing urban planning efficiently and effectively.

The 1966 Land Acquisition Act gave the HDB compulsory powers to acquire private lands for public housing and other public purposes. This, too, was not an easy task. However, in Singapore, the government fulfilled its word regarding the use of newly acquired lands. People could see the results and, over time, supported the government's actions. From 1960–1979, through compulsory acquisition for public purposes, the government share of land ownership increased from approximately 30% (crown lands left behind by the British Colonial Government) to 70%. Over this same period and subsequently in the 1980s, the population saw benefits accrue to them in the form of affordable public housing, public spaces, amenities, infrastructure services and employment that lifted a large number of the citizenry, especially those in lower-income brackets. The government operated in a transparent manner, made the law simple enough to be understood by all and delivered results. As early as the mid-1960s, a similar dynamic happened with usage of the CPF (Central Provident Fund or the compulsory savings programme overseen by the government) for the people to purchase public housing. Financing through the CPF was an innovative measure that gave the HDB the means to undertake an audacious, systematic and comprehensive approach to building decent and subsidised housing for the majority of Singapore's population.

Clarity is courage

In the past, and even today, Singapore's urban planning and housing development programme has had its fair share of critics. In the 1960s, for example, voices around the world criticised high-rise, high-density public housing, calling them "vertical slums". Regardless of this negative sentiment, Singapore's government and planners knew they had no choice other than the high-rise route, given that land would not miraculously expand in Singapore to accommodate a growing population. If they were to house the entire country and a future growing population, they would have to rise above the chorus of world opinion. At the same time, they must not be blind to the handicaps of high-rise housing, but understand and address them through carefully thought-out planning and design.

Until the late 1980s, another common criticism of the urban milieu of HDB estates and other urban areas characterised Singapore as clinical and without liveliness as a city. As head of the HDB at the time, the principal author urged his colleagues to ignore all the well-meaning noise. Europeans, for example, could complain about Singapore's aseptic settings because they themselves had the luxury of centuries to nurture lively and creative cities. Singapore's leading planners did not doubt that liveliness and vibrancy would come, but the key in the early phases was to resist the seduction of enticing words from outsiders and to develop a thick skin against the chorus of well-meaning critics. Planners must not turn their cities hastily into theme parks. It is most important to always focus on the fundamentals. This then creates a catalytic chain reaction, at the end of which is broader contentment, prosperity and the foundation for precisely the kind of liveliness and creativity that the best of cities aspire to have. Indeed, the principal purpose of physical planning and architecture is more to create an experience than an image. Experience includes liveability, a beautiful and ecologically sustainable environment, and economically viable places. Good architectural imagery, including buildings that are well-proportioned and resonant at the human level, can be added to enhance the experience of being in a city or in large housing estates.

In lieu of a conclusion: Thinking about the future, now

The Singapore urban planning story will continue to evolve, and hopefully it will continue to improve. In looking back at what has been accomplished, a few lessons stand out.

1) The primary purpose of architecture and planning is more to provide a good experience for the users rather than to create design images. It is not about building monuments for oneself. "Form follows function", as the aphorism goes, but the principal author has reframed it as "form follows function and fun". In the HDB, form addressed how residents might best work, live, play, learn and move. To create a meaningful experience for the customers and endusers, urban planning created a hierarchy of spaces such as city, region, town, neighbourhood and precinct, and, at the micro-level, void decks and "courtyards in the sky". The scales of these spaces reflected the diverse needs of human beings. In addition,

careful thought was given to cultivating emotional ties to precincts, squares and gardens. Squares and gardens were integrated not only in residential, but also in commercial centres, thus facilitating civic and commercial interaction.

2) In addition to hierarchy of space, good planning requires optimised distribution of amenities. In Singapore, plazas, gardens and sports fields of different sizes were planned to have an optimal service radius, allowing them to serve maximal (but different) catchment areas. These spaces might serve a decorative purpose, but more importantly, they enhanced the living environment, offered respite and recreation for children and adults, and facilitated a range of activities for users' physical and social well-being.

3) The HDB did not just create a roof over people's heads. The social dimension of urban planning extended the goals of public housing construction to include, first and foremost, safety and security, along with green spaces, community building, social cohesion, stability and a higher quality of life. Planning in Singapore has shown that, no matter how big a city is, the human scale remains the same. The basic unit is the precinct. This is a key principle of urban planning. One must think of creating "urban cells", where each unit has sufficient human numbers, energy and activites to become self-sustaining.

4) The catalytic chain effect of good urban planning cannot be overestimated. In Singapore, the HDB generated a catalytic chain reaction of material results that will continue to inform the country's future. It underlines the value of strong leadership and effective public policy, which was evident in the positive impact including housing for the nation, successful resettlement, an upgraded construction industry that has evolved to become a regional player, a commercial industrial infrastructure, good jobs and economic growth, a vibrant property market, a strong foundation for creativity and a highly liveable city. Because the bones of urban planning are right, the edifice built on top can shine. HDB first built housing for the "poorest", but this was only the beginning of bigger and brighter aspirations. Today, even unexpected delights come from the HDB. For example, residents have created artistic works to adorn their estates. In Clementi, 500 families organised a painting activity and the resulting lively canvases were exhibited on HDB walls. This is community and creativity at their best. HDB motifs have also appeared in original designs for household products and fashion, showing how HDB has captured the imagination of artists and entrepreneurs.

Singapore must resist the allure of its own success. It has achieved much that is laudable and excellent in urban planning, but there is always room for improvement. Indeed, great cities do not stay in stasis, but continue to evolve, with leaders who are always observing, learning and making improvements. Before looking outside, Singapore's leaders, planners and citizens would do well to first know and understand what the city has already done, and done well, and how it got there. The city's own track record should give people confidence in Singaporean talent and ability, while at the same time serve as a reminder to leaders and planners to stay humble and hardworking.

Today, some Singaporeans express rising unhappiness. This is partially the result of living in the limited environment of a single-city state, with very little to experience for direct comparison. Some may be the victims of "perfectionitis". They are unable to appreciate what they have, and because they expect everything to be "perfect", nothing is and will be. We must remember that, as we strive for perfection, it us only human that we may achieve results that are excellent but fall short of perfection. Going forward, it is important for Singapore's leaders and citizens to cultivate perspectives, enhance appreciation, and improve communications between government and people.

Clarity and courage will be important for the future, as they have been in the past. Planners must resist global fads while evolving the fundamental and critical roles of public housing and urban planning for a geographically small, but economically big and still-growing country. Fear should not stymie efforts to continue the tradition of effective planning, including the bold vision of a city-state that might be home to a population as big as 10 million. Leaders and planners must stick to proven principles: Know what our city needs us to do, however difficult; accept the problems, and find and even invent solutions; and believe that we can achieve what appears at first glance to be unachievable. We have already done this. This is the story of Singapore in the past, and is the story we should continue into the future.

References

Housing & Development Board (HDB) (2010, September 22). *HDB Wins Prestigious 2010 UN-Habitat Scroll of Honour Award.* Retrieved 1 November 2014, from http://www.hdb.gov.sg/fi10/fi10296p.nsf/PressReleases/8D132D27FDEFB5CD482577A60 0015451?OpenDocument.

Lee, Kuan Yew (2000). *From Third World to First. The Singapore Story, 1965–2000.* Singapore: Singapore Press Holdings.

Loh, K. S. (2013). *Squatters into Citizens: The 1961 Bukit Ho Swee Fire and the Making of Modern Singapore.* Singapore: National University Press.

World Bank (2012). *Urban Development.* Retrieved 1 October 2014, from http://wbi.worldbank.org/wbi/about/topics/urban.

PART II
Inclusivity and Social Progress

Chapter 7

Social Mobility in Singapore[1]

Tan Ern Ser

This chapter examines social mobility in Singapore and its relationships with social stratification, inequality and the Singapore Dream. Using the analogy of a game as a conceptual guide, the chapter begins with a discussion of the changes in social mobility that have taken place in the last 50 years. This historical perspective is then related to current issues in social mobility. The chapter ends with an evaluation of the mobility game in Singapore and several policy recommendations.

From Third World to middle-class society in a complex global environment

Singapore is a capitalist society, which means that, by definition and in practice, it is also a class society. A class society is in turn an unequal society, a social arrangement likely to be deemed as undesirable from the perspective of social justice. However, inequality is in itself not necessarily a social problem, if the institution of unequal rewards is based on meritocracy — provides incentives for people to live up to their potential, and to perform their best for themselves, their family, community and nation — as well as established measures aimed at ironing out extreme inequality. Such a positive arrangement entails the presence of equality of opportunity for social mobility and the prevention of entrenchment of poverty; failing which, inequality

---

[1]Author Note: This chapter is recast and expanded from "The Mobility Game in Singapore: Poverty, Welfare, Opportunity, and Success in a Capitalist Economy" by Tan Ern Ser which first appeared in *Poverty and Global Recession in Southeast Asia* edited by Aris Ananta and Richard Barichello (2012), pp. 153–163. Reproduced here with the kind permission of the publisher, Institute of Southeast Asian Studies, Singapore, <https//bookshop.iseas.edu.sg>.

will rear its ugly head as a source of social tension, leading to social instability and perhaps social disintegration.

To the government's and people's credit, Singapore has by and large performed well economically over the last 50 years. In the late '70s and the '80s, Singapore was even one of the highly celebrated four Asian Dragons or newly industrialising economies (NIEs), together with Hong Kong, South Korea and Taiwan. The buoyant economy has launched Singapore on an upward trajectory from Third World to First World (Lee, 2000), resulting in full employment, rising income for most Singaporeans, expanding opportunities for education and upward social mobility, and transforming Singapore into a middle-class society.

While this transformation is much admired globally and obviously beneficial to the post-war generations of the citizenry, it also has the effect of raising expectations — with the middle-class level becoming the bottom line — which cannot be easily fulfilled. The implication here is that whereas previously, most Singaporeans were likely to experience some degree of upward mobility and confident of achieving more in their own and the next generation, there is now a sense that inequality spells unequal opportunity. This sense occurs in the current context where the economy produces less low-hanging fruits, while competition for higher-hanging fruits becomes tougher and the burden of caring for an ageing population greatly intensifies. Simply put, it is becoming more difficult to play the mobility game and achieve the Singapore Dream that has been the preoccupation of most Singaporeans since the early '70s. If this is indeed the case, then there are good reasons to examine more closely the mobility game, together with the Singapore Dream.

Social background matters for social mobility

Social mobility is influenced by contextual and psychological factors as well as class origin. Most studies on social mobility have consistently demonstrated that family background matters (Chen, 1973; Quah *et al.*, 1991). What parents, particularly fathers, do for a living has a strong influence on how their children perform in school and eventually in the labour market. Undoubtedly, there is a host of other contributory factors which can enhance one's mobility chances; however, they all boil down to the fact that a person's access to economic, social and cultural capital[2] has a significant impact on his or her future career and life trajectory.

My own study (Tan, 2004), as well as earlier studies by Chen (1973) and Quah *et al.* (1991), suggest that despite official policy aimed at equalising opportunities in

---

[2]Economic capital includes financial assets or resources; social capital refers to the advantages derived from social networks, connections or ties; while cultural capital refers to educational credentials and useful knowledge, including linguistic competence (Bourdieu, 1984).

Singapore, family background continues to have a strong influence on educational and occupational attainment among Singaporeans. Indeed, Ko (1991, p. 224) found that "about one fifth of the variance in education may be explained by the three background variables (father's education, father's occupation, and mother's education)". This is hardly surprising, given that for practical reasons, the provision of opportunities tends to focus primarily on economic capital, rather than social and cultural capital. More specifically, even if economic capital could be equalised — some of which may be used to enhance social and cultural capital — it is unlikely that one could prevent the advantages associated with social networks, such as kinship and friendship ties, and access to lifestyles, knowledge, skills and strategic information from boosting the mobility chances of offspring of well-connected, well-educated, financially well-endowed parents.

However, this is not to suggest that people without the appropriate credentials and merits, academic and otherwise, could climb up the social ladder simply by hanging on to the coat-tails of their parents; rather, all things being equal, social and cultural capital may well tip the balance in one's favour. Consequently, meritocracy is not compromised, even when non-meritocratic, ascriptive factors can have a significant influence on social mobility. There is, however, one important exception to the meritocratic principle. Specifically, because of the institution of private property inheritance, a key feature of capitalist society, one could become a business owner simply by being born into wealth, and paradoxically be in a position to hire and control professionals and managers who possess far higher credentials than themselves, but unfortunately lack the privilege of family wealth.

Using a game analogy

This chapter will not take the approach of continuing to prove ad nauseum that family background matters or that the policy and practice of equalising opportunities, or even promoting economic growth with job creation, has led to greater absolute mobility or even relative mobility. Instead, I would be using a game analogy as a tool to understand social mobility and the related issues of poverty and welfare in Singapore. I believe this approach provides a useful conceptual device for connecting various mobility-related factors and processes in a way which can help us identify the challenges facing, and extrapolate, the future of social mobility and the Singapore Dream.

We begin by describing the key features in the concept of a game. A game is characterised by having rules, goals, and players with differing abilities and motivations. The rules specify how the game is to be played and the processes that one needs to go through in order to win at the game. The game also provides resources and opportunities accessible to players, although there is nothing to stop players from mobilising their own or family resources to perform well in the game.

The mobility game has different categories of winners and losers, as well as players who fall by the wayside. It allows the possibility of people opting out of the game for lack of interest, motivation, ability or resources. However, this does not necessarily imply that the players who exit the game have abandoned their mobility aspirations. For example, they may have decided to move overseas in search of "greener, more user-friendly pastures" wherein to participate in some other countries' mobility games. The advent of globalisation has in fact facilitated this process, even as it encourages the inflow of foreigners, thereby increasing the number of players or competitors involved in the Singapore mobility game. However, not everyone needs to participate in the mobility game. There is a small category of non-players, people who could afford not to play the game because they are independently rich through past successes or through inheritance, or a combination of both of these.

Apart from having a multiplicity of different kinds of players or non-players, another interesting aspect of the game is that it is somewhat structured, yet compatible with the notion of self-reliance. This appears to be a contradiction, but only seemingly so, because while most Singaporeans believe in and are expected to be self-reliant, they depend on the government to ensure that the mobility game and its structure of opportunity remain fair, accessible and viable.

Having described how the concept of a game may be applied to social mobility, I shall next describe the Singapore Dream and mobility game from a historical perspective and discuss the changes that have taken place over the last 50 years.

The mobility game in Singapore: Facilitating success

For much of its known history, Singapore has been a society of migrants, although the net immigration figures vary from time to time, depending on prevailing policies and economic conditions, local, regional and global. By and large, immigrants come to Singapore to seek better opportunities for themselves and their children, just as Singaporeans leave their homeland in search of greener pastures elsewhere.

Some immigrants did become enormously wealthy, thereby becoming the subjects, even folk heroes or icons, of popular history. Because theirs were "rags to riches" stories, similar to those penned by Horatio Alger in the United States, their life histories not only become an inspiration to others, but also point to the possibility of long-range upward social mobility in Singapore, understood as a land of opportunity (cf. Chinoy, 1955).

In reality, the probability of long-range upward mobility is quite small. However, this fact is not a serious concern, since what matters is that the "rags to riches" stories convey a strong sense that Singapore is an open, meritocratic system where one's station in life does not have to be permanent, and that one could take control of one's destiny through sheer hard work and determination, along with some element of luck. This is in fact the fundamental principle of the mobility game, that social background is not destiny and that there are ample opportunities available to whoever has the ability, motivation and stamina to propel oneself upwards.

In the Singapore context, the state has been and is the controller and manager of the mobility game. It sets the rules and provides much of the resources and opportunities necessary to play the mobility game. It has also taken on the responsibility of ensuring that there are sufficient rewards to keep the mobility game meaningful and viable. Specifically, the rule of the game can be summarised in one word — meritocracy, or reward for merit in educational and job performance. The resources and opportunities refer to access to good quality, subsidised education unrelated to ability to pay, as well as to middle-class jobs.

Consequently, while opportunities are not exactly equal (as I have explained earlier), many Singaporeans, regardless of family background, have been able to move up the educational ladder. The large majority of Singaporeans ends up receiving at least a secondary education, and increasingly, with many even a tertiary education.[3] There is no doubt that a high and growing proportion of Singaporeans have availed themselves of the opportunities and managed to move up the social ladder. Coupled with the successful economic strategies that have produced spectacular economic growth rates worthy of an Asian Dragon and contributed to employment creation, the policy of equalising opportunities has led to Singapore becoming a middle-class society, characterised by growing affluence and a rising standard of living comparable to that of First World countries (Lee, 2000). In short, Singapore has had a viable mobility game in which all players have a fair chance of winning, in the forms of securing decent jobs and a reasonably high, but accessible standard of living, regardless of starting points.

It is clear that the viability of the mobility game hinges largely on the capability of the economy to consistently deliver sufficient, decent-paying — even high-paying — jobs which match the aspirations and expectations of young Singaporeans armed with educational credentials. For those with university education, the expectation upon graduation is not to obtain merely a job, but to embark on a secure, middle-class career trajectory.

Using the progress in education and jobs described above as the criterion for successful mobility, the late '70s and early '80s would constitute the golden age of the mobility game in Singapore. That was the period of double-digit economic growth rates, phenomenal employment creation, large bonuses and annual wage

---

[3]There is, however, no necessary correlation between educational attainment and occupational attainment. Indeed, the government is concerned that there will be an oversupply of university graduates relative to the demand for university graduates who are expected to possess specific skills required by businesses or industries. This possible mismatch between expectation and reality could hurt the mobility game, should it be perceived to be unable to deliver what it promises to those who thought they have faithfully played the game since their childhood days. The government-appointed committee, ASPIRE (acronym for Applied Study in Polytechnics and ITE Review) has recommended that there should be multiple pathways, including those not requiring a degree, for achieving occupational success, or, in the context of this chapter, playing the mobility game.

increments, together with a tight labour market where job-hopping, rather than unemployment, was a national concern. That period also corresponds to when the 5 Cs (cash, credit card, condominium, car and country club membership), which symbolises the good life and the Singapore-equivalent of the American Dream, first emerged and became a prominent feature on Singapore's social and cultural landscape.

The Singapore Dream also conveys the comforting idea that class origin does not determine destiny, at least not to any significant extent. In the popular imagination, therefore, class inequality, while present, does not quite matter. Indeed, some people would mistake equality of opportunity for social egalitarianism or class equality itself. Correspondingly, inequality became largely a non-issue in a meritocratic society upheld by expanding equality of educational and employment opportunities. The latter has in turn led to significant absolute mobility, even when relative mobility has remained somewhat unequal. The impressive absolute mobility was most visible in terms of housing and education, even as the presence of unequal relative mobility was rendered invisible. More importantly, the undeniable fact is that most Singaporeans were socially mobile, and visibly so, even if the range, degree and probability of mobility were not equal across the classes. Notwithstanding this, Singaporeans were often exhorted by the government to compare their material situation with that of the past or parents' generation, rather than across classes, which could result in the politics of envy and thereby social instability.

Whether it was because Singaporeans accepted the government's exhortation or they could not do otherwise, there was to be no politics of envy in Singapore. In fact, Singaporeans were until the last decade often characterised as politically apathetic, preoccupied with achieving the Singapore Dream. At the level of everyday life, most Singaporeans were caught up with the idea of upgrading, or doing better intra- and intergenerationally. This upgrading mentality is focused on at least two "big ticket" items: moving to a larger HDB[4] apartment — or better still, even crossing the visible and symbolic class divide between public and private housing — and between public and private transport by purchasing an automobile.[5] In sociological terms, the language of upgrading translates into upward social mobility involving working-class persons or families joining the swelling ranks of the middle class, thereby contributing to the transformation of Singapore into a middle-class society.

Within this middle-class society, living in smaller sized HDB apartments, that is, three-room or smaller flats, was getting out of fashion, while the demand for private condominium apartments rose substantially to such an extent that even the HDB

---

[4]HDB is the abbreviation for Housing & Development Board, the public housing authority. Unlike public housing elsewhere, the majority of HDB dwellers own the flats they live in.

[5]The Singapore Dream and mobility game could be understood as involving the crossing of the visible and symbolic class divide between public and private housing and transport.

felt obliged to design and build so-called middle-class housing (executive apartment blocks, followed by executive condominiums).[6]

At the same time, the government agonised over how best to meet the automobile aspirations of Singaporeans, without at the same time allowing too many cars on already crowded roads, even as it focused much attention on the issue of enhancing company loyalty and productivity via company welfarism, organisational culture and life-time employment — long before the term "life-time employability" became fashionable. Because these attributes were seen as the factors contributing to the Japanese economic success story in the '70s, it is no wonder that Japan was touted by some academics — a prominent example being Vogel (1979) who wrote the bestseller *Japan as Number 1* — and policy-makers as an institutional model worthy of emulation. Nowadays, employing organisations are no longer expected, nor can they afford, to guarantee life-time employment; while individual employees are expected to constantly reinvent and upgrade themselves in order to stay relevant, productive and employable.

The mobility game in Singapore: Dealing with poverty and welfare

Not surprisingly, that period in history when the economy was most vibrant saw poverty as an issue taking a backseat as droves of Singaporeans played the mobility game, having full confidence that individual self-reliance and government-sponsored opportunities constitute the sure-win formula for achieving the Singapore Dream. Poverty is therefore often implicitly deemed to reflect moral shortcomings, in the form of laziness and irresponsible behaviours, or somewhat more generously, to bad luck, misfortunes, lack of natural ability or unsupportive family members, causing some to fall through the cracks, rather than a failure of the system, which in the Singapore case refers to capitalism, to deliver decent paying jobs, and the mobility game, which is perceived to be fair, equitable and viable.

Correspondingly, poverty and low income are seen as the absence of mobility that could be addressed by measures aimed at "levelling up",[7] rather than be encouraged by measures aimed at redistribution and narrowing income inequality. It should be noted that while inequality is generally seen as socially undesirable, it is not exactly a "dirty" word — even if some politicians sometimes feel obliged to

---

[6] A crude indicator of how flat size corresponds to class is median household income. That of residents of one- to three-room flats is below the national median household income of S$4950 in 2008 (Department of Statistics [DOS], 2009). Based on this criterion, those residing in four-room or larger HDB flats could be considered "middle class", while those in private housing, "upper middle class". It is noteworthy that, along with income and employment insecurity, and rising cost of living, the government has found it necessary to resume the building of smaller HDB flats.

[7] "Levelling up", together with "sharing success", is in fact the key theme of an official publication released by the Ministry of Information and the Arts in 1996 (MITA, 1996). This booklet focuses on key social programmes established by the Singapore government.

express disapproval of it in public statements — since support for capitalism and meritocracy presupposes unequal rewards and outcomes as the basis for motivating people to seek to perform well in roles that contribute to economic growth and individual and family well-being. This mirrors the functionalist perspective on social stratification,[8] which is generally considered to be theoretically problematic but comes across as sensible and ideologically defensible.

It should also be pointed out that this ideology, when reinforced by numerous success stories of upward social mobility, provides the justification for the approach to welfare provisions adopted in Singapore. The rhetoric is that an effective and sustainable welfare policy is one that offers opportunities for Singaporeans to become self-reliant materially, rather than one which inculcates a "handout" mentality, and perhaps perpetual dependency. Hence, we often hear the cliché that rationalises why welfare policies should aim at "teaching a person to fish", which will enable him to take care of himself, rather than "give him fishes", which will encourage dependency at the level of individuals and families, and in turn an unsustainable welfare system, although with good intentions, but incapable of delivering on its commitments in the longer term, without bankrupting the country's financial reserves.

The mobility game toughened in Singapore

From the discussions above, the fundamentals of the mobility game do come across as primarily sound, viable and sustainable. Unfortunately, while the game is internally consistent, logical and reasonable — thereby enjoying a high degree of legitimacy — it is not entirely foolproof. For one thing, the decent paying jobs — including middle-class jobs — it is expected to deliver in sufficient quantity to a growing population of tertiary-educated, middle-class Singaporeans may be harder to come by as a result of global recession, competition or restructuring. This concern is succinctly reflected in the serious tones resonating throughout the pages of the report issued by the high-powered Economic Review Committee (ERC) chaired by then Deputy Prime Minister Lee Hsien Loong (ERC, 2003).

Moreover, as noted earlier, it is not practical and sensible under capitalism, which treats private ownership, inheritance and market as sacrosanct, to bring about a totally level playing field. Some players would enjoy greater advantages than others via their access to economic, social and cultural capital. Nevertheless, as long as the game manager is able to "pump" in sufficient prizes, it does not really matter that some are moving faster and further than others just because they have access to more resources. As long as players feel that they are experiencing some degree of

---

[8]The functionalist perspective argues that unequal rewards are necessary to motivate people to make the sacrifice of going through rigorous training and eventually assume the "functionally more important positions" in society.

upward mobility and are able to upgrade their material well-being periodically, they would continue to have confidence in the mobility game, despite the imperfections.

This seems to be the orientation that Singaporeans adopt towards the mobility game. Obviously, during the golden age of the mobility game in the late '70s and early '80s, their confidence did have a strong basis. Since the recession of 1985–86, however, the cycle of "boom and bust" seems to operate at shorter intervals. Over the last quarter of a century, from 1985 to 2009, Singapore has experienced the economic repercussions caused by the 1997 Asian financial crisis, the September 11 terrorist attacks in the United States in 2001, and, subsequently, the housing sub-prime crisis and tremendous financial meltdowns. As we are all very familiar by now, recessions and meltdowns do bring about a trail of destructions, manifested in the forms of job and income insecurity and erosion of retirement savings, affecting both individuals and families.

In the earlier economic crises, the general perception is that working-class jobs are the least secure as the Singapore economy embarked on the process of restructuring to face the challenges of global competition and technological changes. So long as this view was prevalent, it did not affect the fundamentals and the perceived viability of the mobility game. However, in more recent years, due to economic fluctuations, which had led to some contraction in the economy, people in middle-class jobs — collectively known as PMETs[9] or professionals, managers, executives and technicians — too experience retrenchments in significant numbers (Boon, 2014). The fact that PMETs received much attention in recent national budgets and media reports provides a strong indication that job and income insecurity is no longer primarily a working-class affliction, but one that affects middle-class Singaporeans as well.

It does appear that the secure, comfortable middle-class career trajectory sought after by Singaporeans is now in retreat somewhat, given the changed global economic environment characterised by frequent fluctuations and intense competition, which entail economic restructuring and flexibility. Instead of a clear career ladder, middle-class aspirants often find themselves having to compete very hard for shorter-term, contract positions. Once in a job, they are constantly subjected to performance evaluation and expected to be adept at multitasking, yet to not expect employment security. Where life-time or at least long-term employment was once the norm, they are now expected to constantly upgrade their skills, or even to reskill, in order to stay employable, failing which they could face the prospect of job redundancy or skills obsolescence in middle age (Hing, 1997). Moreover, the fact that one could suffer job loss in middle age does amplify the

---

[9]Most recently, the government is concerned that young Singaporeans armed with a degree, but possessing no relevant skills, may not be able to land a PME job within an expected time-frame. The acronym "PME" refers to the preferred job levels of university graduates. It excludes technician jobs, represented by the "T" in "PMET".

problem severalfold, given that ageism may rear its ugly head in subtle, muted forms, notwithstanding official exhortations and measures.

Most certainly, the mobility game is no longer an easy game to play, nor are the rewards a high degree of security and a comfortable middle-class existence; yet the option to drop out of the mobility game is not a realistic one. For one thing, most Singaporeans have committed themselves to acquiring the trappings of a middle-class lifestyle, which includes home ownership and in many cases, automobile ownership as well. Moreover, if they happen to be in the sandwiched generation,[10] they would have ageing parents with longevity and long-term adolescence as dependents. To add to this problem, the ageing parents may not be in good physical health and therefore in need of constant caregiving as well as medical attention often without the benefit of health insurance.[11] At the same time, they are committed to helping their children succeed in the mobility game. This entails having a household budget to ensure that their children perform academically well enough to eventually enter university, preferably the highly subsidised local ones. The emphasis parents place on their children's educational success has in fact spawned a sizeable tuition industry, which reportedly is now worth a billion dollars, as compared to S$650 million a decade ago (T. Tan, 2014).

Clearly, from the mid-'80s onwards, the Singapore Dream has increasingly come under serious threat not only in the forms of economic fluctuations, stiff global competition and technological changes, but also cost inflation, low fertility and a rapidly ageing population, giving rise to the need to further liberalise the inflow of migrants and foreign labour. All of these processes have contributed in one way or another to the widening income gap, employment and income insecurity, higher cost of living, and lower elderly support ratios. While these challenges to the mobility game have, for better or for worse, not quite turned the Singapore Dream into a nightmare, they have produced some degree of anxiety, disillusionment and frustration among Singaporeans. Apart from the sense of insecurity, even a fear of downward mobility, there is a concern that the widening income gap, and possibly the hardening of class boundaries, would act as a dampener on upward social mobility for those on the lower and middle segments of the social ladder, resulting in class origin largely determining destiny once again.[12] At the same time, as we have noted earlier, Singapore has become a middle-class society with a growing

---

[10]The term refers to those who are in an unenviable position of having to take care of elderly parents and schooling children.

[11]The recently introduced Pioneer Generation Package (PGP), together with MediShield Life, which will be implemented in 2015, will to some extent help to lighten the financial burden of the sandwiched generation.

[12]For a recent debate on unequal relative mobility in Singapore, see Irene Ng's (2011) opinion piece in *The Straits Times*, together with rejoinders from Cheong Wei Yang, a director at the Ministry of Education (*The Straits Times*, 2011), Yip Chun Seng (2011), a Ministry of Finance economist, and Minister of Education Ng Eng Hen (2011) in his parliamentary speech. I have written a discussion piece (Tan, 2015), commenting on this debate, in my response to Irene Ng's (2011, pp. 25–49) recent paper on "Education and Social Mobility in Singapore".

tertiary-educated population which aspires to decent paying, high prestige jobs, and secure and comfortable living standards.

The surfacing of these issues indicates that the language of class has become fashionable again on the social and political landscape in Singapore. These issues can be understood as reflecting the concerns of the lower class and the middle class.

Lower-class Singaporeans are concerned about low, stagnant wages, high cost of living, and inequality of opportunity associated with rising income inequality, while middle-class people harbour fears and anxieties about not being able to live the secure, comfortable life they believe they deserve from having been relatively successful in the mobility game. The latter are also just as, if not more, worried about their children not being able to live the Singapore Dream given the phenomenal rise in property and private vehicle prices over the last decade or so, and concerned that a university degree, while necessary, may no longer fetch a premium price in the job market. Some of these concerns are, rightly or wrongly, attributed to the competition posed by foreign workers and professionals for jobs, housing and amenities. In addition, as alluded to earlier, middle-class people who belong to the sandwiched generation have numerous financial fears or concerns that often coexist, including handling the healthcare costs of their ageing parents (particularly if the latter do not possess medical insurance), funding the long-term adolescence and education of their children, grappling with inflation, wage stagnation, the threat of income and employment insecurity, as well as shouldering various financial commitments. There is also the concern of being subjected to means testing and sometimes without the benefits of government subsidies.

The mobility game: Evaluation and policy recommendations

When assessing the mobility game, I recognise that hindsight is usually better than foresight. During the golden age of the mobility game, when the economy had just emerged from a low base and when the demographic profile was much younger, it was relatively easy to develop and sustain a viable mobility game and perhaps think that the good times could continue indefinitely. At the level of individuals, the mobility game was also easier to play and the probability of attaining a secure, comfortable middle-class career trajectory and lifestyle fairly good. Consequently, Singaporeans were totally obsessed with the idea of upgrading and achieving the "good life" — the Singapore-equivalent of the American Dream. To be sure, a large and growing proportion of Singaporeans did succeed in the mobility game.

Unfortunately, while Singaporeans were preoccupied with climbing up the "ladders", they did not pay much attention to the "snakes", such as medical costs for ageing parents, education costs of long-term adolescence children and meltdowns of personal assets, nor did they entertain the thought that job and income security, and in turn the middle-class lifestyle they hold dear, may be far less permanent than they had always thought.[13] Downward mobility in middle age may turn out to be the cruel reality where an earlier generation had looked forward to enjoying the fruits of their labour in old age. Perhaps, during the golden years of the mobility game, very few of the upgraders or upwardly mobile really understood that the mobility game could someday, and soon, lose its glitter, and that while they focus on asset building, they did not notice that their liabilities constitute a potential time bomb ready to explode at a time when they are least able to respond.

I am not sure if the upgraders would fall low enough to benefit from assistance normally extended to the poor or low-income category. I believe they would do all they can to cling on to their middle-class lifestyle, rather than allow themselves to sink into a lower class.

In my view, given that the legitimacy of the government depends on its ability to maintain the viability of the mobility game, more than its ability to help those who fall by the wayside, it makes sense for the government to ensure that, even as Singaporeans are advised to and given the opportunity to stay employable, there will always be sufficient middle-class jobs.

Moreover, I have previously argued that the government should also extend more help towards current middle-class, middle-age people in the sandwiched generation, thereby enhancing their capacity to handle some of the liabilities (for instance, medical costs of their elderly parents, and perhaps even grandparents) they happened to inherit, with some degree of assurance that they would not lose a large chunk of what they have earned and saved from diligently playing the mobility game over the years. Thankfully, there are now new policy measures, such as the Pioneer Generation Package and the soon to be implemented MediShield Life, which may help to some extent to lighten the financial burden of the sandwiched generation, and in turn that of future generations.

I believe that because the government's legitimacy lies in its ability to maintain Singapore as a middle-class society, it must do its utmost to ensure that Singaporeans do not suffer irreversible downward mobility. I am not sure if this is too much or unreasonable to ask or if I am just being unrealistic and unnecessarily nostalgic of a past that can never return.

Let me also venture to suggest something which could be deemed quite outrageous and may even smack of elitism. I have observed that "problem families"[14] do not have the capacity to help their offspring play the mobility game. While it is commendable that the state has taken upon itself to help "problem families" and their offspring, I cannot help but think that Singaporeans ought to do some serious financial budget planning before they decide to start a family; otherwise, not only

---

[13]I am using the analogy of the game of "snakes and ladders" in which the former leads to regression, while the latter allows progression to the end point.

[14]By "problem families", I have in mind family units set up by couples who are incapable of looking after themselves, yet went on to produce children who are exposed to an environment severely lacking in economic, social and cultural capital.

would this result in themselves and their offspring being incapable of playing the mobility game, but they may also end up in the poor or low-income category and needing welfare on a long-term basis.

Moving forward

It is hard to foretell if there can be another golden age during the next 50 years, characterised by a viable mobility game and Singapore Dream. Should this prove unlikely, then, *ceteris paribus*, we may have to settle for a different kind of middle class society in Singapore, a social arrangement which takes on one or a combination of the following forms: a large, "kiasu" (i.e., afraid to lose out) middle class, perpetually feeling the anxiety of losing the lifestyle they hold so dear; one better adjusted to a more competitive world and well-equipped to access the high-hanging fruits; or perhaps one settling into a "good enough", achievable standard of living with a scaled-down Singapore Dream.

For the lower class, despite the prevailing "self-reliance" model, there are various social policy measures aimed at preventing the entrenchment of poverty and provision of financial and educational support to enhance the mobility opportunity of their children. But such measures are not always successful in helping the children break through a home environment unconducive to inculcating high occupational aspirations and achieving academic excellence. What matters more is a conscious and concerted effort focusing on boosting their social and cultural capital, besides providing economic capital, which will enable them to avail themselves of educational opportunities, and facilitate their achieving some degree of upward social mobility.

Clearly, class position and its consequences have important implications for the social orientations of Singaporeans and the kind of social policies that could help bring about individual and social well-being, and in turn a more resilient society, characterised by not merely the absence of social tensions, but more importantly by the presence of strong social ties and solidarity among citizens, and solid social compact, involving a high degree of confidence and trust between the government and the people.

References

Boon, R. (2014, October 23). Graduate Employment: Degrees of Relevance. *The Straits Times*. Retrieved 16 February 2015, from http://www.straitstimes.com/news/opinion/eye-the-economy/story/graduate-employment-degrees-relevance-20141023.

Bourdieu, P. (1984*). Homo Academicus*. CA: Stanford University Press.

Chen, P. S. J. (1973). *Social Stratification in Singapore*. University of Singapore, Working Paper no. 12.

Cheong, W. Y. (2011, February 23). Singapore's Meritocratic Education System Promotes Social Mobility. *The Straits Times*. Retrieved 16 February 2015, from http://www.moe.gov.sg/media/forum/2011/02/singapores-meritocratic-education-system-promotes-social-mobility.php.

Chinoy, E. (1955). *Automobile Workers and the American Dream*. NY: Doubleday.

Department of Statistics (DOS) (2009). *Key Household Income Trends, 2008*. Singapore: Department of Statistics.

Economic Review Committee (ERC) (2003). *New Challenges, Fresh Goals: Towards a Dynamic Global City*. Singapore: ERC.

Hing, A. Y. (1997). Industrial Restructuring and the Reconstitution of Class Relations in Singapore. *Capital and Class*, 62, 79–120.

Ko, Y. C. (1991). Status Attainment. In S. R. Quah, S. K. Chiew, Y. C. Ko & M. C. Lee, (eds.), *Social Class in Singapore* (pp. 220–243). Singapore: Centre for Advanced Studies and Times Academic Press.

Lee, K. Y. (2000). *From Third World to First: The Singapore Story 1965–2000*. Singapore: Singapore Press Holdings Editions.

Ministry of Information and the Arts (MITA) (1996). *Sharing Success: Government Programmes 1990–1995*. Singapore: MITA.

Ng, E. H. (2011, March 7). Social Mobility — The Singapore Story: Past, Present and Future. FY 2011 Committee of Supply Debate. Retrieved 16 February 2015, from http://www.moe.gov.sg/media/speeches/2011/03/07/fy-2011-committee-of-supply-de-1.php.

Ng, Y. H. I. (2011, February 16). Singapore Education System: Growing Worry of Social Immobility. *The Straits Times*. Retrieved 16 February 2015, from http://www.newshub.nus.edu.sg/news/1102/PDF/IMMOBILITY-st-16feb-pA25.pdf.

Quah, S. R., Chiew, S. K., Ko, Y. C. & Lee, M. C. (1991). *Social Class in Singapore*. Singapore: Centre for Advanced Studies and Times Academic Press.

Tan, E. S. (2004). *Does Class Matter? Social Stratification and Orientations in Singapore*. Singapore: World Scientific.

Tan, E. S. (2012). The Mobility Game in Singapore: Poverty, Welfare, Opportunity, and Success in a Capitalist Economy. In Aris Ananta & Richard Barichelb (eds.), *Poverty and Global Recession in Southeast Asia* (Chapter 6). Singapore: ISEAS.

Tan, E. S. (2015). Comments on Irene Ng's Paper on "Education and Social Mobility" in Singapore. In Faizal bin Yahya (ed.) (2014), *Inequality in Singapore* (Chapter 3). Singapore: World Scientific.

Tan, T. (2014, November 9). $1 Billion Spent on Tuition in One Year. *The Sunday Times*. Retrieved 16 February 2015, from http://www.nie.edu.sg/newsroom/media-coverage/2014/1-billion-spent-on-tuition-one-year.

Vogel, E. (1979). *Japan as Number One: Lessons for America*. MA: Harvard University Press.

Yip, C. S. (2011). *Intergenerational Income Mobility in Singapore*. Singapore: Ministry of Finance. Retrieved 16 February 2015, from http://www.app.mof.gov.sg/ig-income-mobility.aspx.

Chapter 8

The Soul of Nation Building in Singapore: Contributions from Social Work

Ang Bee Lian

This chapter examines how the field of social work has contributed and can contribute to nation building in Singapore. The chapter focuses on the "soulful" part of nation building, which is a necessary aspect of nation building and complements other critical aspects such as those related to military and economic efforts.

The soul of nation building

A nation is built through a complex confluence of conditions and cultures under a distinctive set of pressures. One view is that nation building in Singapore, quite like others in this region, started with a decolonisation experience. Post-colonial leaders had the arduous task of engineering a sense of nationalism among our population. Singapore's approach towards nation building could be said to have begun in the wake of the Republic's separation from Malaysia. Singapore's leaders then were faced with the task of shedding Singapore's pre-independence identity and replacing it with a viable "progressive" identity, with social welfare as part of the foundation for a new nation.

For progress to take place, the social well-being of people has to be taken care of and social welfare institutions are often used to respond to the needs of society and its members for health, education, economic and social well-being. Some view social welfare as a "first-line support to enable individuals to cope successfully with a changing economic and social environment and to assure the stability and development of social institutions" (Romanyshyn & Romanyshyn, 1971, p. 34). Many societies use the institution of social welfare to provide all citizens with opportunities to participate fully in society and to achieve their maximum potential. In this regard, social welfare includes those provisions and processes directly concerned with the improvement of the quality of life, the development of human resources, and the treatment and prevention of social problems. It involves social services to individuals and families as well as efforts to strengthen or modify social institutions and social welfare functions to maintain the social system and to adapt it to changing social realities.

Social welfare provisions therefore encompass diverse public and private social services. For example, the social welfare system may provide family and child welfare services, medical and health provisions, legal services, criminal justice activities and income supports. Social welfare may provide these services as social utilities that are available to all people and groups as the rights of citizens. In addition, social welfare services may meet specialised needs or address the unique problems of particular groups of people.

Ideally, social welfare responds by providing adequate income, housing, education, healthcare and personal safety. The beneficiaries of social welfare are not restricted to any one group of people. Social welfare provides benefits for the whole population. Some examples include education services and Singapore's distinctive Central Provident Fund (CPF) system and education targeted at everyone. This frame of reference suggests that users of public utility services, including social welfare, are citizens with rights rather than people who are deprived, deviant, helpless and stigmatised.

Social work has been summarily described as key to social welfare by being agents for helping the distressed, disadvantaged, disabled, deviant or dependent and it influences changes in systems to promote safety and help individuals realise their potential. Social work therefore has significant contributions to the soul of nation building through intervening in policies, programmes and services that promote the welfare and well-being of people.

Singapore's strategy towards nation building was centred largely on the establishment of a legitimate authority and the creation of a national identity. This embodied the need for effective and efficient government, and the creation of new "national" values. Specifically, nation building embodied material and utilitarian concerns of administration and resource control, and the development of a collective identity (and values) that would enable individuals to associate with the state. Singapore's first priority focus was on the ability to protect and develop one's resources and then grow economically to progress as a nation. While these aspects of nation building are important, they alone do not create the soul of a nation. Military and economic capability to defend one's country and a closely-knit society are instrumental in making a nation viable but not sufficient.

Social work's contribution to nation building may be understood in terms of how it has contributed and can contribute to the building of the soulful part of the nation. It played a defining role in influencing the structure for the protection of the vulnerable in society and in attending to the social needs of its people. These could be seen in the areas of protection of children, women and girls since the early days, the care of children and those who are disadvantaged, and the rehabilitation of those who are involved in social ills or have committed offences. Social work was instrumental in advocating the rehabilitation approach within legislation and community involvement. Thus, social work safeguarded the values of protection of the vulnerable, mutual help, caring for others and the fostering of community spiritedness. This was especially evident through the work of child protection services, welfare services for the destitute, support for families, and the community development and outreach work of ground agencies. In the building of an eventually strong economy, social work's contribution in the early years lies in the support systems that were put in place including the crèches, and public assistance and welfare schemes that support families as the adults worked in the newly-formed industries.

Social legislation to protect the vulnerable

If there is one decisive imprint in the history of nation building where social work made its greatest impact, it would have been in the introduction and review of various social legislations. Among the very first of these were the Children and Young Persons Act and its predecessor. The social work perspective shaped significantly the foundation that balanced the tension of protection, rights of parents and the restoration of well-being of families.

This Act, which was among the first social legislations, went through the most reviews and amendments. With each amendment, the social work contribution was to entrench a deeper adherence to the interest of the child as the primary principle. The amendment in 1992 was momentous in including a new provision to punish severely those who contributed to the delinquency of children and young persons. This was deemed necessary to prevent people, including uncaring parents, from using their children to hawk, promote illegal gaming and traffic in drugs, and other heinous activities.

Other social legislations which received significant contributions from social work included the Destitute Persons Act, the Women's Charter and the Probation of Offenders Act. These legislations and their subsequent reviews underwent expert scrutiny from social administrators and professionals. In particular, social workers worked closely with policy-makers and legislation drafters to ensure that the intent and spirit of the Act, and its underlying values, were adequately translated and represented in the powers and provisions that were drafted into the law. The calibrated balance of rights and responsibilities, of state and family ownership of social issues, of what is private to the family and what is the role of the state, were secured through protracted and reflective analysis. To a large extent, the first generation of social workers were in that moment in history where the crossroads of policy, legislation and implementation brought out the best in their social work training. They were living an applied science where the head and the heart met to secure better protection for the vulnerable who count on the law for protection.

The Destitute Persons Act was enacted in 1965, when poverty was rampant. Under the Act, if one did not have a place to stay or a means of subsistence, the person can be provided care and attention in a welfare home. This seemed like the humane way of approaching homelessness which is a social problem faced by many countries. Subsequent amendments made begging by a habitual beggar an offence punishable with a fine or even a short imprisonment. But this in itself will not change a habit. The contribution of social work was to address a longer-term resolution of some of the preconditions that required shelter in a welfare home. One of the significant changes that ensued in the amendments was the appointment of a review committee in each welfare home to monitor the case of each resident under review. If after the review, a resident was found suitable for discharge conditionally or unconditionally, he would be released. This applied discipline into ensuring that the problems of residents were addressed and that individuals were not unwittingly detained without incisive work done to have residents regain their independence and to gain employment where this was appropriate.

A social legislation that addressed the needs of older people was the Homes for the Aged Act. The pressure to ensure that older people in residential care were adequately cared for arose when various types of housing were used to provide shelter. The standard of care varied very widely. When families could no longer care for older people they had to resort to private nursing homes or, for the more fortunate, homes run by charitable organisations which were of better standard. The government's homes then were also filled to capacity. In the light of the emerging challenge, the Homes for the Aged Act was introduced in 1988 to bring the homes under supervision and regulation. This, together with the building of more homes, addressed the problem of older persons living in homes under unregulated conditions and for unregulated private nursing homes to flourish with impunity before that period.

A groundbreaking incision in a piece of social legislation could well be the review of the Probation of Offenders Act. In it, and for the first time in history, volunteers were prescribed powers which enabled persons in the community to be trained to carry out statutory work. This allowed the authorities to tap on volunteers to strengthen the interventions in casework involving offenders, with the ultimate goal of rehabilitation. Under the Community Probation Service, the Minister may appoint a person who is not employed as a police officer or prison officer to be a volunteer probation officer. These volunteers were carefully selected for their positive attitude towards offenders and given training on rehabilitation of offenders on probation. They were given powers to supervise probationers. By letting the volunteer probation officers handle some of the cases that require less intense supervision, the probation officers were able to focus their attention on the more severe or complex cases. This was the start of a more conscious delineation of what a volunteer can do and the introduction of better deployment of human resources to optimise the cost of delivering social services.

The Maintenance of Parents Act enacted in 1995 attracted equally great interest from the social work fraternity including social work students. A group made their submission to the Select Committee when the Bill was sent for further consultation.

The group's articulation of the concept of a Tribunal was taken on-board and incorporated into the Act. The idea was that the Tribunal, with its membership including people from the community, would bring a less austere atmosphere to the hearing and make it less intimidating for older persons. This was just one of many examples of how social work training, which emphasises sensitivity to issues involving interpersonal relationships, had contributed to effective solutions of social problems.

Social work's contribution to nation building

In the early years of Singapore's independence, the country's population was heterogeneous, being made up of immigrant people from different countries and hence differed in terms of ethnicity, language and religion. The population was made of many groups, with ethnic groups being the most obvious. The government has always been concerned that ethnic segregation and ethnic enclaves will divide the nation and contribute to interethnic conflict due to the absence of a common sense of community. For example, in 1989, the government implemented an explicitly ethnic-based public housing policy that ensures ethnic diversity in housing estates by stipulating quotas or limits on the proportion of residents of the same ethnicity within a housing estate.

Social work contributed to the process of creating a Singapore national identity out of the diverse people by fostering mutual help and support and thereby developing a community. One important initiative in community development was the formation of the Residential Committees (RCs). It is not widely known that social work in fact played a significant role in the development of the RCs.

RCs were set up in various precincts to foster neighbourliness and build a new sense of community as citizens were relocated to high-rise flats from their *kampongs* in the national public housing programme. The work of these precinct-based committees in organising residents to foster neighbourliness was among the first forms of large-scale systematic community development work in Singapore. Some of these efforts have been documented by Dr S Vasoo (Vasoo, 2002), who was also personally involved in the development work on the ground, particularly those related to RCs and associated organisations. Vasoo is a lecturer in social work at the National University of Singapore since 1979 and also formerly a Member of Parliament from 1984 to 2001. A number of the community workers who worked alongside community leaders were trained in social work and had among their mandate the nurturing of grassroots leadership to foster mutual help and support.

Given the diversity of ethnicity, language, religious beliefs and culture in the Singaporean society, cultural knowledge and sensitivity were critical when serving those in need or distress. The early years of social work required interviews and home visits to be made to various ethnic groups and it was not unusual for neighbours to serve as interpreters. Many who worked with families in casework or in determining eligibility for welfare learned to speak more than one language. They also learned to respect and work within the cultural boundaries and practices of each ethnic group. Over time, however, the boundaries separating the cultures have become blurred. While this could have been in part due to the gradual emergence of a Singaporean identity, there were also external influences on Singapore society and modernisation that likely affected the different cultures in similar ways. Although there are many commonalities across the different ethnic and cultural groups in Singapore today, a good cultural knowledge and sensitivity of each ethnic or cultural group remains relevant for social work to effect change.

Social work has contributed to nation building by helping to foster a sense of belonging to the local community, which in turn helped enhance the sense of belonging to the country. This sense of belonging to the community is more than an emotional attachment to a place or fond memories. It is closely related to other social values that the government was trying to imbue among the people, many of which are also consistent with the personal values being promoted by social work.

One of the government's various efforts to strengthen people's sense of belonging and bind the different ethnic and cultural groups together as a nation was the propagation of a set of Shared Values in 1989[1] to "evolve and anchor a Singaporean identity" by incorporating various elements of the country's cultural heritage, attitudes and values. A White Paper on the Shared Values (Shared Values, 1991) was presented and adopted in parliament in January 1991.

The intent of the Shared Values was to identify common key values so that all communities would gradually develop more "distinctively Singaporean characteristics" over time. The main theme underlying the set of Shared Values emphasised communitarian values and reflected Singapore's heritage. Unfortunately, there was insufficient follow through to entrench these values which could have been sealed in or embedded into the foundation of what could have constituted the design of the social fabric of the nation. However, the values did pervade policy implementation. The values were very similar to the ones that the social work profession upholds such as respect for the individual and family, building consensus, and forming community support for the vulnerable and compassion for the disadvantaged.

Another attempt in codifying the foundation of nation building could be traced to 1997, when the then Prime Minister Goh Chok Tong called for a national visioning

---

[1]The five shared values are 1) Nation before community and society above self: Putting the interests of society ahead of the individual; 2) Family as the basic unit of society: The family is identified as the most stable fundamental building block of the nation; 3) Community support and respect for the individual: Recognises that the individual has rights, which should be respected. Encourages the community to support and have compassion for the disadvantaged individual who may have been left behind by the free market system; 4) Consensus, not conflict: Resolving issues through consensus and not conflict and stresses the importance of compromise and national unity; and 5) Racial and religious harmony: Recognises the need for different communities to live harmoniously with one another in order for all to prosper.

exercise, known as Singapore 21 Vision, to deepen Singaporeans' sense of belonging to the country and progress beyond material achievements and to establish a society with people at its very centre. Singapore 21 espoused five key ideas: that every Singaporean matters to society, that strong families are the foundation for building a strong society, that Singapore should be a cosmopolitan city with opportunities for all, that every individual should share a "Singapore Heartbeat" and be emotionally rooted to the country, and that citizens should take the initiative to impact society. Singapore 21, which involved a wide range of people with different backgrounds, provided a comprehensive list on what the individual, society and government could do to further the process of nation building and the building of an inclusive society. The effort engaged citizens to be more involved in nation building and signalled the value in engaging the citizenry in a process of consultation.

Against these nationwide efforts to foster a closely-knit society for nation building, social workers played a key role by participating in the development of programmes, consultations, feedback, visioning and policy development. Social workers were among the designers, shapers and artisans of programmes, schemes and processes. These pioneers are known for their astute observations and skills in designing schemes that aim to help families with their social problems while maintaining self-respect and self-determination. As much as possible, the conditionality that came with receiving help fostered self-reliance as the eventual goal.

Singapore's social safety net

Social work has also made significant contributions to issues of a social safety net in Singapore. From the perspective of social work, the challenge in providing a social safety net is selecting the appropriate model of human service provisions. The social work perspective would deem a model appropriate if it nurtures the strengths in individuals, families and communities to safeguard their well-being by raising their resources and enhancing their self-determination to realise their potential.

In recent years, many governments had to confront the dual challenges of an ageing population and rising expectations from their citizens. Globalisation has also added complexities to these challenges, with some blaming free trade and open markets for widening income inequality and causing median wage stagnation. Amidst this global context, Singapore continues to adhere to and implement a policy of social inclusion that is driven by supported self-reliance. Self-reliance and a healthy work ethic are virtues that benefit both the individual and the society. Having access to good jobs and the opportunities to apply one's talent and skills at work contribute to social well-being at both the individual and societal levels. These virtues could have also driven private initiative and enterprise. But as needs and demand for human services grow, how does one foster social inclusion and safeguard the culture of supported self-reliance? Prior to addressing this question, it is useful to examine three pillars that support the principle of social inclusion.

Subsidy in education

Subsidised education is a key component of Singapore's approach to social inclusion. Premised on the belief that education promotes social mobility, the Singapore government has focused much attention on ensuring equal opportunity to quality education. Education is heavily subsidised to prevent wide differences in educational opportunities between the better off and those who are less well-off due to differences in their ability to pay. Recently, the heavy subsidies have been extended to child development at the preschool level. Singapore's education system, therefore, is an important vehicle of social inclusion to achieve a "levelling up" effect for those from lower-income households.

Home ownership

A second pillar of social inclusion is the provision of housing that is affordable to the vast majority of the population. This is achieved through the CPF system, which is a centrally managed, compulsory pay-as-you-earn savings scheme. In addition, low-income families receive a state-sponsored grant to buy public housing flats, which are subsidised by the government and purchased under the terms of a subsidised loan. These policies were formulated and implemented on the belief that housing is an appreciating asset that promotes social mobility, financial security, and a sense of pride and belonging.

Singapore's use of public housing for nation building is distinctive. Indeed, there are no other governments in the world which approach nation building primarily through building homes for its people and subsidising it heavily to enable home ownership. In response to an ageing population in Singapore, housing infrastructure is being redesigned to enable ageing-in-place and also to enable elderly with frailty and who require assisted-living to continue living in their current homes. The infrastructure improvements include enhancing elderly accessibility within public high-rise apartment buildings (e.g., expanding elevator access in apartment blocks) and within neighbourhood precincts (e.g., improving walkways).

Wage supplement to low-income workers

Faced with growing income inequality, Singapore has adopted a "workfare" model instead of the traditional "welfare" model. Under a traditional welfare approach, the state insures citizens against a range of risks, especially unemployment and illness. In contrast, under a workfare approach, benefits are targeted at low-wage workers.[2] Linking government transfers to work reduces the problems associated with unconditional transfers to those who are able to work and have gainful

---

[2] The Workfare Income Supplement scheme is adapted from the model originally introduced in Wisconsin, United States. See Poh (2007).

employment. The reason for this approach is that workfare could work better at redistributing incomes, while preserving the work ethic and promoting self-reliance for the able-bodied.

Some may argue that Singapore's system of social security is too heavily vested in housing, which means less cash savings are allocated for retirement. Others have also cautioned that workfare payments may unintentionally result in reduced productivity by causing businesses to retain more lower-skilled workers (in order to benefit from the government subsidies provided by the workfare scheme) than might otherwise have been the case. There is also the concern that Singapore's social safety net is insufficient for certain vulnerable groups such as the disabled, the aged destitute and the unemployable. In my view, the toughest challenge could well be that if inflation is factored in and government aid is factored out, how can we help vulnerable families advance to a lower-risk state of functioning that will offer them a realistic chance of achieving progress?

A widening income disparity, an ageing population and the integration of foreigners are some of the key social issues which Singapore policy-makers have to deal with. The Singapore government's approach to these challenges, which is probably unique among governments in the world, is a state-supported social safety net woven out of the principles of personal and family responsibility. While proven successful in the past, this approach will need to be constantly reviewed and revised when necessary due to several emerging issues related to the family institution. For example, can Singapore continue to hold on to the tenet that "family is the first line of support"? In fact, issues of what constitutes "family" in the domain of human services continue to challenge those who administer assistance schemes. There is increasing pressure to expand the definition of family to more accurately reflect contemporary social and demographic realities. In addition, trends of low birth rates, later marriages, and the increasing number of divorces raise questions about whether the family institution can be strengthened so that it can be relied on as the main provider of material and emotional support to its members.

Workfare, which was introduced in 2007 as an income supplement scheme, has soon turned into a permanent social safety net. Other forms of relief, ranging from housing grants to training and education subsidies, have helped some low-wage workers by enabling them to have more cash in hand and providing them opportunities to upgrade their skills for better jobs. However, there are some Singaporeans who cannot find work, even if they are able and willing to. Some economists believe that the volatility of the new economy would mean more workers could be unemployed for longer periods due to economic dislocation. That is, Singapore's current system would come under further stress if the speed of retraining and redeployment cannot catch up with the changing global volatility.

In the longer term, we should be concerned with whether intergenerational mobility can be improved and how to ensure that low-income families do not resign to their station in life through a lack of aspiration. These families must be encouraged to emphasise education for children and skills upgrading to achieve a better quality of life.

It is clear, and we know, that we cannot exclusively rely on market mechanisms. We need both (appropriate) social policy and the market to complement each other, which is a challenge that calls for constant calibration by policy-makers. As economist Amartya Sen puts it: "the invisible hand of the market has often relied on the visible hand of government" (Sen, 1987). The nation building efforts have shown that market principles are necessary to help a government work better, and a good government is necessary to help markets work better. Singapore may not always get the balance right. Pragmatism, experimentation and adjustments must continue as the government plays its role managing the relationships between public policies and the market. To do this effectively, the responsibility of government may have to expand in the areas of enabling, regulating, stabilising and legitimising markets in order to achieve better societal outcomes that ultimately benefit the quality of life and well-being of the people.

Social service and the "Many Helping Hands"

As social needs grow, so must social service. With more agencies delivering a variety of social services, the "Many Helping Hands" approach adopted in Singapore has functioned relatively well in balancing state intervention and the space for ground initiatives. The concept of "Many Helping Hands" first appeared in a chapter of the book *The Next Lap* published in 1991 and also released as the Principal Addendum to the Presidential Address. The book was a result of the deliberations of a cabinet sub-committee chaired by the then Acting Minister for Information and the Arts, George Yeo. The sub-committee, known as the Long Term National Development Committee, drew on the ideas by several previous national-level committees formed in the late 1980s including those in the 1989 reports of six Advisory Councils on the 1) the disabled, 2) the elderly, 3) the youth, 4) sports and recreation, 5) culture and the arts, and 6) family and community life. The concept of "Many Helping Hands" builds on the philosophy that community bonds are built when the able and more well-off help the less able and less well-off, creating social networks and social capital. The concept is based on the values of mutual help, reciprocity and giving to society. In addition, as evident in the quote below from *The Next Lap*, the care and compassion demonstrated through acts of helping should build trust and mitigate the social divides among the segments of society that are experiencing different rates of progress

> Many Helping Hands is the Singapore Way of helping that small segment of our community who cannot keep pace with the rest of the population. They are found in every society, however affluent and progressive. Such families lag behind the rest of the population. They are in danger of becoming destitute, despite the comprehensive social security net in the

form of the Central Provident Fund Scheme which provides protection in old age, major illness, incapacity and premature death of a breadwinner (*The Next Lap*, 1991).

The Advisory Councils, which were composed of leaders from the public, people and private sectors, recommended that the government provide one-for-one financial assistance to volunteer welfare organisations (VWOs) to deliver social services that required the impetus to expand their services. The aim of the one-for-one support was to build a foundation for shared responsibility where the public, people and private sectors work together to jointly provide social services. It was intended to foster community involvement and active volunteerism that would lead to the development of a compassionate society, which is one that looks after its disadvantaged members and helps them to be useful members of society or live lives of dignity.

Requiring agencies to raise the other half of the funds from the public produced two consequences. First, agencies would need to communicate their cause to the public and therefore, in the process, should raise awareness about social issues and support for their work. Second, the tension created by the formula would help to distil clarity of the need for the service and provides the traction for consumption of services.

This partnership in social service provision allowed the government to increase and build on social welfare *through* social agencies using its own brand of strong state-supported welfare without making Singapore into a traditional welfare state. This arrangement in a way placed a premium on ensuring that there is a close working relationship between the government and the VWOs. The system of helping the needy through VWOs had to deliver because the social contract between the government and citizens is at stake. The interdependence between the state and the social agencies has made the partnership arrangement reasonably successful and many VWOs and religious organisations were able to provide effective services to those in need. In addition, many VWOs were able to communicate their cause and convince sponsors to be involved in doing social good and build bonds in the community, often in ways that produced benefits that surpassed the financial formula.

The "Many Helping Hands" include the state that set the legal, regulatory and financial parameters, the VWOs that directly serve the social needs of communities, and the boards and organisations that take care of governance, volunteers, staff, donors and funders. The focus is in coordinating the different parties who intend to help in a way that ensures adequate and timely delivery of services to those in need. The human arm may be used as an analogy to explain the important roles played by the state and the various key stakeholders. The upper part of the arm represents the donors and the funders, including the state. They are the muscles that build and help to strengthen the limb work. The hand and fingers represent the social agencies and volunteers. They are the ones who are directly in touch with the target. Being on the ground, they are able to respond more nimbly, with immediacy, empathy and compassion. Every part of the arm, including the limb and muscles, is intertwined, with each supported by the other in order to be responsive and effective. They may have similar goals but each of them can be distinctive and yet complementary. The state is part of the muscles, but it is also the palm that connects the arm and the fingers. It connects and channels resources from the upper arm to the different fingers. The state also plays the role of enabler by supporting ground initiatives that enhance community participation and facilitate connections between the givers and the recipients of help. In addition to ensuring adequate financing for the social sector, the state also invests in manpower development including initiatives with a long-term view such as mid-career retraining, sabbatical leave schemes, scholarships and various professional and organisational leadership schemes.

Challenges in balancing tensions

Policy tensions are healthy when they are examined and debated because the end result is likely a deeper understanding of the issues which will in turn help produce effective solutions. In recent years, two significant policy tensions related to social services have surfaced. The first concerns the roles of the state and family in the "heavy-lifting" care of family members. This is sometimes presented as the tension for greater intervention from government on one hand and the preservation of the role of the family and community. The second tension is that of centralised integrated support that tends to provide more efficient service delivery versus a less organised and uneven system that tends to involve wider community participation.

Both the above tensions are related to the need to review the effectiveness of the "Many Helping Hands" approach due to growing demands for social services as well as a sector with increasingly diverse social services but also of uneven capabilities. The policy tensions need careful examination and debate because it is important to better understand how communities are built in the Singapore context and how community spiritedness relates to the soul of a nation. Here is where social work, as well as other related disciplines and professions, could make a significant contribution to the next phase of nation building by working closely with policy-makers to assess the next steps forward.

References

Poh, J. (2007). Workfare: The Fourth Pillar of Social Security in Singapore. *Ethos*, 3, 48–55.

Romanyshyn, J. M. & Romanyshyn, A. L. (1971). *Social Welfare: Charity to Justice*. New York: Random House.

Sen, A. (1987). *On Ethics and Economics*. Oxford: Blackwell Publishing Ltd.

Shared Values (1991). Singapore: Singapore National Printers (Call no. RSING 306.095957 SIN).

Singapore: The Next Lap (1991). Singapore: Times Editions (Call no. RSING 959.5705 SIN).

Vasoo, S. (2002). New Directions of Community Development in Singapore. In N. T. Tan, and K. Mehta (eds.), *Extending Frontiers: Social Issues and Social Work in Singapore* (pp. 20–36). Singapore: Eastern University Press.

Chapter 9

Social Impact of Policies for the Disabled in Singapore

Reuben Wong and Wong Meng Ee[1]

The definition and framing of "disability" is a subject of much controversy (Scotch, 1988; Leonardi *et al.*, 2006; Oliver & Barnes, 2012). "Disability" has been constantly defined and redefined according to the needs and dominant values of the time and place. Scotch (1988, p. 168) notes the importance of government-sponsored definitions, where "the definition of disability is essentially determined by public policy". National associations, governments and international organisations have all weighed in on this issue since the birth of "disability" studies in the West (mainly in the US, UK and Scandinavia in the 1960s). In this process, international organisations have tended to set the pace and parameters for understanding and defining "disability" across the world. As Michael Barnett and Martha Finnemore (1999) have argued, international organisations today, despite their apparent weaknesses, are powerful expert institutions that set standards and norms for the world.

In this chapter, we offer some reasons for the mindset change in both Singapore's government and society between 1965 and 2015 — from viewing persons with disabilities as unfortunate economic liabilities on society and state, to viewing them as human beings deserving of dignity and state support. We take issue with the "outside-in" explanation of the diffusion of ideas. We argue that two *domestic* factors — first, an ageing population; and second, civil society activism — were more important than international socio-cultural, political and structural factors in

[1] Our deep appreciation to Clement Law, Louis Lim, Ng Sufen, Rohini Arun Samtani and Karan Kamath for research assistance; Victor Zhuang for offering helpful comments; and the "Politics of Enablement" Reading Group (FASS R-108-000-055-646) that held meetings in the College of Alice and Peter Tan, NUS, between October 2012 and February 2014.

explaining the mindset shift which led to the state's signing of the UN Convention for the Rights of Persons with Disabilities (UNCRPD) in December 2012. Some might consider this the story of a neglected segment of Singapore's population, one hitherto deprived of attention and resources, but which has become visible in recent years (Zhuang, 2007). We argue that the attendant policy change in three areas critical to independent living in Singapore — education, employment and accessibility — are making Singapore a more inclusive and compassionate society for persons with physical and cognitive challenges.

Discourse in Singapore

How has Singapore reacted to the "universal" or international normative definition of disability? The Singapore state tends to focus on economic prerogatives, and to discourage a rights-based, socio-political understanding of disability. Persons with Disabilities (PWDs) are often seen as objects of charity rather than as subjects with rights (AWARE, 2012). For instance, Singapore has no equivalent to the Americans with Disabilities Act (ADA) or the UK's Disability Discrimination Act (DDA). Yet, despite its economic pragmatism and lack of protective legislation, Singapore has not been immune to global trends on norms and standards for disabled populations, especially from international organisations and the developed world. The UN-sanctioned International Year of the Disabled (1982) was followed by the Decade for People with Disabilities (1983–92) and the Asian and Pacific Decade of Disabled Persons (1993–2002), all of which were officially celebrated and marked in Singapore.

Tracing the historical trajectory of Singapore's approach to PWDs, in 1988, an Advisory Council for the Disabled (ACD) — chaired by then Education Minister Tony Tan — defined Persons with Disabilities as "those whose prospects of securing, retaining places and advancing in education and training institutions, employment and recreation as equal members of the community are substantially reduced as a result of physical, sensory and intellectual impairments" (Committee Report to MCYS, c.2011). This definition was based on the World Health Organization's 1980 definition, and on the International Labour Organization's 1983 recommendation on Vocational Rehabilitation and Employment of Disabled Persons.

In 2004, the then Ministry of Community Development, Youth and Sports (MCYS) refined the ACD's 1988 definition to include "developmental" disability. According to a Committee Report (Enabling Masterplan Steering Committee) on the MCYS website, Singapore's current definition of PWDs is:

> [t]hose whose prospects of securing, retaining places and advancing in education and training institutions, employment and recreation as equal members of the community are substantially reduced as a result of physical, sensory, intellectual and developmental impairments (Committee Report to MCYS, c.2011).

The demographic trend of increasing numbers of elderly persons, an issue of major concern to Singapore authorities, has had positive consequences for the disabled community. Catering to the needs of an ageing population has strengthened the case for inclusivity in the last decade. For example, one way to convince authorities, organisations and individuals of the advantages of barrier-free environments was to explain the cost implications of a fall, a heightened risk for the elderly. The occurrence of falls should decrease with fewer hazards in the built environment. In 2001, Kenneth Parker noted that where attendance at a Singapore Accident and Emergency (A&E) department cost S$70 for the individual and S$150 for the government; this rose to S$4,000 and S$7,000, respectively, if a fall resulted in a fractured femur (Parker, 2001).

Additionally, Singapore's current "Code on Barrier-free Accessibility" (Public Works Department, 1995) was developed as a usable working document. The first version included the increasing population of "the elderly" in its scope mainly because the numbers of disabled people alone were insufficient to justify its mandatory status. Although older persons may not be technically "disabled", they become "less able" as a natural part of the ageing process. It should be noted that this Code does not regulate the interior of dwellings. That said, revision to the Code included advisory information on design for elderly persons, children with disabilities, pregnant women and parents with young children. Further, it also includes more mandatory requirements to cater to the vision-impaired and hearing-impaired users. These measures will undoubtedly be of benefit to the elderly; concordantly, they will also benefit many PWDs, although they are not the intended beneficiaries of these measures (Parker, 2001).

However, the Singapore government did not fully embrace what disability scholars call the "social model". The social model is a paradigm in disability studies which views disability as a social construction and advocates changes in society and policies to adapt to the needs of such individuals so as to include them more fully in society. While making great strides in PWDs' access, the Singapore government was less decisive in bringing its laws in line with international norms set by the UN. For example, while it moved on legislating compulsory education for Singaporean children in 2003, it rejected a petition by the Joint Committee for Compulsory Education for All to include children with special needs under the Compulsory Education Act (JCEEA, 2004). The reasons given included the high costs, and the difficulty of enforcing the law on parents who could not afford the time or transport fees to send their special-needs children — who sometimes needed special modes of transport — to school.

Singapore, however, was open to changes in global standards. International developments such as the 2006 UN Convention on the Rights of Persons with Disabilities (UNCPRD) have increased the pressure on Singapore to better conform to international norms. Although formally enacted in 2007, Singapore indicated its intention to sign the Convention only after 153 other states had done so. When asked in September 2012 whether Singapore could have acted earlier rather than follow after 153 earlier signatories (by acceding to the UNCPRD before the end of 2012), Prime Minister Lee Hsien Loong admitted that:

> 'In retrospect, we are always too slow. I think we have to continue to move. It's not easy because it's not just money. There's also the trained people and the social attitudes which have to shift' ("Govt to Sign", *The Straits Times*, 2012).

Special education

Special education in Singapore has historically been led and provided by voluntary welfare organisations (VWOs) starting in 1947 with classes for children with leprosy (Quah, 1993; Wong & Crawford, 2011). Since then, the founding of various VWOs championing for different causes and disabilities have represented and advocated for educational provisions for children with disabilities where up till 1988, students with disabilities were educated at 11 special education schools (Lim & Tan, 1999). A recommendation of the "Report of the Advisory Council on the Disabled: Opportunities for the Disabled" (hereafter "Report of Advisory Council") in 1988 stated that "whenever appropriate and feasible, special education should be provided within the regular education system. A child should only be placed in a special school if he cannot be well educated in a regular school" (Report of Advisory Council, 1988, pp. 37–38).

Some exceptions were made for students with sensory and physical disabilities who were able to cope with the mainstream curriculum (Report of Advisory Council, 1988). In those situations, support in resources, facilities and resource teachers were in place in a handful of mainstream schools designated to support these students (Mathi, 1996; Wong & Chia, 2010). While the principal, teachers and parents had the discretion to decide if the school was able to support a student with disabilities (Report of Advisory Council, 1988), it was not unusual for the school to make the final decision. Low awareness, limited resources and the lack of available expertise in the years preceding and ensuing the ACD's recommendations arguably contributed to the limited advancement despite the recommended policy for what would today be termed "inclusion".

In time, the distinction in education where students with disabilities were placed in "special education" (or SPED) schools while students without disabilities were in general education, led to a segregated, dual system. Consequently, students with special needs — depending on the child's ability and needs — attend schools along a continuum that ranges from total segregation to partial integration to total inclusion (Lim & Nam, 2000). This arrangement continues today and generally, students with moderate and severe disabilities are taught in one of 20 special schools (MOE, 2014a). These schools are run by 13 VWOs, which are supported by the Ministry of Education (MOE) and the National Council of Social Service

(NCSS) (*ibid.*). Special education schools are typically organised with smaller class size ratios, greater numbers of teacher aides, specialised therapists and resources to support students' specialised needs (Poon *et al.*, 2013). The mission of SPED schools is "to provide the best possible education and training to children with special needs so as to enable them to function optimally and integrate well into society" (*ibid.*).

The 20 SPED schools cater to the diverse range of disabilities, with some schools delivering multiple programmes. Schools offering programmes for students with autism spectrum disorders are the largest number at 17 while there are nine programmes for students with intellectual disabilities. There are three programmes for the hearing impaired, three for those with multiple disabilities and one for students with visual impairments (MOE, 2014b). Students with sensory impairments, e.g., hearing and visual impairments who qualify for mainstream secondary school have eight designated schools of choice (MOE, 2014c). These designated schools are staffed with resource teachers and are equipped with a range of assistive technologies to help students with sensory impairments. These typically include FM systems for students with hearing impairments and screen readers and close-circuit televisions (CCTV) for students with visual impairments (MOE, 2014d). Availability of assistive technology devices is one part of the equation; the other part is to provide awareness, training and knowledge to teachers, specialists and the users themselves (Wong & Cohen, 2011). Without collaboration across stakeholders, the potential of assistive technology cannot be fully realised (Wong, Chia & Law, in-submission). For students unable to integrate into mainstream schools, vocational outcomes are an important part of the special education curriculum. Preparation as well as vocational education is provided. Presently, there are the ITE Skills Certificate and the Singapore Workforce Skills Qualification available in selected industries. Both are national certifications with the opportunity for open employment or to further upgrade to the National ITE Certifications (MOE, 2014e).

Significant efforts towards inclusive education, however, have been made since Lee Hsien Loong became Prime Minister. In his inaugural 2004 address, he pledged a more open and inclusive society under his government for persons with disabilities. Lee was more explicit with his vision of inclusion at the opening of the Cerebral Palsy Centre that year:

> Every society has some members with disabilities. How the society treats the disabled, takes care of them, and helps them integrate into the mainstream, reflects the kind of society it is. We want ours to be a society that cares for all its members; one that does not ignore the needs of those who are born or afflicted with disabilities (Lee, 2004).

The first of the initiatives aimed at inclusion was the introduction of Special Needs Officers in 2005 (renamed Allied Educators, Learning and Behavioural Support [AED LBS] in 2009) to support mainstream teachers working with students with mild to moderate dyslexia and high functioning autism spectrum disorder

(ASD). All primary schools and one-third of secondary schools are resourced with at least one AED (LBS). They are trained to support the learning and behavioural needs of children with disabilities via in-class support, individual or small group intervention (e.g., literacy skills, social skills, study and organisational skills), transition support as well as case management (MOE, 2012). The second was the Teachers Trained in Special Needs (TSN), where 10%–20% of teachers in each primary and secondary school are trained to serve as resource persons in supporting students with disabilities in their schools. They provide individual or small group support within classrooms; monitor the academic progress of students with disabilities; and share expertise and resources with other teachers and parents (MOE, 2012).

The spirit to promote greater inclusion is also observed in efforts introduced to bridge the SPED-mainstream school divide. Special schools located near mainstream schools have a satellite programme where students able to benefit from mainstream curriculum have the opportunity to attend both schools. These partnerships offer social inclusion for these students and where prerequisites for transfer are met, and evidence for success is convincing, students are encouraged to transfer to mainstream school (Poon *et al.*, 2013).

The increased shift towards greater inclusion in Singapore is evident with the introduction of the post-2004 initiatives. With the ratification of the UNCRPD in 2013, we can expect to have even greater efforts made to extending inclusion in our education system. Lim, Wong and Tan (2014) argue that, as inclusivity is acted upon, the following four factors need to be considered in the Singaporean context:

1) Screening and identification of disabilities is not compulsory, and increasingly, mainstream teachers take on the responsibility of encouraging families to have their child assessed by registered psychologists;
2) Screening and assessment tend to be expensive, not affordable by most families who are willing to take the step;
3) It is challenging for most families who may wish to contest their children's referrals to special schools; and
4) There is no law requiring an individualised education programme for each student.

Regarding screening and identification, the need for early intervention has been recognised in the Enabling Masterplan 2007–2011 and recommendations put forward in the Enabling Masterplan 2012–2016. Some recommendations included in the latter masterplan are: the establishment of early detection points in the community to include primary healthcare professionals, preschool professionals, and the family service centres for young children with developmental problems and those at risk. Recommendations also call for more regular screening, as well as for children who are medically at risk to be referred for early childhood intervention shortly after diagnosis, and also to involve caregivers as active members of the child's development through greater information.

Where disabilities are acquired or manifested later along the school continuum, efforts to have children screened or assessed are less straightforward. Especially for disabilities that are developmental in nature or less conspicuous, efforts to determine impairment continue to be in part exacerbated by parental resistance to assessment from fear of confirmation through diagnosis. While it is not unusual for parents to have an idealised view of having a typically-developing child (Rogers, 2007), news of their child being disabled is often received with consternation (Heiman, 2002; Wong, 2012).

This is where the network of detection points suggested for early intervention needs to also be extended at least to partners including the allied educator team, TSN and psychologists. Clearly, where there are existing role distinctions, enhancement of collaborative efforts is one ongoing avenue for improvement. The post-diagnosis educational guidance (PDEG), where counsellors provide emotional support to parents and guidance on the available educational options for their child and the application process to special education schools, is a positive step forward. Additionally, the Multi-Agency Advisory Panel (MAAP) recommended streamlining of application and enrolment processes, which minimises the administrative burden for parents (MOE, 2013). However, these efforts also continue to entrench the existing practice. Building professional capacity then is a further and likely outcome in the time ahead as parental demands increase in the backdrop of a more educated general population with higher expectations. The possible transformation of roles could involve allied educators taking on more of a special education teacher role in mainstream education. For this to happen, professional training will be necessary to build from the existing one year Diploma in Special Education to a programme that corresponds with their mainstream teacher counterparts, so that special educators are equal partners with mainstream teachers and are equipped to support a greater diversity of inclusion practice options in the mainstream. Already, parents of students with disabilities strongly perceive the need for their children to be placed in mainstream education instead of special education if they are to have a chance to transition to the competitive Singapore society (Wong, Poon, Kaur & Ng, 2014). At the same time, parental aspirations are also shaped by societal norms and ethos.

The value of mainstream education is predicated on the meritocratic system that has contributed and shaped the organisation of the Singapore society. Since Singapore's independence more than 40 years ago, meritocracy and multiculturism have shaped government and society at large (Chuah, 1997; Tan, 2008). This is manifested through the competitive education system which sorts and organises for human resource allocation. The civil service, for example, has been largely organised through this system (Quah, 2010). With meritocracy entrenched so strongly in the Singapore society, it is not unusual that parents of children with disabilities also have similar aspirations to have their children be part of general education in order to have the best post-school opportunities to participate in mainstream society (Wong *et al.*, 2014; Wong, in-submission).

As greater attention is now given to better understand the aspirations and opportunities of the youth, the Applied Study in Polytechnics and Institute of Technical Education (ITE) Review (ASPIRE) Committee was formed principally to focus on opportunities for polytechnic and ITE students. Fundamental for today's youths are a desire for opportunities to upgrade, good career prospects and good salaries. Indranee Rajah, the Senior Minister of State for Education, reported that some takeaways for the committee included:

- Real skills and intangible qualities matter. They must meet industry needs. The committee will study how to tighten the nexus between what is taught and what is required in the workplace.
- Upward progression for polytechnic and ITE graduates is important. However, this will have a counterproductive effect if there was a single-minded chase for the degree route amongst polytechnic and ITE students. Instead, a multiplicity of pathways would be more feasible to offer options to:

    1) Pursue further studies immediately; or
    2) Work first, and pursue further studies later, preferably in a related sector; or
    3) Work and progress upwards through professional certifications and training, even without the need for a degree.

- Continuing education and training (CET) and skills upgrading is important. The committee will study how to help polytechnic and ITE graduates navigate the vicissitudes of the future through CET, industry certifications and short courses that will add to their repertoire of skills and keep them in high demand.
- Staying at the cutting edge matters. Ways must be explored for polytechnic and ITE educators to continue to be at the cutting edge of industry skills and practices.
- Industry participation and collaboration is vital. Close cooperation with the employers and industry must be studied.
- Providing information so that the student can make the right career choices is important. Since education is now a lifelong continuum, this includes career guidance not just for school, but also throughout working life, so that people can find the careers that are best suited to their strengths and circumstances at different stages of their lives (Rajah, 2014).

At the core of the ASPIRE Committee's work is student abilities and aspirations, availability of training and matching these to the needs of the competitive and changing job market. While "ability" is a key determinant for merit rewards in meritocratic Singapore, it is imperative also to expand the definition of "ability" in order for students with special needs to express their ability to contribute to the Singapore society. It is through the enlargement of the conventional definition of ability that inclusivity can be realised. This also helps to reduce the pressure of the SPED-mainstream dichotomy, thus allowing teachers in special education schools to carry out their role without a sense of isolation (Crawford & Wong, 2011). Similarly, teachers working with students with disabilities in the mainstream schools, who have been found to express reservations, ambivalence and even negative attitudes towards inclusion (Thaver & Lim, 2014; Yeo, Chong, Neihart & Huan, 2014) can learn to better appreciate the universality of inclusion.

Employment

The Report of the Advisory Council on the Disabled (1988) also offers direction for employment. At the core of its recommendations, the twin importance of training and employment for persons with disabilities were acknowledged. "Disabled people, like able-bodied people, should receive training opportunities to enable them to undertake work best suited to their abilities, and achieve maximum work potential" (Report of Advisory Council, 1988, p. 43). To achieve this outcome, the committee recognised vocational rehabilitation as a continuous and coordinated process which includes vocational assessment and guidance, pre-vocational and social skills training, vocational training, job placement and follow-up. For a nationally trained programme, the committee regarded persons with disabilities as categorised into the following:

• Those capable of being trained in skilled work on equal terms with able-bodied workers.
• Those who would be at a competitive disadvantage if trained on equal terms with able-bodied workers.
• Those who require work training within production sheltered workshops.

These categories were reflective of a climate when the separation of abilities was distinctive and which reinforced the marginalisation of persons with disabilities (Barnes & Mercer, 2005). At the same time, this was the direction that vocational rehabilitation was conceptualised in a time Singapore's economy was in the momentum of growth (Pang, 1980) which focused more on developing the economic needs of the country.

Until recent years, employment considerations for PWDs have been a largely neglected aspect in disability policy. Unlike areas such as healthcare, education and physical accessibility, the employment of PWDs is considered to be the "final frontier", a cause to be advanced only when the other elements have fallen into place. However, this is a questionable approach. Does society have to have all other disability provisions in place before the issue of employability can be considered? Alternatively, does instituting a long-term vision of equitable employment for PWDs provide a more focused goal for disability policy as a whole? We argue for the latter perspective.

In our capitalist society, the social position of individuals and the attitude of others towards them are greatly determined by their occupation and economic output. Unemployed or economically inactive people are not only accorded less respect by others, they are also often seen as a "burden" to the rest of society. For PWDs especially, their inability to access the general employment sphere serves to reinforce their societal exclusion. This does not merely trap them in an economically dependent situation, but also heightens their feelings of inferiority and personal worthlessness. Many PWDs end up internalising the belief that they are an undesirable presence in society (Abberley, 2002; Barnes & Mercer, 2005; Roulstone & Barnes, 2005).

Making space for PWDs to contribute economically in the country's workforce has several key benefits. Not only does this positively alter their self-perceptions, but more crucially, also creates an inclusive environment in which the wider population can gradually shift their attitudes towards PWDs and come to view them as valued members of society.

A crucial platform for the advancement of PWD employment stems from the United Nations Convention on the Rights of Persons with Disabilities (UNCRPD). One component of the UNCRPD focuses on employability issues, demonstrating a global awareness and commitment towards improving the employment prospects for PWDs. According to the Convention, PWDs have the right to "... work, on an equal basis with others; this includes the right to the opportunity to gain a living by work freely chosen or accepted in a labour market and work environment that is open, inclusive and accessible to persons with disabilities. States Parties shall safeguard and promote the realisation of the right to work ...".

The UNCRPD contains general guidelines that governments can adapt to suit the needs of their own countries, as opposed to having to adopt specific laws. At its core it calls for certain values and a shift in attitudes towards PWDs. It must be noted that while Singapore has ratified this UN convention in August 2013; there is still a long way to go to live up to these international standards.

Prime Minister Lee Hsien Loong spoke about Joan Bowen Cafe which is an example of a social enterprise during the National Day Rally Speech in 2011. He used the cafe to epitomise active citizenry in Singapore, where people did not just rely on the government to solve problems but took the initiative to do something about them. President Tony Tan met social entrepreneurs during his presidential election campaign in July 2011, and mentioned Dignity Kitchen — School of Hawker Training (Disabled and Disadvantaged) and Professor Brawn Cafe as impactful ideas that showed how disabled people could be helped to help themselves.

Another company, Laksania (started in 2008 by Sim Sin Sin of Secret Recipe Cafe Pte Ltd) is a social enterprise whose social mission is to help people who have been marginalised by their mental or physical disability to gain employment. Since then, Laksania's Central Kitchen has become a therapy ground for many of these marginalised groups who have found work and are encouraged to be self-reliant. Besides on-the-job training in various aspects of F&B, staff have gained important interpersonal and life skills that aid them to be financially independent. Laksania serves a variety of different tastes in Laksa with influences from all around the region such as Penang, Kelantan and Sarawak, and Singapore Laksa.

While such enterprises have been thrust into the limelight in recent years, several questions need to be resolved. First, government support for training the PWDs in these organisations. Second, the long-term sustainability of these enterprises. Third, these enterprises' limited reach (these few organisations cater only to a very small proportion of the PWD population).

Another model is open employment, but this is limited to a tiny population of very high-functioning persons with disabilities — typically individuals with high cognitive abilities but also with physical impairments. They have been able to find employment on their own in the open market. Some of these success stories have also been publicly celebrated in high-profile national events. For example, Dr Yeo Sze Ling (A*STAR researcher) was singled out for commendation at the 2013 National Day Rally 2013. Dignity Kitchen, a pioneer among social enterprises in Singapore, has attempted to close the supply-demand gap by training the underprivileged and disabled in marketable F&B (Food and Beverage) skills, and helping them find jobs in the food and beverage industry. Over 100 "students" with physical or intellectual disabilities have graduated from this social enterprise, after being trained by special instructors for eight weeks. Besides continuing to work in Dignity Kitchen, many have found jobs in other restaurants such as Boon Tong Kee, Aston's, Ma Maison and Spize — this was mentioned in Prime Minister Lee's national day rally.

For most persons with disabilities who cannot find white collar jobs, sheltered training and employment opportunities need to be developed. Bizlink Centre is a non-profit organisation that provides comprehensive employment services for disadvantaged people, especially the disabled. Bizlink Employment Placement Division provides job placement and job support services. In particular, for PWDs, Bizlink provides one-stop employment and job assessment services. Bizlink acts as a bridge to connect people with disabilities to potential employers and businesses. It runs a sheltered workshop that provides sheltered employment for more than 120 PWDs. Since 1994, Bizlink has successfully placed more than 5000 PWDs into employment in Singapore.

The Movement for the Intellectually Disabled of Singapore (MINDS) offers job placement and job support for handicaps with intellectual disabilities, as well as a range of supported employment programmes. MINDS helps find open employment for clients with moderate to severe intellectual disability. Their centres try to get national certification for their clients in a bid to enhance their employability. MINDS Social Enterprise was started in 2000 to create employment opportunities for the people with intellectual disability as an additional avenue to secure employment for the Movement's clients. It has proven to be a viable alternative of creating employment for its clients, resulting in the formalising of some in-house industries and transforming them into platforms of sustainable employment for many people with intellectual disability. MINDS Social Enterprise was established with the aim to improve the quality of life of adults with intellectual disability. The Society for the Physically Disabled (SPD) does the same for persons with physical or sensory disabilities.

The Centre for the Physically Challenged (CPC) aims to provide rehabilitation, training and employment opportunities for the physically challenged to enable and empower them to live a productive, meaningful and independent life and to be a full contributor to the community. What sets the CPC apart from the other organisations providing employment to the physically challenged is that a carefully selected portion of its members are put on a holistic programme starting from the time they join until the time they are settled in their new employment. Members of the CPC are usually referred by hospitals, SG Enable (formerly the Centre for Enabled Living) and other volunteer organisations.

SG Enable was set up in 2013 to strengthen the government's focus on PWDs and serve as a focal point of need. Enhancing employment opportunities for PWDs is one of its key missions. The agency is building on pre-existing models of open or sheltered employment (i.e., workshops) which are usually run by voluntary welfare organisations or social enterprises, as enhancing employment is one of its key missions.

The Singapore government's efforts at boosting the employment prospects of PWDs have been evident not only in vocational training in special education schools, but also in giving financial and tax incentives to companies to employ such individuals. For example, SG Enable's Open Door Fund — a grant for employers to hire more PWDs — saw government spending of S$3.5 million between 2012 and 2014. Policies such as the Special Employment Credit (16% of the employee's wages will be credited to the company by the government if they hire people who have graduated from special education schools) and the Handicapped Earned Income Tax Relief have also been implemented in the past few years to promote the employment of PWDs.

The various aspects of improving the lives of PWDs are intricately interrelated and they need to be aligned. For example, there is a need to ensure that skills (e.g., independence, money matters, computer literacy, customer service) taught in special schools are aligned with potential jobs that may be available to PWDs. It is true that not all PWDs can be employed (e.g., those with moderate to severe disabilities). The goal is to effect a change in societal mindset so that a broad spectrum of organisations will actively consider PWDs for employment options and they are doing so not because of government incentives for firms to hire or some top-down government actions. Some organisations have been actively hiring PWDs, and their efforts should be more widely recognised.

Accessibility

The most significant progress made in disability policies in Singapore is probably the development of a more equitable and accessible "built environment". Most of this progress was facilitated by the anticipation of an ageing population. The relevant policies on built environment that benefit elderly persons, which make economic sense, also benefit the disabled community.

Before 1989, Singapore had no legally-enforceable code that required buildings to be made accessible to the disabled or the elderly (Harrison, 1997). During the early years of Singapore's independence, a key priority was basic housing for the nation. When implementing the massive rehousing projects handled by the then Singapore Improvement Trust, which subsequently evolved into the Housing & Development Board (HDB), lifts were considered an unaffordable luxury. As a result, many old HDB blocks either did not have any lifts or had lifts that would only stop at certain levels.

The state's view on physical accessibility for the disabled during this period in time is perhaps best reflected in the 1983 discussions on whether Singapore's first Mass Rapid Transit (MRT) Line should provide access to the disabled. In an interview with *The Straits Times* on the planning developments of the MRT, Mr Lim Leong Geok, the then executive director of the MRT Corporation, explained that the MRT "cannot cater for the handicapped" because "the trains will stop ... for only a short time — 30 seconds at the longest ... so one has to be reasonably agile to get in and out of the trains" (Dhaliwal, 1983). This revelation sparked a flurry of letters questioning the MRT's decision on the matter relating to access for the handicapped. Of particular note was Dr Thomas Tan's letter — entitled "MRT: 30 seconds is enough for the handicapped" — in which he highlighted his observation that the handicapped in New York City had no issue with using the New York subway. He attributed the problem to "attitudes" and argued that Singapore risked remaining a "small-hearted nation" should attitudes towards the underprivileged hitherto remain unchanged (Tan, 1983). In a series of replies, the MRT Corporation and the state stood firm on the decision to bar the wheelchair-bound access to the MRT. Issues of safety, reliability and access to and from MRT stations were cited as reasons as to why the "MRT is not the proper solution" to address the "needs of these people on a comprehensive basis" (Loke, 1983). The MRT's efficiency and reliability for the able-bodied were considered far more important than catering to the less-abled in society. Dr Tan's advice that "the greatness of a nation is measured by how it treats its weakest members" thus fell on deaf ears.

Yet in 1981 — the year declared by the United Nations as the International Year of Disabled Persons — a study team mooting the feasibility of a barrier-free environment for the disabled and the aged had been set up. Consisting of members from the Ministry of National Development, the then Ministry of Social Affairs, the Singapore Council of Social Services and the Singapore Institute of Architects, the team used costings and cases from HDB, URA and private building projects to show that it would only cost developers 1% more to make new buildings more accessible. Despite the negligible additional cost involved, architects and developers did not make their buildings more accessible voluntarily. As a result, the study team recommended legislating that stakeholders in the built environment must conform to certain standards in creating barrier-free environments for all, which eventually led to the 1990 Code on Barrier-Free Accessibility in Buildings.

It is important to note that the 1990 Code was passed to benefit the elderly population. This was stated clearly in the code as well, as it was "designed with special provision to serve the elderly and the physically handicapped". In subsequent years, the code was constantly revised and updated to "better suit local conditions" (1995 Code on Barrier-Free Accessibility in Buildings) and to "update it to comparable standards in the leading developed countries" (2002 Code on Barrier-Free Accessibility in Buildings). The Codes also became more comprehensive as they sought to justify the rising costs involved with each additional mandatory specification. Further, the 2002 Code also catered to "those with visual impairment, the aged and elderly, and families with young children".

Interestingly, the 2002 Code sought to "minimise mandatory requirements whenever possible", with the inclusion of four sets of non-mandatory requirements for the expanded target group. It was hoped that through "greater awareness and public education, market forces will determine the demand for buildings that will meet the needs of the various interest groups". This position was in line with the policy-makers' belief in a Laissez-faire economic system. The experiment was not met with much success. Even as the Building Construction Authority (BCA) introduced the Universal Design Awards in 2007, it was decided that these non-mandatory requirements needed to be made mandatory and further expanded. This was finally done in the 2013 revision.

Another milestone was reached in 2004, when the code was reviewed to place additional emphasis on the "lack of barrier-free inter-connectivity between buildings and from buildings to infrastructure". This reflects an important shift in the perception of the spatial rights for disabled persons. Instead of having the right to an accessible environment only in their private spaces (i.e., homes and offices), the 2004 Code further gave them the right to accessibility in the public realm such as public parks and transport networks. This important shift shows how policies are increasingly enacted to reflect a shift toward a more inclusive society.

This policy shift has also led to tangible differences regarding societal perception of the disabled in terms of the social stigma associated with disabilities. PWDs' increased visibility in public places allows for a better understanding of their needs and the challenges that they face. This also has the potential to foster greater recognition of the rights of PWDs.

Despite the impressive progress made in creating an equitable built environment, one of the major obstacles to achieving a truly accessible built environment is the retrofit of buildings built before 1990. Although government support — such as the Accessibility Fund and the Barrier-Free Accessibility (BFA) Upgrading Programme — were set up to help defray the cost of retrofit, many old buildings remain currently inaccessible to the disabled. Fundamental design incompatibility such as the split-level HDB blocks, and the excessive funds required for retrofitting projects, are two main factors that have resulted in low take-up rates. Unlike countries like Norway, Singapore does not have a fixed deadline as to when these old buildings must be retrofitted to universal design standards. Without a fixed deadline, the onus is on private owners and building managements to decide if they should invest money in retrofitting their facilities. Unfortunately, the market demand for these retrofitting projects has not reached a level where profit-driven companies are willing to fork out extra money for them. As a result, the difference in the level of accessibility between new code-abiding buildings and old buildings remains stark. Given the limited income of some PWDs, it is a challenge for them to afford newly built homes in Singapore's expensive real estate market.

In essence, the Building Construction Authority's policies in universal design can be summed up as a "carrot-and-stick" approach. On the one hand, legislation (the Code) is used as the stick to ensure that architects and developers conform to a certain standard in making the built environment accessible. On the other hand, the BCA Universal Design Mark certification scheme (formerly the BCA Universal Design Awards), which "accord[s] recognition to stakeholders for incorporating user-friendly features in their developments", is the carrot. This approach is similar to the BCA's efforts in promoting an environment-friendly built environment under the GreenMark scheme, where building codes stipulate minimum standards for building energy efficiency. The certification scheme also recognises developers who go the extra mile to make their buildings more sustainable.

Unfortunately, when applied to universal design, this approach has not seen similar levels of success. Private developers, who build the majority of the private apartments in Singapore, remain unmotivated to go the extra mile in applying universal design principles. As compared to green buildings, which result in immediately visible cost savings in building maintenance in the long run, more accessible buildings do not appear to result in any significant cost savings in the long run. Profit-driven companies are thus hesitant to do more than what the code stipulates; some have done so reluctantly, as observed in their response to BCA's alteration of the minimum corridor width from 1.2 m to 1.5 m ("Wheelchair Access", *The Straits Times*, 2014).

Moving forward, it is our hope that architects and developers take on the responsibility of ensuring that buildings are designed to be PWD-friendly. The built environment has the immense potential to include and exclude. Thus, architects and developers need to recognise the responsibility they have in ensuring that people with different physical abilities are not excluded from the spaces they create. The universal design principles should be viewed as a socially responsible mode of action and not an economic burden.

The market can also play a part in encouraging this push for a more accessible built environment. For the market to respond in this manner, consumers would need to create enough demand for these facilities. If Singaporeans stand up for the interests of PWDs and demand that the property they buy be designed in accordance to universal design principles, developers would respond accordingly. Evidence for such consumer effects is seen in the green movement.

Encouragingly, there are currently some signs of demand for responsible architecture. Units in The Hillford, which is Singapore's first retirement resort, were sold out within the first day of launch (Siau, 2014). According to analysts, the success of The Hillford could "open the floodgates for [more] retirement resorts" (Siau, 2014). While the Hillford resort was not primarily targeted at PWDs, having housing options that benefit the elderly will also benefit PWDs because the groups of individuals have similar physical access requirements.

The government can also take a similar approach. For example, Norway's action plan for universal design and increased accessibility uses economic and other non-legal instruments to enhance accessibility in public buildings. According to this plan, the different public bodies which disburse grants that relate to physical infrastructure are to ensure that grants are only given to recipients who conform to the high standards of the accessibility criteria.

A more holistic view and strategy is also necessary in improving the inclusiveness of PWDs in Singapore. The government is providing significant resources to ensure that buses are wheelchair-accessible by 2020. However, to have a real impact on inclusivity of PWDs in Singapore, we need to provide PWDs with appropriate educational facilities and address issues of social stigma. We can perhaps learn from the Norway example. The Norway Action Plan uses a "sector responsibility" principle that identifies the responsibilities of each government Ministry with regard to improving the inclusiveness of PWDs and imposes a deadline for drafting an action plan on these ministries (Norwegian Ministry of Children and Equality, 2009). This Inter-Ministerial strategy resulted in a more coordinated effort.

Singapore has spent the last 14 years improving the country's physical environment and there has been much improvement in this aspect of enhancing inclusivitiy for PWDS. It remains to be seen how the built environment and other areas such as education and employment can be aligned to achieve the overall goal of a more PWD-inclusive society.

Conclusion

Ignorance, superstitions and beliefs about retribution for sins in a previous life or punishment for the sins of one's parents have often been at the root of discrimination against persons born with disabilities. The rise of capitalism and the inability of PWDs to contribute effectively to the demands of capitalist production have further contributed to the marginalisation of PWDs. The "medical model" in the early years sought to isolate and "fix" PWDs. The pendulum swung towards a "social model" in the 1980s and 1990s with the concomitant rise of human rights and welfare state systems.

International definitions of disability, especially those that carry the prestige and weight of the UN or the WHO, are important statements that express the standards and norms by which communities around the world measure their conformity with global best practices. The periodic and frequent changes to definitions of "disability" reflect the contestations that have taken place (and are still taking place) between "medical" and "social" models of disability. Further, the compatibility (or incongruence) of extant definitions of "disability" or "disabled person" employed by national and local authorities, with existing laws, norms and notions of disability — or local "culture" — is a reflection of the degree of change that the relevant institutions aim to see achieved in that society or community. In many cases, national and local communities have attempted to align themselves as far as possible, with globally accepted definitions — financial cost being the usual ultimate consideration.

Being a highly trade-dependent society with an aversion to welfare state thinking, Singapore has been somewhat behind the curve of the social model. Unfortunately, it is unlikely to move as far as most Western countries given that the belief or perception that disability is a personal/family tragedy, rather than a social issue, is still very strong in Singapore. Nonetheless, some elements of the social model have been incorporated into Singapore's disability paradigm. For example, the increasing focus on policies that aim to change society, the advocacy for inclusivity, and the push for barrier-free accessibility and accessible buses are all aspects of "change" which the social model would advocate. The definition of disability in as early as 1989 espoused the idea of a social model of disability in Singapore, although it stops short of the rights-based model common in the West.

The increasing proportion of the elderly in the Singapore population has moved policies towards greater inclusivity for the elderly which also benefit PWDs. The demands of many interest groups and the spread of international norms of disability rights have also moved Singapore's policies towards a greater consideration of PWDs as persons of worth. It looks like the trend towards viewing PWDs as individuals who have rights and can make meaningful contributions to society — similar to elderly individuals with various impairments — will continue.

References

Abberley, P. (2002). Work, Disability and European Social Theory. In C. Barnes, M. Oliver & L. Barton (eds.), *Disability Studies Today* (pp. 121–38). Cambridge: Polity Press.

AWARE (2012). *October 25th, 2011 Roundtable Discussion: Inclusion for Persons with Disabilities*. Retrieved 10 October 2014, from http://www.aware.org.sg/2011/10/roundtable-discussion-women-in-the-disablities-movement.

Barnes, C. & Mercer, G. (2005). Disability, Work, and Welfare: Challenging the Social Exclusion of Disabled People. *Work, Employment and Society*, 19(3), 527–545.

Barnett, M. & Finnemore, M. (1999). The Politics, Power, and Pathologies of International Organizations. *International Organization*, 53(4), 699–732.

Birkenbach, J. (2012). The International Classification of Functioning, Disability and Health and Its Relationship to Disability Studies. In N. Watson, A. Roulstone &

C. Thomas (eds.), *Routledge Handbook of Disability Studies*. London and New York: Routledge.

Chua, B. H. (1997). *Communitarian Ideology and Democracy in Singapore*. London: Routledge.

Committee Report to MCYS (c.2011). *Definition of Disability and Prevalence Rate of Persons with Disabilities in Singapore*. Retrieved 15 November 2012, from http://app.msf.gov.sg/Portals/0/Files/EM_Chapter1.pdf.

Crawford, F. & Wong, R. (2011, July 22). Parents Are Only Part of a Bigger Issue. *Today*.

Dhaliwal, Rav (1983, November 17). Not for Disabled. *The Straits Times*, p. 18.

Enabling Masterplan 2007–2011 Steering Committee (2007). *Enabling Masterplan, 2007–2011*. Singapore: Ministry of Community Development, Youth and Sports. Retrieved 16 January 2015, from http://appl.mcys.gov.sgPublications/Enabling Masterplan20072011.aspx.

Enabling Masterplan 2012–2016 Steering Committee (2012). *Enabling Masterplan 2012–2016: Maximising Potential, Embracing Differences*. Singapore: Ministry of Community Development, Youth and Sports. Retrieved 16 January 2015, from: http://appl.mcys.gov.sgPoliciesDisabilitiesPeoplewithDisabilities/EnablingMasterplan20122016.aspx.

Govt to Sign UN Pact on Rights for the Disabled (2012, September 27). *The Straits Times*, pp. A8–A9.

Harrison, James D. (1997, Winter/Spring). Housing for the Ageing Population of Singapore. *Ageing International*, 32–47.

Heiman, T. (2002). Parents of Children with Disabilities: Resilience, Coping, and Future Expectations. *Journal of Developmental and Physical Disabilities*, 14(2), 159–171.

JCEEA (2004). *A Case for the Inclusion of Children with Special Needs in Compulsory Education*. Singapore: Joint Committee for Compulsory Education for All.

Lee, H. L. (2004). Speech by Prime Minister Lee Hsien Loong at the opening of the Spastic Children's Association of Singapore's Cerebral Palsy Centre. Retrieved 16 January 2015, from National Archives of Singapore website, http://a2o.nas.sg/stars.

Leonardi, M., Bickenbach, J., Ustun, T. B., Kostanjsek, N. & Chatterji, S. (2006). The Definition of Disability: What Is in a Name? *The Lancet*, 368(9543), 1219–1221.

Lim, L. & Nam, S. S. (2000). Special Education in Singapore. *Journal of Special Education*, 34(2), 104–109.

Lim, L. & Tan, J. (1999). The Marketization of Education in Singapore: Prospects for Inclusive Education. *International Journal of Inclusive Education*, 3(4), 339–351.

Lim, S. M., Wong, M. E. & Tan, D. (2014). Allied Educators (Learning and Behavioural Support) in Singapore's Mainstream Schools: First Steps towards Inclusivity? *International Journal of Inclusive Education*, 18(2), 123–139.

Loke, Tammie (1983, November 26). Wheelchair-Users Will Have Difficulty. *The Straits Times*, p. 25.

Mathi, B. (1996, February 8). 20 Schools Have Facilities for Disabled. *The Straits Times*, p. 25.

Ministry of Education (MOE) (2012). *Support for Children with Disabilities*. MOE, Singapore. Retrieved 16 January 2015, from http://www.moe.gov.sg/education/programmes/support-for-children-special-needs/.

Ministry of Education (MOE) (2013). More Support for Students with Special Needs. Press release, MOE, Singapore. Retrieved 16 January 2015, from http://www.moe.gov.sg/media/press/2013/03/more-support-for-students-with-special-needs.php.

Ministry of Education (MOE) (2014a). *Special Education in Singapore*. MOE, Singapore. Retrieved 16 January 2015, from http://www.moe.gov.sg/education/special-education.

Ministry of Education (MOE) (2014b). List of Special Education Schools. MOE, Singapore. Retrieved 16 January 2015, from http://www.moe.gov.sg/education/special-education/schoollist/.

Ministry of Education (MOE) (2014c). Educational Pathway for Students with Sensory Impairment. MOE, Singapore. Retrieved 16 January 2015, from http://www.moe.gov.sg/education/special-education/path/.

Ministry of Education (MOE) (2014d). *Assistive Technology*. MOE, Singapore. Retrieved 16 January 2015, from http://www.moe.gov.sg/education/special-education/assistive-technology/.

Ministry of Education (MOE) (2014e). *Vocational Education*. MOE, Singapore. Retrieved 16 January 2015, from http://www.moe.gov.sg/education/special-education/vocational-education/.

Norwegian Ministry of Children and Equality (2009). *Norway Universally Designed by 2025*. Norwegian Ministry of Children and Equality.

Oliver, M. & Barnes, C. (2012). *The New Politics of Disablement*. Basingstoke: Palgrave Macmillan.

Pang, E. F. (1980). Employment, Development and Basic Needs in Singapore. *International Labour Review*, 119(4), 495.

Parker, K. J. (2001). Changing Attitudes towards Persons with Disabilities in Asia. *Disability Studies Quarterly*, 21(4), 105–113.

Poon, K. K., Musti-Rao, S. & Wettasinghe, M. (2013). Special Education in Singapore: History, Trends, and Future Directions. *Intervention in School and Clinic*, 49, 59–64.

Public Works Department (1995). Code on Barrier-Free Accessibility in Buildings 1995. Building Control Division, Public Works Department, Singapore.

Quah, J. S. T. (2010). *Public Administration Singapore Style*. Singapore: Talisman.

Quah, M. L. M. (1993). Special Education in Singapore. In M. L. Quah, S. Gopinathan & S. C. Chang (eds.), *A Review of Practice and Research for All in Singapore. Country Report Submitted to the Southeast Asian Research, Review and Advisory Group (SEARRAG)* (pp. 89–102). Singapore: National Institute of Education.

Rajah, I. (2014, May 26). Speech on ASPIRE at the Debate on President's Address 2014. MOE, Singapore. Retrieved 16 January 2015, from http://www.moe.gov.sg/media/speeches/2014/05/26/aspire-related-speech-by-ms-indranee-rajah-at-the-opening-of-the-2nd-session-of-the-12th-parliament.php.

Report of the Advisory Council on the Disabled (1988). *Opportunities for the Disabled*. Singapore: Ministry of Education.

Rogers, C. (2007). 'Disabling' a Family? Emotional Dilemmas Experienced in Becoming a Parent of a Learning Disabled Child. *British Journal of Special Education*, 34(3), 136–143.

Roulstone, A. & Barnes, C. (2005). *Working Futures: Disabled People, Policy and Social Inclusion*. Bristol, UK: The Policy Press.

Scotch, R. K. (1988). Disability as the Basis for a Social Movement: Advocacy and the Politics of Definition. *Journal of Social Issues*, 44(1), 159–172.

Siau, Ming En (2014, January 18). All 281 Units of the Hillford Sold out on First Day. *Today*, p. 1.

Tan, K. P. (2008). Meritocracy and Elitism in a Global City: Ideological Shifts in Singapore. *International Political Science Review*, 29(1), 7–27.

Tan, Thomas (1983, November 21). MRT: 30 Seconds Are Enough for the Handicapped *The Straits Times*, p. 15.

Thaver, T. & Lim, L. (2014). Attitudes of Pre-service Mainstream Teachers in Singapore towards People with Disabilities and Inclusive Education. *International Journal of Inclusive Education*, 18(10), 1038–1052.

United Nations Convention on the Rights of Persons with Disabilities (2006). Retrieved September 2014, from http://www.un.org/disabilities/default.asp?id=61.

Wheelchair Access: Do Wider Corridors Make Sense for Private Projects? (2014, March 24). *The Straits Times*, p. C1.

Wong, M. E. (in-submission). Disability in Singapore. Navigating through the Rat Race. Manuscript submitted for publication.

Wong, M. E. & Chia, N. K. H. (2010). Education of the Visually Impaired in Singapore: An Overview of Primary and Secondary Programs. *Journal of Visual Impairment and Blindness*, 104, 243–247.

Wong, M. E., Chia, N. K. H. & Law, J. S. P. (in-submission). Collaboration in Providing Assistive Technology Support for Students with Visual Impairment: Experiences of Special School Teachers of Students with Visual Impairments in Singapore. Manuscript submitted for publication.

Wong, M. E. & Cohen, L. (2011). School, Family and Other Influences on Assistive Technology Use: Access and Challenges for Special School Students with Visual Impairments in Singapore. *British Journal of Visual Impairment*, 29(2), 130–144.

Wong, M. E., Poon, K. K., Kaur, S. & Ng, Z. J. (2014). Parental Perspectives and Challenges in Inclusive Education in Singapore Secondary Schools. *Asia Pacific Journal of Education*. DOI: 10.1080/02188791.2013.878309.

Wong, R. (2012). Patients' Rights, Caregivers' Dilemmas. Singapore: CENTRES (Clinical Ethics Network for Training, Research and Support), NUS, 11, 8–9.

Wong, R. & Crawford, F. (2011, July 18). Educating All Children — Without Exceptions, *Today*, p. 12.

World Health Organization (WHO) (1980). *International Classification of Impairments, Disabilities, and Handicaps: A Manual of Classification Relating to the Consequences of Disease*. Geneva: World Health Organization.

Yeo, L. S., Chong, W. H., Neihart, M. & Huan, V. S. (2014). Teachers' Experience with Inclusive Education in Singapore. *Asia Pacific Journal of Education*. DOI: 10.1080/02188791.2014.934781

Zhuang, Kuan Song (2007). *Enabling the Singapore Story: Writing a History of Disability in Singapore*. Singapore: NUS History Honours Thesis.

Chapter 10

Foreign Domestic Workers in Singapore: A Neglected Social Issue?

Shirlena Huang and Brenda S. A. Yeoh

Foreign domestic workers are a conspicuous presence in Singapore. A stroll through any residential neighbourhood any day of the week will reveal these women accompanying their young charges to childcare or school, taking a slow stroll with an elderly charge for the latter's daily exercise, hanging out the laundry, washing their employers' cars, shopping for groceries, or in small groups chatting as they walk their employers' dogs. On Sundays, they become even more visible in public parks, shopping malls, places of worship, training centres and other public areas as they enjoy a day off. Indeed, foreign domestic workers, or "maids" as they are widely referred to in Singapore, are now a crucial part of Singapore's care and housekeeping landscape, enabling scores of Singaporean women (and, more indirectly, men as well) to go out to work each day or simply enjoy more quality time. Ironically, while visible in this physical sense, too often, the contributions and plight of foreign domestic workers in Singapore — as in many other major cities around the world — are often overlooked. Not surprisingly, foreign domestic workers have been paradoxically described as the "invisible backbone" of many metropolitan economies in which they are found (Sternberg, 2014).

The story of modern Singapore's economic success will not be complete if we focus solely on the contributions by Singapore citizens. In this chapter, we widen the lens of nation building to include the role played by migrant women who work in many Singapore homes to fill the care vacuum created when citizens are unwilling or unable to take on this work. Comprising mainly nationals from less developed economies in Southeast Asia, these women migrate across borders to take up what is generally regarded as undesirable and low-level service work. Following Said (1978), scholars (e.g., Aguilar, 1999; Hogan, 2009; van der Veer, 1995) have argued that the presence of migrants provides a useful reflexive and refractory lens, a "mirror of sorts", to reveal how members of the host society view themselves. Thus, in the first part of the chapter, we highlight how constructions of the migrant "other" in Singapore are also very much about constructions of the national "self". We then move on to highlight two key areas — prompted by the durable presence of foreign domestic workers over the last few decades — that deserve more attention in Singapore, *viz*, challenging the gendered notions of care and domestic work associated with the home sphere, and recognising the growing role of civil society in an area left largely unattended by the state. We conclude by discussing some policy and social implications.

A brief history of domestic servitude in Singapore

Singapore's dependence on migrant domestics is certainly not a recent phenomenon. Wealthier households in British Malaya (including Singapore) employed Hylam cooks and houseboys, *ayahs* and *dhobis* from India, as well as *amahs* and *mui tsais* from China. In particular, the "black and white" *amah* of pre-independent Singapore is nostalgically remembered as a legendary "superior servant" (Gaw, 1988). With the supply of migrants drying up after the Second World War because of more stringent immigration conditions, only wealthier families could afford an *amah*; middle-class households turned to employing young local girls and women from Singapore's rural areas as servant girls and laundry women. However, even this changed in the years after Singapore's independence.

The rapid growth of the manufacturing and service sectors in the late 1960s and 1970s siphoned off many women into jobs in the formal economy. As a result, Singapore's female labour force participation rate (LFPR) grew rapidly, reaching 39.3% in 1980 (Khoo, 1981). Collectively, the high female LFPR, accompanied by the growing proportion of dual-income families and insufficient alternatives for childcare and household work, soon led to a care deficit in the domestic sphere (Iyer *et al.*, 2004). In 1978, the state stepped in to facilitate the supply of transnational waged domestic labour by granting work permits for the first time to allow a limited recruitment of domestic servants from Thailand, Sri Lanka and the Philippines (Cheng, 1984) to help ease the burden of working women in Singapore. Over time, the sources of foreign domestic workers expanded to include countries such as India and Indonesia (now the largest source) and, in more recent years, Myanmar and Cambodia. Given current trends — major advances in women's education, increasing career opportunities for Singapore women, as well as rising aspirations in Singapore society towards middle-class lifestyles sustained by dual-career family structures — it appears that foreign domestic workers in Singapore are here to stay.

However, from the state's perspective, foreign domestic workers are not a long-term solution to Singapore's care deficit on the domestic front, as apparent from the many measures that have been put in place over the years to control their numbers and ensure that foreign domestic workers remain only a transient workforce. In the earliest conceptions of the "Foreign Maid Scheme", they were not allowed to stay beyond four years, and exceptions were considered only on a case-by-case basis and only "where the risk of these foreign maids settling here permanently is minimal, such as in the case of an elderly foreign maid or one who is married with a family in her home country" ("Four-year Stay", *Singapore Monitor*, 1983). As explained by the then Ministry of Labour, the "objective" was "to minimise the chances that they will strike up relationships with Singaporeans and wish to settle here... [The four-year limit is] necessary to ensure foreign workers do not sink roots in Singapore and are repatriated on time" ("Maids Can Stay", *The Straits Times*, 1986). With the rise of nuclear families and dual-income households, demand for foreign domestic workers, however, was not dampened by these measures: while it took 10 years for the number of foreign domestic workers in Singapore to reach an estimated 20,000 in 1987 (I. Lim, 1987), it doubled in the span of one year to reach 40,000 by 1988 ("Answers to Questions", *The Straits Times*, 1988) and then to almost 50,000 by the end of 1989 ("Foreign Worker Levies", *The Business Times*, 1989). It soon became clear that the state's avowed aim to phase out the Foreign Maid Scheme by 1991 was an unrealistic one (Tan & Devasahayam, 1987). By the year 2000, there were 100,000 foreign domestic workers ("'Social Costs'", *The Straits Times*, 2000). Their numbers have continued to climb steadily and today, there are almost 220,000 foreign domestic workers in Singapore (MOM website) or one foreign domestic worker for every 5.5 households.

Although the demand for foreign domestic workers has steadily increased, the state has steadfastly continued to impose measures to ensure that while needed, foreign domestic workers are strategically maintained as a transient labour force though a series of legislation, including regulations that circumscribe the women from family formation and sinking roots in Singapore (e.g., they are not permitted to bring in dependents; are prohibited from marrying Singapore citizens and permanent residents without permission, and from becoming pregnant), as well as a hefty monthly levy (currently more than half of a foreign domestic workers' average starting salary of S$450–S$500) and a S$5,000 security bond to be paid by the employer, the latter of which may be forfeited should the worker transgress conditions of the Work Permit *and* employers are found to have failed to "have done their best to keep the Work Permit conditions, as well as to manage their worker's behaviour in line with the Work Permit conditions" (see MOM website for details).[1] Policy adjustments over the years, however, suggest that the state recognises the

---

[1] Until end-2009, employers would lose their security bond should their foreign domestic workers violate conditions of the Work Permit, e.g., if the foreign domestic worker became pregnant. Since January 2010, however, "MOM has removed employers' liability if the FDW gets pregnant or breaches other Work Permit conditions that relate to her own behaviour" (see Ministry of Manpower, Press Replies, 2011).

role that foreign domestic workers play in devolving the strain from (female) family members not only in the traditional areas of childcare and domestic work, but increasingly in the area of eldercare as Singapore's population has started to age. For example, since August 2004, families employing a foreign domestic for an elderly person (aged 65 years and above) may apply to pay a reduced monthly levy; and in 2012, the state announced that a monthly grant of S$120 would be provided to lower- and middle-income families that needed to employ a foreign domestic worker to care for an elderly family member (see Yeoh & Huang, 2014, for details).

From the inception of the Foreign Maid Scheme, the issue of foreign domestic workers in Singapore has catalysed lively debates on a number of issues in parliament as well as among the general populace, human rights groups and academics, both in Singapore and beyond. On the one hand, their rising numbers have engendered discussions on their impact on Singapore's resources and (potential) influence on Singapore's social fabric and concerns surrounding the social costs of foreign women as carers. On the other hand, Singaporeans' apparent dependence on them and their treatment in Singapore have also fuelled soul-searching amongst Singaporeans as to what the phenomenon says about Singaporeans as a people and Singapore as a society.

Foreign domestic workers as carers: Creating a nation of "soft" Singaporeans?

While foreign domestic workers have facilitated the retention of women and older employees in Singapore's tight labour force and in filling sectors of the economy not favoured by locals, accepting wages well below the national norm, much of the state and public discourse is often predicated on apprehensions associated with Singapore's over-dependence on their growing numbers. Occasionally (especially in the earlier years), the steady demand for foreign domestic workers raised concerns about the burden this would place on public facilities and the country's limited resources, given its small size.

A more recurrent theme in public debate revolves around the rhetoric of projected ill consequences engendered by the presence of "a whole army of maids" (in the words of then Minister of Labour, Lee Yock Suan, quoted in "Foreign Maids Policy", *The Business Times*, 1990) on the social values and moral fibre of Singapore society, particularly in relation to the dynamics of family relations and the sanctity of family values. While earlier parental anxieties revolved around the "undesired habits" that their children might pick up — such as "speaking English with a Filipino accent" (Lee, 1985) or adopting the Filipino "*manana* attitude of procrastination" (Tang, 1988) — the state's concern focused on the unknown long-term effects that using foreigners as childcare givers would have on social values. In particular, anxieties centred on the work ethics of future generation of Singaporeans who "grow up used to having maids to perform all the household duties" as expressed by then Minister of Labour, Lee Boon Yang (cited in Kwek, 1988). Would "maid dependency" lead to a nation of soft Singaporeans so used to being served that the foundational values of being "a rugged society" built through "discipline for survival"[2] would be eroded? Could it ultimately destroy the perception of Singaporeans as "competent, disciplined, hard-working and trustworthy" (in the words of then Prime Minister Goh Chok Tong, quoted in Wong, 1997)?

It was not long before these debates rippled out to implicate the national carrier, Singapore Airlines (SIA). Based on his observations that "Malaysian stewardesses flying for Singapore Airlines fold blankets better than the Singaporean Singapore Girl", one Member of Parliament raised the spectre that the national icon could suffer a downward spiral if a whole generation raised by foreign domestic workers became "Singapore girls" who were unable to fold blankets properly because they grew up "get[ting] their maids to do it for them" ("Malaysian S'pore Girls", *The Straits Times*, 1997, p. 28). As depicted in a cartoon accompanying the feature, in response to a passenger's request to fold his blanket, the SIA stewardess proceeds to fulfil her job by calling upon her "maid" (whom she has brought along on the trip) to do so!

By the late 2000s, a poll conducted by *The Straits Times* seemed to suggest that these fears of a "maid-dependent generation" could not be dismissed: almost all the 50 employers who had been asked "How long would you survive without a maid?" had admitted to being able to survive only a day (10 persons) or at most a month (38 persons) (Arshad & Tan, 2000)! The spirited public debate which followed revealed that Singaporeans had indeed developed "a maid mentality — always expecting someone else to pick up . . . after them" (Daniel Wang, then Commissioner of Public Health, cited in "When It Comes down to Litter", *The Straits Times*, 1997).

A fresh round of public debates around the deleterious effects of Singapore's Maid Dependent Syndrome surfaced in March 2011, when a photograph of a uniformed National Serviceman — walking ahead of his foreign domestic worker who had been tasked with carrying the serviceman's heavy army field pack — seemed to present proof that fears of soft Singaporeans had penetrated its armed forces. The image first surfaced on *STOMP*, a citizen journalism website, before it was (re)circulated on numerous print and new media platforms, along with satirical (re)presentations of the image. The initial reaction of many was that of disbelief. Taking his uniform to be symbolic of the nation, many read the serviceman's "transgression" as negatively affecting "Singapore Armed Forces' deterrence posture, built as it is on an image of steely resilience"; ultimately, it was a "disgrace to Singapore" ("Rethinking a Man–Maid Conundrum", *The Straits Times*, 2011). The episode catalysed a whole series of questions (e.g., "If he can't carry his own field pack, how to depend on this kind of soldier to defend Singapore?"

---

[2]These are phrases from a song that school children in the late 1960s and 1970s were taught.

as posed on the chat forum of news portal *xinmsn*) about whether the army training integral to producing the Singapore soldier — the basic building block of the nation's defence force — was tough enough.

This incident captured the imagination of not only many Singaporeans but also local and foreign news agencies, resulting in satirical representations in both print and social media. A *Straits Times* cartoon showed a foreign domestic worker holding an umbrella over the head of an army recruit (Choong, 2011) while several online sites depicted the domestic worker, field pack in tow, going off to war with her "young sir". Indeed, the incident seemed to confirm, that "behind every successful SAF (Singapore Armed Forces) soldier, there is a maid" ("Row as Maid Seen", *Yahoo News*, 2011), just like Singapore's other famous uniformed personnel — the Singapore Girl. The juxtaposition of a "weak" and "pampered" soldier against a "strong" and "dependable" foreign domestic worker in the photograph ultimately returned the debates to the issue of whether Singapore's "Gen 'Y'", brought up under the care of foreign domestic workers, have become "less resilient" with some framing the issue as part of the fact that *"maids do not come without problems. Many younger Singaporeans are growing up being waited upon at home... and, as some argue, are becoming less resilient and independent"* (Choong, 2011; emphasis added).

A similar discussion of the kinds of values that Singapore parents employing foreign domestic workers for childcare (fail to) convey to their children was precipitated by a Cabinet Minister's recent (May 2014) Facebook post relating an incident he had observed of a teenage girl walking along hands-free beside her foreign domestic worker who had her arms full with a grocery bag, as well as the girl's backpack and umbrella; he asked: "Do we teach our children to treat our helpers with respect, compassion?" (Shanmugam, 2014). Those who responded to the post broadened the discussion to issues about what children learn about treating one another through the way foreign domestic workers in Singapore are treated (i.e., that some people are less valued than others by virtue of their job, nationality or class) and the longer-term consequences of "a generation of spoiled kids raised in Singapore and left in the maid's care" while their parents are busy contributing to a two-income household.[3] As one post asked: "Will this same girl take care of her parents when they are old and handicap[ped?] I think we are digging our own graves."

Singaporeans may not need to wait until they are old to find out the answer. While the state expects the family to be the primary caregiving unit for elderly

---

[3]Interestingly, the Chinese title of "Ilo Ilo", the 2012 award winning film by Singaporean Anthony Chen about the relationship between a Singapore family, particularly the child, and their foreign domestic worker is 爸妈不在家, literally translated as "Dad and Mum Are Not Home". The film is based on his own childhood relationship with his "maid who came as a stranger to our family, and slowly becomes a friend, and then like another mother" (Chen, 2014; translated from Mandarin).

family members, Singapore families are increasingly transferring aspects of this responsibility, particularly that of physical care, to their foreign domestic workers. Chan *et al.* (2012) found that half (49%) of the 1,190 caregivers surveyed in their study employed a foreign domestic worker specifically to care for frail and older family members; significantly, they found that children and "other" caregivers were more likely than spousal caregivers to hire a foreign domestic worker to care for the care recipients. A recent study by the authors found that nurses are often asked by families to teach their foreign domestic workers, rather than family members, how to take care of elderly patients when the latter are discharged from hospital (Huang *et al.*, 2012). In other words, Singapore families that can afford the cost of purchasing care labour are engaging in what Ochiai (2010) has called "liberal familialism", or the outsourcing of filial piety to others whose services can be purchased from the market. While Mehta and Thang (2008, p. 57) rightly note that "the hiring of a maid facilitates the continuity of filial responsibility on the part of the adult children", we must also consider what this may mean for future Singapore society if the availability of foreign domestic workers means that more Singaporeans will abdicate the responsibility of direct filial care for their elderly parents to paid help.

One fallout tied to the outsourcing of filial piety that has already become apparent is the abuse of elderly care recipients by foreign domestic workers, as evident in the many cases reported in the press. While most foreign domestic workers take their caring responsibilities seriously and there are many cases of successful relationships between the workers and their elderly (and young) charges, Singapore does have "the rather unusual phenomenon of elderly women killed or abused by maids, in addition to the numerous cases of maid abuse" (UNIFEM Singapore, HOME & TWC2, 2011, p. 7). That the latter may lead to the former is reflected in Internet discussions whenever such cases are reported in the media. For example, in a recent (March 2014) case of an Indonesian domestic worker who murdered her 87-year-old employer, postings included inquisitorial questions (e.g., "Was she ill-treated till she snapped?" ["Myanmar Maid Charged", *STOMP*, 5 March 2014]) alongside introspective reflections asking for more gracious behaviour on the part of both parties (e.g., "To hurt an 87 year old person is definitely wrong. To kill is even worst [sic]. But to hurl degrading remarks and abusive language to someone is not right either... Employer[s] should understand that maids are just human and have the tendency to err... maids should learn to control their temper and protest if she [sic] may" ["Maid Kills Singaporean Widow", *Yahoo News*, 2012]).

Cases of elder abuse by foreign domestic workers are often related to cultural and/or language differences leading to miscommunications and misunderstandings, as well as the stress of tending to elderly charges who may need constant attention, all of which compounds the pressures on the domestic worker who may also have household chores and childcare responsibilities to fulfil. While not condoning the deplorable acts of murder or abuse, Singapore courts also appear to be willing to recognise the difficult work conditions and weaker positions of foreign domestic workers; judgments have cited the legal concepts of "diminished responsibility" and "provocation" to exonerate foreign domestic workers found guilty of these charges (Cheah, 2009, p. 219). However, as Cheah (2009, p. 220) argues, "While these cases may be well intentioned, by entrenching stereotypes of these maids as naive victims or unhinged murderers and emphasizing the need for controlled maid-employer relationships for the good of larger Singaporean society, these criminal cases affirm the systems of exclusion and control put in place by other governmental authorities against maids in Singapore". It is these exclusions which have positioned foreign domestic workers as the migrant "other" in the first place.

Foreign domestic workers as the migrant "other": Revealing the ungracious Singaporean?

Although brought into Singapore and allowed into the private confines of Singapore homes where they are privy to the most intimate of details of Singapore families, the power geometries between the foreign domestic workers and her Singapore hosts often render her an "outsider" by virtue of her class, nationality and gendered work. Even the preferred term Singaporeans use to describe the job — "maid" rather than "domestic help" or "domestic worker" — connotes the menial positioning of the person, rather than the support she provides through the work she does.[4] The everyday encounters between Singaporeans and foreign domestic workers reveal the racialised, nationalised, classed and gendered dimensions along which Singaporeans are known to typecast this group of workers as an inferior "other", in direct contrast to the assumed superiority of the dominant national "self". This superiority generally manifests itself in the drawing of boundary lines around the worker both in the home and in public spaces. At its worst, it results in the mistreatment, abuse and even death of the migrant worker.

Within the home, employers often expect their domestic workers to know their place by observing the (often unwritten) line of deference between them, hence preserving the social boundaries between the Singaporean as dominant and the "maid" as subordinate. Many employers also attempt to colonise the spaces and times their foreign domestic workers occupy during the work day by specifying a daily timetable (sometimes broken down into half hour blocks or less) of the latter's duties around the home, especially when she is newly-arrived. Some have even been known to ration out the portions of food that the domestic worker is entitled to each day. Often, the timetable is used as a means to eliminate idleness and wasted time on the part of the domestic worker. Online posts by employers confirm that they "expect FDWs to be in constant service during waking hours and breaks are

---

[4]The use of the term "foreign domestic worker" rather than "foreign maid" in our paper is hence a deliberate one.

interpreted negatively as laziness" and "to behave within a certain master-servant framework" (Poon, 2003, p. 15). Periodically, too, foreign domestic workers have been discursively constructed in the press as a predatory *femme fatale* (e.g., "The Maid Dis(A)ttraction. She Shares Your Home. Could She Also Snare Your Hubby?" headline in *The New Paper*, 2003) and who therefore needs to be under restraint and surveillance to preserve the sanctity of the employer's marriage and family. Such imaginations of the modern foreign domestic worker as the potentially promiscuous migrant "other" — in contrast to the *amah* of yesteryear and her vow of chastity (Poon, 2003) — have resulted not just in spatial restrictions within the home (e.g., Lee, 1985, reported that "One maid was told that she should never remain in the same room with the master. Another is not allowed to walk in front of him — not even when she wants to go to the toilet and the trip involves going past a room he is in") but also limits placed on the domestic worker's forays out of the home.

In wider society, the large gatherings of foreign domestic workers in public areas (such as shopping centres, public parks along streets) on weekends heighten the visibility of this group of migrant "others". From time to time, this public visibility has evoked various reactions from Singaporeans, particularly when the workers are perceived to have transgressed public spaces. Thus, shopping centres have "shooed away" foreign domestic workers or "cordoned off" open spaces like atria to prevent them from sitting there (Vasoo, 1998). Signs in food courts have threatened them with being handed to security for simply "waiting around". For example, a poster spotted at the entrance to a local food court located in an office building, in December 2008, stated in uppercase: "THIS IS NOT THE WAITING AREA FOR FOREIGN MAID. UNATTENDED FOREIGN MAID WILL BE HANDED TO THE SECURITY" ("Unattended Foreign Maid", *Migrant Workers Singapore*, 2009). Social clubs have attempted to prevent foreign domestic workers from eating in their dining areas, and condominium management has banned them from using the swimming pools and restricted them to using only the service lifts (with some in the past actually being marked "for maids and dogs"). One of the most well-publicised incidents was brought to the public's attention by a letter to the press written by an employer who, upon bringing her Sri Lankan domestic worker with her to her club's restaurant, had to endure, first from "a waiter and then the captain... the same question: 'Is she a maid?'" The heated exchange of views in public media platforms on the matter generated the lament that "in Singapore, where status and station still matter, foreign maids enjoy little power and privilege" (S. Tan, 2000) and "are treated like modern-day slaves" (Paul, 2000). As our subsequent discussion demonstrates, some of the questions raised during this incident are still pertinent today: Have Singaporeans forgotten the days when white colonials had barred "Chinese and animals" from exclusive club premises (Monksfield, 2000b)? Are Singaporeans indeed "the new colonials" of Southeast Asia (Monksfield, 2000a) who "seem to discriminate against people from poorer countries, while thinking the whites know everything" (Paul, 2000)?

More recently, the mixed reaction to the state's recent imposition of the rule mandating one rest day per week (or compensation in lieu), is indicative of some Singaporeans' continued expectations that the foreign worker can work 24/7 as well as of their deep-seated mistrust of the "migrant other". Although the rule took effect on 1 January 2013, a recent survey found that only 37% received a weekly off-day (Goh, 2014).[5] Employment agents interviewed by the press reported that "seven in 10 employers ask... whether they can withhold giving the day off" and "some employers use the [S]$5,000 security bond as an excuse, saying that if the maid goes out and misbehaves, they will lose the money" (Seow, 2014). Such paranoia is compounded by online surveillance. Members of the public post photos online showing foreign domestic workers having a "void deck date — instead of looking after [the] elderly person in wheelchair" or going on a "date with BF [boyfriend] — together with her employer's child".[6] In contrast, few Singaporeans have stepped up to protest or challenge these popular imaginings of foreign domestic workers as the sexualised "other" woman in Singapore. Thus, the female migrant "other" manages to inspire "man-maid" (as one journalist labelled it; C. Lim, 2001) sexualised anxieties both within the homes and the wider urban landscape of Singapore.

Being able to take weekly off-days is crucial in light of one of the most troubling social issues that Singaporeans' treatment of foreign domestic workers raises, *viz*, that of "maid abuse". Domestic workers not allowed off-days cannot find respite or recuperate from long days of work; neither can they report abusive work conditions. While it is the extreme cases of abuse that hit the media headlines (where physical beatings, mental torture, emotional abuse and sexual crimes, if not death, are involved), abuse in the form of non- or delayed payment of wages, non-compliance of contracts (such as making the domestic worker work outside the employer's home or not providing sufficient food or rest), being made to undertake dangerous work (such as climbing tall ladders to undertake cleaning, or leaning out of a high-rise's window to hang a pole laden with a heavy load of laundry) seldom make the news until they come to light as a result of the domestic worker running away or managing to report her victimisation or, even more rarely, when the case is reported by a neighbour or a passer-by (see Huang and Yeoh, 2007, for details).

Despite amendments to the Penal Code in 1998[7] (in response to the number of maid abuse cases reaching a high of over 190) resulting in increased fines and jail terms, and with Singapore's courts taking "an uncompromising stance against errant employers" found guilty of exploiting and abusing their foreign domestic

---

[5]This figure compares favourably to the 13% that received a weekly rest day in 2011 (Goh, 2014).

[6]The photos described here were posted on the "Singapore Seen: Caught in the Act" webpages of Singapore Press Holding's *STOMP* website which encourages "citizen journalism".

[7]The amendments of the Penal Code in 1998 resulted in enhanced penalties for various forms of offences against foreign domestic workers, including causing grievous hurt, wrongful confinement and the outrage of modesty.

workers (ADF v PP [2009] SGCA 57), cases of "maid abuse" continue to be reported regularly in the press. Particularly appalling situations of abuse "tend to provoke intense soul-searching on the part of the nation" (Poon, 2003, p. 15). An example is the case of a domestic worker whose food intake had been limited so severely that she lost 20 kg in her first six months of work; when she asked for more food, her female employer punched, slapped and kicked her, leading to her jumping out of her employer's third story flat in desperation, and injuring herself (Ibrahim, 2014). In referring to this incident, an editorial commentary in *The Straits Times* highlighted that the Ministry of Manpower's (MOM) handbook for foreign domestic workers advises them "to 'tell (their) employer nicely' that they'd like more to eat. The recommended phrasing: 'Ma'am, I am still feeling hungry. Please give me more food so that I will have energy to do my work. Thank you'". The piece concluded wryly that — "It is rather sad that, to persuade 'ma'am' to sympathise with her hungry maid, food has to be translated as 'energy to do my work' rather than a basic human right". Similarly, in challenging Singaporeans to "stand up for domestic workers rights", local academic Teo You Yenn (in an opinion piece for *The Straits Times*, by Teb, 2014), felt the need to appeal to readers to do so "because our culture and values are at stake" and to consider "who . . . we want our children to be" rather than arguing on the basis of foreign domestic workers' basic human rights.

Reinforcing gendered notions of domestic work

To some extent, the fallback option of employing foreign domestic workers that Singapore — like many other well-off economies around the world — has taken to help ease the burden of domestic responsibilities, including childcare and eldercare, is linked to the availability of this flow of female labour from neighbouring countries. Feminists have long-argued that by employing another female to take over household and care duties in the home rather than expecting men to help take up the slack, middle-class women are merely entrenching patriarchal notions that such work is primarily women's responsibility. In other words, this gendered mode of labour substitution in the home protects men from having to step up to share in the burdens of the maintenance of the home, especially in the physical aspects of housework, child-rearing and eldercare.

In Singapore, despite the breakthroughs that women have made in the workforce and the rise of dual income households — women's overall LFPR in 2013 was 58.1% and even higher (ranging from 67%–88%) for those in the 25–55 age range (MOM, 2013) — the home is still seen as the primary province of women, regardless of whether they are female family members or foreign domestic workers. Notably, the Singapore state does allow the selective entry of male foreign domestic workers "if households have strong reasons" for employing them, such as if there are elderly men in households who need care, particularly if they are semi- or non-ambulant, or if there are "strenuous tasks like looking after a large garden" (A. Tan, 2013a

& Abu Baker, 2014). However, societal expectations that the burden of housework and care work is best left to women, have recently been made even clearer by the low demand for such male foreign domestic workers in Singapore.

In response to Singapore's greying demographic and an apparent "strong demand for male helpers to take care of elderly men whom . . . more petite maids may have difficulty handling", a local employment agency announced at the start of 2013 that it was "ramping up recruitment to bring in about 60 male domestic workers from Myanmar in June . . . the first time an agency [was] bringing in male foreign domestic workers on a regular basis" (A. Tan, 2013a). These workers would have completed a 45-day training course in Yangon, the same course that women being trained for domestic work overseas would undertake (A. Tan, 2013b). Follow-up press reports suggested that the take-up rate for the male domestic workers was slow: some employers had given up the idea either because the approval for male foreign domestic workers was done by MOM on a case-by-case basis (taking up to three months as opposed to a few days for females), or because female family members felt uncomfortable with the idea of a live-in male worker, or because male foreign domestic workers were disinclined to do housework (despite their training), with some requesting for a change of employer when asked to do so (Abu Baker, 2014).

Part of the reluctance to employ men as domestic workers relates to our current understandings of domestic and care work as essentially feminised, especially when undertaken in the unpaid setting of the family home. In particular, care work is idealised as feminised work because women, whether family members or foreign domestic workers employed to serve as low-paid, surrogate caregivers, supposedly possess the desired attributes of face, touch and voice that contribute to their social construction as the "naturally" more empathetic and nurturing gender (Huang *et al.*, 2012, p. 208). This view of care work limits how we understand what men do as constituting care and also explains men's resistance to, and sometimes complete abdication of, parenting and eldercare responsibilities involving physical care, thereby leaving the conventional gendered division of labour intact (Yeoh & Huang, 2014, p. 260). Further, the highly gendered nature of state policy in allowing women to enter Singapore as domestic workers — except on an exceptional basis when the physical strength of a male carer is needed — is complicit in reproducing the notion of domestic and care work as women's work. Indeed, allowing women to be employed as domestic workers as a default, while equally trained men are assessed on a case-by-case basis, simply reinforces these gendered notions.

Unfortunately, the association of the work as feminised — and often deemed as work that should come quite "naturally" to women — follows care and other domestic work into the market, resulting in its undervaluation when commoditised. Hence foreign domestic workers — indeed all domestic workers — receive very low wages for the hard work they do. The work is repetitive, mundane and often described as "3D" (dirty, dangerous and difficult/demeaning); most Singapore employers freely acknowledge that it is not work they would undertake for the pay or under the conditions that the foreign domestic do. Further, while the state has provided guidelines for the working conditions that those employing foreign domestic workers should follow, it does not specify a salary rate (preferring to leave it to market forces) or cover the employment of these women under the Employment Act (unlike those of other foreign workers who come in under the work permit scheme) because it is work done in the private sphere of the home. Nor does the state distinguish between "skilled" and "unskilled" domestic workers, unlike those of other foreign workers in other sectors of the economy, by a lowering of the levy. Sternberg (2014, n.p.) has argued that "[w]hy this job is unseen or remains unseen and unregulated is in many ways attributed to the capitalist logic: something that does not generate value or facilitate its exchange is devalued or rendered socially invisible. It is difficult to quantify, measure, and assign a value to the tasks performed by the domestic workers in capitalist terms"; hence "[d]omestic work is not recognized as employment in the traditional sense; it is performed in someone's home, not in a conventional workplace".

Bringing change to the civil activism landscape

Despite being employed in the country since 1978, Singapore's modern-day foreign domestic workers and their issues were, until the recent decade, largely ignored and excluded from the main focus of civil society developments. Their marginal position in society and their location of work within employers' homes, often without an off-day, rendered the majority of them and their issues nearly invisible to Singapore society. Ironically, it took a case of "maid abuse" of unprecedented proportions — that of 19-year-old Indonesian, Muawanatul Chanasah, who was beaten and starved for a period of nine months leaving her body with more than 200 bruises and weighing only 36 kg at her death (Ho & Chong, 2002) — to catalyse Singaporeans into action. Indeed, foreign domestic workers may be said to have been a trigger for broader changes within the landscape of the women's movement in Singapore, beginning with the "emergence of The Working Committee 2 (TWC2), an ad hoc civil society group focused specifically on the rights and welfare of foreign domestic workers in Singapore" that was formed in 2003 in direct response to "the shock and outrage" at the treatment Muawanatul had received at the hands of her male employer *and* to the "bystander silence" of the other members of his household (his wife and sister) as well as the callousness and apathy of the neighbours, particularly one man who claimed that despite suspecting Muawanatul was being abused, it was not his business to report it (Yeoh & Annadhurai, 2008, p. 555). Thus, as Yeoh and Annadhurai assert, "Concerns about 'maid abuse' and the working conditions to which these women are subjected . . . have in recent years galvanized incipient civil society action and the formation of non-governmental organizations offering services as well as taking up advocacy positions to promote the rights of transnational domestic workers (2008, pp. 550–1)... From the marginal position and near-invisibility of just a few years ago, transnational domestic worker issues have gained much more prominence and the current civil society landscape pertaining to these workers have become more variegated (2008, p. 555)". Today, there are diverse service-oriented groups[8] but limited advocacy organisations associated with foreign domestic worker issues.

Prior to the formation of TWC2 (first as The Working Committee 2, but later evolving into Transient Workers Count Too), civil society activism around foreign workers' issues more generally, and foreign domestic issues more specifically, was muted and issues around foreign domestic workers' generally neglected in the agenda of local civil society groups. Indeed, up to the year 2000, "activism" relating to foreign domestic worker was mainly linked to religious organisations (initially focused around Christian and Catholic churches and groups catering predominantly to Filipino domestic workers and later, mosques catering to Indonesian workers when their numbers started to grow) providing social and spiritual support as well as "ambulance" services; these groups were not formally involved in the advocacy of workers' rights. Also, until recently, women's groups such as the Association of Women for Action and Research (AWARE)[9] and Singapore Council of Women (SCW) focused on local women's issues, giving low priority to migrant women (Lyons, 2007; Yeoh & Annadhurai, 2008). Currently, other than TWC2 which takes a clear advocacy stance and the Humanitarian Organisation for Migration Economics (HOME) which has some advocacy functions, most of the other civil society groups' focus are service-oriented and focus on creating spaces and opportunities for foreign domestic workers to socialise as well as to learn English and acquire new skills useful for their current employment (e.g., cooking, sewing, eldercare) or in preparation for their return and reintegration home (e.g., bookkeeping, computing, entrepreneurship).

How effective have these civil society groups been in raising public awareness and filling the vacuum in areas where the state has left unattended, or not done enough, for foreign domestic workers? In Yeoh and Annadhurai's (2008) assessment, the impact of service-oriented groups has been limited to the provision of support services for domestic workers (ranging from the courses they organise for workers to take on their off-days, to the relaying of information on problematic cases to the authorities and respective embassies, and providing spiritual counselling when

---

[8]Examples of such service-oriented groups include the An-Nisa Activity Group in the Masjid Sultan, Aidha, Archdiocesan Commission for the Pastoral Care of Migrants and Itinerant People, FDW Association for Skills Training, Filipino Ongoing Development Program, Filipino Overseas Workers in Singapore, Holy Family Filipino Community, Mujahidah Centre of Learning, Novena Filipino Community, and a range of fellowship groups in Protestant and Catholic churches located across Singapore (Cheah, 2009; Lyons, 2005; MOM, n.d.; Yeoh & Annadhurai, 2008).

[9]Notably, all the core founding members of TWC2 were members of AWARE (Yeoh & Annadhurai, 2008).

workers face problems). In terms of advocacy, TWC2 and HOME have been the two most active and prominent groups promoting the rights and welfare of foreign domestic workers in Singapore, as well as giving the workers and their issues more visibility and voice. While the problem of "maid abuse" still remains, we would agree with observers (e.g., Lyons, 2005; Gee & Ho, 2006) that these advocacy groups can be credited for some of the changes in legislation (e.g., increasing the minimum age for foreign domestic workers, the implementation of mandatory off-days) and other measures (e.g., the setting up of a Foreign Manpower Management Division to look after the welfare of foreign workers, mandatory orientation courses for first-time employers) that the state has put in place to increase the protection of foreign domestic workers in Singapore.

The impact and effectiveness of civil society, however, has been limited by their need to work within the state's OB ("out of bounds") markers (Yeoh & Annadhurai, 2008) and having little "fire power" to effect rapid change. In addition, many Singaporeans continue to have a general apathy and even insensitivity to the circumstances of foreign domestic workers. For example, MOM issued a circular in September 2003 to employment agencies instructing them not to put foreign domestic workers on display along shop fronts, or to display photos of the women describing their qualities (on the basis that it "created international disrepute for Singapore, as we are perceived not to have accorded the foreign domestic workers basic human dignity")[10] (Gee & Ho, 2006, p. 138). Any effect this had did not last long as MOM was again "prompted . . . to express its concern over 'incidents of insensitive advertising and inappropriate display'" ("Accord Maids Dignity", *The Straits Times*, 2014) in mid-July 2014 by a foreign news agency report highlighting that having women displayed in shop windows under banners declaring "Fast delivery" and "$1 maids" that promised fast and cheap agency services, likened the women to commodities. While most agencies removed such insensitive ads within a couple of months after MOM requested all agencies "to ensure all ads accord maids 'basic respect and human dignity'" (Boh, 2014), one wonders how long the effects of this latest advisory will last.

As one journalist argued, "As a developed nation on the cusp of turning half a century next year, Singapore can, and should, do better in how it treats foreign domestic workers" (A. Tan, 2014). Indeed, why do Singaporeans require a state advisory to be issued before they do the right thing? And why was the state's follow-up advisory issued only *after* an international news report on the issue? How many more years of development will it take before "Singaporeans accord sufficient dignity and respect to domestic workers who contribute significantly to help keep households humming and care for the young, elderly and those with disability" ("Accord

---

[10]Note the primary emphasis on Singapore's reputation rather than the more basic issue of the workers' dignity.

Maids Dignity", *The Straits Times*, 2014)? These are questions that should give Singaporeans some pause for reflection as the society moves into its next 50 years.

Moving forward

> With an expected increase in the number of resident households with young and/or elderly, and an increase in number of households where both spouses are working, we anticipate that demand for FDWs will rise from 198,000 in 2011 to about 300,000 FDWs by 2030. However, the supply of FDWs could be constrained as demand from other countries also grows. The job opportunities in the major FDW source countries could also improve, or these countries could impose new requirements and restrictions on those who work in this sector (National Population and Talent Division [NPTD], Prime Minister's Office, 2012).

Foreign domestic workers comprise a pool of labour that plays a major role in sustaining the social reproduction of the everyday lives of Singapore families and, in so doing, indirectly contribute to the productive sphere by enabling Singapore residents to engage in paid work and build careers. Singaporeans' demand for foreign domestic workers will continue to grow to meet the challenges of an ageing population and other caregiving needs in Singapore households. While this deepening care deficit crisis will continue to entrench Singapore's reliance on the foreign domestic worker for social reproductive work, there is no guarantee that it will continue to enjoy the availability of foreign women willing and able to work here as domestic workers, especially if Singapore is seen as a society where, despite the "severe punitive measures meted out over the years through the prosecution of employers by the MOM and by public shaming in the media, there are still many cases of FDW abuse and unfair work practices including wage deductions and withholding wages" (Lien Foundation for Social Innovation, 2011, p. 61).

Singapore has in recent years made positive strides in dealing with its "foreign maid anxieties", and the state — with inputs from a growing movement in civil society — has brought about some significant and laudable improvements in the regulatory regime governing the conditions of foreign domestic workers employment. Indeed, Singapore seems to have moved on from its earlier preoccupation with the unintended consequences of employing foreign domestic workers on Singapore's social fabric to a concern with the treatment of foreign domestic workers themselves. There is, however, space for more change. Certainly, more progressive labour legislation that will help safeguard the rights and welfare of foreign domestic workers *as employees* should be put in place, such as establishing a minimum wage, mandating medical coverage and specifying maximum working hours. It is also important for the state to begin to highlight the proper treatment of foreign domestic workers as a basic human right, rather than with reference to how "maid abuse" hurts Singapore's international image and reputation.

At the most fundamental level, Singaporeans need to recognise the value of all forms of work and cultivate a due regard for the dignity of the people who perform that labour. This will ensure that there is no discrimination based on the gendered nature of care and domestic work, where it is performed, or that it is work fit only for migrants. As a first step to eschewing such patriarchal notions, women's contribution to the household — whether in the form of care labour as a family member, or when it is provided as a paid service, whether by migrant workers or locals — needs to be recognised, valued and properly valorised in monetary terms. At the same time, we must move away from our asymmetric reliance on women's labour to shore up the home front and expect men to step up to contribute to its social reproduction. As we have argued elsewhere (Yeoh & Huang, 2014, pp. 260–261), "men's roles in nurturance and the provision of care to their families also need to be acknowledged and affirmed as a significant element of masculine identities and a crucial resource". This will not only open up possibilities for more flexible gender roles and relations but also and provide the necessary support in families as Singapore moves into its next 50 years with an ageing structure, without increasing the reliance on foreign domestic workers.

In addition, drawing the attention of policy-makers and civil society groups to the gender connotations and consequences of relying on foreign domestic workers as Singapore's solution to the care crisis in the home is a necessary part of working towards more emancipatory notions and practices of civic inclusiveness. However, according dignity to and providing greater inclusionary rights for foreign (domestic) workers, even as transients, should be reflected not only in state legislation and civil society's efforts, but also as part and parcel of the ordinary Singaporean's life as Singapore matures as a society. Even as we finalise this paper, an article in *The Straits Times* (Choon, 2014) reports that "more maids say they do not get enough to eat".

A more inclusive and gracious Singapore must move towards more liberal ideals of human rights and be more embracing of diversity. It would do well to value not only those who are successful "in terms of academic or material attainments" but also, as the state set out as part of its aspirations for Singapore in the 21st century, be a society that continues to "widen our definition of success to go beyond the academic and the economic" to include "enduring traits such as character, courage, commitment, compassion and creativity" (Government of Singapore, 1999, pp. 18–19, 23). One measure of how successfully Singapore, in its next 50 years, meets the challenge posed in the *Singapore 21 Report* to "embrace a spirit of continual self-improvement, learning and daring to make the difference — to ourselves, our community and our country" (Government of Singapore, 1999, p. 23) will be how it values and treats the foreign domestic workers in its midst.

References

Abu Baker, Jalelah (2014, September 14). Plan for Male Helpers Hits Snag. *The Sunday Times*, p. 2.

Accord Maids Dignity All Workers Deserve (2014, July 19). *The Straits Times*, p. A40 (Editorial Commentary).

Aguilar, F. V., Jr. (1999). The Triumph of Instrumental Citizenship? Migrations, Identities, and the Nation-state in Southeast Asia. *Asian Studies Review*, 23(3), 307–336.

Answers to Questions on Filipino Maids Ban (1988, February 24). *The Straits Times*, p. 12.

Arshad, Arlina & Tan, Theresa (2000, October 13). They've Got It Maid. *The Straits Times*, p. 53.

Boh, Samantha (2014, September 11). Maid Agencies Clean up Their Act. *The Straits Times*, p. B1.

Chan, A., Østbye, T., Malhotra, R. & Hu, A. J. (2012, May). *The Survey on Informal Caregiving: Summary Report*. Singapore: Ministry of Community, Youth and Sports.

Cheah, W. L. (2009). Migrant Workers as Citizens within the ASEAN Landscape: International Law and the Singapore Experiment. *Chinese Journal of International Law*, 8(1), 205–231.

Chen, A. (2014). The Making of Ilo Ilo (Interview in Mandarin). Bonus feature in *Ilo Ilo* (DVD), distributed by Scorpio East Entertainment.

Cheng, S. H. (1984). *Changing Labour Force of Singapore*. Council for Asia Manpower Studies Discussion Paper Series no. 84–04. Philippines: University of Philippines.

Choon, Chang May (2014, October 25). Food for Thought: Maids' Sustenance. *The Straits Times*, p. B9.

Choong, William (2011, April 1). Army of Maids behind Our Boys in Green? *The Straits Times*, p. A2.

Foreign Maids Policy Relatively More Liberal (1990, January 16). *The Business Times*, p. 2.

"Foreign Worker Levies to Go up by $50 Next Year (1989, December 20). *The Business Times*, p. 1.

Four-year Stay for Maids Can Be Extended (1983, February 11). *Singapore Monitor*, p. 6.

Gaw, K. (1988). *Superior Servants: The Legendary Cantonese Amahs of the Far East*. Oxford: Oxford University Press.

Gee, J. & Ho, E. (2006). *Dignity Overdue*. Singapore: Select Publishing.

Goh, C. L. (2014, April 15). The Debate in 2 Minutes. *The Straits Times*, p. B6.

Government of Singapore (1999). *Singapore 21 Report: Together, We Make the Difference*. Singapore: Prime Minister's Office, Government of Singapore.

Hogan, J. (2009). *Gender, Race and National Identity: Nations of Flesh and Blood*. New York: Routledge.

Ho, Karen & Chong, Elena (2002, July 20). Starved, Battered, Dead ... 9 Months of Maid Abuse Went Unnoticed. *The Straits Times*, p. H1.

Huang, S. & Yeoh, B. S. A. (2007). Emotional Labour and Transnational Domestic Work: The Moving Geographies of 'Maid Abuse' in Singapore. *Mobilities*, 2(2), 195–217.

Huang, S., Yeoh, B. S. A. & Toyota, M. (2012). Caring for the Elderly: The Embodied Labour of Migrant Care Workers in Singapore. *Global Networks*, 12(2), 195–215.

Ibrahim, Zuraidah (2014, April 20). What's Your Maid Eating? *The Straits Times*, p. 35.

Iyer, A., Devasahayam, T. W. & Yeoh, B. S. A. (2004). A Clean Bill of Health? Filipinas as Domestic Workers in Singapore. *Asian and Pacific Migration Journal*, 13(1), 11–38.

Khoo, C. K. (1981). *Census of Population 1980*. Singapore: Department of Statistics.

Kwek, Geneieve (1988, February 2). Govt Not in Favour of Minimum Wage. *The Straits Times*, p. 1.

Lee, Geok Boi (1985, March 24). Foreign Aide and Influence. *The Straits Times*, p. 1.

Lien Foundation for Social Innovation (2011). *Unmet Social Needs in Singapore: Singapore's Social Structures and Policies, and Their Impact on Six Vulnerable Communities*. Singapore: Lien Centre for Social Innovation.

Lim, Cindy (2001, January 9). She Makes Your Bed. Gie Me an Ugly Maid. *The Straits Times*, pp. L1 & L4.

Lim, Ivan (1987, February 7). Act Doesn't Cover Maids but 'They Are Doing Well". *The Straits Times*, p. 13.

Lim, Joyce (2003, December 28). The Maid Dis(A)ttraction. She Shares Your home. Could She Also Snare Your Hubby? *The New Paper*, pp. 12–13.

Lyons, L. (2005). Transient Workers Count Too? The Intersection of Citizenship and Gender in Singapore's Civil Society. *Sojourn: Journal of Social Issues in Southeast Asia*, 20(2), 208–248.

Lyons, L. (2007). Dignity Overdue: Women's Rights Activism in Support of Foreign Domestic Workers in Singapore. *Women's Studies Quarterly*, 35(3/4), 106–122.

Maid Kills Singaporean Widow after Being Called Stupid (2012, February 16). *Yahoo News*. Retrieved 16 February 2015, from https://sg.news.yahoo.com/maid-kills-singaporean-widow-being-called-stupid-053853598.html.

Maids Can Stay Longer If Reasons Are 'Exceptional' (1986, October 13). *The Straits Times*, p. 14.

Malaysian S'pore Girls 'Fold Blankets Better' (1997, August 25). *The Straits Times*, p. 28.

Mehta, K. & Thang, L. L. (2008). Visible and Blurred Boundaries in Familial Care: The Dynamics of Multigenerational Care in Singapore. In A. Martin-Matthews & J. E. Phillips (eds.), *Aging and Caring at the Intersection of Work and Home Life: Blurring the Boundaries* (pp. 43–64). New York and London: Lawrence Erlbaum Associates.

Ministry of Manpower (MOM) website, www.mom.gov.sg.

Ministry of Manpower (MOM) (n.d.). *Your Guide to Employing a Foreign Domestic Worker*. *Singapore*: Foreign Manpower Management Division, MOM.

Ministry of Manpower (MOM) (2011). *Truth about Security Bonds*. Press Replies. Retrieved 15 February 2015, from www.mom.gov.sg/newsroom/Pages/PressReplies Detail.aspx?listid=187.

Ministry of Manpower (MOM) (2013). *Labour Force in Singapore, 2013*. Singapore: Manpower Research and Statistic Department, MOM.

Monksfield, Gim Leng (2000, July 21). We're Acting Like British colonials. *The Straits Times*, p. 68.

Monksfield, Gim Leng (2000, October 26). I Spoke up to End Discrimination. *The Straits Times*, p. 65.

Myanmar Maid Charged with Murder of 85-Year-Old Woman in Bukit Timah Condo (2014, March 5). *STOMP*. Retrieved 16 February 2015, from http://singaporeseen. stomp.com.sg/singaporeseen/this-urban-jungle/murder-of-87-year-old-woman-in-bukit-timah-condo-woman-24-arrested.

National Population and Talent Division (NPTD) (2012). Occasional Paper on *Projection of Foreign Manpower Demand for Healthcare Sector, Construction Workers and Foreign Domestic Workers*. Singapore: NPTD, Prime Minister's Office.

Ochiai, E. (2010). Reconstruction of Intimate and Public Spheres in Asian Modernity: Familialism and Beyond. *Journal of Intimate and Public Spheres*, Pilot Issue, 2–22.

Paul, Jacinta (2000, July 22). Holding on to Colonial Attitudes. *The Straits Times*, p. 84.

Poon, A. (2003). Maid Visible: Foreign Domestic Workers and the Dilemma of Development in Singapore. *Crossroads: An Interdisciplinary Journal of Southeast Asian Studies*, 17(1), 1–28.

Rethinking a Man-Maid Conundrum (2011, April 4). *The Straits Times*, p. A20.

Row as Maid Seen Carrying Singapore Soldier's Pack (2011, March 30). *Yahoo News*. Retrieved 19 January 2015, from https://sg.news.yahoo.com/row-maid-seen-carrying-singapore-soldiers-pack-20110330-010402-008.html.

Said, E. (1978). *Orientalism*. New York: Pantheon.

Seow, Joanna (2014, April 16). Some Bosses 'Reluctant' to Give Maids Weekly Day off. *The Straits Times*, p. B6.

Shanmugam, K. (2014, May 17). The Values of Our Children. Retrieved October 2014, from https://www.facebook.com/k.shanmugam.page/photos/a.699705796742620.1073742 052.203314719715066/699705813409285/.

'Social Costs' of More Maids Explained (2000, September 15). *The Straits Times*, p. 71.

Sternberg, C. (2014). Who's Got Your Back? Domestic Workers in Chicago. AAG Newsletter, October. *Association of American Geographers*. Retrieved October 2014, from http://news.aag.org/2014/domestic-workers-in-chicago.

STOMP — A Singapore Press Holdings Website. Retrieved September 2014, http:// singaporeseen.stomp.com.sg/singaporeseen/this-urban-jungle.

Tan, Amelia (2014, July 14). Recruitment of Maids Could Do with Extra Spit and Polish. *The Straits Times*, p. A20.

Tan, Amelia (2013a, January 28). Maid Agency Hiring Male Caregivers. *The Straits Times*, p. A2.

Tan, Amelia (2013b, May 12). First Male Helper from Myanmar Starts Work. *The Sunday Times*, p. 19.

Tan, Sebastian (2000, July 25). Treat Foreign Maids with Dignity. *The Straits Times*, p. 49.

Tan, T. T. W. & Devasahayam, T. W. (1987). Opposition and Interdependence: The Dialectics of Maid and Employer Relationships in Singapore. *Philippine Sociological Review*, 35(3/4), 34–41.

Tang, K. R. (1988, February 14). Maid Values, Good or Bad? *The Straits Times*, p. 2.

Teo, You Yenn (2014, March 18). What Are You Teaching Child by the Way You Treat Maid. *The Straits Times*, p. A22.

The Maid Dis(A)ttraction. She Shares Your Home. Could She Also Snare Your Hubby? (2003, December 28). *The New Paper.*

Unattended Foreign Maid Will Be Handed to Security (2009, February 8). *Migrant Workers Singapore.* Retrieved 19 January 2015, from http://migrantworkerssingapore. blogspot.sg/2009/02/unattended-foreign-maid-will-be-handed.html.

UNIFEM Singapore, HOME & TWC2 (2011). *Made to Work: Attitudes towards Granting Regular Days Off to Migrant Workers in Singapore.* Singapore: The Singapore National Committee for the United Nations Development Fund for Women, Humanitarian Organisation for Migration Economics, and Transient Workers Count Too.

van der Veer, P. (1995). Introduction: The Diasporic Imagination. In P. van der Veer (ed.), *Nation and Migration: The Politics of Space in the South Asian Diaspora* (pp. 1–16). Philadelphia: University of Pennsylvania Press.

Vasoo, Sharon (1998, March 30). Sunday Blues for Loiterers. *The Straits Times*, p. 1.

When It Comes Down to Litter, Do You Have a 'Maid Mentality'? (1997, June 10). *The Straits Times*, p. 24.

Wong, Kwai Chow (1997, August 25). Able S'poreans Helping Others Instead of Returning Home. *The Straits Times*, p. 28.

Yeoh, B. S. A. & Annadhurai, K. (2008). Civil Society Action and the Creation of 'Transformative' Spaces for Migrant Domestic Workers in Singapore. *Women's Studies: An Interdisciplinary Journal*, 37(5), 548–569.

Yeoh, B. S. A. & Huang, S. (2014). Singapore's Changing Demography, the Eldercare Predicament and Transnational 'Care' Migration. *TRaNS: Trans — Regional and — National Studies of Southeast Asian*, 2(2), 247–269.

Chapter 11

Social Issues in Developing a Community in Singapore

Mohamad Maliki Bin Osman

Five decades ago, it would have been hard to imagine that Singapore — then a fledging nation troubled by high unemployment, urban slums, poor infrastructure, lack of proper sanitation, and an unskilled labour force — would make the leap from a developing nation into a thriving First World global city in the space of just five decades. For many of us born during that period, we literally saw the city transform before our very eyes. Despite our small land mass and the seemingly insurmountable challenges we faced in the 1960s housing about 2.5 million people, Singapore is now one of the few highly liveable cities that have combined highly dense urban structures with high standards of living, providing a good quality of life for a population of 5.5 million.

Similarly, it would have been hard five decades ago to imagine today's Singapore in terms of social and community development. In the 1960s, we were confronted with fundamental problems — dealing with ethnic tensions and racial riots, curbing population growth, and meeting basic health, education, housing and social needs. Many older Singaporeans will relate stories about how community life existed in the past, peppered with common phrases like *"gotong royong"* (mutual help) and *"kampong spirit"* (village spirit). Then, the community existed amidst common issues of survival in an environment of great economic uncertainty. Natural village heads (often the village elders) emerged and community issues were resolved with these village elders' strong leadership. While the community was often defined geographically (with each village boundaries marked out), it was not uncommon for the villages to be ethnically homogeneous.

Today, the community is more geographically defined although ethnically diverse. With 85% of Singaporeans living in HDB housing estates, it is natural that community work in Singapore takes on a strong locality development model focus.

The establishment of the People's Association (PA) was directed at ensuring communities remain cohesive, given the socio-economic and ethnic diversity that exist in each of them. Grassroots organisations (GROs) were formed in each geographical community to organise community activities that enable the different ethnic communities to connect and bond, and at the same time deepen trust and celebrate diversity. Over the years, these activities evolved into mass activities, reflecting mobilisation capabilities of these GROs. However, racial and religious harmony alone does not ensure strong communities, although it may ensure mutual respect and tolerance. It is the same for mass activities.

There is much more to community development than organising mass activities for people of different ethnic groups to intermingle. This has become evident with the changing profiles and aspirations of the people. Social issues have become more complex and increasingly require community engagement and intervention, often beyond what the government alone can do. Addressing the felt needs of residents requires understanding the local manifestations of social issues in specific community contexts. Engendering deeper trust in the community requires understanding how the community can be strengthened to develop mutual self-help and resilience. To help achieve such understanding, this chapter will examine some key issues involved in the efforts to develop a community and address social issues.

Emerging social issues

Singapore has made significant achievements over the last 50 years in terms of responding to various social issues that emerged. The problems associated with poor living conditions were solved when people were relocated to apartments with modern facilities including clean water and electricity. People received good quality education and skills training that enabled them to be gainfully employed. The population explosion problem was addressed through unpopular but effective family planning policies. Ethnic tension was reduced and social harmony was enhanced through various interethnic community programmes.

Given the obvious nature of the fundamental issues that confronted the country in the early years of independence, the criteria for success or failure were clear. Today, it is less clear how to define success and measure progress in tackling social issues and developing communities. What is our situation today? What are the issues that face us now, after 50 years of development? Moving forward, what are the emerging social issues that require attention?

Presently, Singapore is undergoing a transition phase where the economy is being transformed to achieve quality growth, create better jobs, and ensure citizens remain economically competitive. The economic transformation is guided by the societal goals of creating opportunities for all Singaporeans and building a fair and inclusive society. Despite its developmental success, Singapore has not achieved the productivity and income levels of an advanced economy. While Singapore's productivity level is higher than that of Hong Kong, our productivity level is about 70% of today's global productivity leaders — the US, Japan, Switzerland and Sweden. At the same time, the Singapore society is increasingly facing the pressures of rising income inequality, increasing aspirations of the young, social tensions as diverse populations congregate, and an ageing population and shrinking workforce due to falling birth rates and higher life expectancies.

Recognising these challenges, the Singapore government has embarked on an economic restructuring and introduced policies and initiatives to achieve quality and inclusive growth. To create better jobs and raise incomes (and address issues of income inequality), greater emphasis have being placed on productivity and innovation through support schemes. For example, the Productivity and Innovation Credit Scheme aims to enhance companies' productivity levels by providing incentives to encourage companies to share productivity gains with their workers through higher wages. The government has also introduced schemes to develop industry capabilities and enhance workforce competencies such as investment in skills and training, tax incentives for innovation, and programmes to help businesses grow and internationalise. These initiatives would help businesses to move up the value chain. They should lead to the creation of better quality jobs to meet the growing aspirations of a higher-educated young generation. They would also enhance the employability of older workers through skills upgrading.

To build a fair and inclusive society, the government has introduced policies and programmes to promote social mobility, strengthen social safety nets, mitigate inequalities, keep quality healthcare affordable and strengthen community networks. For instance, programmes were introduced to create equal opportunities for every student including those from the very low-income groups to advance through education, and ensure affordable housing and public transport. The government also recently enhanced the Workfare Income Supplement (WIS) scheme to boost incomes and retirement savings of low-wage workers, including heavily subsidised skills and upgrading courses for these workers. The purpose of enhancing WIS was to ensure inclusive growth where all segments of the economy would benefit from the restructuring efforts. As an open and diverse society with different cultures and religions, it is important that Singapore continues strengthening social harmony and deepening the sense of belonging to the country. The prevailing racial and religious harmony cannot be taken for granted. Singapore's own experience following the September 11 terrorist attacks in the United States was a reminder that cracks can easily surface in a multicultural society and lead to ethnic tensions that threaten social cohesion. Singapore must continue to promote and maintain good relations among the ethnic and religious communities. There is a need to deepen Singaporeans' sense of belonging through domains such as arts, heritage and sports as well as community and youth engagement. There is also a need to enhance the efforts to encourage and help new citizens integrate into society and adapt to the Singapore way of life.

A significant challenge facing Singapore is the rapid pace of ageing. This is seen in the fast-declining number of working-age citizens for every citizen aged 65 years and above, from 8.4 in 2000 to 5.9 in 2010. It is estimated that by 2030, there will only be two working-age citizens for every citizen aged 65 years and above (National Population and Talent Division [NPTD], 2013). This trend, along with a falling birth rate, presents significant challenges in the way the city sustains itself and in meeting the needs of an ageing population. Keeping seniors active and ensuring strong social infrastructure within communities will be critical. In addition, the demand for healthcare services is rising with an ageing population and we face the challenge of a shrinking workforce and fewer Singaporeans available to serve in the healthcare sector. Thus, there is an increasing need to better understand and address the relationships linking health and social issues.

Given the rapidly ageing population due to declining birth rates and higher life expectancies, more attention needs to be paid to issues of retirement adequacy. With fewer younger people to depend on for financial support in old age, seniors will have to ensure that they have sufficient savings for their retirement. Poor retirement adequacy has significant impact on the society and community because more Singaporeans will be dependent on the state and fellow citizens to meet their retirement needs. While one of the major goals of the home ownership scheme is to help Singaporeans build a nest egg for their retirement, many may not be able to benefit from this nest egg if they had decided to monetise their assets prematurely. More needs to be done at the community level to develop financial literacy programmes to help Singaporeans make informed choices and plan for their future retirement needs.

As Singapore progresses to be one of the world's most sustainable and liveable cities, the process is more than providing modern physical infrastructures, ensuring economic development and promoting environmental conservation. It is people and communities that make cities come alive. There are critical social and community challenges that go beyond physical infrastructure development. These challenges relate to questions on how to build the soul of the city, the emotional resonance of the people with the physical, emotional and social spaces, and the ability to anticipate and respond to social issues faced by the people. Answers to these questions are likely to be found in building communities where mutual support and self-help provide social connectedness and a sense of belonging. Community building is even more crucial for Singapore in the next few decades given the increasing cultural diversity associated with the changing population demographics. There is a need to build and strengthen local communities to deepen the sense of emotional connection to make the everyday life meaningful and purposeful. At the most micro-levels, these local communities refer to the neighbourhoods. Finally, there is a need to ensure that Singaporeans feel, at both the individual and community levels, that their needs are understood and met. To effectively meet these community needs as felt by the people, a better understanding of the role of the community and the nature of various community development efforts is needed.

Conceptual issues in community development

The literature on community development makes the broad distinction between a community by locality (e.g., neighbourhoods, housing estates, towns) and a community by shared sentiments (e.g., ethnic- and/or faith-based communities) (Rothman, Ehrlich & Tropman, 2001). Singapore's housing and other social policies have resulted in a unique blend of communities by shared sentiments existing within the community by locality, to ensure coexistence of the former within the latter. Having ethnic and religious communities share the same geographical spaces would create opportunities to bridge these communities as larger geographical communities are being built in Singapore.

The PA's network of GROs is also structured along geographical lines, with the most micro being the HDB block. These GROs are tasked to build the community that they belong to and bridge the various ethnic, faith and other communities to ensure racial and religious harmony.

Over the years, we have seen GROs' operation, primarily through the organisation of community events that aim at bringing people together and bonding them. Levels of participation at these events are used as proxy indicators of the strength of the community. That is, people come to the event and they are assumed to be interacting and making more new friends and thereby bonding together and achieving social cohesion. However, are these valid proxy indicators? Does participation indicate social cohesion? Does minority participation indicate a greater level of bridging between ethnic communities within that geographical community? Does it strengthen the geographical community? Is the community cohesive enough such that social issues and problems within the community can be identified and addressed collectively by the residents and relevant stakeholders? Is the community able to respond to social issues that emerge at the community level? Is community problem solving an indicator of community cohesion and strength? Does it translate to stronger neighbourly relations with residents prepared to support one another in finding solutions to common community problems and social issues as well as in times of crisis? These are important practical questions of social cohesion and community bonding that underline the question on the validity of using participation at community events as a measure of community development.

A few years ago, when asked at a public dialogue session about the Singaporean's sense of civic consciousness, Prime Minister Lee Hsien Loong replied:

> One very important factor is whether or not we really have a community where people feel that they know one another, that there are friends... And that's what we have been trying to do with the grassroots in all our constituencies, with our RCs, our neighbourhood committees. The purpose is not just to do taiji and brisk walking, although that's good. The purpose really is to have neighbours who care for one another and look out for one another (Prime Minister Lee Hsien Loong, 27 March 2010, at the public dialogue event *Prime Minister's Dialogue with REACH Contributors* held at Grassroots Club, Singapore).

PM Lee's reply essentially described the process of building and strengthening communities such that mutual self-help amongst residents can be enhanced. His reference to the neighbourhood recognises that the immediate geographical boundary is the best way to view communities in our effort to strengthen them. There is much truth in the Chinese saying "远亲不如近邻" (*yuan chin bu ru jin lin*), which means "the far relative cannot compare to the near neighbour", because neighbours, regardless of differences in ethnicity or other characteristics, are better able to provide support for one another and in a more timely manner than distant relatives given the proximity of neighbours. A network of strong and mutually supportive neighbourhoods will result in a stronger, more cohesive, and larger geographical community and in turn a stronger Singapore community. The critical concept for building such communities is social capital, which refers to a community's quality social interactions and relationships, strong sense of reciprocity norms, and mutual social trust (Coleman, 1998; Putnam, 1993, 1995).

Community development researchers have concluded that the smaller the size of the geographically defined community, the better the chance to build communities through building relationships (Mattessich & Monsey, 1997). Accordingly, researchers have proposed the concept of micro-communities.

In the context of Singapore where more than 80% of its residents live in public housing estates, the concept of micro-communities would refer to the smallest unit in a housing estate — the HDB block. An accumulation of blocks will form the next level of community (e.g., the RC zones' boundaries), which in turn accumulate to form the larger community (the divisional boundary).

The intensity of building relationships is strongest at the most micro-level (i.e., the block) as this is where the neighbourhood spirit can be first established. At each level of the micro-community, the process of building the community enhances as the systemic interaction of the micro-communities will result in a stronger larger community. This concept can also be applied to private housing estates where a micro-community refers to a street or two comprising about 100 households.

In addition to structural components such as size and composition, the process component of community has been a key focus in the literature on community development. The process that has been examined in most detail is known as community building.

Community building has been defined by Gardner (1993) as "the practice of building connections among residents, and establishing positive patterns of individual and community behaviour based on mutual responsibility and ownership". Building communities requires an organised effort at community organising. It is a process that includes "identification of local resources, the gathering of information about the community, the development and training of local leaders to prepare them to serve effectively as representatives of the community and as full partners in an initiative, and the strengthening of the network of the various interests both internal and external to the community" (Joseph & Ogletree, 1996).

Based on an extensive literature review, Mattessich and Monsey (1997) suggested a list of 28 factors that could influence the success of community building. They classified these factors into three broad categories — characteristics of the community (e.g., the community's awareness of an issue, small geographical area), characteristics of a community-building process (e.g., good system of communication, systematic gathering of information and analysis of community issues) and characteristics of the community organisers (e.g., an understanding of the community, relationship of trust).

What is the state of community building in Singapore? Who are our community workers and how much do they know about their community? Do they systematically gather information and analyse community issues and how do they respond to these issues? What would be the relationship between social issues at the national level and impact and management at the local community level? To address these questions, we need to relate micro-communities to an approach that focuses on both needs and assets in people and the community.

The micro-community and the needs- and assets-based approach

The community has much potential in providing ground-up support and direction to responses to social issues that emerge. Concerns over widening income inequality at the national level will manifest itself with communities facing issues of low-income families from vulnerable backgrounds, seeking to find stability and overcome day-to-day crisis. Issues of an ageing society may manifest itself in the community in several forms. One example is the problem of mobility faced by vulnerable elderly who are living alone or with an elderly partner with little or no social support. Another example is retirees looking for opportunities to find meaningful activities to remain socially active and connected. These and other social issues, which are manifested concretely at the community level, can be adequately addressed through effective community-building and development efforts. The following sections will describe and illustrate how this can be accomplished by developing micro-communities and adopting a needs- and assets-based approach.

Rising income inequality: Supporting the vulnerable

The vulnerable in the community may face challenges of structural unemployment and a host of other social problems such as addiction, anti-social behaviour, mental health issues and unstable housing arrangements. How does the community respond to a situation when it is confronted with members who face such dire circumstances that require substantial resources that may involve close supervision and personal guidance?

The community can play an important role in supporting such families in need. A good example is Project 4650. This is a community initiative involving many agencies and community partners to coordinate support for families residing in interim rental housing (IRH) in the eastern part of Singapore, as they work through or wait for their long-term housing ("Puttling the HEART", *The New Paper*, 2013). These are vulnerable families who came into the community "unannounced". When the IRH scheme in the area started, the community was overwhelmed. The families had many complex issues such as divorce, large families with young children, heads of households in prison, mental health problems, and addictions including drug abuse and problem gambling. The community came together and worked with government agencies, social workers, and volunteers to provide help with the objective of bringing stability to these families and assisting them to meet their multiple challenging needs. Social workers and agencies delivered life skills programmes such as workshops on parenting and financial budgeting, while the staff at the local community centre provided administrative and coordinating support.

Resident volunteers from the community, including young professionals, responded to the call to serve as befrienders and assist the young children of these families every night through the Homework Cafe programme ("Get Help with Homework", *The Straits Times*, 2013). Both the recipients (i.e., children from the vulnerable families) and the givers of help (i.e., befrienders) benefitted from the programme. One example is Mr Lim YQ, a 26-year-old medical researcher, who came every night to help. Mr Lim said that helping the children had not only helped him mitigate the negative effects of his work stress but also provided him motivation for his job.

In addition to financial assistance, the community volunteers organised a weekly collection of bakery products from a nearby bakery to be redistributed to these families. The assistance reduced the financial strain on these families. The care and concern shown by the community volunteers also provided important social support to these families.

This project illustrates strong community engagement and support. The important learning point is the question on how the strong level of community support came about. How was the community able to reach out to the young professionals and community volunteers to agree to come every night to provide educational support to children of these families? Part of the answer to this question is the community leaders' sincerity, passion and willingness to reach out to and connect with their fellow residents. The community leaders also took ownership of the community issue before them and did not diffuse the responsibility to others.

More importantly, a large part of the answer lies in the adoption of the community-building principles. Illustrating Joseph and Ogletree's (1996) conclusions, the community recognised that it has resources from within (e.g., befrienders who are prepared to serve in the community) and it connected itself to various partners both in and outside the community to jointly develop intervention programmes based on information gathered about the vulnerable families. Community leaders also decided to undergo training to acquire the necessary social and interpersonal skills to connect with these challenging families. As articulated by

Gardner (1993), the community leaders together took ownership of the issues and bonded themselves closer as leaders. They shared the efficacy belief that they could build a stronger community by building stronger relationships amongst the residents through meeting the needs of the most vulnerable members of the community.

Micro-community: Grounded and ground-up response to emerging issues

It is important to build community through strengthening relationships amongst residents at the most micro-level. This is consistent with the literature review by Mattessich and Monsey (1997) which concluded that there is an inverse relationship between the size of the community and the quality of the outcome of community-building efforts.

In building the micro-community, access to relevant information about the community is crucial to be able to identify needs and resources to meet these needs. This was a critical feature in the success of Project 4650. The community leaders systematically developed "*The community directory*", which is a database of residents' profiles. The database includes occupations and skills which are important community resources, as well as resident needs as reflected by their profile and self-report of assistance that they might have sought from relevant agencies. Residents are asked if they would be willing to contribute their expertise to a neighbour if they were called upon to do so. Informed consent is always sought. Individuals with specific needs are matched with resources within the community, connecting fellow members of the community for mutual self-help. This in turn enhances informal community social support.

The following is an example of how useful the community directory was in enhancing informal social support in one community.

> Mdm J, 38, was suffering from chronic diabetes. She has several toes amputated and required regular dressing. She needed assistance to walk downstairs and to pay for transport (a taxi) to take her to the polyclinic nearby. However, as her husband was earning just under S$1000 and the family was in tremendous debt she was unable to afford medical care, nor the transport fees. A visit to the home enabled the MP to recognise that one of his residents was in tremendous need. The block directory showed that within her block, there was a taxi driver and a retired nurse. They were willing to come and provide her nursing aid and free transport to the hospital. The visits by her neighbours reduced the isolation that she felt. They maintain daily contact by phone or a home visit.

The development of the community directory is premised on the belief that the community is full of people resources — doctors, lawyers, teachers, police officers, nurses, taxi drivers and people from many other occupations — that can and should be harnessed to build stronger communities. Much more can be done if residents see themselves as part of a larger community, believe that they have a stake in it and can make a difference, and organise their efforts to leverage on these combined resources.

One key purpose of the community directory is to expand the informal networks among residents within their own blocks through the sharing of resources. This also enhances social connection between neighbours. In the sharing of resources, there is no exchange of financial payment. What it also exemplified is the use of natural resources that exist in the community. The identification of a resource enabled residents to act and this in turn allows for community improvement. It also builds on the level of trust amongst them and enhances reciprocity.

Beyond individual needs, community members with skills and resources can also be tapped on to provide services to fellow residents. Lawyers within the community have stepped forward to provide pro bono legal advice services to fellow residents. Geriatric medical specialists have been called upon to help design a comprehensive community silver blueprint programme to meet various needs of elderly in the community.

Analysis of community data is key to successful community-building processes. Aggregated data combining several micro-communities within a larger precinct will give community leaders a deeper insight to the profile and possible emerging needs within that community. For example, the analysis may show that there are many elderly in the community living alone or with their spouse only. Some may have children who come and visit them in the weekend while others do not. Some may be vulnerable and may need support.

The importance of community data analysis can be illustrated in an analysis that led to the collaboration between a local community and a healthcare institution. The healthcare institution analysed data of elderly patients visiting the hospital and found a worrying trend — the increasing number of elderly patients being readmitted to the hospital. Further analysis showed that these elderly were indeed living alone or only with their elderly spouse. They were vulnerable to falls or did not have the necessary support to ensure that they adhere to their prescribed medical treatment regime. There was a gap in the integration of social and health support services for these elderly. They are medically ready to be discharged but need follow-up supervision and social support to ensure compliance with their medical treatment plans. Without this medical compliance, they will continue to remain vulnerable and likely to be eventually readmitted to the hospital.

To address this emerging problem in the community, the local community leaders and the health institution developed the "Neighbours for Active Living" programme which aims to strengthen the social health services integration to meet the needs of such vulnerable elderly ("Elderly Patients", *The Straits Times*, 2014). The programme's key pillar is the provision of social support for these elderly from two teams — professional community health team and volunteer befrienders. To reach out to potential befrienders, the community directory is used. Housewives, semi-retirees and others who have indicated interest to be a community volunteer from the database were approached. Those keen were then sent for the appropriate training to ensure that they understand their roles and have the skills to befriend these vulnerable seniors.

In short, there is much potential in building micro-communities to address emerging social issues and solve problems through a needs- and assets-based approach. As the government continues to develop policies and national schemes to meet the needs of a rapidly ageing society, communities can and should play their important role to respond to local needs of the people.

Strengthening community through co-creating solutions and enhancing government–citizen engagement

While communities of the past function through mutual support and self-help, today's community is often faced with the challenge of managing the use of common spaces. When the use of common space is not properly managed, it can pose a threat to the social cohesion in the community. Some examples of issues related to the use of common space are dealing with limited parking spaces in private housing estates, the decision to place a community facility like an elderly nursing home or a childcare centre near to residents' homes, and the decision on upgrading the estate. The management of such issues has the potential to strengthen or weaken the community. Frequently, these local issues surface as a social problem that the government is expected to solve. Government agencies are often placed in the difficult situation of being both the regulator and the implementer of policies. Given the contentious nature of these issues, a decision either way made by the government agency is likely to be perceived as favouring one group over another. These perceptions could negate previous community engagement efforts.

Despite clear challenges, the problem of use of common spaces provides an opportunity to bond and strengthen the community by involving residents and government agencies to co-create solutions. For such solutions to occur, some government agencies would need to exercise more flexibility and be less risk-averse and more innovative.

Issues of use of common space often surface at regular public engagement sessions with members of the community conducted by politicians or government agencies. However, community engagement could and should go beyond these formal sessions. In the context of micro-communities, engagement can come in the form of regular dialogues, where residents in that neighbourhood or housing block would come together to discuss local issues with the community organisers and the relevant government agencies. Some examples of these issues include transport and vehicle parking problems, inconsiderate pet problems, and noise pollution. Such dialogue sessions are most useful when they go beyond identifying problems faced by the residents to result in residents forming task groups to find solutions. The following are some actual examples of useful dialogue and public engagement sessions that resulted in effective solutions.

Addressing noise nuisance:

During a block dialogue, residents complained about the noise disturbance created by youths sitting at a community hall stretching into the midnight hours. The options presented were to demolish the facility or to provide for a controlled use, such as providing fencing around the hall and to stop use after a certain time. As it was a community facility, a collective decision would have to be achieved. A task force made up of residents and grassroots leaders was formed and their task was to seek feedback and support from residents in the nearby vicinity on the proposed solution. The feedback and support is particularly important for the proposed controlled use option which requires residents to take ownership of opening and closing the fenced area on a daily basis. The task force proceeded to seek feedback from residents. They obtained overwhelming support from residents for the controlled use option. The task force then identified residents to take turns to be responsible for the opening and closing of the fenced facility. The proposed controlled use procedure was then implemented with assistance from the local town council. The result was a collective agreement on the use of the common space that minimised noise nuisance in the community. This is an example of community ownership of a local issue that involves a community-driven solution.

Addressing indiscriminate parking:

A community in a private estate was facing a problem of indiscriminate vehicle parking. A task force made up of residents, community leaders and government agency representatives was formed to address the problem. The task force members discussed the nature of issues involved in the indiscriminate parking and they also assessed the car population in the estate. They brainstormed possible solution options and then surveyed residents on the options identified. Based on the survey and subsequent discussions, the taskforce developed and shared with all residents in the community a "Code of Conduct", which detailed the dos and don'ts of parking along the public roads. The taskforce also discussed with the relevant government agency issues of implementing enforcements. The outcome was a significant improvement in the way residents parked their cars and a reduction in the frequency of the enforcement notices issued to residents which had earlier caused much unhappiness to the vehicle owners in the community.

The above are but two of many real life examples of effective community engagement efforts which suggest that community issues on the use of common spaces can and should be addressed at the most local level. This involves empowering residents to take ownership and responsibility. The engagement approach does imply a longer decision-making process as compared to the approach where government agencies alone make and execute the decisions. However, the longer process is worthwhile because of its high potential in strengthening communities in multiple ways such as providing residents an effective voice and identifying new community leaders.

Community leaders as first responders

Community leaders and volunteers are critical to the effectiveness of the community-building process. Thus, it is important to understand the values and motivations that guide and drive their community-building behaviours. Values and principles are foundational in community-building efforts. In addition to influencing community-building behaviours in implicit ways, values and principles provide the explicit justification for decisions and direction for behaviours. They may also serve as a source of motivation, passion and conviction for actions.

There are three dimensions of values and principles that are critical in community leadership and volunteerism. They are service orientation, relationship building and ownership of community processes.

Service orientation is one of the most basic attributes of effective community leaders. Service-oriented community leaders are motivated by a genuine desire to help residents resolve problems and improve their well-being. This genuine desire is important because they tend to facilitate efforts to establish rapport and social relationships with residents. Successes in these efforts contribute to the development of empathy and interpersonal understanding, which are often necessary for the accurate identification of critical issues and particularly residents' needs.

When community leaders possess a genuine service orientation, they are likely to exhibit service attitudes and behaviours that earn them trust and appreciation from the residents whom they serve.

The second dimension is the value placed on relationship building with residents. Relationship building is fundamental to building social capital in a community. As explained by Putnam (1993, 1995) and Coleman (1998), social capital refers to a community's quality social interactions and relationships, strong sense of reciprocity norms, and mutual social trust. Strong social capital enables a community to be cohesive and resilient.

It is important to recognise that relationship building is not about the community leader's resources or ability to organise mass events for residents to participate. Instead, relationship building requires the community leader to establish one-on-one relationhips with residents through intensive but personally meaningful interactions with them. Some examples of the type of significant activities that the community leader needs to engage in to form these quality social relationships are house visits, gathering feedback from residents, and conducting welfare and needs assessment. Understanding the essence of relationship building also implies recognising and treating mass activities and other community events as a means to foster quality interactions among residents and not as ends in themselves. It also means providing community events as sites of initial interactions that may subsequently develop into informal but strong social networks among residents where there is mutual self-help and social trust.

The third dimension is the principle of "ownership" with regard to community issues and solutions. Ownership refers to both the outcome and process of community building. Social capital is effectively built through relationship building facilitated by the service orientation of community leaders when all people in the community — community leaders, volunteers, residents — take ownership of the community issues including the problems and the solutions. Ownership involves a sense of duty or responsibility as a member of the community to help identify and address issues that affect the well-being of the community. It also involves a commitment to action and implementation when a solution option has been collectively adopted by the community.

The effectiveness of the Singapore model of community building in the local geographical locality is highly dependent on the attitudes and actions of the community leaders who are themselves residents in the community. The model is dependent on residents who are willing to avail themselves to serve the community. More importantly, the model is dependent on having a constant critical mass of community leaders and volunteers who place a strong value on the principles of service orientation, relationship building and ownership. The model requires community leaders and volunteers to understand their role as change agents and catalysts in community building and not merely event or activity organisers. They need to have interpersonal skills to reach out to fellow residents, capabilities in identifying community trends and issues, and awareness of and access to community resources to address issues. Given the personal sacrifices and resource-intensive nature of community-building efforts, they would need relevant physical, social and emotional support. Thus, a systematic volunteer management system is needed to ensure that community leaders and volunteers could do their work effectively and to provide ways to sustain their motivation through developing positive experiences. An effective volunteer management system should also develop volunteers who will inspire other residents to become volunteers.

Challenges and priorities

In conclusion, there are various challenges and priorities for Singapore to focus on when developing a community. At the community level, there is much potential for community leaders to develop strong communities through building strong micro-communities that would facilitate mutual self-help and effective collaboration with relevant government agencies to address community issues. There is a need for more community leaders to reflect on and better appreciate their roles and value systems as they continue to interact and connect with their fellow residents.

At the national level, there have been increasing public discussion on and more calls for help for vulnerable Singaporeans, reducing income inequality and increasing social mobility, ensuring retirement adequacy, honouring the pioneer generation, increasing opportunities for all Singaporeans, and solutions to other social issues. There are no easy solutions to these issues. As Singapore reviews and examines these issues, the country should be guided by the basic question of what people want as a society. Reflecting on and answering this question will help Singapore better prioritise the various policy and intervention efforts.

Without the support of Singaporeans and the community, the government alone will not be able to address these social issues adequately. The individual, the community and the government need to work together effectively to co-create solutions. For this to occur, we need to focus more attention on developing communities in Singapore.

References

Coleman, J. S. (1988). Social Capital in the Creation of Human Capital. *The American Journal of Sociology*, 94, 95–120.

Elderly Patients Get a Hand from Neighbours (2014, January 24). *The Straits Times.* Retrieved 16 February 2015, from http://yourhealth.asiaone.com/content/elderly-patients-get-hand-neighbours.

Gardner, J. (1993). *Community Building: An Overview Report and Case Profiles.* Washington, DC: Teamworks.

Get Help with Homework at This Cafe (2013, July 4). *The Straits Times.* Retrieved 16 February 2015, from http://news.asiaone.com/news/edvantage/get-help-homework-cafe.

Joseph, M. & Ogletree, R. (1996). Community Organising and Comprehensive Organising Initiatives. In R. Stone (ed.), *Core Issues in Comprehensive Community Building Initiatives.* Chicago, IL: Chapin Hall Centre for Children.

Mattessich, P. & Monsey, B. (1997). *Community Building: What Makes It Work. A Review of Factors Influencing Successful Community Building.* Saint Paul, MB: Fieldstone Alliance.

National Population and Talent Division (NPTD) (2013). A Sustainable Population for a Dynamic Singapore: Population White Paper. Prime Minister's Office, Government of Singapore.

Putnam, R. D. (1993). The Prosperous Community: Social Capital and Public Life. *The American Prospect*, (13), 35–42.

Putnam, R. D. (1995). Tuning in, Tuning out: The Strange Disappearance of Social Capital in America. *Political Science and Politics*, 28(4), 664–683.

Putting the HEART in the Heartland: Community Support Programme Helps Needy Families in Bedok South (2013, November 25). *The New Paper.*

Rothman, J., Ehrlich, J. & Tropman, J. (eds.) (2001). *Strategies of Community Intervention*, 6th ed. Itasca, IL: F. E. Peacock.

Chapter 12

Developing Civil Society in Singapore

Gillian Koh and Debbie Soon

This chapter examines social issues related to developing civil society in Singapore. We begin with a description of the current day scene. We then provide a brief summary of the history of civic activism so that the context of our description can be set out clearly. We conclude by discussing the emerging trends in civil society and possible future directions.

The current scene of civil society

"Avoid clash between Wear White and Pink Dot groups, says Mufti" (Nur Asyiqin, 2014a). The highest authority of Singapore's Muslim community advised mosque management boards and staff not to get caught in the crossfire between a pro-family Muslim group calling itself the Wear White community on one side, and the people organising the annual Pink Dot picnic in support of the Lesbian-Gay-Bisexual-Transgender (LGBT) community, or the "Freedom to Love" movement, on the other side. The next picnic was due to be held on 28 June 2014 and an Ustaz Noor Deros had urged Muslims who were due to have their first evening prayer that same evening to mark the start of their holy fasting month the next day, to take a stand against the liberal views that Pink Dot represented. His campaign also drew the support of Reverend Lawrence Khong of the Faith Community Baptist Church and the LoveSingapore network of Protestant Christian churches who also urged congregants to wear white that weekend to support the preservation of traditional notions of love and family. The Pink Dot picnic was itself first held in June 2009 to rally the public in protest against the rise of a Christian conservative movement against the gay lifestyle. The Pink Dot organisers asked Singaporeans who wished to support the "freedom to love" to wear pink and attend the picnic at Singapore's

Speakers' Corner — Singapore's only free speech and demonstration location. They reiterated in 2014 that it was "a secular event that embraces all Singaporeans" (Nur Asyiqin, 2014c).

The Muslim and Christian supporters of the Wear White campaign felt that LGBT activists had, over the past years, become "unashamedly public and loud in its agenda" and that they (i.e., supporters of the Wear White campaign) too should make a stand to say that the lifestyle went against the moral code of Islam and other faiths — the "sanctity of the family", they explained, needed to be defended (Philomin, 2014; Nur Asyiqin, 2014b). Of course, the specific case of the 2014 picnic was that it also coincided with the sacred time of the year for Muslims.

The Minister-in-Charge of Muslim Affairs, Dr Yaacob Ibrahim assured Muslims that the institution of the family was something that he would want them to support but, recognising the multicultural nature of Singapore society, he urged them to also see how it was important to let people have their choices and take the "gentle" approach to managing differences (Sim, 2014).

The situation described above is emblematic of many things related to the development of Singapore's civil society scene in 2014. In the rise of independent civic activism in Singapore, most of the ground-up energies tended to be directed towards the government; they aimed at changing public policy, administrative rules and laws. The circumstances that gave rise to the Pink Dot movement and the LGBT developments since 2009 on the other hand, have seen formal and informal groups mobilising in the online and real world to take on each other. This intra-civil society conflict is one of the major developments in the sector in recent times. It is also emblematic of the force of social media in mobilising opinion, activism and protest rallies through which otherwise reticent Singaporeans are encouraged to make small but significant gestures to support a social cause with important social and legal ramifications. While the inaugural Pink Dot picnic drew a crowd of 2,500 people, the 2014 event mobilised, at its peak, 26,000 people. As for the other side, Muslim and Christian groups rallied their supporters online, received publicity for their Wear White counter-movement and got people to participate in online petitions, pledging their support for the traditional notion of family.

While the confrontation between the Wear White and Pink Dot movements speaks of the intra-civil society conflict, the Bukit Brown and the Green Corridor movements (both occurred in 2011) were emblematic of the opposite — the collaboration within civil society around the conservation of nature and heritage and efforts to stave off the government's re-development of these areas. Bukit Brown cemetery comprising 100,000 graves, including those belonging to many of Singapore's Chinese pioneers, had been earmarked for removal since the government's Urban Redevelopment Authority's Concept Plan 1991 to make way for 15,000 flats to house 50,000 people in 40 to 50 years' time from publishing of the Plan.

To Singapore's nature and heritage enthusiasts, the cemetery was home to the country's social memories as well as living flora and fauna. With most of Singapore's historical cemeteries already redeveloped, the Singapore Heritage Society (SHS) and the Nature Society (Singapore) (NSS) had conducted audits of the area's unique value. The SHS published a record of the area — Spaces of the Dead: A Case from the Living. Informal groups organised regular walking tours of the area to heighten public interest in it. In September 2011, when the government announced the development of a new four-lane dual carriageway to ease traffic congestion and later that in doing so, some 5% of the graves would be exhumed, these groups were on their haunches, ready to persuade the government to consider alternatives to such a plan. In the course of doing that, groups such as SOS Bukit Brown and All Things Bukit Brown arose alongside the formal groups to protect "100%" of Bukit Brown (Lim, 2011; Chua & Li, 2012; Goh & Sim, 2012).

While the government engaged the formal and informal groups on the plans, it later explained that if the conservation groups thought there was the prospect that the engagement would result in a change in plans, they were misguided — the government's intention was simply to inform the groups of the plans. What did emerge of the engagement however was a tweak to reduce the number of graves that would be sacrificed and the introduction of an "eco-bridge" designed to minimise the impact on the flora and fauna when an existing road through the cemetery is to be expanded. The SHS and other activists nonetheless expressed great disappointment while the Minister-in-Charge explained that there had been a mismatch in expectations in the engagement process.

In similar fashion, the Green Corridor movement began with nature conservationists recording the value of the area covered by the Malayan Railway Track (or the "KTM railway land") that ran from the northern to the southern top of the island in an unbroken chain. The NSS published its proposal — The Green Corridor. A Proposal to Keep the Railway Lands as a Continous Green Corridor (2010) — with contributions from architects and the former President of the SHS as well. Recognising that the KTM railway land would be returned to the Singapore government, civic activists tried to steal a march on the handover to suggest proposals for sensitive redevelopment that would preserve the full corridor and become an icon of the country's biodiversity and social history.

When the government did eventually receive the KTM railway land back in July 2011, these activists were ready with their social media campaigns to generate interest and, ultimately, support for conserving the railway land by mobilising the public to visit these areas and associated historic buildings. The alternative would be to break up the strip with commercial redevelopment and housing.

The same government Minister involved in the Bukit Brown movement convened consultations with the NSS, and other proponents of conservation in July. The outcome was that not all of the corridor would be conserved and that the eventual plans would be found in the URA's Master Plan in 2013. There was also to be a public design competition for innovative ways to redevelop the tract (eventually concluded in March 2012). In 2013, the Minister said that the issue of conservation and development was "highly subjective and contextual". He added "[o]ne may strongly believe that a particular green area or an old building should be conserved. Someone else may not share the same attachment and ask 'what is the big deal?'". He said that the government would aim to develop and conserve to achieve a win-win arrangement but that was not always possible (Sreedharan, 2013). Since then, the URA's Land Use Plan 2013 has been released. It refers to the Rail Corridor as providing inviting routes for joggers and cyclists for access to recreational and heritage sites (URA, 2013).

From this second set of movements on conservation, we also note the use of research-driven advocacy; direct engagement between government and activists on specific proposals; and again, a mobilisation of the public to see, touch and feel the causes involved.

Civic activism has grown to be lively in Singapore over the past 50 years. Energies are not only directed toward areas that deal with values, such as the LGBT issue, the Anti-Death Penalty Campaign and the NoToRape campaign against marital rape. Civic movements such as the Animal Rights Campaign and the "I'm FINished" campaign against the consumption of sharks fin indicate that the full spectrum of concerns animates civil society here.

In 2013, the "No to 6.9 million" White Paper protest movement pulled together civic activists, political activists and ostensibly a good number of the public to protest against the government's long-term population plan. This was on the back of broad-based public uneasiness against what was considered an all-too-liberal immigration policy that was deemed to have caused crowdedness in public infrastructure, change in the cultural and social landscape but most critically, the protestors claimed, depressed wages and career prospects for Singaporeans who were out-competed by cheaper foreign labour at all levels of the occupational ladder. This movement was a full frontal attack against the government's population strategy and economic strategy. The claim in the protest rallies, of which, up to the time of writing, there have been four, was that the government had lost its way in serving citizens. The zenith of the movement saw estimates of about 7,000 people gathered at Speakers' Corner. Like the two other sets of movements cited above, this cause was also vigourously promoted in the online space.

Has civil society had any transformative power in Singapore, politically? Judging by the mobilisation of opinion and the changes in legislation (in 2012–2014 the death penalty regime was reformed, laws protecting animal welfare were strengthened, and frameworks to ensure fair employment practices and wage growth for Singaporeans introduced), this ground-up activism across several policy arenas has shaped the social and political system here in stark contrast to conditions at independence. There are those who seek to answer that question by whether the support for alternative political parties and oppositional politics has increased. It may still be too early to tell. What is clear is that civic advocacy and the state's response has transformed specific issue areas and on that score, the answer can only be in the affirmative.

The case is best made through a contrast of the current day scene with the scene of 1965 or even before that. In the next section of this chapter, we provide a brief summary of the history of civic activism so that the context of what has been described above can be set out clearly. We end the chapter by coming back to where we began — what are the emerging trends in civil society and what does the future hold over the next decade or so?

It should be clear that our working definition of civil society in this chapter is that it includes all forms of voluntary organisation, whether formally constituted or not, that lies between and is independent of the state and the family. Each group or organisation is held together by shared values, interests and purposes, and seeks to mobilise resources and people to achieve those. Often, in Singapore, the term is broadened to include the work of voluntary welfare organisations, charities and other groups that attend to or provide social services to the needy and disadvantaged in society. Chua (2003a) considered this the welcomed half of civil society, as the state sees this primarily as a subsector that does not question its frameworks of policy or the political system but takes the state's cue and also, the state's contracts to achieve their interests and purposes. The other unwelcomed half comprises activists who exist precisely because they wish to change policy, legislation or the worldview of the public and the government.

It should be noted however that in practice, the distinction is not quite so clear-cut. There are groups that toggle between partnership on one end of the relationship spectrum with the state, and independence from and resistance against the state on the other. Two groups are good examples to illustrate this point. The Tsao Foundation has provided powerful policy advocacy vis-à-vis the government on ageing issues with a particular emphasis on needy elderly women and yet complements the state's efforts to provide social and medical care to seniors (Tsao, 2013). The second group is ACRES which is an animal rights and conservation group. It is a powerful advocacy group for the protection of endangered species. It called out the lack of enforcement against the illegal trade in such species and led efforts to strengthen the animal rights regime in the country. Yet, it has also provided services to the government in the area of animal rescue. Most recently, just as the legislation to strengthen the animal welfare regime was being proposed in parliament, the founder of ACRES, Mr Louis Ng declared that he had joined the ruling People's Action Party (PAP) to expand his activism to cover community interests (Tan, 2014; Wong, 2013b). While this might be cause for some cynicism about the status of his organisation and its work (with some asking if this was a "sell-out"; see for instance, Lay, 2014), it is equally true that there are many other individuals and groups that have emerged in recent times to resist the state in such areas as arts censorship and media freedom. This case of Ng just provides a flavour of the full complexity and colour of civil society in Singapore today.

Having examined the current state of affairs of civil society, the next section will take a historical developmental perspective to explain how things came to be.

Civil society development: Historical context

We will examine the development of civil society in Singapore beginning from the pre-independence period through the post-independence years under the three respective Prime Ministers.

Civil society in pre-independent Singapore

Even as it waxed and waned in the time of British colonial rule, civil society in post-World War II and pre-independent Singapore was marked by vigorous activism carried out by trade unions, student groups, immigrant and ethnic-based organisations, and mercantile associations.

According to historical accounts, the first signs of civil society were people's efforts to ensure the protection of mercantile interests such as the maintenance of Singapore's free port status in those early days of colonial history from 1819 to 1867. Such activities set the tone for interest groups to influence public policy. Subsequently, ethnic and immigrant groups such as those in the Chinese, Straits Chinese, Eurasian, Indian and Malay communities also emerged as Singapore prospered as a trading hub for the hinterland; these groups were subject to differential treatment and degrees of control by the British and later the Japanese in World War II. The immediate aftermath of the Japanese occupation saw the onset of critical issues of social provision because of rapid population growth and the large social disruption the war brought. This paved the way for the emergence of a militant union movement that campaigned for the betterment of working and living conditions (Gillis, 2005), and certainly, the movement for self-determination.

Constitutional reforms introduced in the last throes of British rule paved the way for a more competitive party system, which saw civil society groups interact with and mobilised by political parties in the anti-colonial struggle (Gillis, 2005). The People's Action Party (PAP) would come to dominate Singapore's political landscape in its post-independent history because of that interaction with communist elements that had built up centres of power in trade unions and student movements. The departure of its leftist members because of the disagreement over aspects of the merger into Barisan Socialis (BS), as well as the eventual detention of these activists and their peers in the lead up to the merger with the Malayan mainland, meant that the PAP had no more leverage over those centres of power (Turnbull, 1989). This was something the PAP had to rebuild in short order.

Under the leadership of Lee Kuan Yew, the PAP recovered with a twofold approach to re-establishing its power bases (Gillis, 2005). First, it would dismantle the power structures supporting the left-wing faction. The BS-controlled Singapore Trade Union Congress was deregistered and in its place, the National Trades Union Congress was set up. The newly formed Singapore Association of Trade Unions that supported the BS was denied registration on the premise that it had been used for illegal purposes.[1] The activism of student groups from the Chinese middle school, the University of Singapore and the Nanyang University was marginalised by means of legislative reform[2] and by the subsuming of university student unions under the Education Ministry's control. This period also saw the imposition of limits to academic freedom and commentary (Gillis, 2005). Ethnic-based civil society groups were either co-opted (such as the Singapore Chinese Chamber of Commerce) or marginalised (like the Straits Chinese British Association).

Second, the PAP then moved to establish new means of connecting with the ground through the use of British-built community centres. These community centres came under the oversight of the para-political institution, the People's Association (PA) that the PAP formed. The strong activism of the women's lobby in the 1950s led by the Singapore Council of Women and political parties against polygamy led the PAP to take on the slogan of "one man one wife" to recognise gender equality in its election manifesto. This eventually led to the passing of the Women's Charter outlawing polygamy in 1961 (Singam, 2003). The PAP was successful in mobilising support at the ballot box for the merger with Malaysia in 1963. Singapore became an independent nation in 1965 however, when it became clear that the socio-political differences between the PAP's vision of a racially equal Malaysian Malaysia could not be reconciled with UMNO's outlook of a Malay-dominated Malaysia (Turnbull, 1989, pp. 279–283).

Civil society in independent Singapore under Lee Kuan Yew

The first era of independent Singapore under the leadership of first Prime Minister Lee Kuan Yew saw a strong developmental imperative which favoured social and political stability for the good of economic development (Koh & Soon, 2011). As such, civil society in newly independent Singapore was subdued given how the PAP had extirpated it from the ground.

Civil society activity began to emerge in the mid-1980s in the areas of gender and ethnic representation, in direct response to government policy and proposed legislation. These were the first signs of the development of a vertical relationship that civil society had with the state in independent Singapore. The formation of a

---

[1] This was after the arrest of several trade union leaders, in what is known as Operation Cold Store, and seven SATU-affiliated unions were deregistered (Gillis, 2005).

[2] In 1966, the Internal Security Act was amended to require all students desiring to be part of an institution of higher learning to first obtain an approval letter from the Director of Education (Gillis, 2005).

women's group — the Association of Women for Action and Research (AWARE) — in 1985 was precipitated in reaction to the "Great Marriage Debate" where Lee proposed programmes that would encourage higher birth rates among graduate women (Lyons, 2004). The Association of Muslim Professionals (AMP) was set up in October 1990 as a consequence of the view that the PAP's Malay-Muslim members had not sufficiently represented the interests of the Malay community nor improved its lot in the country (Chua, 2003b).

The state would also nonetheless signal the limits to which civil society would be allowed to operate. This period also saw the censure of the Law Society for publicly commenting on the proposed amendment to the Newspaper and Printing Presses Act that sought to restrict the circulation of foreign publications engaging in domestic politics; saying that it afforded the Minister of Communication and Information significant powers. This led to a stern reprimand from then Minister of Communication and Information, Wong Kan Seng, that it was not the place for professional associations to comment on legislation and public policy. The Legal Professional Act was soon amended to reinforce this position, so that it would not be allowed to interfere in the running of government and in policy formulation, except when invited to do so by the government (Rodan, 1996). This was taken as an object lesson to the rest of civil society — stick to your stated mission and stay out of policy debate and politics.

Another object lesson was on its way that had the same effect of "disciplining" of civil society. This was the Marxist Conspiracy of 1987 when it was construed that the Catholic church had strayed into political agitation against the state's economic and foreign labour policy. A group of Catholic workers and others — 22 people were deemed to have been influenced by Liberation Theology and associated in various ways with political dissident in exile, Tan Wah Piow, to destabilise Singapore. Critics of the episode argue that what was at issue was how the government tried to eliminate political dissent by framing the activism as a Marxist plot, when that was not the case (Barr, 2008; Wijeysingha, 2012). Also at issue was how these individuals were detained without trial under the Internal Security Act, and were alleged to have been forced to confess to the government's case against them (Bellows, 1989). This happened under the leadership of Lee, although he would later reveal that it was his deputy Goh Chok Tong and his team who were in charge (Chong, 1991).

The state would, with this incident, take the opportunity to set in place the boundary line where civil society could tread — first, that the line between church and state should be clearly drawn and kept separate; that faith-inspired political activism would not be welcomed. Second, that the state would have no qualms against using the full force of its laws to detain those who wished to destabilise the state and society and therefore, that civil society was not a free-for-all but it could only carry on within what the state and what the duly-elected government had defined as the national interest.

Civil society development under Goh Chok Tong

Singapore's second Prime Minister, Goh Chok Tong, assumed the reins of leadership in November 1990. This era would be marked by "greater freedom for Singaporeans to make their own choices, and to express themselves", but not for "actions which rock the boat" (Goh, 1990). Those actions considered constructive and welcomed tended to be in the areas of social service, community-oriented self-help or more broadly, what was termed "Total Defence". Although there was more space for civil society groups to act in its vertical relationship with the state, this would happen within a boundary still very much determined by the government.

The government's view on state-civil society relations was reinforced in a seminal speech by then Acting Minister for Information and the Arts, George Yeo, in 1991. In an arboreal metaphor, Mr Yeo likened the presence of state institutions to the all-pervasive influence of the "banyan tree", which, he said, was necessary to "prune . . . so that other plants [like civic institutions] can grow". The message however was that while space would be freed up for expression and volunteerism, it would be done cautiously: "We cannot do without the banyan tree . . . We need some pluralism but not too much because too much will also destroy us. In other words, we prune judiciously." Yeo explained that the changes would be set in the context of "Total Defence" so that the spirit of community self-help will allow Singapore to develop its "soul" (Yeo, 1991).

The general impetus to provide greater space for expression stems back to the 1984 General Election, where the PAP vote share declined by 12.9%. The need to garner support from the middle classes became apparent, and the PAP did this in Goh's era through the promise of a "more refined, more compassionate, kinder and gentler" society (Goh, 1990) and by means of a more consultative and consensus seeking political style, made months before he became the Prime Minister in 1990 (Koh, 2009, 94). However, it seemed that the PAP's reading was that such an idea of liberalising the social and political space did not quite resonate with other segments of Singapore society through its interpretation of the 1991 General Election results. In an unprecedented fashion since independence, four opposition members were successfully elected to parliament, and the PAP's portion of the vote share dipped to 61%. (Arguably, this was also the intended outcome the political opposition's "by-election" strategy of allowing the PAP to return to power on Nomination Day which would embolden voters to take their chances and elect non-PAP candidates.)

Given that the constituencies that went to the opposition were home to the working class, the PAP read its defeat as a backlash from conservative "Chinese heartlanders" (Koh, 2009). As such, the discussion of liberalising space for civil society did not resurface again until the PAP did better at the polls in the 1997 General Election, where its share of the popular vote went to 65%, and it regained two of the four constituencies that went to the opposition in 1991. The discussion about widening the room for civil society would pick up again with the launch of a major public consultation exercise, under the purview of the Singapore 21 (S21) Committee. One of the thrusts of its recommendations was for Singapore to welcome "active citizens". It was an attempt to appeal again to middle class Singaporeans' sense of political competence and interest in shaping governance in their country.

However, this period was also marked by what was called the Catherine Lim Affair which saw Goh set yet another boundary marker on the room for civil society. In 1994, Dr Lim commented about how Goh's promise of consultative government had given way to Lee's authoritarian iron fist as manifested in a debate about ministerial salaries. She was castigated for overstepping the mark in doing this. She had crossed the "out of bounds" markers (OB markers) by making personal attacks on political leaders, and sniping from the sidelines. Goh challenged her and any others who wished to politicise matters to properly declare their interests in seeking to take on the government and contest in elections (Tan, 2009). This seemed like a different role than what civic activists would recognise as being a public intellectual — the role that Lim had assumed. Together with the Marxist Conspiracy, the Catherine Lim Affair led members of civil society to believe that there was a certain way that government leaders wanted them to operate; to understand the topics and the processes which were considered unacceptable. Lyons (2008) provides valuable insights and evidence into the effect that these had in the operations of AWARE. While its decision-makers, Lyons argues, sought to avoid the same fate of the 1987 Marxist conspirators, and "spent considerable time formulating and re-formulating its strategies in anticipation of the state's response" (p. 257), "Goh Chok Tong's public treatment of Catherine Lim reinforced the Exco's message that the state had the power to shut AWARE down whenever it liked. His comments regarding OB markers merely provided a common language with which to name an already internalised mode of behaviour" (p. 260).

Nonetheless, within the non-legal and therefore "soft" bounds through the Catherine Lim Affair, the Goh administration was marked by its routine use of public consultation to incorporate views from across society in reviews of policy — sometimes, single-issue ones and sometimes, omnibus reviews. There were channels by which civic activists that chose to, could sit around the table with policy-makers and share their views, concerns and suggestions. After all, it was Goh's time when the Feedback Unit was established (Koh, 2009). As a result of advocacy for the freedom of expression, the government also introduced a platform for free speech — the earlier discussed, Speakers' Corner in Hong Lim Park. The Nominated Member of Parliament (NMP) scheme was introduced to provide a formal channel in the legislature where people of standing and noted representatives of the civic and business sectors could shape debate on public policy and legislation (save for three key limits on their power in the areas of no-confidence motions, money bills and constitutional reform) (Lee, 2002; Rodan, 2009). At least two members of a leading policy discussion group then, called The Roundtable, were NMPs. Several members of AWARE also took up NMP positions. The President of the NSS, Dr Geh Min, was also an NMP. Each used the platform to good effect not only in the House but also in policy formulation consultation processes because of their standing as NMPs (Zuraidah, 1998; Chan, 2013).

This period also saw the government deal with online activism as the arrival of Web 1.0 and later 2.0 changed the way in which people mobilised opinion and activities. Sintercom (or the Singapore Internet Community) was set up as a space for the free discussion of politics and policy in Singapore with no partisan agenda. Although Sintercom was initially welcomed by the state, its founders decided to shut it down when asked to register under the Broadcasting (Class Licensing) Scheme in the backdrop of the emergence of other websites like Think Centre and Singapore Window and later The Online Citizen, emerging with an anti-establishment tone in the lead up to the 2001 General Election. Websites dealing with politics in Singapore would be required to come under the jurisdiction of the scheme and would be held responsible for the content on their sites and required to refuse foreign funding for their activities.

The internal stakeholders of Sintercom closed it down in the face of the ambiguity of rules when the Broadcasting Authority refused to comment what material would be construed as having crossed the line as acceptable commentary. However, a week after Sintercom had been taken off the World Wide Web, some other parties revived it as New Sintercom on the Geocities service platform in the United States although it was not ever like it was before (George, 2006).

For the first time, there was a formal networking process among civic activists — a one year collaboration called The Working Committee (TWC) in 1998 (Singam *et al.*, 2002). This effort at horizontal level peer-to-peer networking was focused on helping members understand each other's areas of interest and advocacy. It was also focused on sharing lessons on working effectively and discussing approaches to interacting with the government. The journey of collaboration, learning and networking of TWC has been captured in the book — *Building Social Space in Singapore* by Singam *et al.* (2002).

In Goh's era, the concept of "civil society", defined as "civic society", was positioned as the crux of what would contribute to the larger sense of Singapore identity. Back to the speech by George Yeo in 1991, it seemed that the idea of people seeking to cultivate strong social ties at the local level, volunteering to promote social good was the preferred model rather than political notion of "civil society" that has as its starting point, the political rights to freedom of speech, expression, association and of media freedom — a distinction discussed by Nair (1993). Chua says of the distinction: "... the difference between the two terms, 'civic society' and 'civil society', is not some inconsequential play of words, but an indication of one's political stance on the appropriate balance in the relationship between state and society in Singapore" (p. 63). "Civic society" was to be read in conjunction with the broader many helping hands approach, put in place so that Singaporeans would be encouraged to assist "that small segment of our community that cannot keep pace with the rest of the population" through the efforts of voluntary welfare organisations (*Singapore: The Next Lap*, 1991, pp. 117–29). In its vertical relationship with civil society, public intellectuals saw Mr Yeo's speech as a strong nudge in favour of the depoliticised mode of civic society.

As discussed, the notion of civic society and state relations did not resurface till after the 1997 General Election in the S21 exercise. In its vision of Singapore's future, the S21 committee instituted "active citizenship" as the fifth pillar of its framework, which further reinforced the notion of civil society as civic society (*Singapore 21*, 1999). This time, state actors emphasised the importance of a cooperative approach, as opposed to a confrontational take to state society relations. David Lim, the Minister-in-Charge of operationalising S21 contended that the "confrontational approach generally results in a win-lose outcome, or worse, a lose-lose outcome" ("NGOs Should Cooperate, Not Confront", *The Straits Times*, 2000). Simon Tay, who was from the independent political and policy discussion group, The Roundtable, referred to earlier, and an NMP, proposed barring the use of violence — "confrontation can also be a contest of ideas ... And a contest of ideas is absolutely critical for Singaporeans to develop thinking minds and for volunteers to feel that they have a say" ("Contest of Ideas Critical", *The Straits Times*, 2000). Some members of The Roundtable queried in an article in Singapore's main English broadsheet, *The Straits Times*, if all the government wanted was many helping hands, rather than thinking heads (George & Tan, 1998). To be fair, the state, at this point, was already inviting the thinking heads of the likes of the members of NSS to contribute to its green plans for the country (Francesch-Huidobro, 2008).

Months before then Deputy Prime Minister Lee Hsien Loong would take over the mantle of leadership in 2004, he addressed the issue of state-society relations in his speech to the Harvard Club. He said the government would open the space for "further civic participation" and "promote a political culture which responds to people's desire for greater participation, in a manner which supports Singapore's growth as a nation". He said he would welcome robust debate on policy issues as long as civic activists stayed away from personal attacks on leaders (Lee, 2004a). He picked up on the issue of the role of thinking heads and suggested that a shift would be on its way.

Civil society development under Lee Hsien Loong

Lee Hsien Loong became Prime Minister in August 2004, and pledged in his swearing-in speech that there would be "an open and inclusive Singapore" (Lee, 2004b). Since then, civil society has been marked by further liberalisation although others will be quick to point out that it has not been in some straight-line upward vector towards openness. Speakers' Corner was modified to allow for other uses than speeches and eventually for demonstrations. This however has to be paired with the introduction of the Public Order Act (2012), which includes the definition of a single person as an assembly or procession, who would be required to register to obtain a permit to organise or participate in a public assembly and procession (Ministry of Home Affairs [MHA], 2009; "Citizens Hope for Transparency", *Channel NewsAsia*, 2009).

In its vertical relationship with civil society, this period has seen the government go beyond the mere proscription of acceptable limits of participation to partner as well as dialogue on a larger nationwide scale with Singaporeans.

The current administration has sought to promote the co-creation of public programmes to enhance the public engagement process. Examples of the former range from the National Environment Agency's mobilisation of "Litter-Free Ambassadors" to spread the word on keeping Singapore litter-free, to the involved role that animal rights activists were given to design public engagement on a strengthened animal rights regime. Like under Goh with the omnibus policy reviews, Lee embarked on a year-long nationwide engagement process known as *Our Singapore Conversation* "to define what sort of country Singaporeans want and how they can achieve it" (Lee, 2012).

This effort happened in the wake of the watershed General Election of May 2011, where the ruling party's share of the popular vote dipped to its lowest since independence, and where a Group Representation Constituency (GRC) went to the opposition for the first time (Ortmann, 2011). It has been argued that the "new normal" of increased political pluralism has arrived (Tan, 2012).

This period has seen the growth of online discussions and activity, and attempts by the state to demarcate the boundaries and "norms" this time, in the virtual space. The government tried to have the blogging community to develop a code of community norms which was rejected. It went on to introduce legislation to regulate online news websites. It also sought to bring these news websites into the Broadcasting (Class License) Scheme if they were not already under it — *The Independent* (Singapore) and *Breakfast Network* were asked to register (Hussain, 2013). The former decided to comply, and the latter resisted and decided to abandon plans to launch as a news website. The editor, Bertha Henson, questioned the rules and the process and continues to comment on politics and policy on her personal blog *Bertha Harian*.

This era would also see the growth in diversity of horizontal peer-to-peer relationships in the form of collaboration between civil society groups across different sectors as discussed in the first section of this chaper. Other areas of successful civic campaigns that benefitted from that collaboration include the example of UNIFEM (now UN Women), and local groups focused on migrant worker issues like Transient Workers Count 2 (TWC2) and the Humanitarian Organization for Migrant Economics (HOME) working towards changing legislation to ensure the foreign domestic maids in Singapore now have a mandated one off-day per week written into their contracts ("Day-Off", 2014).

The unfolding future

What of the future then? There are at least four key driving forces that will continue to act on civil society in Singapore and its vertical relationship with the state beyond 2014.

The first and most obvious is the effect of changes in communications technology and specifically, the use of social media and whatever emerges after that puts the power of information and mobilisation in the hands of individuals. While existing research suggests that such media serve best to reinforce and mount traditional non-online political action where relationships already exist before the online connection (Skoric *et al.*, 2009), we also recognise that on important shared areas of policy concern, such as the White Paper protest and also the Pink Dot movement, it has the force to cause sizeable demonstrations of solidarity. It also means that alternative causes and policy agenda can be placed out there among the body politic and it is no longer the sole prerogative of the government to do that. This trend not only implies that the means for alternative communities, centres of opinion and mobilisation to arise quickly and with force, exists. It also implies that the government competes against a noisier and complex field of non-state actors as it exercises its power to govern; these are actors who feel that they can and should be setting the policy and political agenda. Many also set out to address community concerns in practical ways through it. We think of the support ordinary citizens were providing each other in the Haze Crisis, 2013 — offers of masks and air-conditioned accommodation were made through social media ("Room for Civil Society to Grow", *Channel NewsAsia*, 2013).

The second driving force is the changing value orientation of younger Singaporeans. Not only are Singaporeans better educated and better travelled with each generation but there are also theories about how the millennials born in the two decades before the year 2000 and generations living after a society has transcended the most difficult stages of development anywhere in the world, are different in their outlook to life and work than preceding generations. In a nutshell, they tend to value mental and emotional well-being beyond mere material provision — a higher order preference; they tend to be relatively more democratic in orientation and aspiration — they expect to find tolerance for diversity of views and lifestyles; they also place more importance on areas of human rights, environment, conservation and other "post-material" concerns — they are more civic-minded yet also liberal ("Generation Boris", *Economist*, 2013; Wilke & Saad, 2013). This trend, yet to be fully played out here, suggests that succeeding generations of citizens will not only take the material for granted but they will also not accept it if other areas of public policy are sublimated as "secondary" to economic survival and growth — what they think defines the PAP's policy agenda. The positive implication of this trend is also that this generation will wish to be involved, to participate actively and attend to what they care about as they feel it is their "right" to do so, and to see their aspirations come true.[3]

The third driving force is the extent to which the fruits of socio-economic development are equally distributed through society and its impact on social cohesion and the notion of being "one nation". Despite the discussion of the post-materialist values above, the key to understanding the landscape is that the material is no less important — it is just taken for granted which means double-pressure for any governing regime in Singapore. On top of that, there is a very strong egalitarian ethos that defines Singaporean society. The PAP government itself has said since it began ruling Singapore that it is committed to ensuring that all can share in the country's success. In that vein, there are public intellectuals who are concerned that with globalisation as well as large financial and economic disruptions in the global economy, income gaps are widening and that many are not sharing in the country's gains. They are also concerned about how policies reinforce the impact of those gaps, where the rich get richer and the poor get poorer — or what is called social stratification.[4] This has kept the government focused on ensuring that social assistance and social safety nets are strengthened and that the poor and disadvantaged get more help that is targeted at ensuring that their poverty and disadvantage is not replicated in the next generation. The Finance Minister is at pains to explain the subtleties of Singapore's overall tax and fiscal system as one that is progressive — you have to view the full package rather than feel the proverbial elephant from the regressive GST end of it (Shanmugaratnam, 2014, pp. 43–56; 2013a, pp. 12–24; 2013b, pp. 1–4). The transfer payments as well as the direct subsidies to many public goods tilt the playing field towards those who need the most help to "level up", the Minister has explained. As long as it is perceived that the government is sincere in its efforts, and also that global economic shocks do not undermine such efforts, this issue will not become a cause around which vigorous civic activism arises.

The fourth driving force is simply the effect of demands on the governance system that the forms of diversity and complexity discussed above impose on it. In the early years of independence, the government rallied citizens and businesses around the need to address the "survival crisis". In the mid-1980s, the Goh administration said it faced the "problems of the management of success" which was about how the government would meet not just the basic needs but even the aspirational material goals and desires of an affluent society. Today and looking ahead, the task at hand is not simply delivering public goods or meeting the aspirational

---

[3]For an up-to-date review of the changing value orientations of Singaporeans, see Tambyah and Soo (2013).

[4]For an examples of such efforts, see Manu *et al.* (2013) and Low and Vadaketh (2014).

goals — material and non-material sense for one part of its constituency, but if indeed social stratification takes root in the next 10 years, then it will be meeting the needs of "different Singapores"[5] — the experience of life can become quite distinctly different from say one group of people at the lower class, to another group in the middle class and yet another group in the upper class. Where should the government target its efforts? Will an informed and "big-minded" citizenry arise to appropriate the space to take care of itself where possible? Or will the shift be towards universalistic forms of state support from cradle to grave, yet leaving more than enough space for a lively civil society to play its part? With effective state intervention and socio-economic transformation, society becomes increasingly differentiated, with some parts of it wanting more autonomy from the state and other parts wanting greater state intervention and provision for their welfare. With each new form of state intervention, the government opens itself to questions about whether it is indeed able to stand above any of the particularistic demands of a segment of society because it simply cannot intervene equally to please every constituency equally (Koh, 1997), or can it? This questioning of its legitimacy may be the result of civic activism but paradoxically, the solution to this dialectical momentum of an interventionist state may also be civil society. Why?

The state may choose to trim or curb the areas that it is prepared to intervene in and reduce the call on its governance capacity. Some areas may be best served by civil and "civic" society and certainly, the current PAP government would wish for them to do so within a broad framework that it sets and to do it peaceably vis-à-vis other parts of society. This has been the case with the area of social services where the government is a contractor of services and takes the many helping hands approach. It is not an uncomplicated route as a recent controversy about sexuality education provided by an external vendor in a junior college illustrates (Lee & Tan, 2014). What it has done is to ensure that the education and employability to the poor and disadvantaged is improved, through the opening up of education routes for special needs people for instance, and the promotion of social enterprise.

Some areas will be wrested by civil society because it believes it is the more appropriate locus of expertise and authority on the issues and it simply invites the state to lend its resources for what is construed to be a cause that serves the public good — think of the local conservation movements that have arisen to memoralise housing estates that are being redeveloped (Zaccheus, 2014).

In the areas of values, race and religion, the status quo in the framework of management is maintained. The example of the gay movement is where the government has already stated its position — status quo to the position in the legal statutes that homosexual acts between two men is a criminal act, yet advocacy to change that continues. The online outpouring to allow Muslim women to wear the

---

[5]See a discussion of how Singapore is experienced differently depending on where one stands in the income spectrum by Lien (2009).

hijab in the public healthcare sector in 2013 also resulted in the reiteration that there can be no change to the rule of universality in the formal uniformed sectors of which healthcare would considered to be a part of (Kok, 2013).

In other areas, civil society activism continues to be focused on ensuring that the government will address issues viewed as shared concerns. Think of the area of migrant workers and human trafficking, where there has also been a confluence of international interest. The government has changed policy and legislation in response to long-running campaigns by civic activists to do so. The government has also taken steps to be more firm in enforcing the rules that are already in the statute books — there have been spates of prosecutions for abuses in wage payments to migrant workers; adjustments to statutory requirements for the housing of workers; and clarification and expediting of worker compensation for workplace injury of foreigners. More should be done, say the civic activists, but the government says it should proceed in ways that ensure decisions are enforceable and fair to all parties concerned.

In all cases, the emphasis is placed also on educating corporate and individual citizens about the issues at hand, be they the treatment of foreign workers, fair employment practices for Singaporeans as well, creating inclusive workplaces for special needs people, as well as in areas of environmental and heritage concerns. These are all areas that civil society can do best, and would not be out of joint with the current Lee government's efforts to build an "inclusive" Singapore.

What then are the areas of activism and their likely impact on intra-civil society relations and state-civil society relations that will have greater force over the next decade? While the answer to this question might result from the interaction of the driving forces cited above, there are others that have emerged and can be discussed briefly. The first will be the area of the "culture wars". These are areas of public interest that are usually viewed from the lens of moral and religious values and therefore particularly difficult to address; they are usually positions that are deeply held, mutually exclusive and therefore polarising. Think here of debates about the homosexual lifestyle, assisted suicide or euthanasia, and the death penalty (Lim, 2014).

The second area of activism and resistance to the state is in the area of media freedom and censorship. The year 2013 was a particularly challenging one where, as discussed, the government implemented a new regime to regulate news websites and also tried to have the Singapore Internet community adopt a code of conduct for self-regulation. When new legislation on news websites was announced in early June 2013, 150 Singapore websites and blogs joined in the #FreeMyInternet campaign and blacked out their sites in protest; there was an online petition to have the regime withdrawn and a protest rally was held at Hong Lim Park that was attended by an estimated 1,500 people to show their displeasure of what was perceived as a tightening of control. From 2013 to 2014, a blogger called Roy Ngerng rallied Singaporeans around the issue of the integrity of the Central Provident Fund system. In doing so, he alleged that the Prime Minister (PM) had been defrauding citizens and not granting them a fairer return on their compulsory savings. The High Court found him guilty of defaming the PM (Nur Asyiqin, 2014a). It remains to be seen if it becomes a cautionary tale of how not to conduct one's public advocacy even if it is in the online space or whether it stimulates a stronger movement toward the freedom of expression for Singaporeans.

The third area will be when there is a spillover of politics and political developments from lands beyond our shores, which is mixed with the migration that has taken place into the country. As a global city and with foreigners comprising a third of the total population, this is an area that could be challenging to manage. After the Malaysian General Election of May 2013 resulted in protests there about election fraud, Malaysians in Singapore mounted two illegal public protests on 8 May and 11 May, just as the diaspora in Sydney, Melbourne and Taipei had done. The police issued a warning after the first incident that while foreigners were allowed to work and live in Singapore they had to abide by the laws of the land and more critically — "They should not import issues from their own countries into Singapore which can disturb public order as there can be groups with opposing views." In its public statement, the police also reminded all concerned that action would be taken against those who broke the law and it could result in termination of work passes or visas. Nine people were specifically warned for "actively participating" in the illegal gathering at Merlion Park (Boon, 2014). Yet, 21 Malaysians persisted and mounted another protest on 11 May and were arrested for it. The government revoked the work pass of one and the visit passes of two of them. What is more important is that a Singaporean migrant worker activist went on to organise a rally at Speakers' Corner in sympathy, arguing that foreign workers should not be denied a political voice — it was their human right. Seven Malaysians involved mobilised the support of a Malaysian Member of Parliament and the Chief Minister of Penang also made a public appeal to the Singapore government to take the case of the protesters "not from a criminal angle but from a human rights perspective" ("Penang Chief Minister Pleads", *Today*, 2013). This led Singapore authorities and eventually a Home Affairs Minister to reiterate how Singapore would not allow foreigners to stage political activities in Singapore that contravene its rules and certainly brook no foreign interference in its affairs (Wong, 2013). It not would allow Malaysian politicians to petition for leniency, "seek special treatment and to further politicise what is essentially a domestic law and order issue in Singapore" ("Merlion Park Illegal Gatherings", *Today*, 2013). What is to be done however when bona fide citizens take up the cause on behalf of the foreign population, or in sympathy to a political cause elsewhere or even, appeal to foreign governments to address social or political issues in Singapore? These are not new challenges but can be particularly confounding given the question of national sovereignty by which such actions are viewed.

Related to that is a fourth area of civic activism that arises from the impact of immigration on Singapore's national and multiracial framework of social identities and on the civic landscape. The government's call for foreigners to integrate well into their host society has been at the heart of many debates on how this should happen (Yap, *et al.*, 2015; Nur Diyanah, 2014; Koh & Soon, 2014). The impact of this on local-born Singaporeans, where different ethnic groups have different levels of attachment to racial and national identity (Mathew, 2013), remains to be seen. Immigrants take pride in the culture and social norms they arrive with and the challenge is whether they are prepared to adopt the existing multiracial framework and adapt to its diversity. Immigration is also likely to add impetus to the growth of new migrant associations and the strengthening of old ones. However, immigrants bring with them different schemas of how citizens and community groups relate to the authorities in their home country, and without notions of how they "should" operate here and strong pathfinders to guide them; all these factors add yet another layer of complexity to the relationship between ground interests and the government as we look ahead.

We hope that this chapter has given a flavour of the deep challenges and complexities that are thrown up with a developing civil society in Singapore. It speaks of the political development of a people but also of the demands that will be placed on the Singapore state and government to respond effectively. An effective response would allow civic activism to result in a more socially inclusive and compassionate Singapore where citizens renew their commitment to the good of the collective, but not the tyranny of the majority. It should cause the common space and sense of identity and pride in the community to grow, not narrow. Tolerance, civility and yet some measure of social order will ensure that the full-flowering of human potential is not too lofty a goal for Singapore, beyond her 50th birthday.

References

Boon, W. (2014, March 7). Police Warn Foreign Nationals against Importing Their Countries' Issues into S'pore. *Today*. Retrieved 11 November 2014, from https://global.factiva.com.

Barr, M. (2008). Singapore's Catholic Social Activism. In M. Barr & C. A. Trocki, (eds.), *Paths Not Taken. Political Pluralism in Post-War Singapore* (pp. 228–247). Singapore: NUS Press.

Bellows, T. (1989). Singapore in 1988: The Transition Moves Forward. *Asian Survey*, 29(2), 145–153.

Chan, R. (2013, February 7). Assess Impact on Nature: NMP. *The Straits Times*. Retrieved 7 November 2014, from https://global.factiva.com/.

Chong, A. (1991). *Goh Chok Tong, Singapore's New Premier*. Petaling Jaya, Selangor Darul Ehsan, Malaysia: Pelanduk Publications.

Chua, B. H. (2003a). Non-Transformative Politics: Civil Society in Singapore. In D. Schak (ed.), *Civil Society in Asia* (pp. 20–39). Aldershot, Hampshire, England: Ashgate.

Chua, B. H. (2003b). The Relative Autonomies of State and Civil Society in Singapore. In G. Koh & G. L. Ooi (eds.), *State-Society Relations in Singapore* (pp. 62–76). Singapore: Eastern Universities Press.

Chua, G. & Li, X. Y. (2012, March 30). Navigating a New Terrain of Engagement. *The Straits Times*. Retrieved 7 November 2014, from https://global.factiva.com.

Citizens Hope for Transparency in New Public Order Law (2009, April 20). *Channel NewsAsia*. Retrieved 5 November 2014, from https://global.factiva.com.

Contest of Ideas Critical, Says NMP (2000, March 6). *The Straits Times*. Retrieved 1 November, 2014, from https://global.factiva.com.

Day-Off: About the Organizers. *Day-Off Campaign*. Retrieved 1 November 2014, from http://dayoff.org.sg/weare_2.shtml.

Francesch-Huidobro, M. (2008). *Governance, Politics and the Environment*. Singapore: Institute of Southeast Asian Studies.

Generation Boris (2013, June 1). *Economist*. Retrieved 10 November 2014, from http://www.economist.com / news / britain / 21578666 - britains - youth - are - not - just - more - liberal-their-elders-they-are-also-more-liberal-any.

George, C. (2006). *Contentious Journalism and the Internet: Towards Democratic Discourse in Malaysia and Singapore*. Singapore: Singapore University Press, in association with University of Washington Press, Seattle.

George, C. & Tan, K. (1988, May 17). Barriers to a Web Society. *The Straits Times*. Retrieved 2 March 2015, from http://global.factiva.com.

Gillis, E. (2005). *Singapore Civil Society and British Power*. Singapore: Talisman.

Goh, C. L. & Sim, R. (2012, March 20). Naysayers Want All Works Halted. *The Straits Times*. Retrieved 7 November 2014, from https://global.factiva.com.

Goh, C. T. (1990, June 13). Deputy Prime Minister's Speech on President's Address in Parliament. Retrieved 31 October 2014, from http://www.nas.gov.sg/archivesonline/data/pdfdoc/yybg19910620s.pdf/.

Hussain, A. (2013, December 17). MDA, Breakfast Network Continue to Cross Swords. *Today*. Retrieved 1 November 2014, from http://www.todayonline.com/singapore/mda-breakfast-network-continue-cross-swords/.

Koh, G. (1997). Bureaucratic Rationality in an Evolving Developmental State: Challenges to Governance in Singapore. *Asian Journal of Political Science*, 5(2), 114–141.

Koh, G. (2009). Pruning the Banyan Tree? Civil Society in Goh's Singapore. In B. Welsh, J. Chin, A. Mahizhnan & T. Tan (eds.), *Impressions of the Goh Chok Tong Years in Singapore* (pp. 93–106). Singapore: NUS Press.

Koh, G. & Soon, D. (2014, November 10). S'poreans Share the Ability to Embrace, Adapt to Diversity. *Today*. Retrieved 11 November 2014, from https://global.factiva.com/.

Koh, G. & Soon, D. (2011). Civil Society in Singapore. In T. Chong & S. Elies (eds.) *An ASEAN Community for All: Exploring the Scope for Civil Society Engagement* (pp. 111–137). Singapore: Friedrich Ebert Stiftung.

Kok, X. H. (2013, November 6). Hijab Issue: Govt Must 'Balance Community Requirements'. *Today*. Retrieved 11 November 2014, from https://global.factiva.com/.

Lay, B. (2014, October 21). PAP Just Won the Animal Lovers Vote by Acquiring ACRES Founder Louis Ng. *mothership.sg*. Retrieved 10 February 2015, from http://mothership.sg/2014/10/pap-won-the-animal-lovers-vote-by-acquiring-acres-founder-louis-ng/.

Lee, H. L. (2004a, January 6). Speech by Deputy Prime Minister Lee Hsien Loong at the Harvard Club of Singapore's 35th Anniversary Dinner — Building a Civic Society.

Retrieved 31 October 2014, from http://unpan1.un.org/intradoc/groups/public/ documents/APCITY/UNPAN015426.pdf.

Lee, H. L. (2004b, August 13). Swearing in Speech by Prime Minister Lee Hsien Loong. Retrieved 1 November 2014, from http://www.mfa.gov.sg/content/mfa/over seasmission/tokyo/press_statements_speeches/2004/200408/press_200408_5.html.

Lee, H. L. (2012, August 26). Prime Minister Lee Hsien Loong's National Day Rally 2012. Retrieved 7 November 2014, from http://www.pmo.gov.sg/content/pmosite/ mediacentre/speechesninterviews/primeminister/2012/August/prime_minister_leehs ienloongsnationaldayrally2012speechinenglish.html#.VFSebPmUeDo/.

Lee, P. & Tan, A. (2014, October 9). Disputed Course to End by Dec: MOE. *The Straits Times*. Retrieved 11 November 2014, from https://global.factiva.com.

Lee, T. (2002). The Politics of Civil Society in Singapore. *Asian Studies Review*, 26(1), 97–117. DOI: 10.1111/1467-8403.00122.

Lien, L. (2009). Reaching out to Low-Income Groups in Singapore. In T. H. Tan (ed.), *Singapore Perspectives 2009. The Heart of the Matter* (pp. 35–44). Singapore: World Scientific.

Lim, J. (2011, May 30). Bukit Brown to Make Way for Housing. *The Straits Times*. Retrieved 7 November 2014, from https://global.factiva.com.

Lim, L. (2014, July 20). Let's Not Open the Doors to 'Culture Wars'. *The Straits Times*. Retrieved 1 November 2014, from https://global.factiva.com.

Low, D. & Vadaketh, S. T. (2014). *Hard Choices. Challenging the Singapore Consensus*. Singapore: NUS Press.

Lyons, L. (2004). *A State of Ambivalence: The Feminist Movement in Singapore*. Leiden: Brill.

Lyons, L. (2008). Internalised Boundaries: AWARE's Place in Singapore's Emerging Civil Society. In M. Barr & C. A. Trocki (eds.), *Paths Not Taken. Political Pluralism in Post-war Singapore* (pp. 248–263). Singapore: NUS Press.

Manu, B., Ho, S. C., Low, D., Tan, K. S., Vadaketh, S. & Yeoh, L. K. (2013). Background Paper: Inequality and the Need for a New Social Compact. In S. H. Kang & C. H. Leong (eds.), *Singapore Perspectives 2012. Singapore Inclusive: Bridging Divides* (pp. 125–158). Singapore: World Scientific.

Mathews, M. (2013). Insights from the IPS Survey from Race, Religion and Language. Retrieved 11 November 2014, from http://lkyspp.nus.edu.sg/ips/wp-content/ uploads/sites/2/2013/04/Insights-from-the-IPS-Survey-on-Race-Religion-and- Language.pdf.

Merlion Park Illegal Gatherings a Domestic Law and Order Issue: MHA, MFA (2013, May 29). *Today*. Retrieved 11 November 2014, from https://global.factiva.com.

Ministry of Home Affairs (MHA) (2009, March 23). Overview of The Public Order Act. Retrieved 7 November 2014, from http://www.mha.gov.sg/news_details.aspx?nid= MTM5OQ==-3BtUG+2xe3A=.

Nair, S. (1993). Political Society. Commentary, 15–19.

Nature Society (Singapore) (2010, October 21). The Green Corridor. A Proposal to Keep the Railway Lands as a Continous Green Corridor. Retrieved 10 November 2014, from http://nss.org.sg/documents/TheGreenCorridor101103.pdf.

Newspaper and Printing Presses Act. Cap. 206. Retrieved 11 February 2015, from http://statutes.agc.gov.sg.

NGOs Should Cooperate, Not Confront (2000, February 27). *The Straits Times*. Retrieved 7 November 2014, from https://global.factiva.com.

Nur Asyiqin, M. S. (2014a, June 21). Mosques Told Not to Get Caught in LGBT Crossfire. *The Straits Times*. Retrieved 21 July 2014, from https://global.factiva.com.

Nur Asyiqin, M. S. (2014b, June 25). Muslim Student Group Backs 'Wear White'. *The Straits Times*. Retrieved 7 November 2014, from https://global.factiva.com.

Nur Asyiqin, M. S. (2014c, June 27). Police Issue Public Advisory to 'Keep the Peace' at Pink Dot Event. *The Straits Times*. Retrieved 7 November 2014, from https://global.factiva.com.

Nur Asyiqin, M. S. (2014d, November 8). Blogger Roy Ngerng Found to Have Defamed PM Lee. *The Straits Times*. Retrieved 11 November 2014, from https://global.factiva.com.

Nur Diyanah, A. (2014, November 7). Move beyond Identifying Singaporeans Based on Ethnicity. *Today*. Retrieved 11 November 2014, from https://global.factiva.com.

Ortmann, S. (2011). Singapore: Authoritarian but Newly Competitive. *Journal of Democracy*, 22(4), 153–164. DOI:10.1353/jod.2011.0066.

Penang Chief Minister Pleads for Leniency for M'sians Nabbed (2013, May 31). *Today*. Retrieved 10 November 2014, from https://global.factiva.com.

Philomin, L. E. (2014, June 24). Church Must Work with Like-minded Groups to Oppose Pink Dot: Pastor. *Today*. Retrieved 7 November 2014, from https://global.factiva.com.

Public Order Act 2012. Singapore. Retrieved 11 November 2014, from http://statutes.agc.gov.sg/.

Rodan, G. (2009). Goh's Consensus Politics of Authoritarian Rule. In B. Welsh, J. Chin, A. Mahizhnan & T. Tan (eds.), *Impressions of the Goh Chok Tong Years in Singapore* (pp. 61–70). Singapore: NUS Press.

Rodan, G. (1996). State-society Relations and Political Opposition in Singapore. In G. Rodan (ed.), *Political Oppositions in Industrialising Asia* (pp. 95–127). London: Routledge.

Room for Civil Society to Grow in Singapore (2013, August 15). *Channel NewsAsia*. Retrieved 19 January 2015, from https://global.factiva.com.

Shanmugaratnam, T. (2014, March 5). Transcript of Budget 2014 Debate Round-Up Speech by Deputy Prime Minister and Minister for Finance, Mr Tharman Shanmugaratnam on 5 March 2014. Retrieved 11 November 2014, from http://www.singaporebudget.gov.sg/portals/budget_2014/download/FY2014_Budget_Debate_Round-Up_Speech.pdf.

Shanmugaratnam, T. (2013a, March 7). Transcript of Budget 2013 Debate Round-Up Speech by Deputy Prime Minister and Minister for Finance, Mr Tharman Shanmugaratnam on 7 March 2013. Retrieved 11 November 2014, from http://app2.mof.gov.sg/data/budget_2013/download/FY2013_Budget_Debate_Round-Up_Speech.pdf.

Shanmugaratnam, T. (2013b). Building an Inclusive Society. In S. H. Kang & C.-H. Leong (eds.), *Singapore Perspectives 2012* (pp. 1–4). Singapore: World Scientific.

Sim, W. (2014, June 22). Be Big-hearted, Avoid Dividing Society: Yaacob. *The Straits Times*. Retrieved 7 November 2014, from https://global.factiva.com.

Singam, C. (2003). Civic Traditions in Singapore: A Feminist Perspective. In G. Koh & G. Ooi (eds.), *State-Society Relations in Singapore* (pp. 28–37). Singapore: Eastern Universities Press.

Singam, C., Tan, C., Ng, T. & Perera, L. (2002). *Building Social Space in Singapore: The Working Committee's Initiative in Civil Society Activism*. Singapore: Select Publishing.

Singapore 21: Together, We Make the Difference (1999). Singapore: Singapore 21 Committee c/o Prime Minister's Office (Public Service Division). The Government of Singapore.

Singapore: The Next Lap (1991). Singapore: Times Edition, The Government of Singapore.

Singapore Parliament Reports (2011, February 14). Gazetting The Online Citizen, Parliament no. 11, Session no. 2, Vol. no. 87, Sitting no. 16, Sitting Date. Retrieved 2 November 2014, from http://www.lawnet.com.sg.libproxy1.nus.edu.sg/.

Skoric, M. M., Ying, D. & Ng, Y. (2009). Bowling Online, Not Alone: Online Social Capital and Political Participation in Singapore. *Journal of Computer-Mediated Communication*, 14(2), 414–433. DOI: 10.1111/j.1083-6101.2009.01447.x.

Sreedharan, S. (2013, March 12). One-tenth of Singapore Will Be Green. *Today*. Retrieved 7 November 2014, from https://global.factiva.com.

Tambyah, S. K. & Soo, J. T (2013). *Happiness and Well-Being. The Singapore Experience*. Oxon: Routledge.

Tan, A. (2014, October 21). Animal Rights Activist Louis Ng Joins PAP. *The Straits Times*. Retrieved 1 November 2014, from https://global.factiva.com.

Tan, K. (2009). Who's Afraid of Catherine Lim? The State in Patriarchal Singapore. *Asian Studies Review*, 33(1), 43–62. DOI: 10.1080/10357820802706290.

Tan, K. (2012). Singapore in 2011: A 'New Normal' in Politics? *Asian Survey*, 52(1), 220–6.

Tsao, M. (2013). Mapping out an Age-friendly Singapore. *Social Space*, (6), 4–9. Retrieved 8 November 2014, from https://centres.smu.edu.sg/lien/files/2013/11/SocialSpace2013-2014_MaryAnnTsao.pdf.

Turnbull, C. (1989). *A History of Singapore, 1819–1988*, 2nd ed. Singapore: Oxford University Press.

Urban Redevelopment Authority (URA) (2013, January). Retrieved 10 November 2014, from http://www.ura.gov.sg/uol/publications/research-resources/plans-reports/Concept Plan2011/land_use_plan_2013.aspx.

Wilke, J. & Saad, L. (2013). Older Americans' Moral Attitudes Changing, Gallup. Retrieved 10 November 2014, from http://www.galup.com/poll/16288/older-americans-moral-attitudes-chaing.aspx?version+print.

Wijeysingha, V. (2012, June 2). Dr Vincent Wijeysingha: Lies of the 'Marxist conspiracy'. Retrieved 8 November 2014, from http://exchersonesusaurea.blogspot.sg/2012/06/dr-vincent-wijeysingha-lies-of-marxist.html.

Wong, T. (2013a, 10 July). Breaking Local Laws; Foreigners Cannot Use S'pore for Political Activities: Iswaran. *The Straits Times*. Retrieved 10 November 2014, from https://global.factiva.com.

Wong, T. (2013b, October 19). Louis Ng: 'Pushing the Govt into a Corner Will Backfire'. Retrieved 5 November 2014, from http://www.singapolitics.sg/supperclub/louis-ng-pushing-govt-corner-will-backfire.

Yeo, G. (1991, June 20). Civic Society — Between the Family and the State. Retrieved 1 November 2014, from http://www.nas.gov.sg/archivesonline/data/pdfdoc/yybg19910620s.pdf.

Yap, M. T., Koh, G. & Soon, D. (eds.) (2015). *Migration and Integration in Singapore. Policies and Practice.* Oxon: Routledge.

Zaccheus, M. (2014, 10 November). Bid to Save 2 Historical Areas in Queenstown. *The Straits Times.* Retrieved 16 February 2015, from http://www.straitstimes.com/premium/singapore/story/bid-save-2-historical-areas-queenstown-20141110.

Zuraidah, I. (1998, May 2). Civic Groups Relate Their Experience. *The Straits Times.* Retrieved 8 November 2014, from https://global.factiva.com.

PART III
Principles and Social Processes

Chapter 13

Social Justice in Singapore:
Some Personal Reflections

Tommy Koh

In the past 50 years, Singapore has gone through a revolution: physically, socially and economically. The slums have been replaced by high-rise HDB estates. All Singaporeans have a roof over their heads. They have access to clean drinking water and modern sanitation. The economy has been diversified and modernised. Unemployment is a non-issue. The per capita income has gone up by a 100 times. The diverse population has bonded as one united people. There is a high degree of acceptance of ethnic, cultural and religious differences. Mutual respect and tolerance have become part of our DNA. Singapore is therefore a success story, a great success story.

The question which I have been asked to answer in this essay is whether Singapore is a socially just society. My answer is both yes and no.

Singapore is a socially just society

I would like to begin by arguing that Singapore is a socially just society for the following reasons.

No discrimination against women

First, there is no discrimination against girls and women in Singapore. Women have achieved equality with men in education, employment, equal pay for equal work, marriage, divorce, custody of children, leadership positions in both the public and private sectors, etc. The only two areas in which women are under-represented are in politics and boards of directors.

Racial and religious equality

Second, there is no discrimination against persons based on their race, colour, language or religion. This is a rare achievement in our bigoted world. In many countries and in different parts of the world, we are witnessing turmoil and conflict due to tribal, ethnic and religious differences. Unscrupulous politicians have used the tribal, racial and religious cards to gain power.

Basic human needs

Third, all Singaporeans have access to employment, housing and healthcare. In contemporary Europe, youth unemployment is a major problem. This is, fortunately, not the case in Singapore. Singapore has one of the most successful housing policies in the world. There are practically no homeless people in Singapore. 90% of Singaporeans own their own homes. Over 80% live in public housing estates. The World Health Organization once ranked Singapore as having the sixth best healthcare system in the world (The World Health Report, 2000).

Rule of law

Fourth, the rule of law is strong in Singapore. The judiciary is independent. All citizens, irrespective of their race, religion, gender and social status, can be confident that they will enjoy the equal protection of the world. They can trust the courts to be impartial and to render justice in accordance with the law.

Meritocracy

Fifth, meritocracy is the governing principle when it comes to examinations, recruitment, appointment, promotion, etc. The system is fair and transparent. No person from any minority group needs to fear that his or her merit will not be given the same weight and consideration as a competing candidate from the majority group.

Right to education

Sixth, all children have the opportunity to attend a good school. It is, of course, true that not all schools in Singapore are of equal quality. The neighbourhood schools are obviously not in the same class as the elite schools. However, the average school in Singapore is better than the average in most other countries. This has been repeatedly confirmed by international comparisons. Singapore students in our neighbourhood schools have out-performed their peers in maths, science and reading comprehension. In a recent competition conducted by the Organisation for Economic Co-operation and Development (OECD), Singapore's students even topped the world in problem solving (OECD, 2014).

Singapore is not a socially just society

I would now like to argue the opposite case. I want to argue that Singapore is socially unjust for the following reasons.

Inequality of income and wealth

First, Singapore is socially unjust because of the growing inequality of income and wealth. One universally accepted measure of inequality is the Gini coefficient, with 0 representing perfect equality and 1 representing perfect inequality. Taking all the government transfers into account, the Gini coefficient of Singapore is 0.41 in 2013 (Department of Statistics [DOS], 2014). According to the 2013 Legatum Prosperity Index, Singapore is the world's 18th most prosperous country (Legatum Institute, 2013). According to the World Bank Development Indicators, the lowest 20% of Singapore's population account for 5% of the country's income whereas the top 20% account for 49% (World Bank, 2014).

Earning below a living wage

Second, Singapore is socially unjust because many hard-working Singaporeans are not paid a living wage. By a living wage, I mean a wage which enables the worker to maintain himself and his family in material sufficiency and to live with dignity. Singapore does not have a poverty line. However, many countries and political entities, such as Canada and Hong Kong, hold the view that a person who earns less than half the median income can be considered poor. The median income of Singapore is S$3,705 in 2013 (DOS, 2014). Half the median income is S$1,853. According to our statistics, 440,000 of our workers earn less than S$1,853.

No minimum wage

Third, Singapore does not have a minimum wage. The Singapore government has repeatedly opposed the introduction of a minimum wage on the grounds that it will increase unemployment and deter foreign investment. These arguments do not seem to be supported by the facts. Japan, South Korean, Taiwan and Hong Kong have adopted the minimum wage system without increasing their unemployment or decreasing their foreign investment. Another explanation often offered for the growing disparity of income is that it is caused by globalisation and technology. While it is true that these two forces are part of the reason, it is not the full story. Otherwise, all countries would be as unequal as Singapore. The fact is that some very successful countries, such as Japan and Switzerland, are very egalitarian. The Gini coefficient of Switzerland, which does not have a minimum wage, is 0.33.

Children growing up in poverty

Fourth, Singapore is socially unjust because many of our children are growing up in poverty. Professor Joel Kotkin is a respected scholar of cities. During his visit to Singapore in 2010, Professor Kotkin was reported by *The Straits Times* (Basu, 2010) to have said: "A third of the children in inner city London live in poverty. It is this kind of inequality Singapore should guard against."

Poor children in our schools

Fifth, I think we should take Professor Kotkin's warning to heart. Many of our children go to school with no pocket money to buy lunch. The Straits Times School Pocket Money Fund (SPMF) is expected to disburse S$8 million this year to assist 14,000 students in our schools. The Chairman of SPMF, Mr Han Fook Kwang, said: "The large numbers who continue to need help is a stark reminder of how, despite Singapore's economic growth, there remain many people who have been left behind" (Seow, 2014). Since 2000, the SPMF has disbursed about S$42 million to help 128,000 needy children and youth.

Needy students in tertiary institutions

Sixth, poverty is a problem which transcends our primary and secondary schools. I am personally involved in administering two trust funds to benefit needy students in our educational system. I am surprised by the number of needy students in our universities, arts colleges and other tertiary institutions. The time has come for the Singapore government to establish a commission to look into the problem of poverty in Singapore, with a special focus on how we can help our needy students to stay in school and complete their education. Our meritocratic system requires that we ensure that students from poor families have a chance to develop to their full potential.

Conclusion

As a society, Singapore is both socially just and unjust. To address social injustice, we need to tackle many issues related to income distribution. In the past few years, the Singapore government has made more attempts to uplift those with lower income such as increasing government transfers and introducing to some sectors a progressive wage model that involves a wage floor and a wage ladder that links progression with job scope and skills. It remains to be seen if these measures are effective or more fundamental changes are required.

I want to conclude by telling a story. On the 30th of October 2014, Volume 3 of *The Little Red Dot* was launched. This new volume contains essays on Singapore written by foreign diplomats who had served here as Ambassadors or High

Commissioners. One of the essayists is Ambassador Yang Wenchang of the People's Republic of China. His essay is entitled, "The Lasting Taste of Olive". Ambassador Yang recalled a meeting with then Prime Minister Lee Kuan Yew. He asked Mr Lee for his vision of Singapore. Mr Lee said he wanted to build a Singapore which resembled an olive, with a very large middle class and very few people at the top and the bottom. Does the income distribution profile of Singapore resemble an olive? The answer is no. It resembles a pear instead. To put it simply, the olive is the profile of a socially just society and the pear is the profile of a socially unjust society. How did our olive become a pear?

References

Basu, Radha (2010, October 13). Great Hawker or Great Scholar for a Great City. *The Straits Times.* Retrieved 5 March 2015, from forums.condosingapore.com/ showthread.php/10093-Great_hawker_or_great_scholar_for_a_great_city.

Legatum Institute (2013). *The Legatum Prosperity Index, 2013.* Legatum Institute.

Organisation for Economic Co-operation and Development (OECD) (2014). *PISA 2012 Results: Creative Problem Solving: Students' Skills in Tackling Real-Life Problems (Volume V).* France: PISA, OECD Publishing.

Seow, Joanna (2014, October 5). ST Fund Plans to Raise More Aid. *The Straits Times.* Retrieved 5 March 2015, from http://www.schoolpocketmoneyfund.org.sg/ web/media-coverage-article199.php.

Singapore Department of Statistics (DOS) (2014). *Press Release, 18 February 2014: Key Household Income Trends, 2013.* Singapore: DOS.

The World Health Report (2000). *Health System: Improving Performance.* Geneva, Switzerland: World Health Organization.

World Bank (2014). *World Development Indicators. Milennium Development Goals. Eradicating Poverty and Saving Lives.* Retrieved 19 January 2015, from http://wdi.world bank.org/table/1.2.

Chapter 14

Doing Good in Singapore

Willie Cheng and Sharifah Mohamed

In Singapore, the term, "doing good" is often associated with the social sector,[1] in particular charities. Of late, it has been juxtaposed with "doing well",[2] a reference to the private (or enterprise or business) sector and its traditional emphasis of performing well financially. Together with the public sector (which we can also call the "ruling well" sector), the three sectors form the pillars of an economy. As Figure 14.1 shows, the social sector does not exist in isolation; instead, it is an interdependent part of the overall economy, just as it comprises interdependent components within it.

To discuss the history and emerging trends of "doing good" and the social sector in Singapore, we have organised this chapter in three sections:

- The Social Ecosystem: Who are the main players of the social ecosystem in Singapore?
- Macro Trends: What are the key patterns and trends that have shaped Singapore's social sector to date?
- Moving Forward: What are the forces and considerations that could affect the social sector in the next 10 to 50 years?

---

[1]Sometimes, it is also called the "people sector", making up the three P's sectors: people, private and public sectors. However, the term "people sector" carries with it a certain political undertone.

[2]Prime Minister Lee Hsien Loong was recently quoted as saying at CDAC's Charity Dinner on 24 October 2014: "We all have a shared responsibility to do good when doing well."

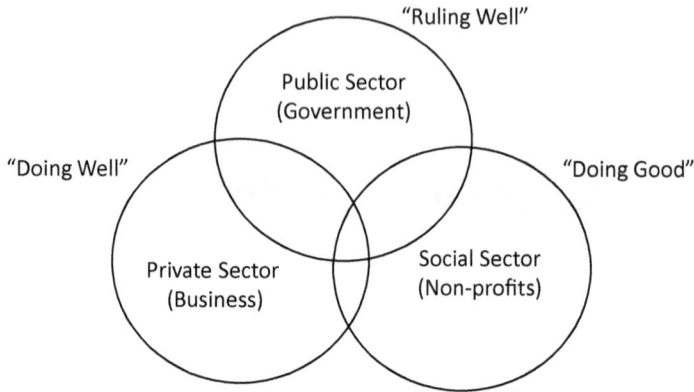

Fig. 14.1   Three Pillars of the Economy.

The social ecosystem[3]

An ecosystem is a system whose members benefit from each other's participation via symbiotic relationships. By taking an ecosystem approach to the social sector, we obtain a holistic and integrated perspective of how the different players do, and indeed, should interact.

Figure 14.2 shows what the social ecosystem and its players might look like. At the core of the social ecosystem are the social purpose entities (the helpers) who seek to positively impact their beneficiaries (the helped), and the capacity builders (the helpers' helpers) who seek to facilitate the missions of these social purpose entities. Surrounding the core players are the community (individual and corporate volunteers and donors), the media, and the government who collectively provide the resources (time and money), support (including legitimacy), and scrutiny to ensure that the core players function as intended. The government has multiple roles, including that of regulator.

Beneficiaries

Beneficiaries and their causes are the raison d'etre of the social ecosystem. Yet, we sometimes lose sight of this vital group because they have the smallest voice and they are also not always well-defined.

In Singapore, it is fair to say that the man in the street thinks of beneficiaries quite narrowly in terms of the poor and needy of society. For others, the group

---

[3]The social ecosystem framework and part of the content for this section and the next section is drawn and condensed from the chapter by Cheng, "Transitions within the ecosystem of change", in Cheng and Mohamed (eds.) (2010).

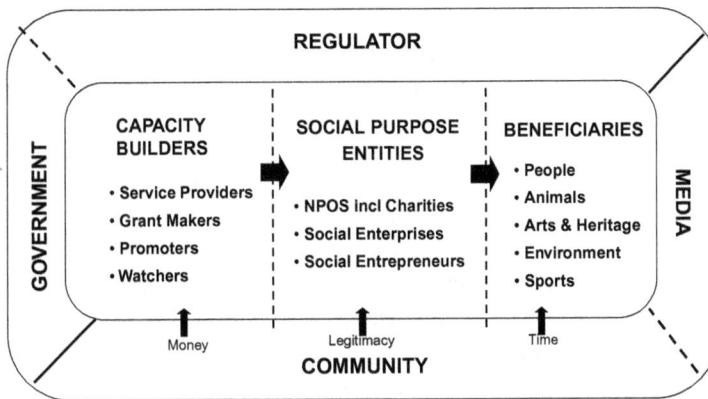

Fig. 14.2   The Social Ecosystem.

is slightly broadened to include those who fall within the scope of the "social service" subsector, the segment of the population targeted by the Ministry of Social and Family Development (MSF) and the National Council of Social Services (NCSS).

A 2011 study by the Lien Centre of Social Innovation (LCSI), *Unmet Social Needs In Singapore*,[4] identified six vulnerable communities largely from the social service sector:

- The disabled. There are around 131,000 disabled persons in Singapore, and in need of a central registry for outreach programmes.
- The mentally ill. It is estimated that one in six individuals suffers from a mental disorder. The challenges include cultural stigma and the burdens of caregivers.
- Single-person-headed poor households. About 116,000 households are headed by singles, divorced or widowed individuals (seven out of 10 being women). For a long time, the government's help schemes with their pro-family criterion have bypassed this group.
- Silent workers. These are Singaporeans who have to live by the country's cardinal rule of self-reliance but who may still not earn enough for their upkeep. An estimated 122,000 households live on a per capita monthly income of S$500.
- Foreign workers. There are 850,000 lower-skilled or semi-skilled foreign workers, of whom about 180,000 are foreign domestic workers. While they contribute to two economies (their home countries and Singapore), their basic dignity and legal rights in Singapore leave much to be desired.
- New communities. In the last three decades, while Singapore's population grew 2.3 times, the foreign workforce grew by a staggering multiple of 64. Today, there

---

[4]The description of the six vulnerable communities and data provided are taken from this document (Mathi & Mohamed, 2011).

are 500,000 permanent residents and 1.6 million non-residents (Department of Statistics [DOS], 2014). Some of the citizens (about 20,000 in 2013) (Kotwani, 2013) are new migrants. Recent initiatives to integrate these new communities will take time to produce impact.

Beyond the poor and needy of society, the scope of those who can be classified as beneficiaries from a legal standpoint is very wide. In Common Law, charity covers four main purposes: the relief of poverty, the advancement of education, the advancement of religion and "other purposes beneficial to the community not falling under any of the other heads".[5] The last catch-all clause has been broadened, over time, to cover almost anything to do with community good, including youth, elderly, arts, health, the environment, heritage, animals and sports.[6]

The size of the different beneficiary groups depends on the measurement basis. For example, from a financial standpoint, most of the money received by Singapore charities go to education (60%), followed by religion and others (animals, think tanks, environment, self-help groups) (14%), social and welfare (13%), health (6%), arts and heritage (6%), and sports (2%).[7]

Social purpose entities

Social purpose entities describe the organisations and individuals who seek to change society for the better.

The main type of organisations often go by labels such as non-profit organisation (NPO), non-governmental organisation (NGO) or civil society organisation (CSO), which are often used interchangeably. They primarily serve as vehicles for the needs of the beneficiaries to be met.

There are several forms in which NPOs can be legally constituted in Singapore: a company limited by guarantee (under the Companies Act), a society (under the Societies Act), a trust (under the Trustees Act), a co-operative (under the Co-operative Societies Act), or, more rarely, a legislated body with its own Act. Some NPOs are trade bodies or associations. Those NPOs that are primarily undertaking charitable work are usually granted tax beneficial status, either as

---

[5]These four categorisations of the four broad charitable causes were enunciated by Lord Macnaghten in a landmark UK case, *Income Tax Special Purpose Commissioners v. Pemsel* in 1891, and is the starting point for the definition of charity in jurisdictions like Singapore and that of over 60 countries that inherit the common law system of England.

[6]For example, in 2005, the Singaporean government announced that "the advancement of sport, where the sport advances health through physical skill and exertion" will be within the ambit of "other purposes beneficial to the community".

[7]The figures here are extracted from the *Commissioner of Charities Annual Report 2013*. It measures the distribution of charitable income (donations, fees and grants, in total S$12.6 billion) across the various groups. When grants and fee for services are excluded, religion and others take up the lion share of donations (48%), followed far behind by social and welfare (19%), education (15%), and health (11%).

a registered charity (its surplus are not taxed) and/or as an institution of a public character (IPC) (donations to the organisation are tax-deductible for the donors).

NPOs focused on charitable causes have long been a mainstay in Singapore. Examples include Thong Chai Medical Institution (1868), Kwong Wai Shiu Hospital (1910), Little Sisters of the Poor Home for the Aged (1935) and the Salvation Army (1935). In 1982, the Charities Act was enacted and required such organisations to be officially registered for attendant tax benefits and to be regulated. As of the end of 2013, 2,142 charities and 599 IPCs (most IPCs are also charities) were registered under the Act.[8]

The profiles of these charities are:

- 1,280, or more than 60%, are religious organisations and others,[9] while 359, or 17%, are social and welfare organisations.
- Most are small charities: 51% have annual receipts of less than S$250,000.
- The top 120 charities that receive over S$10 million a year each account for 85% of the charity sector's total receipts of S$12.6 billion.

Another type of social purpose organisation is the social enterprise, a profit-making business with a social mission. Social enterprises create social impact and generally redistribute their profits back to the community. These are covered in further detail in the next section.

Among the individuals working in the sector, there has been a buzz in recent years about the rise of social entrepreneurs.[10] These are people who can effect systemic, large-scale social change through innovative approaches. While Singapore can lay claim to a few social entrepreneurs along with several organisations seeking to foster their development, the segment is still largely nascent.[11]

Capacity builders

As the name suggests, capacity builders are the intermediaries that help build the capacity of the social sector. They are needed in any marketplace to improve its efficiency although their forms may differ. For the social sector, these intermediaries

---

[8]The most recent data on charities and IPCs in this chapter are extracted from *Commissioner of Charities Annual Report: For the year ended 31 December 2013*.

[9]We understand that about 85% of this combined category is "religious organisations" while 15% is "others". Therefore, religious organisations would be slightly more than half of all charities.

[10]Social entrepreneurs (individuals) should not be confused with social enterprises (organisations). Not all social enterprises are run by social entrepreneurs (only those who are innovative and have major impact), and not all social entrepreneurs run social enterprises (in fact, few do).

[11]For example, the Schwab Foundation's Social Entrepreneur of the Year Award was given to Jack Sim of World Toilet Organisation in 2006, Kenny Low of O School in 2007 and Sarah Mavrinac of Aidha in 2008. It was discontinued after that.

include (in descending order of maturity of development): service providers, grant makers, promoters and watchers.

Service providers provide NPOs with needed goods and services such as premises, printing and computing. However, there are some that focus primarily or exclusively on social sector clientele and gear their products and services for non-profits. Examples include Social Service Training Institute (training), The Hub (shared offices) and UM-MC Asia (consulting).

Grant makers are organisations that receive and aggregate money from donors, big and small, and give them out as grants to charities. They ensure accountability of the NPOs by putting in place a rigorous process.

Grant makers have more than doubled their giving over the past decade, from S$296 million in 2001 to S$644 million in 2013. The largest grant maker in Singapore, by far, is the Singapore Tote Board. Established in 1988, the Tote Board has given out annual grants of between S$500 million and S$1 billion in recent years.[12] Far behind is the Community Chest, set up in 1983, which provides a common pool of funds for Voluntary Welfare Organisations (VWOs). In 2013, it disbursed S$81.5 million to 84 VWOs running 223 social service programmes that support 300,000 beneficiaries. Next are the well-known foundations such as the Lee Foundation, the Tan Chin Tuan Foundation and the Lien Foundation. In recent years, corporate foundations have also emerged with companies such as Singapore Press Holdings, Capitaland and NTUC Fairprice. In addition, two community foundations were recently established: the Singapore Community Foundation and SymAsia Foundation.[13]

Promoters seek to grow and develop the sector, or a specific segment within it. The major promoters in Singapore are subsector based[14] and usually government related. The largest is NCSS, the umbrella body for some 400 VWOs. The other subsectors have similar bodies: the National Arts Council (NAC) for arts, National Heritage Board (NHB) for culture and heritage, National Environmental Agency (NEA) for environment and Sport Singapore for sports. Some promoters have functional roles that cut across the subsectors. For example, the National Volunteer & Philanthropy Centre (NVPC) promotes volunteerism and philanthropy across the entire non-profit sector, and LCSI seeks to catalyse innovative responses to social needs.

---

[12]The Singapore Tote Board's *Social Investment Report 2012/2013* shows that donations approvals is S$569 million in FY2010, S$606 million in FY2011 and S$1,074 million in FY2012.

[13]Community foundations allow for donor-advised funds which function like sub-foundations within the larger umbrella foundation. Singapore Community Foundation is set up by NVPC and SymAsia Foundation by Credit Suisse.

[14]We will be, sometimes, using the term "sectors" and "subsectors" to describe these vertical segments of the social sector. The industry generally refer to these as sectors. However, for clarity, we have sought to use the word, "subsectors" to clarify that these are one part of the larger social sector.

Finally, watchers facilitate informed giving by analysing and monitoring the performance of NPOs. This is the least developed segment in our social ecosystem. In other developed countries, broad-based rating agencies such as Charity Watch and Guidestar aggregate information about NPOs and provide performance ratings that are loosely analogous to the Standard & Poor's of the commercial world. The closest to the work of these rating agencies is the Independent Charity Analysis framework developed by NVPC.[15]

Community

The community provides the social ecosystem with underlying support through the giving of time, money and legitimacy. Within the community, there are several distinct players: individual givers (volunteers and donors), corporate givers and the media.

NVPC was formed in 1999, and its biennial nationwide individual giving survey since 2000 provides a good idea of how the spirit of giving by individuals as well as corporations has grown in the last decade.

In 2000, only 9.3% of Singaporeans reported having volunteered in the previous 12 months. After 12 years, supported by active campaigning by NVPC and others, the volunteering rate climbed to over 32% in 2012 (NVPC, 2013). This compares well with the US participation rate of nearly 30% but still falls below the UK's of above 40%. However, the findings of an international survey on giving by Charity Aid Foundation (CAF), placed Singapore 75th among 135 countries surveyed on the volunteer participation rate.[16]

For donations, Singapore's international placing in the same CAF survey was better at the 17th position. In monetary terms, Singaporeans have nearly tripled their individual giving in the last decade, from S$438 million in 2004 to S$1.1 billion in 2012 (NVPC, 2005, 2013). The most recent NVPC survey also shows that half of the donation dollars went to religious organisations and 14% to overseas causes. Interestingly, while those with more may give more in absolute terms, it is the reverse in relative terms: those earning below S$1,000 per month give the highest proportion (1.82%) of their income to charity compared to those earning the most (1.03%) (NVPC, 2013).

---

[15]See next section, subsection "Doing Good Well: Demands for Accountability of Charities" on further information on the Independent Charity Analysis by NVPC.

[16]See Charity Aid Foundation, *World Giving Index 2013* where 135 countries were surveyed and Singapore's volunteerism rate was determined to be 17% (rather than 32%). Do note that the different volunteerism figures of the different countries are usually based on different methodologies of determining participation and thus are not always directly comparable without a clearer understanding of the underlying differences.

Corporate giving has also increased in the last decade. Based on tax deductible donations, corporate philanthropy has nearly doubled in a decade from S$325 million in 2004 to S$644 million in 2013. A 2012 NVPC survey shows that seven out of the top 10% of companies support employee volunteerism.[17] Other forms of corporate giving are less common: donations-in-kind (38%), purchase of goods and services from the non-profits (25%), provision of company's services for free (23%) and complimentary use of corporate assets and resources (15%).

The media plays an important role in lending legitimacy to the work of NPOs as news reporter, critic or advocate, and even as participant. Indeed, it has become noticeably supportive of NPOs in the aftermath of the NKF saga in 2005.[18]

Government

The government is a unique player in the ecosystem. It has multiple and, sometimes, conflicting roles as regulator, funder, promoter and participant.

The regulatory role is necessary for order and order-keeping. For charities which receive funds from the public, it is particularly important for the regulator to ensure that they operate for public benefit and not private advantage, and that there is public confidence in charities.

In Singapore, NPOs are subject to multiple regulators. First, depending upon the type of legal entity in which an NPO is constituted, the regulator could be the Accounting and Corporate Regulatory Authority for companies limited by guarantee, the Registrar of Societies for societies, the Registrar of Co-operative Societies for co-operatives or the Monetary Authority of Singapore for trusts. If the NPO is further registered as a charity or an IPC, it will be additionally regulated by the Commissioner of Charities (COC) and the COC office (also known as the Charities Unit of the Ministry of Culture, Community and Youth). Supplementing the COC, three ministries and two statutory boards function as Sector Administrators to oversight charities within their domain.[19] In addition to these regulators, NPOs need to observe regulations pertinent to specific activities (for example, certain fundraising solicitations are governed under the House to House and Street Collections Act)

---

[17] Corporate Giving Survey (2010). This study surveys members of the Singapore Business Federation which numbers more than 18,400.

[18] See section below (Macro Trends — Doing Good Well) on the NKF saga and the involvement and the response of the media.

[19] The five Sector Administrators to assist the COC in overseeing the charities and IPCS in their respective subsectors are: Ministry of Education (education), Ministry of Health (health), Ministry of Social and Family Development (poor and family), Sport Singapore (sport) and People's Association (citizenship and community development). Meanwhile the COC directly oversights charities and IPCs in arts, heritage, animal welfare, environment, religion and any others which do not fall neatly under the five sectors.

Governments are generally a major funder of the social sector in most countries. On average, they contribute 35% of the social sector's global revenue through grants and contracts to NPOs.[20] Singapore's government spending on the social sector is much more generous: In 2012, government grants alone accounted for S$6 billion or nearly half of the S$12.6 billion receipts of the charity sector. The S$500 million to S$1 billion annual donations by the Singapore Tote Board, a government body, form a substantive part of the S$2.3 billion donations collected by charities. In addition, it is likely that government contracts account for a significant proportion of the remaining S$4.3 billion recorded as "other receipts". Our guess would be that two-thirds of the receipts of the sector comes from governmental sources.

The government also promotes the sector even as it seeks to manage it, especially in areas where such promotion fits its broader agenda of communal support and state building. Over the years, it has driven and supported initiatives which promote aspects of the social sector, such as:

- The formation of the National Volunteer Centre, which later became the NVPC, to promote volunteerism and philanthropy.
- Two *Enabling Masterplans* in 2007 and 2012 which have resulted in a slew of initiatives to embrace persons of disabilities and to help them realise their potential.[21]
- A *National Mental Health Blueprint, 2007–2010* that has resulted in numerous preventive programmes at the community level.[22]
- The formation of the Council for Third Age (C3A) to promote active ageing in an increasing elderly population.
- The establishment of the Comcare Enterprise Fund and the Social Enterprise Association to help create sustainable social enterprises.
- The increase in tax deductions for donations to IPCs from 100% to 200% (2007 to 2010), and then to 250% (from 2011 onwards).[23]

Finally, as a participant, the government can directly provide social services that some NPOs may consider their domain. For example, MSF runs two juvenile residential homes, the Singapore Boys' Home and Singapore Girls' Home, not dissimilar

---

[20]The data cited in this section of global averages are from the Johns Hopkins Comparative Nonprofit Sector Project, a study of nonprofit activity across 46 countries of the world — see Centre for Civil Society Studies website in the References section; Salamon (2006); and Salamon, Sokolowski & Associates, Global Civil Society (2004).

[21]The first *Enabling Masterplan* was for the period 2007–2011, and the second for the period 2012–2016. The plans chart the development of programmes and services in the disability sector to enable persons with disabilities to better integrate into society. The agency set up to oversight the implementation of the masterplans is SG Enable (www.sgenable.sg).

[22]The Blueprint aims to promote primary prevention, improve the delivery of psychiatric services, develop mental health professionals, and promote mental health research amongst others.

[23]The levels of 200% and 250% translate into about 50% benefit (in the cost of their donations) to tax payers at the top end of the individual income tax bracket.

to those run by charities such as Boys Town, AG Home and Muhammadiyah Welfare Home. However, this is not common. By and large, the government has tended to depend on VWOs and other NPOs to carry out the work.

Macro trends

Over the last 50 years, the social sector has evolved. The players involved have shaped the changes in the sector even as they themselves have been shaped by the dynamics of their interactions.

Several years ago, LCSI sought to capture the early history of the social sector. Figure 14.3 provides its summary of the key milestones in the evolution of the sector presented within the three main themes of development: ethnic, religious and individual-based benevolence; social welfare and civic activities; and government and social advocacy (Mohamed, 2008).

The last decade, especially, has been transformative for the social sector in several respects. From our observation of this rich history of Singapore's social sector, we abstract five major patterns:

1) Doing good better: There have been demands and responses by NPOs, in particular charities, to be more transparent and accountable in their fundraising, in their use of funds, and in the outcomes.
2) Doing good and doing well: There is an increasing convergence of the social sector and the business sector in their approaches, models and value systems.
3) Ruling well the do-gooders: The state has been dominant and pervasive in the social sector, and will likely seek to continue to be so.
4) Campaigning despite constraints: Advocacy is increasing with the rise of civil society, but there are still many constraints to its growth.
5) Faith in action: The religious communities have been pioneers of charity work and social action, and now hold the fort on moral values.

Doing good better: Demands for accountability of charities[24]

For a long time, charity was viewed simply as "doing good". Based on this paradigm, when an organisation (the charity) or an individual (the social worker or volunteer) is "doing good", it or he/she should be similarly treated with compassion. Even if the actions and results might be less than efficient or effective, these should be tolerated. Donations are given out of generosity rather than as a reward for "doing good" well.

This changed in 2005 with what became known as the National Kidney Foundation or NKF saga. During the civil trial of a libel suit initiated by NKF's

---

[24]Much of the content of this sub-section is drawn from two chapters, "NKF: The Saga and Its Paradigms" and "Doing Good Better" in Cheng (2009).

Ethnic, Religious and Individual-Based Benevolence	Social Welfare and Civic Activities	Social Advocacy

1819	Clan and religious-based philanthropy predominant		
1942 (WW2)	DECLINE OF COMMUNITY GROUPS		
1945	COMMUNITY GROUPS RESUMED ACTIVITIES		
1946		First multi-service agency in welfare provision [Social Welfare Department]	
1949		[Children's Social Centres]	
1952	[Lee Foundation]	[Community Centres]	
1958	SINGAPORE COUNCIL OF SOCIAL SERVICE		
	[Shaw Foundation]		
1959 (Self-Govt)	PEOPLE'S ASSOCIATION oversees grassroots organisations		
	Gradual maturing of social services arena		
1980s	SOCIAL WELFARE DEPARTMENT incorporated into MINISTRY OF COMMUNITY DEVELOPMENT		
	[Lien Foundation]	[Community Chest]	[AWARE]
			[Feedback Unit]
	[Yayasan Mendaki]		[1987 "Marxist Conspiracy"]
1990s	SOCIAL COUNCIL OF SOCIAL SERVICE restructured as NATIONAL COUNCIL OF SOCIAL SERVICE		Advent of non-government organisations with greater advocacy role
	[CDAC & SINDA]	[S'pore International Foundation]	
	←—————— SINGAPORE 21 ——————→		
		Community Development Councils	[The Nature Society]
			[The Working Committee]
	NATIONAL VOLUNTEER & PHILANTHROPY CENTRE		
2000s	←————— REMAKING SINGAPORE —————→		
			[Speaker's Corner]
		[Transient Workers Count Too]	
	←——— DPM LEE HSIEN LOONG'S HARVARD CLUB SPEECH ———→		
	NKF Saga and other scandals Charity Law Reform		

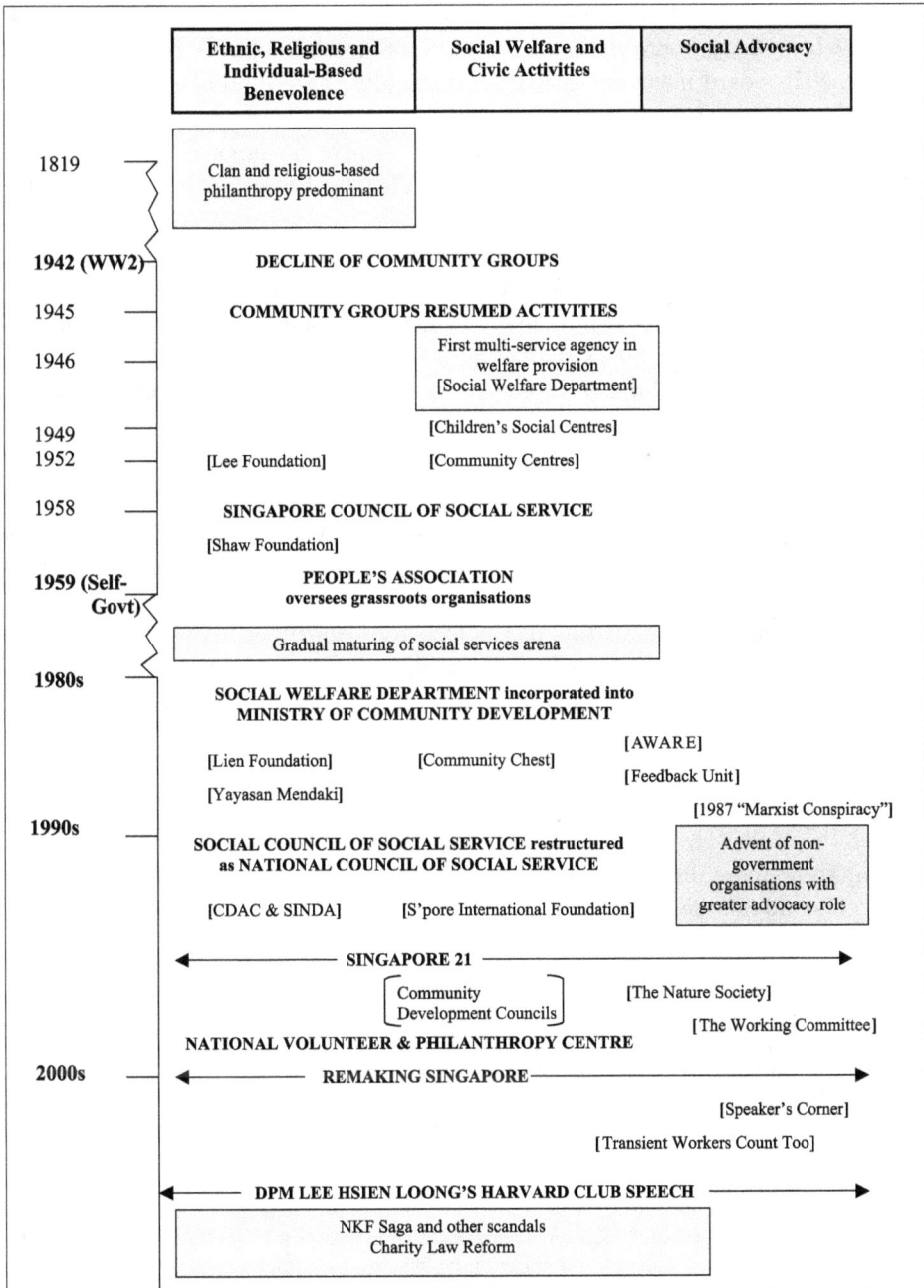

Fig. 14.3   Evolution of the Social Sector in Singapore.

CEO, TT Durai, revelations about his S$600,000 annual salary and the extravagant lifestyle he and the board led at NKF's expense, created a public furore. Durai and several NKF board members were later criminally charged and convicted.

It did not help that other scandals (of a smaller magnitude) followed shortly after the NKF debacle. These involved Youth Challenge, Singapore Anti-Tuberculosis Association, Singapore Association for the Visually Handicapped and St. John's Home for Elderly Persons.[25]

Following the NKF court case, the government reviewed the charity regulatory framework and implemented reforms, including amendments to the Charities Act. The regulators who were seen by many to have been less than diligent in the NKF case became more forceful in dealing with infractions.[26] In 2009, the government charged Shi Ming Yi, the high-profile monk and CEO of Ren Ci, and an aide with criminal breach of trust over a S$50,000 loan and related offences. Ming Yi was convicted and sentenced to six months in jail. In 2012, Kong Hee, the founder and senior pastor of City Harvest Church together with five current and former church members were charged with conspiracy to commit criminal breach of trust for misusing over S$50 million of church money to finance the music career of Kong Hee's wife, Sun Ho. The court case is ongoing.

One reform was the creation of the Charity Council, an advisory body to the COC. The Council has developed a Code of Governance for Charities and IPCs. Since 2007, charities and IPCs have to report annually on their conformance with the Code on a "comply or explain basis". In 2012, the Council introduced the Charity Governance Awards to encourage and recognise the highest standards of governance.

NVPC and other bodies also began promoting "informed giving" — asking donors to be more discerning of the charities they give to, to discriminate between deserving and non-deserving charities, and to be more demanding of those charities

---

[25] In summary, the situations were:

1) Youth Challenge: Executive Director Vincent Lam stepped down from his position after a Commissioner of Charity's inquiry found irregularities in management, financial and governance controls surrounding his remuneration.

2) SATA: CEO Chong Chee Leong and Director for Operations and Technology Paul Wang resigned after they failed to disclose a conflict of interest to the Council on their setup of an IT company to which SATA's service can be outsourced to.

3) SAVH: The Commissioner of Charity found weaknesses in its corporate governance and management, financial and operational controls, and procurement procedures. However, before the results of the investigation was released, NCSS withdrew funding, its IPC status and even created a parallel charity.

4) St. John's Home: The Home lost S$3.88 million from its fixed deposit accounts, believed to have been absconded by a staff. Having found no wilful negligence in the management, the Commissioner of Charities suggested areas for improvement.

[26] There was also a view that it was overly harsh in some cases such as the Singapore Association for the Visually Handicapped.

for accountability of the donations they received. In other words, charities are being told that "just doing good" is no longer good enough, they must be "doing good well". Along with this, there has been greater emphasis, and education, on outcome-based measurements and funding.

In the post NKF environment, a few family foundations, notably the Lien Foundation and the Tan Chin Tuan Foundation, which had been run largely by family and board members, have hired full time staff to run the organisations and professionalise their grant making and administration.

In order to better support informed giving by givers, in 2011, NVPC developed an Independent Charity Analysis framework to analyse Singaporean NPOs and their work. However, the project has not yet gone beyond the production of a few assessment reports of NPOs. The view of some sector observers is that Singaporeans are still largely happy to give out of generosity than be overly demanding and analytical of the performance of NPOs.

Prior to the NKF saga, the media had been largely an impartial observer and occasional reporter of nonprofit work. However, it was an article in its publication, *The Straits Times*, that triggered the NKF's lawsuit against Singapore Press Holding. After the court case, *The Straits Times* and other papers increased their coverage in a way which has been usually positively of charities.

In summary, the NKF debacle was the catalyst for major changes in the Singapore charity sector, moving it from an environment of "just doing good" to one of "doing good well" (see Figure 14.4). As a result of the charity reforms and other actions, public confidence in charities returned two years after the

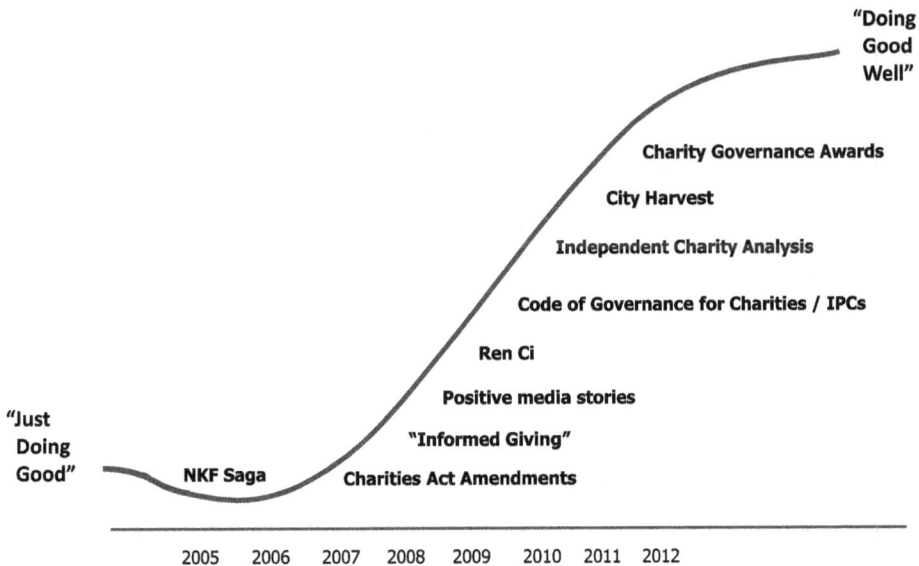

Fig. 14.4 Increasing Demands for Accountability.

scandal,[27] though the ideal of a fully accountable sector and its charities is yet to be reached.

Doing good and doing well: The coming business–social convergence

Traditionally, the business and social sectors have been largely separate. Each has its purpose, basis and culture. The business sector focuses on profits and doing well financially, while the social sector skims past profits to doing good.

However, of late, the two sectors are coming together. Players from each are criss-crossing and influencing one another. The fusion is taking place on at least two levels: the adoption and adaptation of ideas and practices, and the cross-pollination of values.

The influence of the business sector on the social sector is manifested in the calls for NPOs to not just do good, but "do good well". That call started when foundations set up by donors from the corporate sector sought to implement grant-making processes that demand accountability and deliverables from the grantees. In recent years, starting in the US, a new breed of successful businessmen turned big time philanthropists, such as Jeff Skolls and Bill Gates, have pushed for market-based solutions to social issues.

This has included pushing the envelope to apply venture capital approaches to the social sector. Known as "venture philanthropy", the giver, like the venture capitalist, is personally engaged with his or her investee. The focus is on building the capacity of the investee organisation rather than directly on its mission work. Set up in 2011, the Asian Venture Philanthropy Network has 59 organisational members from Singapore.[28]

The influence of the social sector on the business sector is best seen in the many corporate social responsibility (CSR) programmes of Singaporean companies. The early programmes focus mainly on corporate volunteerism and philanthropy. Also Singaporean companies generally lag behind those in other developed countries in the volume and sophistication of their corporate giving.[29]

---

[27] In the NVPC biennial surveys, those with low or no confidence in charities fell from 20% in 2006 (the year of the NKF scandal) to about 11% two years later (after the new charity reforms were introduced) while those with high confidence increased from 28% in 2006 to 40% two years later; the levels have remained at these levels since. See *Individual Giving Survey 2012 Supplement*.

[28] As a sign of the early stage of venture philanthropy in Singapore, less than a handful of the AVPN members in Singapore are pure venture philanthropy funds or organisations, most are organisations which support or seek to practise venture philanthropy. See more at the AVPN website, www.avpn.asia.

[29] In the international comparison in *The State of Giving: Inaugural Study of Singapore's Giving landscape* (2005), corporate giving as a % of pre-tax profits is 0.22% in Singapore, 1.60 % in US, 1.03 % in Canada and 0.95% in UK.

Beyond corporate giving, there have been calls globally for a rethink of the unfettered capitalist model and its mantra of maximising shareholder value. The calls have been made across the board by activists (e.g., the Occupy Movement), consumers (e.g., LOHAS), thought leaders (e.g., Michael Porter), political leaders (e.g., King Bhumibol), religious leaders (e.g., Pope Francis), regulators and leading corporate leaders. As a result, there is a distinct move by many in the business sector towards a more compassionate form of capitalism. The Singapore Institute of Directors' flagship annual conference in 2014, for example, was themed on the "New Capitalism" and its implications for boards and companies.

Perhaps, the most significant manifestation of the increasing convergence of the two sectors is the rise of social enterprise. This business–social hybrid can be started by different groups. Many are set up by charities to provide meaningful work for their beneficiaries and be a funding source. For example, RSVP ProGuide was set up by the Organisation of Senior Volunteers to help its senior members provide consultancy services. Some are set up by business people to create social impact. Bettr Barista, for instance, was founded by a serial entrepreneur to conduct training for marginalised women and youth at risk in careers in the specialty coffee industry. They could also be set up by the government. The Singapore Corporation of Rehabilitative Enterprises provides employment and skills to prison inmates through operations in food manufacturing, catering, laundry, bakery and data entry. Among the most successful social enterprises are those set up by the labour movement such as NTUC Fairprice, NTUC Income and NTUC First Campus.

Today, there are over 200 social enterprises in Singapore (Prakash & Tan, 2014). Over 40% are in service provision. Another 15% are in business support (travel, job placement or event management), 10% are in food and beverage, and another 10% are in education.

The mushrooming of social enterprises is partly due to efforts by different capacity builders. Aspiring and existing social enterprises can seek funding from MSF's Comcare Enterprise Fund, Tote Board's SE Hub or some of the foundations. SE Hub, NUS Enterprise, The Hub and other incubators mentor and nurture budding social enterprises, while the Social Enterprise Association brings them together for a greater collective voice and mutual support.

Corporates such as DBS Bank have made social enterprise a mainstay of their CSR programmes. Competitions organised by the Singapore International Foundation and local academic institutions are pitched at various constituencies of potential social entrepreneurs. There are awards for social enterprises such as the President's Challenge Social Enterprise Award and the Social Impact category of the Singapore Venture Capital Association.

Paralleling this growth is the rise of impact investing. The term refers to the active placement of capital into businesses that generate both financial *and* social returns, which often means investing in social enterprises. Examples include Bamboo Finance and LGT Venture Philanthropy Foundation, both of which have offices in

Singapore.[30] Recently, some efforts have been made to establish a stock exchange for social enterprises (Cheng, 2013).[31]

In other words, a whole support system is being assembled around social enterprises, the quintessential combination of "doing good" and "doing well".

Ruling well the do-gooders: The dominant role of government in the social sector[32]

Since its independence in 1965, Singapore has been, effectively, a one-party state. The rule of the PAP government has been firm and paternalistic, and its presence is strongly felt in the private and social sectors.

The government seeks to determine the role of, and set the agenda for, the social sector. It does this generally through a well-oiled messaging infrastructure, explicit articulation by governmental leaders of what is good for the national interests, being entrenched in key institutions, and majority funding of the sector.

Key social sector organisations are controlled, if not heavily influenced, by the government. To start, an umbrella body is designated for each subsector, for example, NCSS for social service, Sport Singapore for Sports, NEA for environment, NHB for heritage and NAC for arts. Some of these governmental umbrella bodies have both a regulatory as well as a dominant developmental role of their subsectors.

One of the most significant umbrella bodies is NCSS whose operating expenses are primarily government funded. Interestingly, NCSS gave up its regulatory role as Sector Administrator for the social services subsector in January 2010 because "wielding a stick on one hand and handing out sweets with the other is not an easy task and one that certainly does not breed confidence and trust" (Tan, 2009).[33] NCSS' counterpart in the UK, the National Council for Voluntary Organisations, has 10,000 members and is an NGO rather than a government body. In fact, NCSS has its roots as an NGO, the Singapore Council of Social Services; the latter was created in 1958 and effectively nationalised in 1992 by the National Council of Social Service Act. As part of the change, 12 board members including the NCSS President and key office bearers are appointed by the government, while one Vice

---

[30]For example, Transformational Business Network (www.tbnetwork.org) has setup TBN Asia in Singapore in 2014.

[31]The Impact Investment Exchange Asia (IIX) (www.asiaiix.com) eventually went to announce its collaboration to set up the Impact Exchange for social enterprise with the Stock Exchange of Mauritius.

[32]Much of the content for this subsection is drawn from Mohamed (2008) and Lien (2011).

[33]Statement was by NCSS President Kwek Siew Jin.

President and 10 other board members are elected from the general membership of VWOs.[34]

Perhaps, the largest organisation in the people sector is the People's Association (PA), a statutory board established in 1960, the year after the PAP came into power, to promote racial harmony and social cohesion. By legislation, the Prime Minister is the Chairman who then appoints all the other board members.[35] With an annual budget of more than half a billion dollars, the PA's reach is extensive: over 28 community centres, 1,800 grassroots organisations and more than 25,000 volunteer grassroots leaders.

In addition to these subsector developmental agencies and the PA, the government has created key capacity building organisations to promote its agenda of state building and social cohesion while addressing certain social needs. Examples include NVPC (volunteerism and donations), C3A (active ageing), SG Enable (embracing people with disabilities) and Social Enterprise Association (social enterprises).[36] The government provides operational costs and grant-making funds, and also appoints the governing boards of these organisations.

For the larger number of NPOs where board appointments may not be dependent upon the government, their funding would likely be from government sources. Government grants and contracts are, however, given for specific purposes and conditions aligned with the government's direction. For example, the network of 43 family service centres, although owned by various NPOs, are effectively run as part of a national system providing core, homogenous funded programmes endorsed by the government.

Although it is the major funder of the social sector, the government is clear that it does not wish to fully fund an NPO as it wishes for them to also raise some money from the public. Dubbed the Many Helping Hands, the approach develops "self-reliance in a society that is robust, yet compassionate and caring" through "partnership with concerned citizens, corporations, community organisations, religious groups and family members".[37] However, with the high level of funding and directedness of these programmes, Many Helping Hands has sometimes been called Many Hired Hands.

Yet, for all its dominance in the social sector, the government has not traditionally made the sector a high priority, preferring to focus on national economic growth and consolidating Singapore's position in a globalised world. This

---

[34] National Council of Social Service Act (Chapter 195A).

[35] The Chairman appoints the Deputy Chairman (a Minister) and eight other members who form part of the Board of Management. The rest of the Board are four members elected from a group appointed by the Chairman in consultation with some 80 civic organisations. See People's Association Act (Chapter 227).

[36] These organisations are briefly described in the section below "The Social Ecosystem — Government".

[37] Statement by Mr Abdullah Tarmugi, then Acting Minister for Community Development at the World Summit For Social Development Copenhagen, Denmark, 10 March 1995.

approach seemed to change somewhat after the 2011 General Election when the PAP, while retaining its dominance in parliament, had its lowest vote share (60.14%) since independence. One reason proffered for the relatively poor result was the growing chasm between the rich and the poor, and the perceived neglect of the hidden have-nots.

In the 2012 Budget, Finance Minister Tharman Shanmugaratnam announced that Singapore was "stepping up its social policy" to better support the elderly and Singaporeans with disabilities, and to help the lower-income families with social mobility (Budget Singapore 2012). In the 2013 National Day rally, in what has been described as the "tipping point" (Chan & Lian, 2013) of social policy changes in Singapore, Prime Minister Lee Hsien Loong spoke of the need to "shift the balance" from nation building that was premised on "tough love" to one where the community and the government "have to do more to support individuals" (Prime Minister's Office, Singapore, 2013). In 2014, several laws were passed that showed the government's move towards "a more compassionate Singapore": Prevention of Human Trafficking Act, Family Justice Act, and Protection from Harassment Act (Basu, 2014).[38]

Notwithstanding the good work and intent of the government, there are many who believe that the government should not be so heavily ruling the social sector. Nominated Member of Parliament (NMP) Laurence Lien summarises the reasons as follows (Lien, 2011):

- There are areas of social and community interventions that the government simply cannot take on. Unlike a more monolithic governmental system, individual NPOs can provide niche, customised solutions to meet holistic and diverse needs of its beneficiaries. Some needs are also not within the scope of government policies, capabilities and priorities.
- There are areas that NPOs can do better than the state. Where innovation and experimentation are needed, NPOs are better placed at conducting and abandoning as needed. They also have more moral authority with each other and with beneficiaries to effect certain programmes.
- Even if state agencies can be more efficient that NPOs, it should, nevertheless, recognise the autonomy and dignity of each individual and social group. "It is only when individuals are able to exercise self-determination and contribute meaningfully to the communities they live in, that they feel they are fully human, and fully citizens of this country. This is when a place to stay becomes a home" (*ibid.*).

---

[38]The advocacy for some of these laws had been pushed for some time by social activists. Consultations on the legislations with civil society groups also preceded the passing of most of these laws.

The full effects of the recent shift to focus more attention and funding on the social sector remain unclear. A determining factor will be the government's interaction with civil society groups which is taking a different trajectory from the past.

Campaigning despite constraints: The rise of advocacy and civil society[39]

In direct contrast to its enthusiastic support of charity groups that serve the poor and disadvantaged, the government is seen as resistant and even antagonistic towards civil society groups. This was especially so during Singapore's early years when the government considered economic survival an imperative. Responding to advocacy and civil society groups was viewed as a distraction.

Various tools have been used to limit the operating space of civil advocacy. In 1968, the government drew up a framework of industrial relations that was in line with state objectives to rein in the early activist tendencies of the trade unions. Licenses and permits were needed for newspapers and other publications. Defamation suits and the damages awarded were seen as effective in silencing dissent, as was the Internal Security Act, a feature left from the colonial government. The detention of the alleged Marxist conspirators in 1987 under this Act was said to have curtailed the growth of civil society for a long time after.

The 1990s brought economic growth, and the rise of a more educated middle class with greater access to alternative thoughts and ideas through the Internet. Responding to this group, the then Prime Minister Goh Chok Tong promised a more consultative government. He introduced the Feedback Unit (now known as REACH), Speakers' Corner at Hong Lim Park, the NMP scheme and Community Development Councils.

At the same time, Goh's open disapproval of Catherine Lim's essay, "The PAP and the People — A Great Affective Divide", led to the establishment of "out of bounds" or OB markers: a term (borrowed from golf) to denote topics that are not permissible for public discussion. The government's position is that if anyone wishes to delve into such topics, he or she should form or join a political party to challenge state policy. In 2006, blogger Mr Brown wrote an article (Brown, 2006; "Voices" *Today*, 2006) in his weekly opinion column in *Today* concerning the rising costs of living in Singapore. The government labelled him a "partisan player" whose views "distort the truth" and his column was suspended by the paper. The acceptance of OB markers has limited what can be raised in public discourse and has been described by some critics as creating "a suffocating environment where the limits of one's freedom to express is defined by citizens themselves" ("Singapore Media", 2010).

---

[39] Part of the content for this subsection is drawn from Mohamed (2008); Singam, Tan, Ng and Perera (eds.) (2002); and Koh and Soon (2012).

In 2004, the then Deputy Prime Minister Lee Hsien Loong made what was regarded as a seminal speech at a Harvard Club of Singapore anniversary dinner outlining how the government views civil society ("Building a Civic Society", 2004). He spoke of how the government would be "increasingly guided by the consensus of views in the community with regards to morality and decency issues" and will "pull back from being all things to all citizens". He encouraged civic participation through debates on policies and national issues, but warned that criticism which "scores political points and undermines the government's standing, whether or not this is intended" will be rebutted or even demolished so that the government does not "lose its moral authority".

The process of further liberalisation of civil society space in Singapore is therefore not necessarily a linear one. Some critics describe some developments as "one step forward, two steps back". One example of the step forward is Speakers Corner, which was liberalised in 2008 to allow demonstrations and the tolerance of anti-government forums and demonstrations such as the Tan Kin Lian protest on the state's failure to protect investors in the financial crisis (2008), #FreeMyInternet (2013), the Population White Paper (2013) and Return Our CPF (2014). Taking two steps back might be the establishment of the Public Order Act and the installation of CCTVs at the Speaker's Corner in 2009.

Another example of the government's engagement takes place on the online battlefield. Given the rise of new media, the government has made attempts to engage citizens through the net and social media. Several Ministers have their own Facebook and Twitter accounts which they use to broadcast happenings and even policies, and respond to citizens' posts. At the same time, in 2013, the Media Development Authority (MDA) surprised many by requiring individual licensing for websites that report on Singapore news, including some blogging sites. The move was widely criticised by Singapore's online community as another restriction on press freedom ("MDA Clarifies", *Yahoo News*, 2013).[40] In addition, Prime Minister Lee served lawyer's letters to bloggers Alex Au and Roy Ngerng demanding an apology and the removal of certain online articles which were alleged to be defamatory (Jhaipragas, 2014).[41]

The government is particularly sensitive about the agenda of human rights activists. In 2010, human rights advocacy group MARUAH was gazetted as a political association three years after it applied to become a registered society, limiting its fundraising access not just to foreign donors but also effectively to

---

[40]Since the scheme was introduced, several blogging sites were asked to register: Yahoo! Singapore, The Breakfast Network, Mothership. Following the press release by the government on the licensing scheme, several bloggers staged blackouts of their websites in protest, and a group of bloggers, #FreeMyInternet, staged a protest at Hong Lim Park.

[41]Alex Au acquiesced swiftly and escaped court action. Roy Ngerng did so only after posting subsequent media links deemed offensive to PM Lee, and now awaits court trial.

local donors.[42] In 2012, the Singapore Management University suddenly cancelled plans to set up the Handa Centre for Global Governance and Human Rights. There was speculation that the government had a hand in the closure of the centre (Wong, 2012; "SMU Pulls Plug", *Today*, 2012).

Notwithstanding these challenges and constraints, several civil society groups have emerged, championing their causes and contesting the government's practices and policies when needed: Nature Society for the environment, Transient Workers Count Too (TWC2) for migrant workers, Think Centre for political research, Association of Women for Action and Research (AWARE) for women's rights, Association of Muslim Professionals for Malay-Muslim self-help and MARUAH for human rights. In addition, prominent theatre groups and arts organisations such as The Necessary Stage, Substation and Wild Rice explore societal issues that are sometimes controversial, and face censorship or punitive action.

In 2007, Wild Rice staged a political play, *The Campaign to Confer the Public Star on JBJ*, and subsequently saw its funding cut in 2011 and 2012 because its works were deemed "incompatible with the core values promoted by the government and society" (Yusof, 2013).[43] Funding from the NAC returned to its original level in 2013.

That year, the Singapore arts community put up a six-point arts manifesto emphasising the fundamentality of arts in society. One of the six points is that "art can be challenged but not censored" ("A Manifesto for the Arts", *Arts Engage*). The government did not fully agree.

In 2014, MDA accorded a "Not Allowed for All Ratings" classification to Tan Pin Pin's political film, *From Singapore with Love*. This spiked interest in the film and 400 people including Singaporeans watched the film screening in Johor, Malaysia and the film had four sold-out screenings over two days in London (Yong, 2014; Wei, 2014).

One significant civil group is The Working Committee (TWC). It comprises individuals from various NGOs who came together in 1998 to build a national network of civil society activists and organisations. Their year-long discussion helped them learn how the network could and should work together with each other and the government, and the value of advocacy.

In 2001, following news reports of the death of an abused 19-year-old foreign domestic worker, several social activists came together under the umbrella of

---

[42] Braema Mathi, President of MARUAH disagrees that MARUAH is a political association based on the definition in the Political Donations Act (PDA). She also said that fundraising for MARUAH is crippled because not only can it not take in donations from foreign donors (condition of political association under the PDA), the brush of being a political association and being named as a donor will deter interested Singaporean donors who may see it as being anti-state and or being a political party (when it is not).

[43] Funding was cut by S$20,000 in 2010 and a further S$60,000 in 2012.

The Working Committee 2 (or TWC2, which was later re-invented with the same moniker to Transient Workers Count 2) to advocate and support migrant workers.[44]

Again, in 2014, The Working Committee 3 (TWC3) was formed to create the Singapore Advocacy Awards. The awards objective was to "recognise, affirm and celebrate civil society organisations/individuals for its outstanding initiative(s) and positive impact on integration, diversity, solidarity, tolerance and awareness in Singapore". Ten individuals and organisations were honoured in August 2014 at a ceremony: they received a certificate and a contribution of S$1,000 towards their cause ("Advocacy Awards", *The Straits Times*, 2014; Lee, 2014).[45] Unlike most other award ceremonies, there was no Minister or parliamentarian as guest of honour.

To be sure, several individuals and organisations have had some measure of success in their advocacy. One of the most prominent examples was the Nature Society's successful campaign in 2001 to save Chek Jawa, an area on Pulau Ubin, that is known for its rich biodiversity. The government reconsidered its earlier reclamation plans and decided not to proceed.

However, in an almost parallel case, conservation groups such as SOS Bukit Brown and All Things Bukit Brown did not succeed in preserving the Bukit Brown cemetery despite having it included in the 2014 World Monuments Watch list. The government stated that it had to make the "difficult trade-off decision" in "land-scarce Singapore" to create a dual four-lane road that would run through Bukit Brown and which would require the exhumation of 5,000 graves.

Other successful advocacy by civil society groups include:

- A new law in 2013 to give foreign domestic workers a day off every week (or monetary compensation in lieu) after a decade of petitioning by migrant NGOs.
- A rule on the evidence of character in rape cases in the Evidence Act was repealed in 2012 after representations by AWARE (AWARE, 2011; Ramesh, 2012).
- The creation of the Early Childhood Development Agency in 2013 to integrate the government's approach towards early childhood care and education and

---

[44]Although TWC2 and TWC3 (see later below) were formed using the same name of "The Working Committee", the only common person across the three committees was Constance Singam. Braema Mathi, who was part of TWC2 and became its first President, explained that they decided to name it as such in the spirit of the first TWC: "to show that people can come together, do something and eventually disappear, a social movement building approach".

[45]The award recipients were ACRES (animal welfare organisation), All Things Bukit Brown (heritage preservation movement), Braema Mathi (human rights advocate), Chan Li Shan (mental health advocate), Damien Chng (second chances advocate), Eugene Tay (environment advocate), Jeremy Boo and Lee Xian Jie (social issue film-makers), Louis Ng (animal welfare advocate), M. Ravi (human rights lawyer), and Pink Dot (freedom to love movement).

the setting up of 15 government kindergartens after the publication of a Lien Foundation's commissioned study benchmarking early education across the world; the report showed that Singapore ranked 29th out of 45 developed and emerging economies ("Starting Well", *Economist Intelligence Unit*, 2012; Pin, 2012; Ministry of Education [MOE], 2013).

- A Bill on animal welfare put together by a committee of animal welfare activists, grassroots leaders and industry representatives that was tabled in October 2014 after two years of collaborative review (Ee, 2014).

However, it should be noted that civil society is not just about a vertical civil society-to-state relationship where activists campaign, with some general consensus, on a public interest issue towards the government. In recent years, a horizontal peer-to-peer relationship has developed between civil society groups, and between civil society groups and citizens which may campaign against each other.

One example of this was a proposal in 2012 by the government to build scaled eldercare facilities and apartment studios in Woodlands, Toh Yi and Mountbatten, amongst others. Some residents protested their loss of common space, calling for such "death houses" to be Not In My Backyard (NIMBY). Appalled by what they perceived as a lack of civic mindedness, 500 residents in Mountbatten organised a counter-NIMBY movement and created a "In My Backyard" petition, drowning out the voices of some 130 residents who earlier petitioned for the facilities to be moved elsewhere (Chan, 2012). To date, the government remains firm on their plans for these facilities, offering instead other sweeteners in the form of improved recreational facilities for disgruntled residents.

Another example of intra-civil society engagements resulted from the society-to-state campaign by migrant NGOs for a day off a week for domestic helpers. The success of the campaign led to a negative response from maid employment agencies and employers who appealed for fairer terms of employment for themselves. However, the Ministry of Manpower (MOM) stood by its policy change, stating that current arrangements incorporate collective employers' feedback ("Employer's Concerns", *The Straits Times*, 2012).

AWARE, the women's rights organisation has also encountered pushbacks from citizens for its strong push on gender-related matters. In November 2013, it announced its success in getting the Singapore Armed Forces to stop a misogynistic version of a popular marching song. Most of the 700 comments it received on its Facebook page were negative, some calling it a "feminazi group". In April 2014, responding to the government's announcement of enhanced benefits for national servicemen, AWARE said that it "disagrees strongly with any link between support for fundamental needs and an individual's status as an NSman, especially when the military may not be suitable for many people, regardless of their gender". Overnight, it received more than a 100 comments, mostly negative, urging it to consider the issue within the larger context.

Faith in action: Good words and good works from the religious community

With four out of five Singaporeans professing a religious belief,[46] it should not be surprising that religion is an indispensable part of the social sector.

First, as described above, more than half of the registered charities are religious organisations and they attract about half of all charitable donations.[47] As noted, the "advancement of religion" is legally a charitable cause — even if it may be an enigma to some as to how what is fundamentally about a person's own salvation and spirituality equates to helping the poor and needy, the latter concept being what the average man in the street would equate with charity.[48]

Perhaps the nexus of religion to the common understanding of charity is that while religion is primarily about God and the afterlife, they are also fundamentally about bringing out the goodness in man, including being good towards his fellow man. The major religions all preach charitable service to others. For Christians, "love your neighbour" and giving alms without "the right hand knowing what the left hand is doing" are among the commandments of Jesus Christ to his followers. For Muslims, one of the Five Pillars of Islam is to pay *zakat* to the poor and needy and, in the process, purify one's wealth and soul. For Buddhists, compassion and the giving of alms is the beginning of one's journey to nirvana.

In this context, many religious organisations perform charitable works for the broader community, mostly those outside their faith. They often do so through spin-off charities[49] which focus on specific areas and constituencies of needs, most of which are in the social service sector. A large proportion of the VWOs today are faith-based in origin. A 2008 study to trace the religious origins of NCSS members found that 41% (76 out of 188 studied) were best described as Protestant Christian-related organisations, followed by, in order, secular, Buddhist, Catholic, Muslims and Hindu orientations (Mathew, 2008). Among the significant faith-based VWOs are:

- Catholic: Boys Town (1948), Catholic Welfare Services (1959) and Caritas Singapore (2006).

---

[46] Figures are from the Singapore Census of Population 2010. Out of a total population of 3.105 million residents aged 15 years and above, 527,553 (17%) reported having no religion. 1,032,879 (33.3%) Buddhists, 339,149 (10.9%) Taoists, 219,133 (7.1%) Catholics, 350,111 (11.3%) other Christians, 457,435 (14.7%) Muslims, 157,854 (5.1%) Hindus, 10,744 (0,3%) Sikhs, and 10,891 (0.4%) belonging to other religions.

[47] The amount donated to religious organisations do not include those from older institutions such as the Catholic and Anglican churches which are exempted from registering under the Charities Act.

[48] For an explanation of how historically religion became a charitable cause, see Cheng (2012).

[49] Part of the reason was the administrative criterion of secularism in these charities in order to qualify for IPC status and hence, tax-deductible donations.

- Protestant Christian-related: Presbyterian Community Services (1974), Methodist Welfare Services (1981), Touch Community Services (1992) and Singapore Anglican Community Services (2005).
- Muslim: Jamiyah Singapore (1932), Muhammadiyah Association (1957) and PERTAPIS (1970).
- Hindu: Ramakrishna Mission (1928) and Sree Narayana Mission (1948).
- Buddhist: Singapore Buddhist Free Clinic (1969), Singapore Buddhist Welfare Services (1981), Buddhist Compassion Relief Tzu Chi Foundation (1993) and Metta Welfare Association (1994).
- Other: Thye Hua Kwan Moral Society (1978).

Propagating goodness is not just about good works. It also involves the spreading of good words. However, in secular Singapore, while every citizen has a constitutional right to profess, practise or propagate his or her religious belief, the government restricts this right in some circumstances. Certain religious groups such as Jehovah's Witness and the Unification Church are banned. Equally, government leaders are clear about their determination to separate state and religion. The government especially does not tolerate speech or actions it deems could adversely affect racial or religious harmony. The Maintenance of Religious Harmony Act which came into force in 1992 specifically disallows ill will or hostility between different religious groups. In that light, the major religious leaders are usually circumspect about "aggressive preaching or proselytization".[50]

However, when it comes to religiously informed viewpoints on matters of public policy and interest such as euthanasia, stem-cell research, abortion, organ transplant, homosexuality and gambling, religious leaders have spoken up. In March 2004, when the idea of building a casino in Singapore was mooted by the government, leaders of the Catholic Church, the National Council of Christian Churches and Muslim Groups expressed their strong disapproval in view of the negative social consequences. In the event, two casinos were built.

A tense state-religion confrontation occurred in 2013 with the Faith Community Baptist Church (FCBC), an independent Christian church. Senior Pastor Lawrence Khong of FCBC fired a female employee who had committed adultery with a fellow church employee and became pregnant. She complained to the Ministry of Manpower. The Minister decided that she was "dismissed without sufficient cause" and ordered the church to pay compensation of S$7,000. The church paid up, but sought a High Court judicial review of the Minister's decision. The review is pending.

Yet, as they enter the civil society space to advocate for their religiously informed positions, religious organisations have found that they can face greater pushback

---

[50]This is a term used by PM Lee Hsien Loong in his 2009 National Day Rally Speech. The speech provided a good summary of the government's approach to religious harmony and activities.

from other NGOs. The 2009 AWARE saga, in particular, left a deep imprint on civil society and the nation.

A group of Anglican Pentecostal Christians gained control of AWARE's executive committee because they were unhappy with the gay-oriented sex education programme the organisation was running in schools. They wanted, instead, to use the organisation to promote Christian family values. The Christian conservatives were eventually ousted, but not before a very public war of words that not only enthralled the nation but brought to the fore the underlying culture war over values. Observers have theorised that the event reflects the rise of religious groups such as the Christian Right to fill the role as upholder of public morality — a role that the pragmatic state has ignored in recent years to focus instead on more urgent economic priorities (Chong, 2011).

The culture war manifested itself again in July 2014, this time bringing two faiths together in a common stand for family values. Pink Dot SG, an annual event of the lesbian, gay, bisexual and transgender (LGBT) community in Singapore was held at Hong Lim Park. The annual event had drawn increasing numbers since it started in 2009. Pastor Khong of FCBC and also Chairman of the LoveSingapore network of churches in Singapore decided to organise a Red Dot Family Movement at the Padang on the same day as Pink Dot. However, his application for the space was rejected by the authorities and the family festival was instead held as a virtual rally on Facebook. At the same time, a Muslim religious teacher, Ustaz Noor Deros called for a "Wear White" campaign, asking Muslims to "return to their normal disposition". Pastor Khong voiced his support. The Pink Dot 2014 event proceeded without incident with a turnout of 26,000 attendees. Meanwhile, the Wear White campaign saw Muslim mosque goers and some church members don white garb in support of traditional family values in the days following the event (Yuen-C, 2014).

Moving forward

It seems almost foolhardy to predict what the Singaporean social sector landscape will look like in the next 10, let alone 50, years. However, it is possible to identify some key elements and the players that will play a prominent role in shaping the social sector going forward. These include:

- Changing societal needs and how NPOs respond to them.
- The extent and trajectory of advocacy.
- The attitude and approach of the government towards the social sector.
- Collaboration within and outside the sector.
- The extent to which innovation is embraced and exploited.

Changing societal needs and response

Singapore will have a more active and diverse citizenry. Demographics are changing. The young, especially, are more vocal and liberal in their outlook. However, young or old, citizens expect more. Better educated and informed, they will make more nuanced demands about the social fabric. The population is also more mixed with the influx of foreigners who bring a greater diversity of views and value systems.

As demographics change, who the beneficiaries are, and what their needs are, will change. With the increasing income divide, the poor have not gone away. They are just less visible. By their nature too, beneficiaries are not usually seeking help; they need to be sought out and be helped.

NPOs are the key organisations on the ground. To be effective, they need to be responsive to the needs of their beneficiaries. As needs change — and they do in the fast changing world — NPOs must morph to address them.

The healthcare subsector provides a good illustration of changing needs. With medical advances, diseases such as leprosy and tuberculosis are no longer prevalent; instead, new infectious diseases such as Bird Flu and Ebola pose the greatest threat. It will be incumbent on health-based NPOs to review their scope and mission with the changing circumstances.

Indeed, NPOs should work towards the completion of their mission and, thus, their extinction as individual NPOs. (The individual volunteers and staff can move on to address new and greater social needs.)

In working to eliminate a social need, and thus the completion of a particular NPO's mission, there should be greater focus on long-term solutions especially those based on preventative and structural changes, rather than just the immediate relief and treatment of the problem. For example, the number of abused migrant workers will not be reduced just by creating more shelters even if this may be necessary in the immediate term. Instead, the long-term answer lies in educating employers and changing their attitudes toward the exploitation of migrant labour, as well as in ensuring a punitive system and process to redress and discourage wrong doings. In other words, advocacy can be more effective in dealing with long-term issues than just welfare — which has been the mainstay and focus of many NPOs here to date.

While effectiveness should be measured by the mission of the NPO, it is easy for charities to be distracted by the need for fundraising, operational and manpower issues. However, it is unlikely there will be any let up in the new era of "doing good well". Increasingly, more donations are being channelled through funds and foundations, and these grant makers are getting more professional and demanding. In the new thinking, the focus of deliverables on grants is not just output, but measurable outcomes of social impact.

Trajectory of advocacy[52]

As noted above, advocacy, when its goals are achieved, can be more effective (even conclusive) in dealing with social issues in the long term, compared with relief and welfare. Advocacy addresses root causes, whereas relief and welfare often address only the symptoms.

Advocacy is difficult in Singapore. For one, results, especially those which successfully pre-empt the occurrence of bad situations, are not always visible or tangible compared to relief efforts. Then there are all the constraints of advocacy. There is little surprise that so few organisations engage in advocacy to a significant extent. Yet logically, if the social sector is to be more effective, it should engage in more advocacy.

In promoting greater advocacy, civil society could perhaps take to heart the conclusions of the TWC1's study.[53] Activism requires both volunteerism and advocacy, and an effective civil society needs not just civil society players that cooperate with the state without losing their individuality and independence, but also a state which is responsive to alternative views.

Apart from a more vocal populace, advocacy is expected to significantly increase as a result of the power of the Internet and social media. Facebook, Twitter, Instagram, Tumblr and their ilk are enabling citizen engagement and conversations that cannot be easily managed, if at all. They provide the platform for citizens to be agenda-setters. The result is a situation where the government does not necessarily know first or know best.

Advocacy is, of course, both vertical and horizontal. Vertical engagement between civil society and state will partly depend upon the attitude of, and response by, the government. Horizontal engagement between civil society groups as well as with citizens will likely see greater and more intense encounters, given the changing values and a more expressive public. Lines have been, and could be further, drawn between groups with opposing worldviews and values such as the conservatives versus liberals, locals versus foreigners, and minority versus majority. Differences over existing issues like S377A, overcrowding, meritocracy and the cost of living could boil over, even as new and not-so-new issues related to economic restructuring, immigration, retirement, ageing, and dying could surface and polarise society further. Hopefully, the rise of intra-civil society advocacy can be managed to prevent a damaging war of culture and values.

Attitude of government

Without a doubt, the type and extent of government participation in the social sector will impact the latter's growth trajectory. Political leaders will need to

---

[52]The content of this subsection and the next draws partly from Kiat and Soon (2013) and Singam, Tan, Ng and Perera (2002), *op. cit.*

[53]This is summarised in the last chapter of Singam, Tan, Ng and Perara's (2002), *Building Social Space in Singapore*, referred to above.

recognise changes in society when deciding their approach to working with the social sector, and responding to social issues. What has worked in the past may not be as effective going forward. Whether PAP or another political party, the next generation of leaders will not have the same gravitas as the first. The political, economic and social compacts have changed.

At an IPS Conference in 2013, it was pointed out that, anecdotally, there have been more court cases challenging the government in the last five years than the previous 30 to 40 years. Fear of dissent and confrontation with authorities is dissipating. Witness the increasing number and size of rallies challenging government policies and positions at Hong Lim Park in 2013 and 2014.

At the same time, it should be in the government's interest to welcome and nurture constructive advocacy. Differences of views can reveal disconnects and potential policy changes and solutions which are structural in nature, and which are not easily discerned and framed without the orientation and perspectives of stakeholders on the ground.

Former Minister George Yeo recognised this as early as 1991. He used a "banyan tree" analogy to describe the pervasiveness of the state and the need for the government "to withdraw a little" and to prune the banyan tree "judiciously" so that the "other plants" of civil society can flourish (Latif & Lee, 2015).[54] In the years since, the government has, indeed, shown a greater willingness to accommodate different views. It has conducted several "national conversations" and reviews — including Singapore 21 (1991), Remaking Singapore (2002) and Our Singapore Conversation (2012) — to build a common national agenda for moving forward. However, civil society groups have expressed the desire for greater liberalisation and less reversal of the liberalisation measures that have occurred. For instance, many feel that OB markers and the blurred, somewhat arbitrary, boundaries between politics and civil society, and between politics and religion need to be dismantled for there to be open and constructive communication.

In the welfare sector, the government's funding and support is generally much welcomed. Nevertheless, an overdependence on the government's direction and blessings is a real risk to a vibrant sector. The nature of the social sector is that it is made up of a large number of grassroots organisations, each attuned to the needs of their constituencies, and each nimble and responsive to those needs. Innovation has to come from the ground-up, rather than be driven top-down. After all, the purpose of the social sector is to fill the gaps — and there will always be gaps. When NPOs get lazy and wait for directions, the gaps will remain.

Therefore, without reducing its funding of the sector, if the government were to be less dominating, the social sector might have a better chance of becoming more effective, albeit messier.

Here, civil society observers distinguish between state-led and state-supported groups. A state-led group is one initiated by the state with appointed trusted

---

[54] A banyan tree is an Asian tree with a dense canopy, under which nothing grows.

individuals to lead the efforts with the explicit or implicit understanding that instructions from the state will be carried out. On the other hand, state-supported groups are those formed from an idea mooted either by the state or civil society, but the government provides some or much of the financial and other resources while allowing leaders to emerge naturally with the explicit or implicit understanding that the government will not intervene in running the groups or in compelling obedience.

Perhaps the one area that most stakeholders in the social sector wish to see the government continue at the same level is its role as regulator, in particular, of charities. The COC has to balance the need to maintain confidence in charities through tight regulations with the need for an efficient sector which is not tied up in suffocating rules and enforcement. The current COC has been able to walk that tightrope well. However, there can be improvement in the review of the policies that constrain the sector and giving. Chief among the sector's bugbears are the regulations that effectively hamper the generosity of Singaporeans towards overseas humanitarian needs — for example, the requirement for permits for fundraising for overseas purposes, the retention of 80% of funds raised for domestic purposes, and lack of tax deductibility for overseas giving.

Collaboration

Collaborations can take the social sector and its organisations to new heights. The benefits of collaboration are obvious: increased reach, knowledge and skills; cost savings from economies of scale; and expansion of the value proposition of the parties. Collaboration is happening in various degrees, but much more can be done.

First are the collaborations among NPOs. The social sector is a fragmented one. The majority of the 2,142 charity organisations, for example, have less than S$250,000 in annual receipts, employing less than a handful of staff. Less than 20% have more than S$1 million in annual receipts. In each subsector, be it healthcare, elderly, youth, etc., there are a number of overlapping NPOs that perform the same kind of work targeted at essentially the same group of beneficiaries. While this is to be expected — the nature of social work is ground-up initiatives by people with passion for the cause — more can be achieved if organisations come together to share resources and knowledge. This can be done in several ways.

The first is the establishment of associations of NPOs with commonality to each other, to network, learn and advocate with collective strength. While there are a number of trade associations for the various vertical segments of commercial companies, there are much fewer in the social space. For example, in Singapore, there is no association of foundations or grant makers such as the Council of Foundation in the US or the Association of Charitable Foundations in the UK.

The next is bilateral or multilateral cooperation on common programmes and activities of NPOs. This need not be only for NPOs from the same vertical segment. For example, every NPO has back office functions of accounting, audit,

IPC records, IT and human resources. One solution is shared services to encourage these economies of scale. Currently there are shared service providers and schemes by NCSS and other capacity builders to encourage use of shared services. However, the take-up has not been high.

The ultimate form of collaboration is the merger of NPOs. In the commercial sector, mergers are usually driven by financial incentives. Improved valuations do not figure in the social sector, hence mergers happens once in a blue moon.[55] More mergers could happen if personal pride and ownership of the entity were less of a consideration.

Synergies can also be found in cross-sector collaborations. The social sector does collaborate with the other two sectors on a project basis. More tri-sector collaborations are taking place, especially in other countries. A study by Accenture, "The Convergence Economy", provides several case studies of cross-sector collaborations that are creating a new marketplace in international development (Bulloch, Lacy & Jurgens, 2011).

Unfortunately, cross-sector collaborations are often uneven given the relative power of the relationships. Corporates and government tend to have more clout as they bring more financial power and expertise to the table. However, NPOs should not underestimate the power of their reach and understanding of their constituencies and the issues. The most effective form of collaboration occurs when there is mutual respect and a willingness to let each handle their area of expertise.

Social innovation[56]

Innovation is widely recognised to be the game changer to drive the growth of companies and the economy. Economists estimate that 60% to 80% of economic growth comes from innovation and new knowledge.

Innovation is equally relevant and valuable to the social sector. The main purpose of innovation here is to speed up the process of social change. The ultimate goal is to accelerate the process of change so as to achieve systemic change. Indeed, observers believe that some of society's greatest problems such as climate change, widening inequality and an ageing population can only be solved by social innovation.

In simple terms, social innovation refers to new ideas and insights that fulfil unmet social needs. Innovations can be incremental or disruptive, but their impact should be significant. Some world changing social innovations include the Open University, fair trade, micro-finance and humanitarian relief.

---

[55]There are few examples of mergers amongst charities. The last known significant one was the 1963 merger of the Singapore Chinese Sign School for the Deaf and Oral School for the Deaf to become the Singapore School for the Deaf. Another was the 2008 merger of two young charities for youths, Promiseworks and Halogen Foundation Singapore (formerly Young Leaders Foundation).
[56]The content of this subsection draws partly from the chapter by Geoff Mulgan, "Stepping on the Accelerator of Social Change," in Cheng & Mohamed (2010), and Hartung (2012).

To be sure, social innovators and social innovations have existed side by side for years. However, much of Singapore's large scale social innovations such as electronic road pricing, public housing and the Marina Barrage (turning a seawater port area into a freshwater reservoir and recreation site) are driven primarily by the public sector.

Specifically, there are two drivers that could accelerate the process of social innovation in Singapore. The first is the establishment of capacity builders such as innovation centres, catalysts, incubators — essentially innovation-focused organisations that concentrate on understanding and developing the field. Towards this end, in the last decade, organisations such as the LCSI and Social Innovation Park (SIP) have been set up. Some tertiary institutions feature social innovation programmes. The growth of social enterprises has also led to the setting up of companies to implement specific socially innovative solutions as businesses.

Yet, the level of social innovation activity in Singapore is still comparatively low. While some social enterprises are innovative in their offerings and approaches, most are not; they are similar to regular businesses except that many of them seek to employ beneficiaries from the social sector. LCSI and SIP are relatively small organisations. LCSI has focused largely on awareness and education while SIP has a broader focus on social entrepreneurship and social enterprises.

The second driver involves cross-sector collaboration for innovation. Creativity is known to blossom at the crossroads of diverse knowledge domains. In fact, a social enterprise is a hybrid organisation formed at the nexus of social and private sectors. The growth of social enterprises has been spurred by several cross-sector collaborations: seed funds for social enterprises from public sector sources (MSF and Tote Board); the annual Social Collab that brings the social enterprise community together with representatives from the other two sectors; and competitions to encourage social enterprises by academic institutions in partnership with private sector organisations.

In its push for innovation, the government also launched a S$450 million Public Private Co-Innovation Partnership in 2010 to encourage the co-development of innovative solutions between the public and private sector to meet Singapore's longer-term needs.

In short, while the fostering of social innovation remains a nascent industry in Singapore, hopefully the several initiatives that already exist will grow, and the ideal of innovation, in its broadest sense, can be applied to solve many of the most pressing social challenges of our time.

References

A Manifesto for the Arts. *Arts Engage*. Retrieved 16 February 2015, from https://sites. googie.com/site/artsengagesg/manifesto-for-the-arts; https://sites.google.com/site/ amanifestoforthearts/the-petition/in-english.

Advocacy Awards for 10 Groups, Individuals (2014, September 2). *The Straits Times.* Retrieved 16 February 2015, from http://news.asiaone.com/news/singapore/advocacy-awards-10-groups-individuals.

Association of Women for Action and Research (AWARE). Section 157 (d) of Evidence Act: Repeal It (2011, November 1). Retrieved 16 February 2015, from http://www.aware.org.sg/2011/11/section-157d-of-evidence-act-repeal-it/

Basu, Radha (2014, November 16). Signs of a More Compassionate Singapore. *The Straits Times.* Retrieved 16 February 2015, from http://www.straitstimes.com/news/opinion/more-opinion/more-opinion-stories/story/signs-more-compassionate-singapore-20141118.

Brown (2006, June 30). S'poreans Are Fed up with Progress! *Today.* Retrieved 16 February 2015, from http://www.mrbrown.com/biog/2006/07/today_sporeans_.html.

Budget Singapore 2012. Ministry of Finance, Singapore. Retrieved 16 February 2015, from http://www.singaporebudget.gov.sg/budget_2012/budget_speech.html.

Building a Civic Society (2004, January 6). Speech by the Deputy Prime Minister, Lee Hsien Loong at the Harvard Club of Singapore 35th Anniversary Dinner.

Bulloch, Gib, Lacy, Peter & Jurgens, Chris (2011). Convergence Economy: Rethinking International Development in a Coverging World. Accenture.

Centre for Civil Society Studies. Retrieved 9 February 2015, from www.ccss.jhu.edu/index.php?section=content&view=9&sub-3.

Chan, Robin (2012, June 2). Yes, In My Backyard. *The Straits Times.* Retrieved 16 February 2015, from http://xinkaishi.typepad.com/a_new_start/2012/06/.

Chan, Robin & Lian, Goh Chin (2013, August 20). PM Lee's NDR2013 Speech Bold and Necessary, Say Analysts. *The Straits Times.* Retrieved 16 February 2015, from http://lkyspp.nus.edu.sg/wp-content/uploads/2013/06/straitstimes.com-PM-Lees_NDR2013_speech_bold_and_necessary_say_analysts.pdf.

Cheng, Willie (2009). *Doing Good Well: What Does (and Does Not) Make Sense in the Nonprofit World.* New Jersey: Jossey-Bass, John Wiley & Sons.

Cheng, Willie (2010). Transitions within the Ecosystem of Change. In Willie Cheng & Sharifah Mohamed (eds.), *The World That Changes the World: How Philanthropy, Innovation and Entrepreneurship Are Transforming the Social Ecosystem* (pp.7–33). New Jersey: Jossey-Bass, John Wiley & Sons.

Cheng, Willie (2012, July 7). When Churches Are Charities. *The Straits Times.* Retrieved 16 February 2015, from http://heresthenews.blogspot.sg/2012/07/when-churches-are-charities.html.

Cheng, Willie (2013, June 26). Can Stock Exchanges Go Social? *The Straits Times.* Retrieved 16 February 2015, from http://ifonlysingaporeans.blogspot.sg/2013/06/can-stock-exchanges-go-social.html.

Chong, Terence (2011). Filling the Moral Void: the Christian Right in Singapore. *Journal of Contemporary Asia*, 41(4), 566–583.

Commissioner of Charities Annual Report: For the year ended 31 December 2013 (2014, August). Charities Unit, Ministry of Culture, Community and Youth.

Corporate Giving Survey (2010, February 27). National Volunteer & Philanthropy Centre, Singapore.

Department of Statistics (DOS) (2014). Statistics Singapore, Monthly Digest Statistics Singapore September 2014. Ministry of Trade and Industry, Singapore.

Ee, David (2014, October 27). Khaw Lauds MPs' Work on Animal Welfare Bill. *The Straits Times*. Retrieved 16 February 2015, from http://news.asiaone.com/news/singapore/khaw-lauds-mps-work-animal-welfare-bill.

Employers' Concerns Considered, Says MOM (2012, March 13). *The Straits Times*. Retrieved 16 February 2015, from http://www.mom.gov.sg/newsroom/Pages/PressRepliesDetail.aspx?listid=206.

Hartung, Richard (2012, January 1). Thinking out of Boxes for Social Good. Challenge Online. Retrieved 16 February 2015, from http://www.challenge.gov.sg/2012/01/thinking-out-of-boxes-for-social-good/.

Individual Giving Survey 2012 Supplement (2014, March 25). National Volunteer & Philanthropy Centre, Singapore.

Jhaipragas, Bhavan (2014, May 29). Singapore PM Launches Defamation Suit against Blogger. *AFP News*. Retrieved 16 February 2015, from https://sg.news.yahoo.com/singapore-pm-launches-defamation-suit-against-blogger-095645352.html.

Kiat, Tay Ek & Soon, Debbie (2013, November 11). *Report on IPS Conference on Civil Society 2013: Our Future*. Singapore: Institute of Policy Studies.

Koh, Gillian & Soon, Debbie (2012). The Future of Singapore's Civil Society. *Social Space*, (5), 92–98.

Kotwani, Monica (2013, February 25). More than 20,000 Singapore Citizenship Applications Approved in 2012. *Channel NewsAsia*. Retrieved 16 February 2015, http://www.channelnewsasia.com/news/specialreports/parliament/news/more-than-20-000-singapore/590336.html.

Latif, Asad-Ui & Lee, Huay Leng (eds.) (2015). *George Yeo on Singapore and the World: Pruning the Banyan Tee*. Singapore: World Scientific.

Lee, Howard (2014, August 30). Ten Honoured at Inaugural Singapore Advocacy Awards. *The Online Citizen*. Retrieved 16 February 2015, from http://www.theonlinecitizen.com/2014/08/ten-honoured-at-inaugural-singapore-advocacy-awards/.

Lien, Laurence (2011, October). Singapore's Nonprofit Sector: What Should Its Role Be? *Ethos*, (10).

Mathews, Mathew (2008). Saving the City through Good Works: Christian Involvement in Social Services. In Lai Ah Eng (ed.), *Religious Diversity in Singapore* (pp. 524–557). Singapore: Institute of Policy Studies.

Mathi, Braema & Mohamed, Sharifah (2011). *Unmet Social Needs in Singapore: Singapore's Social Structures and Policies, and Their Impact on Six Vulnerable Communities*. Singapore: Lien Centre for Social Innovation.

MDA Clarifies Online News Licensing Scheme amid Criticism (2013, June 1). *Yahoo News*. Retrieved 16 February 2015, from https://sg.news.yahoo.com/mda-clarifies-online-news-licensing-scheme-amid-criticism-031829941.html.

Mohamed, Sharifah (2008). Tracing Singapore's Social Sector. *Social Space*, (1), 16–22.

Mulgan, Geoff (2010). Stepping on the Accelerator of Social Change. In Willie Cheng & Sharifah Mohamed (eds.), *The World That Changes The World: How Philanthropy, Innovation and Entrepreneurship are Transforming the Social Ecosystem* (Chapter 20). New Jersey: Jossey-Bass, John Wiley & Sons.

Ministry of Education (MOE) (2013, March 27). Press Release: Launch of the Early Childhood Development Agency (ECDA).

National Volunteer & Philanthropy Centre (NVPC) (2005). The State of Giving: Inaugural Study of Singapore's Giving Landscape. Singapore.

National Volunteer & Philanthropy Centre (NVPC) (2013, January 13). Individual Giving Survey 2012: Media Briefing.

Pin, Phua Mei (2012, August 24). What's the Fuss about Pre-school Education? *The Straits Times*. Retrieved 16 February 2015, from http://www.singapolitics.sg/fast-facts/whats-fuss-about-pre-school-education.

Prakash, Roshini & Tan, Pauline (2014). Landscape of Social Enterprises in Singapore: Working Paper no. 1 of Social Entrepreneurship in Asia. Asia Centre for Social Entrepreneurship & Philanthropy, National University of Singapore Business School, Singapore.

Prime Minster's Office, Sinapore (2013). Prime Minister Lee Hsien Loong's National Day Rally 2013 (Speech in English).

Ramesh, S (2012, February 14). Evidence Act Changes Passed. *Channel NewsAsia*. Retrieved 16 February 2015, from http://www.channelnewsasia.com/news/singapore/evidence-act-changes-pass192926.html.

Salamon, Lester M. (2006). Government-Nonprofit Relations from an International Perspective. In Elizabeth T. Boris & C. Eugene Steuerle (eds.), *Nonprofits & Government: Collaboration & Conflict* (pp.399–437), 2nd ed. Washington, DC: The Urban Institute.

Salamon, Lester M., Sokolowski, S. Wojciech & Associates, Global Civil Society (2004). Dimensions of the Nonprofit Sector, Volume Two. Bloomfield, CT: Kumarian Press, in association with the Johns Hopkins Comparative Nonprofit Sector Project.

Singam, Tan, Ng & Perera (2002). *Building Social Space in Singapore: The Working Committee's Initiative in Civil Society* Activism. USA: Select Publishing.

Singapore Census of Population 2010, Administrative Report. Department of Statistics (DOS), Singapore. Retrieved 16 February 2015, from http://www.singstat.gov.sg/docs/default-source/default-document-library/publications/publications_and_papers/cop2010/census_2010_admin/cop2010admin.pdf.

Singapore Media: Self-censorship or Else (2010, May 31). Southeast Asian Press Alliance. Retrieved 9 February 2015, from http://www.seapa.org/?p=3272.

SMU Pulls Plug on Human Rights Centre (2012, November 3). *Today*, Retrieved 16 February 2015, from http://www.sammyboy.com/showthread.php?133005-SMU-Pulls-Plug-On-Human-Rights-Centre.

Social Investment Report 2012/2013. Singapore Tote Board. Retrieved 16 February 2015, from http://www.toteboard.gov.sg/Data/ImgCont/1190/Tote%20Board%20Social%20Investment%20Report%20FY2012-2013.pdf.

Starting Well: Benchmarking Early Education across the World (2012, June). *Economist Intelligence Unit*. Retrieved 16 February 2015, from http://www.lienfoundation.org/pdf/publications/sw_report.pdf.

Tan, Theresa (2009, October 30). NCSS Gives up Charities Watchdog Role; Ministry Taking over That Function; NCSS to Focus on Nurturing Groups. *The Straits Times*. Retrieved 16 February 2015, from http://app.msf.gov.sg/Portals/0/Summary/pressroom/13772048-30_10_2009-ST-FIRST-A6.pdf.

Voices: When a Columnist Becomes a 'Partisan Player' in Politics, Letter from K Bhavani, Press Secretary to MICA (2006, July 3). *Today*. Retrieved 16 February 2015, from http://www.mrbrown.com/blog/2006/07/Ietter_from_mic.html.

Wei, Tan Dawn (2014, October 13). Film on Exiles Screened at Film Festival in London. *The Straits Times*. Retrieved 16 February 2015, from http://news.asiaone.com/news/showbiz/film-exiles-screened-film-festival-london.

Wong, Tessa (2012, November 5). SMU Cancels Opening of Research Centre. *The Straits Times*. Retrieved 16 February 2015, from http://www.singapolitics.sg/news/smu-cancels-opening-research-centre.

World Giving Index 2013: A Global View of Giving Trends (2013, December). Charities Aid Foundation, Retrieved 16 February 2015, from http://www.cafonline.org/PDF/WoridGivingIndex2013_1374AWEB.pdf.

Yong, Charissa (2014, October 3). Film-maker Appeals against MDA Rating; Tan Pin Pin Submits Unchanged Exile Film Again for Panel's Review. *The Straits Times*. Retrieved 16 February 2015, from http://news.asiaone.com/news/singapore/film-maker-appeals-against-mda-rating.

Yuen-C, Tham (2014, June 20). Church Network Joins Muslim Group in Stand against Pink Dot. *The Straits Times*. Retrieved 16 February 2015, from http://www.singapolitics.sg/news/church-network-joins-muslim-group-stand-against-pink-dot.

Yusof, Helmi (2013, April 26). Can Singapore Accept Political Art? *The Business Times*. Retrieved 16 February 2015, from http://www.stcommunities.sg/entertainment/show/st-review/can-singapore-accept-political-art.

Chapter 15

Social Media and Social Issues in Singapore

Tan Tarn How

This chapter is about the effect that the rise of social media has on social issues in Singapore. It examines the ways in which this unprecedented communication tool changed how social issues are raised and discussed, and the consequent impact on the issues themselves, the people these issues are about, civil society, citizens and the government. In addition to reflecting on the past and the present state of the intersection and interaction between the medium and its subjects, it attempts to look into what the future holds on these questions.

The chapter discusses four structural conditions that bear on the main question: technology, the political landscape, civil society and citizens. It examines the extent to which these conditions are enabling of or obstacles to the rising awareness, discussion and advocacy of social issues in general, and of the role of the Internet in them.

Social issues defined

What is meant by a social issue? The classic definition by Mills (1959) contrasts "private troubles" of the individual with "public issues" or social issues that "transcend these local environments of the individual and the limited range of his life". He and many subsequent social scientists see a social issue as a public matter where values cherished by publics are felt to be threatened (Mills, 1959). Others also require empirical evidence for a social condition to be called an issue (Crone, 2007).

I argue for a broader use of the term "social issues" to mean problems of society that need to be addressed irrespective of whether there is subjective opposition by people or readily available objective evidence. They include those acknowledged social issues covered in this book, namely, ageing, healthcare, social security, family, race and ethnicity, social mobility, disability, and social justice. They also include other issues such as discrimination, poverty, the environment, racism, human rights, culture and language, censorship, crime, and the justice system.

But the broader definition also covers issues not necessarily in the public eye or articulated by a group calling for change. These "latent" issues await discovery or general recognition. They might — because one does not know for sure since they are latent until revealed to be problems or not — include the high incarceration rate and their social effects on families, homelessness, the Christianisation of the elite and establishment, and soft corruption. By their very nature or as a result of the conditions in a society, such as I contend exist in Singapore, they may remain hidden by intent, ignorance or neglect. In a liberal democracy, latent issues would be rare because of the constant scrutiny of the media, civil society, academia, citizens and government. But in less democratic societies like Singapore the invisibility of social problems needs to be borne in mind.

Government's promotion of IT

Since the dawn of the Internet, the Singapore government has had the foresight to recognise it as a tool for transforming business and government. An avid early adopter and promoter, it has since rolled out successively well-implemented national plans to harness this potential. The first such blueprint, the 1986 National IT Plan, mapped the strategic framework and the requirements for a conducive environment for exploiting IT for national competitive advantage. By 1992, the plan had reaped rewards. Anticipating the phenomenal growth of IT, the National Computer Board, a government agency, released *A Vision of An Intelligent Island: IT 2000 Report*. It said, "in our vision, some 15 years from now, Singapore, the Intelligent Island, will be among the first countries in the world with an advanced nationwide information infrastructure. It will interconnect computers in virtually every home, office, school, and factory" (Mahizhnan & Yap, 2000). Singapore quickly became one of the most connected nations in the world. Today, household broadband penetration is 87%. Singaporeans spend an average of five hours and 16 minutes surfing the Internet each day on laptops and desktops and one hour and 57 minutes on mobile (Aziz, 2014; IDA, 2014). They spend 2.2 hours a day using social media. Some 59% have a Facebook account. They lead the world in percentage with smart phones, 85%, ahead of South Korea's 80%. This means that Internet access is no longer tied to a computer or a fixed-line Internet subscription. Singaporeans are connected all the time and everywhere, as a ride in a bus or subway train will attest. This means that technology in terms of the tools, access and ability to harness its potential is an issue in Singapore.

Social media defined

But what is "social media"? It means websites and online applications that let users create and share content or to network with other people. They include sites mostly launched in the mid-2000s such as those for social networking (Facebook), video sharing (Youtube), photo-sharing (Flickr and Instagram), blogging (Wordpress), crowd sourcing (Wikipedia) and social bookmarking (Delicious). But even social media already existed in the earliest days of the Internet in the early 1980s. People were already sharing and networking using simple services like email and mailing lists (collection of names and addresses to send material to multiple recipients). In the late 1980s, new platforms came on stream such as Usenet, newsgroups and electronic bulletin boards. They are still used and are not very different from some of today's platforms, such as the discussion forums on REACH, the government website for gathering feedback from citizens. The main differences between the older and new technologies are the latter's greater ease of use, multi-media functions that increases the draw and power of the content, customisability by the user, and more interactivity between content producers and consumers. A parallel advance in hardware, such as digital cameras and phones, has added to the possibilities of creating and uploading pictures and videos with ease. The hardware and software combination makes creating and sharing a video, a picture or text literally child's play. This blurring of the traditional line between producer and consumer is one of the transfiguring powers of social media.

The political landscape

Singapore's political landscape, in terms of the government, regulatory framework and extra-legal factors, is unconducive to civil society or citizen engagement in social and political issues. Ever since independence, the ruling People's Action Party (PAP) has run an authoritarian government with tight control on citizens' lives, both public and private. The overwhelming reach of the state means that few social issues are also not political.

In the last two decades since Goh Chok Tong became the second Prime Minister in 1990, the controls have relaxed somewhat, especially in the private realm. It has repeatedly called on Singaporeans to be active citizens. In the last five years, it has allowed more space simply by resisting from stepping into debates that have social but little political significance, for instance, in the struggles between fundamentalist Christians and pro-gay groups. But despite the government's claim and the belief of some citizens that Singapore is a fully democratic state, some scholars still see it variously as soft authoritarian, hybrid (democratic and authoritarian) or electoral authoritarian (recognising that it could be both competitive in electoral politics and authoritarian) (Rodan, 2009; Diamond, 2002; Mohamed & Turner, 2013).

The freedoms of speech, association and action guaranteed in the constitution remain diluted by laws and subsidiary regulations passed as exceptions. Among them are the Societies Act, Penal Code, the Internal Security Act, Sedition Act, Public Entertainment Act and Defamation Act. These laws constrain both individuals but particularly civil society. For instance, groups trying to register as societies may not be allowed to, although some just operate without doing so. Among them are the anti-death penalty activists, the LGBT group — People Like Us (PLU), and the arts advocacy group — Arts Engage (which this author is involved in). Others may have their activities proscribed, such as the political discussion group Socratic Society and the Law Society. The court cases in 2014 of Roy Ngerng for defamation against the Prime Minister and Alex Au for scandalising the judiciary attest to continuing restrictions on speech.

Constraints also exist as non-legal restrictions such as the so-called "out of bounds" or OB markers, loosely defined no-go zones for public discourse. Academics have also been discouraged from entering the fray as a number of them have gotten into trouble for their writings as public intellectuals. The net effect of these strictures — and equally important, the panopticon belief that they exist — is a chilling effect on participating in public issues, especially where there is direct or indirect criticism of the government or its policies. The aspect of Singapore's soft authoritarianism of particular relevance to this chapter is its control of the mainstream media, and its regulation of alternative (largely online) media. The government maintains that these controls are necessarily because editors and journalists are not elected and thus have less moral standing than the elected government to set the agenda. They cannot be the Fourth Estate and must be part of the nation building project (Agency France Presse, 2005). The Newspaper and Printing Presses Act (NPPA) ensures government control of local newspapers and the Broadcasting Act, of television and radio stations. The NPPA and defamation and other laws have also muzzled foreign publications by the brilliant move of hitting them where it matters most, their financial bottom line.

These restrictions have stunted the public sphere, a space where citizens "confer in an unrestricted fashion — that is, with the guarantee of freedom of assembly and association and the freedom to express and publish their opinions — about matters of general interest" (Habermas, Lennox & Lennox, 1964). Public discourse was for many years sparse in quantity, narrow in range and shallow in depth, and where it exists, does so under the government's dictates. That began to change with the advent of the Internet.

Technology and social issues

The Internet poses a challenge to the overall authoritarian structure of the government as well as its specific methods of control. This majority view however has been challenged by doubters of the liberating powers of the Internet, some who even argue that the Internet in fact aids regimes in consolidating their hold on society (Kalathil & Boas, 2003; Morozov, 2011). The power of the Internet — mostly for good but sometimes for bad — is much documented. It lies firstly in its organisational effect as a powerful tool that transcends space and time and makes collaborating and mobilising easier and sometimes out of sight of the authorities. Secondly, its effect is discursive, letting individuals share information and insights, express opinions and access information. Unlike ephemeral coffee shop talk, the Internet is accumulative, publicly accessible and practically permanent. Thirdly, its effect is psychological, engendering community, solidarity and a sense that one is not alone.

The government was mindful that the positive economic and governance dividends come with negative effects. Some argue that Internet should not be and cannot be controlled even in a small country like Singapore (Yeo & Mahizhnan, 1998), but the government has never bought that idea. A year after the Internet was made widely available to the public in 1995, it amended the Broadcasting Act to regulate the online space. It introduced the "Class Licence Scheme" which automatically registers Internet Service Providers and Internet Content Providers, although they can be explicitly asked to do so. In 1997, the comprehensive set of content guidelines called the Internet Code of Practice was issued under the Act. It declared illegal any material "objectionable on the grounds of public interest, public morality, public order, public security, national harmony, or is otherwise prohibited by applicable Singapore laws" (MDA, n.d.). Separately, the government also imposed restrictions on how citizens and political parties can discuss issues during elections. Critics charged that these regulations are too broad and more harmful than helpful to society as they stifle democratic discourse. Some also accused the government of trying to protect itself from scrutiny and to continue its grip on society. The government promised that it would use a "light touch" in enforcement. To its credit, it has largely upheld its word by not cracking down very often. However, in a number of the cases when it acted, it did so with the full weight of the law (Chua, 2007).

Civil society and social issues

Volunteer welfare organisations (VWOs), which provides a range of services to the disadvantaged and underprivileged that do not have an activist agenda, are welcome, indeed supported by the government. They deliver services and engender active citizenry without publicly questioning the conditions that lead to the services being needed or indeed why civil society should offer these services. However, the government's authoritarianism leaves little space for activist civil society.

One group in the post-independence but pre-Internet era was the seminal Singapore Planning and Urban Research (SPUR). Founded in 1965, it played a role in discussing and offering ideas on planning and other issues, but closed a decade later amidst the government's growing distrust of its activities. In the 1980s and 1990s, among the few activist NGOs allowed are the gender equality advocacy group AWARE (formed in 1984) and the Singapore Nature Society (which split from its Malaysian parent in 1991). Even rarer were the three registered societies set up for political discussion: the Roundtable, the Socratic Circle and Tangent. One early instance of civil society use of the Internet for outreach was The Socratic Circle, which in 1995 tried to conduct an online survey that involved non-members. It was told to stop because it was breaching the rule that it could only hold political discussions with members (Gomez, 2006). This is the first documented case where a registered political society was stopped from harnessing the potential of the Internet.

As the Internet became more widely used, it heralded new ways of citizen association that fall in between the formal offline organisations such as Socratic Circle and AWARE, and individuals. At one end, the loosest types of association between individuals are those in mailing lists and online discussions groups. Next are the websites created for the specific purpose of creating a community and engendering discussion, with one or more editors wielding control over form and content. The earliest of such was Sintercom, a website founded by then student Tan Chong Kee in 1994 to discuss political and other issues. Sintercom became a locus of protest against the proposed Internet Code of Practice in 1996, with members of its forum arguing that it would be detrimental to Internet development in Singapore. They also put up a petition in their real names — not a trivial act then — against the draft Code. The users also engaged the government offline in meetings, a move no different from another offline civil society organisation. Most of the clauses in the Code they objected to were written out of the final draft. Sintercom founder, Tan, said, "It was the first cyber petition against a government policy in Singapore and the success caught everyone by surprise. This was a seminal event in Singaporean cyberspace because it showed that Singaporeans on the Net cared passionately about how it would develop and were willing to take considerable personal risks for something they held dear to their hearts". That year, when government wanted Sintercom to register under the Broadcasting Act, Tan promised to "exercise responsibility, intelligence and maturity" in running the site, and the government demurred (George, 2006). However, in 2001, the government asked Tan to register under the Class Licence Scheme but he decided to close it because he found the conditions too onerous (Tan, 2001).

At the next level up are the advocacy groups that are not registered entities, almost all who depend heavily on the Internet for organisation, outreach and mobilisation. The earlier is the gay group PLU, and the new ones that have sprung up in the last few years include those that campaign on the death penalty, the Internal Security Act, the Bukit Brown cemetery and unemployment.

Around the turn of the millennium, two offline groups were formed that leveraged heavily on the Internet: the Think Centre (which looks at politics and human rights) and human rights advocacy group, Singaporeans For Democracy (Gomez, 2006). Additional legislation were then passed to contain political expression engendered by the Internet and prevent it from spilling onto the offline world. These included the Political Donations Act of 2001 that lets the government designate groups as "political associations", that is, barred from receiving money from foreigners. Over the years, five groups have been gazetted, including Open Singapore Centre (OSC) (set up by opposition leaders J. B. Jeyaretnam and Chee Soon Juan), the Think Centre, Singaporeans for Democracy (a now defunct human rights NGO) and MARUAH (another human rights NGO). In 2011, the government gazetted the first blog, the popular news and commentary website, *The Online Citizen*. The government said its "coverage, commentary and analysis of political issues" meant it could "influence the opinions of their readership and shape political outcomes in Singapore". Thus it must be denied funding by foreign elements or sources to "safeguard the integrity of the domestic political process" ("TOC Gazetted", *AsiaOne News*, 2011).

Before the 2001 election, the government also amended the Parliament Elections Act to allow only types of online content specified in a "positive list" and also to bar citizens from engaging in "election advertising" during the election period. When podcast and videocast technology became popular in the lead up to the 2006 election, they were banned during the election period. "Persistently political websites" were also required to register with the government. But netizens widely flouted these rules (Ibrahim, 2009; Tan & Mahizhnan, 2008). The government raised the ban before the 2011 elections on citizens writing about their support for parties or candidates during the election period.

How civil society uses the Internet

How did and do groups use the Internet? For one of the major civil society initiatives of the late 1990s called The Working Committee, it was vital. The group was formed in 1998 by a group of individuals, civil society groups (including AWARE and Nature Society) and VWOs who wanted to build networks and contribute to the development of civil society. The group openly declared that it wanted to use the Internet as a tool. Alvin Tan, one of its founders, said, "The Internet itself made a huge difference because it reduces the need for physical meetings". Decisions could be made via email discussions. The members were volunteers and so found it hard to meet at the same time. The Internet's asynchronous nature (that is, it allows people to work on an issue at the times most convenient for each) was critical in facilitating collaboration across time and place. This flexibility also encouraged more people who might otherwise be afraid to meet commitments to volunteer.

Around that time, Tan, who is also founder artistic director of theatre company The Necessary Stage, also started an online Yahoo e-group called *artscommunity* for artists to discuss political and policy issues mostly but not always related to the arts. The e-group was "very lively, with verbal fights" among its members. "They discussed a lot of issues, not moderated. It was our first phase of democracy and anyone had [the] right to bring up [an] issue, and no one can say what some[one] else cannot say." The e-group was like the online version of The Substation and S11, the coffee shop outside the old National Library, in that both were venues for artists to meet. "It brought together a lot of people, but unlike the small offline discussions which often happen in silos, with *artscommunity*, once you write, 400 or 1,000 know about it straight away." Members debated on issues such as censorship, the death penalty and Gulf War. They organised a few offline events on the above issues, including a No Arts Day. These offline and online activities represented "an intersection of the arts and civil society," Tan says (A. Tan, 2014).

Indeed, *artscommunity* could exist online because leadership was not needed. Attempts to hold regular offline discussions of *artscommunity* members fizzled out because no one wanted to take on the leadership role such as setting the agenda. This shows that online communities have dynamics and existential values of their own that are unique to being virtual and are not necessarily offshoots or mirror images of offline civil society. Eventually, *artscommunity* morphed into its present form, a space for advertising of arts events or calls for collaborators and freelancers in projects for its 4,000 or so subscribers. The discussions on the arts issues and arts policy shifted to smaller and more focused groups such as Arts Engage. Much of the work of Arts Engage is now done online via email and outreach via Facebook, a powerful medium for reaching out to the "contacts of contacts of contacts — a shared social capital".

Another civil society group that relied on the Internet was The Working Committee 2, an advocacy group fighting for equitable treatment for low-wage migrant workers and which borrows its name and spirit from The Working Committee. Spurred on by horrendous cases of abuse of foreign domestic workers, it was founded in 2002 by veteran activist Braema Mathi and others. She says, "When we started it in 2002 it was all via the Internet to get the projects up, to recruit like-minded people, to hold discussions, to plan and organise, to raise awareness via a website. Within a matter of weeks over 120 volunteers signed up" (Mathi, 2014). It was for her, "the best example of how the Internet really enables social movements by interest". Strict guidelines that regulated what it could not do as ad hoc group, led to its registering under the Societies Act in 2003 and being renamed as Transient Workers Count Too in 2004.

The Internet was also crucial to the formation of gay identity and engendering and sustaining activism. It accelerated the coming out of the gay community by offering information and resources to those who hid their sexual identity for fear or other reasons. Alex Au, entrepreneur, gay activist and political blogger, said, "They also found each other, creating a sense of community from previously isolated individuals. Internet chat rooms, online forums and personal websites propelled identity formation and social consciousness, besides serving more personal needs such as finding friends, love and sex. These Internet sites were the virtual equivalent of gay ghettoes; few heterosexuals ever stumbled onto them or cared to stay if they did, but nonetheless, the constant engagement of gay individuals with each other would eventually produce a new generation of 'out and proud' gay Singaporeans, self-assured and vocal about their concerns" (Au, 2009).

LGBT people and their supporters — and their opponents — also took advantage of opportunities offered by the government. In 2002, when the Remaking Singapore government committee held an online forum, homosexuality became the second hottest topic, with over 700 posts from both sides. Also at this time a number of gay and lesbian interest groups were formed on social, sports, faith or other personal issues.

In 1993, the gay advocacy group People Like Us was formed to raise consciousness and build a community. It took courage. Gay men were then still being entrapped by police officers under disguise. The group held weekly forums at the arts centre, The Substation, which it believed were infiltrated by the police, though they never intervened. In 1997, it applied to the Registrar of Societies to be registered but was rejected. PLU then moved the forum online for fear of being charged with operating illegally (Au, 2009). It was unclear if the new move was safer. "What level of activity would constitute an unregistered society? Both the gay community and the government were moving into uncharted territory here." The group hoped they had some protection given the government's open promotion on the use of the Internet. "Subsequent experience has proved this calculation right."

PLU exists on the borderline of legality but is allowed to continue probably because it was not explicitly political or openly campaigning. The larger and more influential groups, such as *The Online Citizen*, have been asked to register or have been gazetted under various regulations as described above. Less influential groups survive in legal no-man's ground such as the Singapore Anti-Death Penalty Campaign and We Believe in Second Chances (also an anti-death penalty advocate). The first was founded by human rights lawyer, M. Ravi, in 2005 and given an additional impetus in 2009 when activist Rachel Cheng and others decided to commemorate World Day Against the Death Penalty and to launch the campaign for 21-year-old Malaysian Yong Vui Kong, sentenced to death in January 2009 for trafficking 42 g of heroin. It has a website and a Facebook page. Zeng said the group had been ignored by mainstream media (Zeng, 2014). Reporters would interview her and her colleagues but would not quote them in their reports, and the newspapers did not publish their letters. Besides events at Speakers Corner, the only channel to reach out is online. "Hence the Internet is a lifeline for us." She believes the online presence creates awareness and lets the campaign connect with strangers, including those who are against the group. "There are the silent observers who can read the debates and think about the issues and the points. That is very important." The Facebook page has a mere 30 likes, but readership of articles can reach 1,000 sometimes. She also monitors comments to articles posted

50 Years of Social Issues in Singapore

online by mainstream media to gauge the mood. She sees some change in attitudes in the last five years, as there are some people now who will step in to defend its position on its behalf. "But there are many other stumbling blocks. In civil society there is a hierarchy of causes. Death penalty is not something that people talk about much, unlike animal rights." Public opinion is against the campaign, as is clear from a survey in 2006 showing that 96% of Singaporeans support the death penalty (Lim & Au, 2006). "People don't fund us, plus the tactics we use are more confrontational. Even other members of civil society were very wary of us at first." The group works with the Think Centre as well as the "less radical" We Believe In Second Chances, which also is online. The latter tends to mount legal arguments whereas her group would argue from philosophical standpoints. The Internet also allows her group to network with and get the support of international groups, such as those in Taiwan and Hong Kong. They have issued statements in support of her campaign and also protested outside Singapore diplomatic missions in Hong Kong. Activist Braema Mathi said of the advocacy group that she is now President of — "MARUAH is the toughest thing I have done, because its deals with human rights". On some issues such as the group's monitoring of media coverage in the 2011 elections, there was more interest. "Other issues such as death penalty and migrant workers don't have the kind of traction. You see the same faces at events. General interest is low." Some civil society groups are also caught in a vicious circle. Not being able to attract funds from the public, they cannot afford full-time staff for outreach and communications, which then hobbles efforts at raising money. This contrasts with groups like Pink Dot SG which has managed to escape that circle.

One episode that illustrates the power and limitations of the Internet and its interplay with the OB markers is over Fateha, a by-Singapore-standards radical advocacy group for Muslim issues. In 2002, it set off alarm bells with its spirited campaign mere months after the September 11 attacks in the United States against the government's policy to not allow Muslim girls to wear the *tudung* in schools, which it declared as unconstitutional. It expressed its intention on its website, fateha.com, to "nationalise and if necessary internationalise Malay issues" by publishing information not discussed in the local mainstream media. Fateha submitted a petition with 3,300 signatures against the no-*tudung* policy. Its Chief Executive Officer, Zulfikar Mohamad Shariff, also spoke on both local and international issues affecting Muslims, including asserting that racial integration had not worked and that the government's support for the US and Israel could have prompted the actions of 15 people detained by the Internal Security Department. But ultimately it was five allegedly defamatory articles he posted on the website that led to the group's unwinding. Members of the group resigned, the website was closed down and he fled to Australia with his family. The result was to cast a pall at least temporarily, over discussion on the Internet, especially on issues related to Islam and terrorism (Tan, 2002).

Reaching out to citizens

Civil society faces challenges in widening their movements by raising awareness and gaining support in the wider community. The Pink Dot SG movement, an annual event which promotes support for the LGBT community in Singapore, is by far the most successful Internet-mediated mass mobilisation of ordinary citizens to date. The first in 2009 was Singapore's first open-air, LGBT-supportive event. It drew between 1,000 and 2,500 people, a record for the Speakers' Corner at Hong Lim Park. By 2014, a new record of an estimated 26,000 people turned up. Pink Dot's appeal is based on a combination of uncontroversial messages that, in the words of one organiser, no one cannot but embrace (such as "Focusing on Families") slick marketing, strategic partnerships with non-LGBT luminaries and other supporters like corporate donors, and careful political (more accurately non-political) positioning. Highly appealing, well-produced videos spread via the Internet got the message home effectively. Its very name, a riff on Singapore proudly and defiantly appropriating the phrase "little red dot" and the inclusion of "SG" advertises its non-confrontational inclusiveness.

Contrast that with other LGBT efforts such as PLU and Indignation, the annual "LGBT pride season" of events by and for the community. Many Singaporeans, wary of politics or social issues, go to Pink Dot because they think it neither a "political" nor human rights event. However, Pink Dot's critics within the gay community have complained that its sanitised imaging was more harmful than not to the community's fundamental cause, especially to those whose sexual identities and behaviour are less acceptable by the general public and thus become the marginalised of the marginalised. One question is the extent to which it is necessary for civil society to dilute its message to gain greater acceptance, and whether that is a compromise worth making.

Internet as a mobilising tool

In Singapore as elsewhere, most people are mobilised for two reasons: when an issue affects them directly, or when someone does something outrageous on an issue that they often do not care about. Social media then becomes a powerful tool for informing and organising. Two issues that have sparked general interest via social media are that of the CPF and retirement adequacy, and the White Paper on Population. Both issues received traction online not just on leading blogs and the online writings of activists such as Leong Sze Hian, Gilbert Goh and Roy Ngerng but also in forums, Facebook, as well as comments to articles in alternative and mainstream media. After Ngerng was sued by Prime Minister Lee Hsien Loong in 2014 for defamation, he raised the extraordinary sum of S$110,000 in slightly over a month, a large part in small donations of several tens of dollars.

As for the White paper, 4,000 turned up in 2013 at Speakers' Corner for the first protest against what they thought was an overly high target population of 6.9 million people set in the government's Population White Paper. The rapid rise in the foreign population and inward immigration, which has led to competition for jobs and overcrowding as well as a perceived threat to Singapore's culture and identity, was a lightning rod issue leading up the last election.

In the past, the government would have been able to close the debate on these two issues by instructing mainstream media to stay off the topic, leaving no other available media and other channels for public debate involving ordinary citizens. But now such a move would only drive people to look for information, to find solidarity and to speak their mind online. As noted above, however, less bread and butter issues such as freedom of speech and human rights find it much harder to attract interest and generate much less support from the public. That the defamation suit against Ngerng attracted so much interest compared to the contemporaneous case against Alex Au for scandalising the judiciary is testament to this.

AWARE is an example of an NGO which eschews mass mobilisation. It chooses, or needs, to operate on the state's terms to ensure some success. "Compromise, reform, and moderacy become rational responses to authoritarian control," writes one critical academic (Lyons, 2007). This is because AWARE owes its existence to the PAP, and being deregistered is always a possibility. It does not engage in a sustained critique of all forms of structural inequality, and focused on self-help programmes, counselling services, and research and education activities. "Using a cautious, back-door approach to lobbying the government means that AWARE is unable to harness a grass-roots support base and must wait patiently for the state to initiate policy change on its own terms. Where this is combined with an inherent middle-class conservatism, which is supportive of the state's developmentalist goals, the opportunities for significant political transformation are limited." The potential of the social media is thus untapped.

Other groups have also taken the "softly, softly approach", choosing to talk directly to the authorities in getting what they want rather than go down the more common route of civil society elsewhere in seeking, as one of its goals, to change public attitudes so as to pressure the government or corporations for change. The Nature Society is a prime example, preferring the behind-the-scenes lobbying to openly criticising and confronting the government. As its website justifiably claims it has had major successes, for instance, "modification of the Singapore Armed Forces Reservists' Association's (SAFRA) golf course design at Kranji Marsh's freshwater wetland". However, one of its major triumphs, in 2001, when it convinced the government to not carry out reclamation of the Chek Jawa mudflats was only possible because of wide support from citizens who independently used social media to raise awareness (Sadoway, 2013). Other groups that have decided to take a back-room, closed-doors approach in place of or together with galvanising public awareness and action are the animal welfare groups. In the last few years, they have found a Minister who identifies with their cause; thus the strategy has reaped rewards. Critics have warned that in the long run, the success of civil society should not be predicated on the personal likes or dislikes of individuals with power and that change in legal and other structures is meaningless without wider changes in society. But pragmatism seems to hold sway.

Groups which have chosen confrontation and the harnessing of public opinion include the several groups of activists fighting for the preservation of the Bukit Brown cemetery in opposition to plans unveiled in 2011 to clear it to build an expressway and housing. Interestingly, the issues led to a loose coalition of formal organisations such as the Nature Society and Singapore Heritage Society and more aggressive non-registered informal groups that sprung up around Bukit Brown (Sadoway, 2013; Soon, forthcoming, 2015). A public fall-out between the groups and the Minister concerned occurred, and after separate vigorous social media campaigns they managed to wring some minor concessions from the government but could not reverse the plan. It is moot to speculate what would have happened if they had taken a more conciliatory approach instead of mounting public opinion against the initial plan.

What is clear is that before the Internet, the state control of platforms of discourses such as the media as well as institutions such as the academia made it extremely difficult for civil society to reach the public directly with their messages or to mobilise via tactics such as petitions. That structural hurdle no longer exists, and it is interesting that those most able to seize the new opportunities are the newest groups of activists such as Pink Dot SG and other gay groups, the newer churches, Arts Engage and Singapore Anti-Death Penalty.

Citizens and social issues

Despite the restrictions on public speech, the Internet from the very beginning gave citizens a tool to come together to discuss political and social issues. From 1980s to 1997 two online forums were used to discuss Singapore's political issues on bulletin boards and newsgroups such as *soc.culture.asean* (started in 1989) and *soc.culture.singapore* (started in 1992 by Nanyang Technological University students) (Tan, 2001). The participants were mostly students overseas who had Internet access via their universities. The government was monitoring the discussions, as shown by the Singapore embassy in London contacting an Essex University student about another student's critical views of the education policy. Students at the National University of Singapore also had a bulletin board where they discussed the 1991 General Election and a 1992 by-election. Gomez writes: "it was after the Internet was widely made available in 1995 and the establishment of various online forums and websites that alternative reporting of election rallies and other election related news became accessible to the wider public." The number of such sites remained very small because considerable technical expertise was needed to set up and run a website in the pre-blog days.

As technology became easier to use, Internet penetration rose and the government offered a little more space, and the citizen socio-political cyberspace slowly grew. The elections have been catalysts. Beginning with the 2006 elections when citizens set up anonymous blogs or continued blogging about the elections in challenge to the rules, the number of socio-political blogs belonging to individual citizens has increased dramatically. The 2011 elections also spurred the growth of such blogs, and saw the emergence of Facebook as a tool for sharing information and for discourse. The use of blogs, Facebook and social media for personal ends such as recording what one had for dinner or lunch or describing family life have spill-over effects to discourse on social and political issues. During the height of the controversy over the gay library books, which is described below, many citizens who do not normally write about social or political matters did so on the matter. A new group of people just joins and enriches the debate.

The two instances in which social media played an even pivotal role in a social issue which did not directly affect the interests of the general public were the so-called AWARE saga and to a lesser extent the National Library Board's "Penguin-gate". The first refers to a surreptitious take-over of the liberal management of the gender equality advocacy NGO by a Christian fundamentalist who objected to its alleged pro-gay agenda, particularly in its sex education classes for schools. The coverage by mainstream media played an important role by stoking feelings of outrage against this clandestine coup, especially when the usurpers denied their true affiliations until forced to reveal them by investigative reporting supplemented by tip-offs from the public, who posted information dug up by netizens. In the lead-up to the Extraordinary General Meeting (EGM), social media in the form of blogs, Facebook and Twitter were used by both the "Old Guard" and the "New Guard" for a membership drive. They and their allies also used social media to whip up wider support. That sometimes backfired, for instance, when private emails and videos to spur on the fundamentalists were leaked, and became major factors in turning many against their crusade (Ghani & Koh, 2011).

The mainstream media played an indispensible part in the saga, but this was the first social issue in which social media came into its own in Singapore. During the EGM, there was even live coverage provided online via *The Online Citizen*, and Facebook and Twitter updates by attendees. This is also one of the few occasions when the government did not intervene, at least until after the reverse takeover by the liberals during the EGM. The saga raised a number of questions that needed to be answered, such as what exactly was the sex education programme that instigated the fundamentalists and what makes a good programme. But after the EGM, when these issues were brought up, the government finally intervened and both the mainstream and alternative online media did not pursue the matter further. Other important questions were also not much discussed: how different interest groups should engage with one another; democratic decision-making in organisations; and the role of religion in public life (Tan, 2009).

The second incident refers to the 2014 controversy over, first, the National Library Board (NLB) removing three gay-friendly books (one of which is about a gay penguin couple) from the children's section. It is an irony that the news of the removal of the books was announced on the Facebook group "We Are against Pink Dot in Singapore" by one of its members, who crowed that he had successfully asked the NLB to remove the books. His post was picked up by others online and then reported in the mainstream media. NLB added fuel to the fire by announcing that it was "pulping" the books, technically accurate librarian jargon, but unfortunate in its connotations to a perplexed public. Judges resigned from literary judging committees, parents organised a "read-in" at the central library, a Cabinet Minister stepped in, and the issue was resolved by moving the books intact to the adult section.

There is one crucial difference between these two cases and Roy Ngerng's fund raising. The former illustrates that with the help of mainstream media, social media could be a powerful force. But when Roy Ngerng appealed for funds to fight his case, the mainstream media did not report on the monetary support pouring in until he was well on his way to achieving his target amount. Social media single-handedly did it for him and in spite of mainstream media. This is an achievement considering that only a third or so of the people read political blogs or use Facebook to read political information (Chang, 2011).

Despite widespread interest and almost blanket coverage of both the AWARE and the NLB controversies, a large part of Singaporeans were not interested in them. Polls after both events showed that 70% did not care about what is going on with the AWARE saga and 40% had not even heard of the NLB incident. It can thus be argued that most Singaporeans generally do not care about social issues except when they are affected. The struggles of the NGOs in general and those on the lower end of the hierarchy of causes in particular testify to that. One explanation offered is that Singaporeans care but that the country is so well-governed and socially harmonious that it has very few social problems in the first place. That may be so, but countries higher on the human development index have more engaged citizens and a livelier civil society then here. Another explanation is that most Singaporeans accept the social contract that they give up their rights and responsibilities in return for economic prosperity. Part of the contract is leaving the discussion and resolution of social issues solely to the government, and "the duty of the passive citizen is merely to consent to the legitimacy of the regime" (Mohamed & Turner, 2013).

When citizens do engage, what is the nature of that debate? In 2007, when parliament considered whether to repeal the law against male homosexual sex, Section 377a of the Penal Code, both sides of the debate organised petitions. The pro-repeal uploaded a video featuring local celebrities to their petition site to help spread the message. The signatures collected, which eventually exceeded 8,000 in number, would be sent in an open letter to the Prime Minister, establishing a direct link between online and traditional participation. Similarly, the anti-repeal group also had an online petition that garnered over 15,000 signatures and an open letter. One researcher concluded that it was "a rather healthy debate of this issue both online and offline" (Skoric, Ying & Ng, 2009).

However, another study on the same debate which analysed the over 2,500 comments on the repeal petition site and nearly 8,000 on the anti-repeal site concluded that the two sides did not come to a real debate. They each deployed different kinds of arguments (rights versus morality), expressed different kinds of concerns and used different patterns of language (Detenber *et al.*, 2014). They were talking at cross-purposes and thus not engaged in a deliberative way that leads to common ground or at least greater understanding, even in an issue so divisive.

Engagement can sometimes be harmful rather than helpful to society, for example on issues such as xenophobia and racism. Here, as elsewhere, the Internet is not just a tool for speaking out against racism and xenophobia but unfortunately also one used to express prejudices and even hate. While there are some voices online that warn against and criticise racism and xenophobia when they crop up, they have not coalesced to form a united voice. There is just one NGO — government sponsored at that — that works against both (Soon & Tan, 2013).

The absence of activist NGOs is also apparent in issues such as poverty and its invisibility (Chan & Basu, 2013), inequality, homelessness, the unemployment faced by mid-level employees in their 40s, and the high incarceration rates. There are, for instance, the occasional alternative online media articles about homelessness. Some articles even make the jump to mainstream media, where it would be much more widely read, such the series on *The Online Citizen* in 2010 drawing attention to the homeless who live in tents in Sembawang and other parks (Chiang, 2010). There are few NGOs which can sustain the discussion on these issues online and offline.

The Internet is a democratising tool that helps give voice to citizens: but only if they have access to it and know how to use it. Quite often than not, those marginalised by social problems have neither access nor knowledge. The only way in which their problems can be made known is if others do it on their behalf. In a state with a weak civil society and a disengaged citizenry, that does not happen. The social problems they are mired in remain latent social issues, out of the public eye.

The government and social issues

Social media has put pressure on the government to be a little more transparent and accountable. This is not easy, as despite assurances that there will be more consultation and that the government will listen more to the people, old habits die hard. It also has had to contend with groups and citizens and alliances between them, such as the case with Bukit Brown, that openly challenge not just its conclusions but also scrutinise the way it works. It has also had to contend with the fact that citizens, either anonymously or otherwise, are not always as compliant as the mainstream media and other institutions. The resistance has put some pressure on the government. Tan, the founder of Sintercom, wrote a decade ago that the Internet was a "de facto carpet" where "whatever gets swept under will turn up in some form or other there". Asked if he still believes that, he says, "Yes, even more so now, even though it is also an overstatement. Not everything will show up, but more and more are doing so" (C. K. Tan, 2014). This has led to a retreat in some areas, such as the space that it allows to citizens during elections to be part of the public sphere. Nevertheless it has not stopped trying to impose new regulations or enforce old regulations on websites (Breakfast Network, 2013; Lee, 2014). As long as the people continue to buy into the old social contract, and the government keeps its end of the bargain by delivering the economic goods, it is unlikely that it would need to make any drastic changes to the soft authoritarian system that has worked so well for it.

Conclusion

This chapter has examined the impact of the Internet and social media on social issues. It leaves much out as it has not aimed for a comprehensive survey of the past or the present, but has used specific incidents and organisations to illustrate the interaction between the radical new technology and society. There are four factors to consider: technology, civil society, government and citizens. Technology has made absolute or near absolute control of public discourse impossible. Civil society has done well in using it as an organising tool, but with very few exceptions, less so as a mobilising tool, and even less so as a tool to change the minds of the general public. Sometimes the last is by choice, because some believe the price of public engagement and mobilisation is to be ignored by government or worse. Sometimes it is not, and is determined by the simple lack of resources and ability to harness the technology. The Internet has also opened up new possibilities, indeed new forms of civil society that sprout and coalesce around specific issues, such as the case with Bukit Brown and the NLB gay books. The government has loosened its control — but only a little. It continues to make it difficult for civil society groups or individual activists and is now seen to be re-tightening the screws again in the lead up to the next election. There is some pressure to change, and it has changed and adapted, but not enough for it to fundamentally alter its time-tested way of doing business. Citizens largely care for themselves (and then mostly in economic terms) and so are generally disinterested in social and political issues outside of their own immediate needs. Civil society thus faces dual challenges – with the government at the top, and with an apathetic constituency below. The government appears to know that, and that is why in their latest calculus, as long as they deliver economically, tightening serves them better than liberalisation.[1]

---

[1] Author note: I wish to acknowledge the help of my assistants Das Nanditha and Siti Nadzirah Samsudin.

References

Agency France Presse (2005, November 1). Ex-PM Goh Defends Local Media after Dismal Survey Showing. Retrieved 20 January 2015, from http://www.singapore-window.org/sw05/051101af.htm.

Au, A. (2009). Soft Exterior, Hard Core: Policies towards Gays. In B. Welsh, J. Chin, A. Mahizhnan & T. H. Tan (eds.), *Impressions of the Goh Chok Tong Years in Singapore* (pp. 399–408). Singapore: NUS Press.

Aziz, M. A. (2014, January 10). Singapore among the Most Active on Social Media: Report. *TODAY*. Retrieved 20 January 2015, from http://www.todayonline.com/tech/singapore-among-most-active-social-media-report.

Breakfast Network (2013, December 10). Singapore Opinion News Site Breakfast Network to Shut down. *Yahoo News*. Retrieved 20 January 2015, from https://sg.news.yahoo.com/blogs/singaporescene/kitchen-closed-161623269.html.

Chan, R. & Basu, R. (2013, October 26). The Invisible Poor. *The Straits Times*. Retrieved 23 March 2015, from http://1kyspp.nus.edu.sg/wp-content/uploads/2013/06/straitstimes.com-The_invisible_poor.pdf.

Chang, R. (2011, October 5). Internet 'Did Not Have Decisive Effect on GE', Says Study. *The Straits Times*. Retrieved 16 February 2015, from http://lkyspp.nus.edu.sg/ips/wp-content/uploads/sites/2/2013/06/ST_Internet-did-not-have-decisive-effect-on-GE_051011.pdf.

Chiang, J. (2010, January 13). People of the Tents. *The Online Citizen*. Retrieved 20 January 2015, from http://www.theonlinecitizen.com/2010/01/people-of-the-tents/.

Chua, H. H. (2007, June 27). Be a Cyber-activist? S'poreans Can't Be Bothered, Says Panel. *The Straits Times*. Retrieved 20 January 2015, from http://www.international.ucla.edu/article.asp?parentid=72601.

Crone, J. (2007). *How Can We Solve Our Social Problems?* 2nd ed. United States of America: Pine Forge Press.

Detenber, B. H., Cenite, M., Zhou, S., Malik, S. & Neo, R. L. (2014). Rights versus Morality: Online Debate about Decriminalization of Gay Sex in Singapore. *Journal of Homosexuality*, 61(9), 1313–1333.

Diamond, L. J. (2002). Elections without Democracy: Thinking about Hybrid Regimes. *Journal of Democracy*, 13(2), 21–35.

George, C. (2006). *Contentious Journalism and the Internet: Towards Democratic Discourse in Malaysia and Singapore*. Singapore: Singapore University Press and Seattle: University of Washington Press.

Ghani, A. & Koh, G. (2011). Not Quite Shutting up and Sitting down: The Singapore Government's Role in the AWARE Saga. In T. Chong (ed.), *The AWARE Saga: Civil Society and Public Morality in Singapore* (pp. 36–50). Singapore: ISEAS.

Gomez, J. (2006). 'Citizen Journalism': Bridging the Discrepancy in Singapore's General Elections News. *Südostasien Aktuell — Journal of Current Southeast Asian Affairs*, 6, 3–34.

Habermas, J., Lennox, S. & Lennox, F. (1964). The Public Sphere: An Encyclopedia Article. *New German Critique*, 3, 49–55.

Ibrahim, Y. (2009). Textual and Symbolic Resistance Re-mediating Politics through the Blogsphere in Singapore. In A. Russel & N. Echchaibi (eds.), *International Blogging: Identity, Politics and Networked Public* (pp. 173–198). New York: Peter Lang.

Infocomm Development Authority of Singapore (IDA) (2014). Statistics on Telecomm Services for 2014 (Jan–Jun). In *Infocomm Landscape.* Retrieved 20 January 2015, from http://www.ida.gov.sg/Infocomm-Landscape/Facts-and-Figures/Tele communications/Statistics-on-Telecom-Services/Statistics-on-Telecom-Services-for-2014-Jan-Jun.

Kalathil, S. & Boas, T. C. (2003). *Open Networks, Closed Regimes: The Impact of the Internet on Authoritarian Rule.* Washington, DC: Carnegie Endowment for International Peace.

Lee, T. (2014, September 30). Singapore Government Asks Prominent Political News Site TOC to Get a License. *TechinAsia.* Retrieved 20 January 2015, from https://www.techinasia.com/prominent-singapore-political-site-toc-license-operate.

Lim, L. & Au, J. (2006, February 12). 96% of S'poreans Back the Death Penalty. *The Straits Times.* Retrieved 16 February 2015, from http://eresources.nlb.gov.sg/newspapers/Digitised/Article/straitstimes/20060212-1.2.5.7.aspx.

Lyons, L. (2007). A Curious Space In-Between the Public Private Divide and Gender-based Activism in Singapore. *Gender Technology and Development,* 11(1), 27–51.

Mahizhnan, A. & Yap, M. T. (2000). Singapore: The Development of an Intelligent Island and Social Dividends of Information. *Urban Studies,* 37(10), 1749–1756.

Mathi, B., personal communication, 9 November 2014.

Media Development Authority (MDA) (n.d). Internet Service & Content Provider Class Licence, In *Regulations, Licensing & Consultations.* Retrieved 20 January 2015, from http://www.mda.gov.sg/RegulationsAndLicensing/Licences/Pages/InternetService AndContentProviderClassLicence.aspx.

Mills, C. W. (1959). *The Sociological Imagination.* United States of America: Oxford University Press.

Mohamed, K. N. & Turner, B. S. (2013). Governing as Gardening: Reflections on Soft Authoritarianism in Singapore. *Citizenship Studies,* 17(3–4), 339–352.

Morozov, E. (2011). *The Net Delusion: The Dark Side of Internet Freedom.* New York: Public Affairs.

Rodan, G. (2009). Goh's Consensus Politics of Authoritarian Rule. In B. Welsh, J. Chin, A. Mahizhnan & T. H. Tan (eds.), *Impressions of the Goh Chok Tong Years in Singapore* (pp. 61–70). Singapore: NUS Press.

Sadoway, D. (2013), How Are ICTs Transforming Civic Space in Singapore? Changing Civic-cyber Environmentalism in the Island City-state. *Journal of Creative Communications,* 8(2–3), 107–138.

Skoric, M. M., Ying, D. & Ng, Y. (2009) Bowling Online Not Alone: Online Social Capital and Political Participation in Singapore. *Journal of Computer-Mediated Communication,* 14(2), 414–433.

Soon, C. & Tan T. H. (2013). Corrosive Speech: What Can Be Done. *Institute of Policy Studies.* Retrieved 20 January 2015, from http://lkyspp.nus.edu.sg/ips/wp-content/uploads/sites/2/2013/06/Report_ACM_Corrosive-Speech-Report_120613-1.pdf.

Soon, C. (forthcoming, 2015). Technology and Change. In C. Soon & G. Koh (eds.), *Civil Society: Our Future.*

Tan, A., personal communication, 8 November 2014.

Tan, C. K. (2001). Singaporeans in Cyberspace: From 1995 to 2000. In L. G. Boi (ed.), *Singaporeans Exposed: Navigating the Ins and Outs of Globalisation* (pp. 38–52). Singapore: Landmark Books.

Tan, C. K., personal communication, 20 November 2014.

Tan, T. H. (2009), Assessing Media Coverage: The AWARE Controversy as a Case Study. *Institute of Policy Studies*. Retrieved 20 January 2015, from http://lkyspp.nus.edu.sg/wp-content/uploads/2013/06/TanTarnHow_on_aware_coverage.pdf.

Tan, T. H. (2001, August 22). Sintercom Founder Fades out of cyberspace. *The Straits Times*. Retrieved 15 January 2015, from Factiva database.

Tan, T. H. (2002, July 6). Probe into Web Articles Spooks Net Community. *The Straits Times*. Retrieved 15 January 2015, from Factiva database.

Tan. T. H. & Mahizhnan, A. (2008). Subverting Seriousness and Other Misdemeanours: Modes of Resistance against OB Markers in the 2006 Singapore General Election. *Media Asia*, 35(4), 207–212.

TOC Gazetted as Political Association (2011, February 17). *AsiaOne News*. Retrieved 15 January 2015, from http://news.asiaone.com/News/AsiaOne+News/Singapore/Story/A1Story20110217-264061.html.

Yeo, S. & Mahizhnan, A. (1998). Developing an Intelligent Island: Dilemmas of Censorship. In A. Mahizhnan & T. Y. Lee (eds.), *Singapore: Re-engineering Success* (pp. 138–148). Singapore: Institute of Policy Studies.

Zeng, R., personal communication, 11 November 2014.

Chapter 16

Understanding and Addressing Social Issues in Singapore

David Chan

Collectively, the chapters in this book have provided a critical examination of a variety of key social issues in Singapore that have continuously captured the attention of policy-makers and the public. The chapters also traced the development of social issues within the historical context of how Singapore has evolved over 50 years of nation building, and explicitly linked this past to our current situation and future possibilities.

A theme that runs through these chapters — whether they are about the social fundamentals of population changes, social progress through inclusivity, or core social principles and processes — is what I called "people matter". I used this as a pun to refer to critical issues that matter to the people and also to emphasise the idea that the way people think, feel and act should matter to policy-making and nation building in Singapore (Chan, 2015a). Indeed, a shared characteristic among the contributors in this book is our interest in people matter and our belief that people matter in policy and public action.

Many readers do not need much or any persuasion on the importance of "people matter" — in both senses of the pun. But the challenges are often about understanding and addressing the various social issues. Or to put it another way: How do we know what matters most (or more) in a specific context of the social issue, and what are the practical solutions or possible approaches?

The contributors in this book explicated several dimensions of the social issues that they discussed. There is much potential in reflecting on the viewpoints expressed and evaluating them, to derive lessons for public policy and discourse in Singapore, and elsewhere, even though one may disagree with some perspectives adopted by the contributors.

The analyses and arguments presented in the different chapters have varying degrees of support from extant empirical evidence. I believe that readers will not, and should not, uncritically agree with each and every viewpoint expressed or position advocated in the chapters, including this chapter. The goal is to advance our understanding of social issues in Singapore so that we can address them effectively in practice. So, a healthy culture of constructive debate must evolve — one where public policies and the arguments for or against them should be evaluated with both rigour and relevance. That means a need to go beyond one's personal beliefs or subjective preferences, to ensure that the evaluation and inference have strong evidentiary basis and realistic practical application. This expectation of robust debate and scrutiny should apply to all parties, including policy-makers, academics, public intellectuals, civil society activists and anyone interested to advocate a position in social issues. In social analysis, we also need to guard against falling into the common trap of confirmatory bias — the tendency to seek out, interpret and remember information that confirms our existing beliefs, positions or actions (Chan, 2013f). In the light of contrary information and strong validity evidence, we should have the intellectual honesty and political courage to revise our prior position.

It is in this spirit of rigour and relevance that I suggest readers to evaluate the critical questions raised by the chapter contributors that require further examination. Many contributors also suggested areas where more research is needed and identified unresolved issues which appear to demand some extent of mindset changes in individuals, the community and the government. In this concluding chapter, I hope to complement the call for rigour in analysis, relevance in applications, and review of mindsets by discussing approaches towards understanding and addressing social issues. That is, the purpose of this chapter is to examine the ways we think about or make sense of social issues and the ways we respond to or tackle them.

To provide a coherent theme for discussion, I will focus my illustrations on population issues although the arguments are often also applicable to other social issues such as social mobility and social cohesion. In the first half of the chapter, I discuss issues by adopting a social and behavioural sciences approach that gives primacy to the way people think, feel and act, including the antecedents and the consequences. Focusing on the dimensions of cognition, emotion and behaviour will provide more holistic, contextualised and people-centric perspectives on the social issues in question. In the second half of the chapter, I propose an adaptive conceptual toolbox to facilitate the efforts to understand and address social issues in Singapore. This toolbox contains a multifaceted strategic focus and principled approach as well as contextualised modes of thinking.

Understanding and addressing social issues:
The example of population challenges

Population changes in Singapore are social fundamentals in that they have significant impact on people's way of life and quality of life. The impact occurs through infrastructure issues such as housing, transport and use of public spaces, economic issues such as jobs, wages and taxes, and socio-political issues such as citizen proportion, value diversity and social cohesion.

Chapters 1 and 4 in this volume provided useful summaries of the evolution of population policies in Singapore and their impact on population growth. It is important to understand these past policy contexts and population trends because current and future population policies do not occur in a historical vacuum. It is true that policy-makers have to adapt to changing circumstances and the past should neither dictate the present nor the future. However, the way we were or have changed in the past 50 years is likely to continue to influence policy-making.

The challenge is for policy-makers to discern between relevant lessons from the past and previously effective approaches that are no longer adaptive due to differences in circumstances (Chan, 2014a). This capacity to discern — which contributes to policy acumen — increases when historical policy knowledge is complemented with a scientific understanding of how individuals and groups think, feel and act in similar and different situations. Hence, there is a lot of potential for policy-makers to work more closely with social and behavioural scientists to understand and address population challenges with regard to population priorities, policies and perceptions.

The need for science and practice to converge is probably most evident in both the communication and content of the Population White Paper (National Population and Talent Division [NPTD], 2013) that was released in end-January 2013. About one year prior to the release of the White Paper, I began participating actively in the research and public discussions on population issues in Singapore. I noted that population numbers are needed as planning parameters for economic and urban development. But my emphases were on the need to go beyond population numbers to examine other fundamental and interrelated population issues. These issues are tied to Singapore's economy as well as national development related to our city-state's physical and social environment. I also argued that understanding and addressing many of these issues require science and practice to learn from each other. Examples include the desirability and implications of different population composition profiles, the challenges of social cohesion and ways to manage local–foreigner integration, nature of national conversations, social mobility, the nature of public emotions and social trust, the social compact between people and government, the development of social capital, and Singaporeans' well-being and quality of life. I discussed these issues both prior to the release of the Population White Paper in January 2013 (Chan, 2011a; 2012a; 2012b; 2012c; 2012d; 2012e) and after (Chan, 2013a; 2013b; 2013c; 2013d; 2013e; 2014c; 2014d; 2014g; 2015c; Chan *et al.*, 2014).

A recurring theme in my writings was the need to pay attention to what we know from science and practice on how people think, feel and act as they evaluate and experience their lives in the context of population changes and challenges. Not surprisingly, and similar to key issues discussed by others in commentary articles in newspapers, these issues that I raised publicly on population policy content and communication did not go unnoticed by the government. For example, Prime Minister Lee Hsien Loong reproduced on his Facebook page two commentaries that I wrote in June 2012 on challenges of cohesion (Chan, 2012b) and ways to manage integration (Chan, 2012c) after he read them in *The Straits Times*. In his accompanying Facebook post, Prime Minister Lee wrote:

> Two thoughtful commentaries on population and integration issues by Prof David Chan of SMU in ST. Prof Chan analyses the difficulties in integrating large numbers of foreigners into our society, and what it is that upsets people. He then goes on to propose sensible approaches to managing the problems and getting positive outcomes for Singapore.
>
> Getting our population and integration policies right is crucial to our social cohesion, economic well-being and sense of belonging. This is why we are encouraging discussion and dialogue on this difficult problem.
>
> We have to recognise the human and emotional reactions that people understandably feel when they see our society changing. We must also acknowledge our economic and demographic realities — our need for enough workers and more talent, as well as our shortage of babies and ageing population. Only then can we anticipate the challenges, and address the problems comprehensively.
>
> Let us work towards a shared understanding of what is at stake, so that we can manage these issues better, and improve our lives in the future (Lee Hsien Loong, 16 June 2012).

The above Facebook post by Prime Minister Lee occurred one year after the 16th Parliamentary General Election held on 7 May 2011 where issues of population growth, infrastructure support and local–foreigner relations took centre stage. In my view, Prime Minister Lee's remarks in the Facebook post was one of various clear expressions soon after the 2011 General Election that the government was aware of and concerned with the anxiety and angst among Singaporeans brought about by the rapid and large inflow of foreigners. As illustrated in the next section, the government's awareness and concern were evident in government responses to public discussions of population issues and specifically those related to local–foreigner relations and social integration. Undoubtedly, internal deliberations among policy-makers and senior public officers would have paid attention, although probably with varying degrees, to these social and behavioural issues in population policies.

In end-January 2013, the Population White Paper (NPTD, 2013) was released to the public. The White Paper outlined the road map for Singapore's population policies to address the country's demographic challenges. Despite the fact that several key social and economic issues were highlighted in the White Paper, the public, the media and also Members of Parliament were focused on the population figure of 6.9 million. This figure refers to the upper limit of a population range mentioned in the White Paper when outlining population trajectories. The specific statement read: "By 2030, Singapore's total population could range between 6.5 and 6.9 million" (NPTD, 2013, Executive Summary). There was much confusion in the public debate regarding the meaning of these population projections.

What was clear was that the release of the Population White Paper immediately provoked strong and sustained negative public reactions. The reactions were predominantly focused on the reasons for and implications of the 6.9 million population figure. The focus on this number led to the public perception of a population policy in favour of a large and rapid inflow of foreigners, even though the White Paper in fact proposed a significant slowdown in the growth of the workforce and population compared to what it had been.

The strong negative reactions should be understood in terms of Singaporeans' prevailing experience of liveability and their quality of life in the recent years prior to the release of the White Paper, particularly in the context of the mismatch between population growth and infrastructure support. As explained in my proposed framework for understanding challenges to social cohesion involving Singaporeans and foreigners (Chan, 2012b), in addition to crowding, there were also citizen anxiety and angst related to clustering of large groups of foreigners in public spaces, competition in school and at work, comparisons of responsibilities and benefits between citizens and non-citizens, and conflict in local–foreigner relations.

But as elaborated below, in addition to the prevailing "5 Cs" context of crowding, clustering, competition, comparison and conflict, the form and substance of the public communication and policy content also contributed to the public reactions. These reactions influenced subsequent public discussions and policy deliberations on practically all major issues such as those involving housing, transport, healthcare, education, manpower and jobs.

The debate on population challenges, with all its intensity and implication, provides a good learning example of the importance of "people matter" in understanding and addressing social issues in Singapore. I will first discuss matters of public communications, followed by matters of policy content.

Population challenges: Public communications

Many, including the government, would agree that public communications on Singapore's population challenges could have been more effective. However, there is less agreement and less clarity on what went wrong in the public communications.

It is probably more puzzling for those who are familiar with the detailed content of the Population White Paper, given the large disconnect between facts and perceptions. For example, contrary to popular belief, there were in fact substantial public consultations prior to the formulation of the White Paper. The White Paper was released on 29 January 2013, after the government had worked on it for about one year and gathered public feedback from over 2,330 individuals representing various stakeholder groups and organisations (NPTD, 2013). Also, contrary to the negative reactions, it was Singaporeans and not foreigner inflow that were at the core of the White Paper. The government considered the White Paper as a comprehensive population policy road map to address Singapore's demographic challenges. It attempted to strike the balance in population policies in order to 1) have enough young Singaporeans to sustain the population and provide for the seniors, 2) create good jobs for increasingly better-educated Singaporeans, and 3) maintain a high quality living environment for Singaporeans.

Given the disparity between facts and perceptions, it is important to understand how the facts were communicated and how the communication can be improved. That is, it is important to think counterfactually and ask how public communications could have been better. The purpose of engaging in this upward counterfactual thinking is not to gripe or assign blame but to learn from mistakes and identify pathways that would lead to a better outcome in future similar situations involving public communications and engagement (Chan, 2014f).

There were several aspects of public communications that could have been done differently and better. One was that public communications should have begun much earlier to prepare the population for the large and rapid inflow of foreigners and engage Singaporeans on the population challenges. Another was the need for effective public engagement to explain and discuss the importance of Singapore staying open and the value of diversity in the population composition profile. The government has publicly acknowledged these two shortcomings. For example, in exactly one year after the release of the Population White Paper, the Minister for Education, Heng Swee Keat, said at an Institute of Policy Studies Conference:

> We need to do a better job of explaining the value of staying open, the value of working with people from different countries, cultures, different groups (Heng, 2014, p. 87).

In addition to being clear, proactive and prompt, public communications also need to be practical and sensitive to public emotions. Communication on local–foreigner integration issues, especially in management of adverse cases, should never be patronising, preachy or provocative. In this regard, it is noteworthy that a powerful feature of communication is the use of labels to categorise, describe and summarise people's attitudes and their expressions. Take, for example, the use of the label "anti-foreigner" to describe what Singaporeans should not be and the sentiments that they should not possess or exhibit. If the label refers to a stereotypical, irrational and unjustified strong opposition towards foreigners, then most Singaporeans are certainly not anti-foreigner. If Singaporeans' concerns and the issues underlying their angst are not clearly acknowledged, then using labels such as "anti-foreigner" and "xenophobic" may actually contribute to producing such sentiments in more Singaporeans (Chan, 2012c). When tackling population challenges in the context of Singaporeans' perceptions of foreigners, xenophobia is a consequence to prevent and not a cause to lament.

In short, the style and not just substance of communication affects whether Singaporeans view the communicator as principled and adaptive, or proud and arrogant. The former type of communicator, but not the latter, will be effective in explaining, persuading, motivating and influencing people. And most importantly, there needs to be a clear citizen-centric focus that directly addresses citizens' concerns and aspirations (Chan, 2012c; 2013a).

Another important but seldom discussed learning point for addressing social issues is the need for effective *strategic* communications. This is not about using the right words or framing issues in simple language. It is also beyond the technical coordination of media releases across different public sector agencies or technical briefings to the media to enable factually accurate reporting. Strategic communications involve judgments on how to integrate public discussions and policy announcements.

It is important to strategically coordinate different public announcements and consultations so that they are integrated in a manner to achieve the intended communication and engagement goals. To illustrate, consider the government's announcement of the Land Use Plan on 31 January 2013, which was two days after the release of the Population White Paper.

The Land Use Plan (Ministry of National Development [MND], 2013) began by referencing the Population White Paper's projection of a population size between 6.5 and 6.9 million by 2030. It was framed as a long-term strategic plan to optimise land use to support the population growth and to ensure a high quality of life. There were many innovative and integrated ideas in the Land Use Plan on optimisation of land use and enhancing people's quality of life. These ideas could have generated constructive public discussions how Singapore can be highly liveable as both a city and a country. There would have been assessments of both constraints and opportunities. These, in turn, would have led to problem-solving and critical thinking mindsets and optimistic attitudes towards finding alternative ways to create a vibrant Singapore. Unfortunately, such discussions did not occur. The public debate was fixated at the 6.9 million population figure in the Population White Paper released two days prior to the Land Use Plan.

Negative reactions came fast and furious. In the parliamentary debate, several Ministers took pains to explain that the 6.9 million figure was simply the upper limit of a range of population projections by 2030 needed for planning infrastructure, and not a target to achieve. But in both parliamentary and public debates, there were confusions over whether these population figures refer to hypothetical situations, plausible possibilities, best- versus worst-case scenarios, planning parameters or population targets, and what all these terms mean.

One could argue that releasing the Land Use Plan two days after the Population White Paper was logical because the population projections were needed to provide the planning parameters to develop a concrete land use plan such as the land area needed to sustain a range of population sizes. But releasing the Population White Paper prior to the Land Use Plan resulted in a negative outcome. For the public and even the Members of Parliament debating the Population White Paper, the unexpected population projection numbers have evoked more than a negative reaction. The numbers activated what behavioural scientists call a prevention focus.

When people are in the state of prevention focus, their thoughts and feelings are focused on preventing adverse consequences, such as those that easily come to mind when thinking of a large and rapid population growth. Indeed, the public attention was fixated on the potential negative outcomes of a large population and the rapid population growth. No attention was given to the ideas and opportunities for good quality of life from optimal land use.

A strategic approach would have, prior to releasing a Population White Paper, presented a draft general national development plan for a substantial period of public discussion on land use and liveability. The plan would focus on ways to ensure a good quality of life in high-density living. This would allow various ideas on land use to receive a fair hearing in terms of constraints, opportunities, innovations and implications. At the same time, the demographic challenges, including issues of local–foreigner relations, could have been raised and honestly discussed at the then ongoing National Conversation exercise. The Population White Paper would be formulated and refined based on the inputs from the public discussions on land use and demographic challenges.

The release of the White Paper would occur after the National Conversation exercise, rightly so as an outcome of discussions among Singaporeans. And at least several weeks or months of public discussion should occur before parliament convenes to debate and vote on the White Paper. This is as opposed to what in fact happened — a five-day interval between the release of the White Paper and the start of the parliamentary debate. A longer interval would have allowed Members of Parliament to solicit and represent a range of views in a constructive debate that address the heart of the matter.

Such a strategic approach would be consistent with and respectful of the National Conversation exercise, which was intended to discuss the kind of society that Singaporeans want and reflect on shared core values such as meritocracy, respect for diversity and social harmony. It would also be consistent with what I called citizen-centricity in population priorities — the idea that citizen well-being and quality of life, including their expressed concerns and aspirations, should be the driver of population policy, and not the population numbers (Chan, 2013a). At the parliamentary debate on the Population White Paper, Prime Minister Lee similarly characterised the government's purpose as follows:

> Our purpose is to do the best for Singaporeans. Singaporeans are at the centre of all our plans and everything which we do is to improve Singaporeans' well-being, their security and welfare. And everything else — whether it is economic growth, whether it is population policies, whether it is your housing, your trains — those are means to this end (Lee Hsien Loong, Singapore Parliament Reports, 8 February 2013).

The five-day parliamentary debate in 2013 on the Population White Paper was a heated one, and it remains debatable today on how much light it has generated for the public on the complex issues of population challenges. More importantly, there is the separate question on the extent to which the critical issues for Singaporeans have been understood and addressed in both the parliamentary and public debates. This relates to knowing the difference between complexity and what I called "criticality". This is an important distinction when understanding and addressing social issues, which will be discussed later in the chapter.

Population challenges: Policy content

The strong negative public emotions experienced and expressed in the population debate did yield much good. The complexity and multifaceted nature of demographic challenges were made more explicit in policy deliberations and public discourse. More fundamentally, the public reactions have surfaced many deeper issues for social analysis. Examples include sustainable economic models, urban planning, manpower management, fair employment practices, social mobility and social cohesion (Chan, 2013g; Chan *et al.*, 2014).

Thus, in understanding and addressing social issues in population matters, it is important to link public reactions to policy content. The inadequacies in public communication can only partly explain the strong public reactions in the population debate. To effectively address negative reactions, one has to focus on policy content to examine how it can be improved.

The way that the government has specifically responded to the negative reactions through revision of policy content is instructive. Overall, the government responded swiftly and adaptively to the public reactions and the deeper issues. There were investments in improving infrastructure, economic restructuring, tightening of foreigner inflow, and steps to assist more Singaporeans and raise social mobility.

In addition to their speed and multifaceted nature, these policy responses clearly involved large expenditures in implementation. It is therefore easy to label these responses as populist. Indeed, it would have been populist had the policy responses been simply pandering to prevailing public sentiments without regard to their quality and sustainability. But a dispassionate social analysis would have revealed that the citizen-centric government actions were also principled — directed at the pain points but guided by meritocracy, fairness, accountability and pragmatism. For example, the inflow of foreign manpower was tightened by slowing the growth rather than turning off the tap. Housing supply was dramatically ramped up, but housing policies were adapted in stages to calibrate the impact on demand and property prices. The Fair Consideration Framework ensures citizens are aware of job vacancies and signals the importance of fair employment practices. It does not mandate hiring Singaporeans in ways that go against meritocracy. University places for Singaporeans were increased, but scholarships for foreign students were not done away with.

Hence, rather than labelling them as populist, it is more evidence-based and fairer to describe the post-Population White Paper initiatives as sustained and sustainable principled efforts to develop the Singaporean core. But it is also fair to say that the strong reactions to the White Paper had fuelled the urgency and creativity underlying many citizen-centric policies.

The extent to which the policy content is adequate is only partly a function of its technical quality such as the rational basis and logical arguments. Adequacy of policy content is also influenced by the likelihood that the policy can be effectively implemented in realistic contexts without compromising or contaminating the policy intent. If and when policies were developed from theoretical analysis and top-down from meeting rooms, with little or no ground-up inputs and therefore an understanding of the contextual realities and the ground sentiments, then the validity of the policy content is likely to be theoretical only. That is, the so-called valid policy would suffer from what I call "validity decay" when implemented in practice. This is one of the reasons why policy revision needs inputs and help from multiple stakeholders outside policy-makers and the public service, to include not just experts and civil society but also relevant segments of the population and the public at large. The goal is not simply the reduction of negative public reactions as an end in itself. Without public support and a "whole-of-society" approach, the technical quality of the policy content *per se* is insufficient for translating policy intent to desired policy outcome.

In this regard, there are several areas in population issues where policy content can be significantly improved. In my view, there is urgency in two important areas that have surfaced since the release of the Population White Paper which require more systematic governmental and societal responses. One concerns foreigners at the workplace and the other concerns ageing.

On foreigners at the workplace, there are several festering issues that, if left unaddressed, could adversely affect local–foreigner relations and turn diversity at work into a liability when it could be an asset. Fundamentally, more attention should be given to the quality of the foreigner inflow, not just the quantity. This issue of quality is inextricably tied to the issue of fair competition as perceived by Singaporeans.

Competition, especially when it is perceived as unfair, threatens social cohesion through adverse impact on local–foreigner relations (Chan, 2012c). From the government's perspective, the global competition for talent and the limited pool of local manpower necessitate opening the doors to foreigners to enlarge the economic pie and create jobs in Singapore. Ironically, responding to the macro-level competition has created the micro-level competition Singaporeans face from foreigners who were attracted here. When left to itself, the micro-level competition could create negative consequences that affect citizen well-being and threaten cohesion.

Social cohesion is threatened when Singaporeans experience feelings of neglect and react negatively when they perceive, rightly or wrongly, that the competition with foreigners is unfair. One example is the belief that foreign employers are hiring or promoting foreigners based on similarity or affiliations rather than merit. Another example is the belief that there are jobs which are no longer feasible for Singaporeans because the pay is depressed to a level acceptable only to foreigners.

Competition from foreigners is not restricted to the workplace. It extends to education, health, housing and other tangible public resources. Competition can be healthy, so the issue is not competition from foreigners *per se*. The issue is unfair perceptions, whether the competition is actually unfair or fair but only perceived as unfair. Perceptions of unfairness strongly affect integration and they are contagious — spreading quickly with multiplier effects on other Singaporeans' perceptions.

More attention is needed to design and implement realistic and effective procedures to attract, screen and select the appropriate foreigners with the desired quality. More attention is also needed to enhance the regulation and education of fair employment practices. In addition, policy-makers and employers would benefit much by drawing practical implications from the well-established research on fairness perceptions which consistently showed that people are sensitive to the fairness of decisions made or the treatment they receive. Research in work contexts has shown that it is important for processes like personnel selection, performance appraisal and compensation to be perceived as fair, because fairness perceptions influence how people react to situations and their leaders. This also applies to public policy implementation and public engagement efforts.

Specifically, scientific studies in the laboratory as well as in actual workplace contexts showed that people are sensitive to fairness in the distribution of outcomes and fairness in the processes leading to those outcomes (for a non-technical summary, see Chan, 2011b). Fairness is also critical in the treatment of the individual, whether it is in the rewards given or help offered. How we evaluate and therefore treat an individual should be based on two considerations. The first is the objective evidence of the individual's performance. The second is the individual's access to opportunities to perform. Taken together, these multiple dimensions of fairness — outcomes, processes, performance and access to opportunities — provide a more holistic value basis for actions to address issues of employment discrimination, development of local talent, social inequality, social mobility and compassionate meritocracy (Chan, 2013g).

Three additional research findings in fairness perception with implications for treatment of Singaporeans and foreigners are noteworthy. First, the negative effects of unfairness are much stronger than the positive effects of fairness. This asymmetry of impact is consistent with the well-established power of negativity bias in human perception. Second, our perceptions of fairness are influenced by how we see or believe our fellow employees or citizens are being treated. Fairness perceptions are contagious: An individual's fairness perception is likely to have multiplier effects on the fairness perceptions of other individuals. Third, fairness effects are stronger when the decisions are perceived as discretionary rather than compelled. If a person eventually gets an outcome he considers fair, but only after he had to go through a grievance process or after he had to appeal to higher authority, the positive effects of that fair outcome would be reduced because it would be seen as having come about only after compulsion from a higher authority. It makes more sense to behave fairly in the first place, than to simply rely on an appeal process to address unfair practices.

In sum, politicians, policy-makers, public officers, and employers need to pay more attention to how people see the process by which policies are decided and implemented, and the way administrative decisions are carried out. This is particularly important in the context of local–foreigner comparisons. There is a robust body of behavioural sciences research to help leaders adopt evidence-based approaches to create processes that enhance fairness perception. Understanding fairness perceptions helps in formulating practical actions and solutions in the contexts of competition and comparisons between Singaporeans and foreigners.

Another area of policy content that requires significant revision is the way that ageing has been construed and presented in the Population White Paper. Demographic challenges associated with an ageing population are real. The government was being responsible in revealing the facts and reviewing the implications. However, a major problem with the policy discussion on population challenges, which reflects the focus of policy content, has been the pessimistic conceptualisation or assumption of ageing as a negative process. In other words, ageing has been construed and presented as a liability, primarily economically and probably also socially. This is a limiting representation and a self-fulfilling one, with a failure to recognise that ageing can be an economic and social asset.

Population policy content and discussion have overemphasised the negatives and neglected the positives of ageing. As elaborated below, this is most evident in the policy emphasis given to the old-age dependency ratio. I will argue that when the positives of ageing are considered alongside the negatives, it is possible to produce policy adaptation and innovation to tackle the demographic challenges in qualitatively different ways that are more effective than existing policies. I propose that, in both policy deliberations and public discussion, we replace the term "ageing problem" with "ageing issues" and construe ageing issues as an adaptation process involving multiple stakeholders including individuals, employers and communities, and multiple aspects of the environment including jobs, organisations, urban planning and policies. More details on this perspective of ageing issues are available in Chan *et al.* (2014).

The Population White Paper and numerous policy speeches or official statements on Singapore's ageing population have highlighted the adverse consequences that would result from increasing old-age dependency ratio for Singaporeans if there are no mitigation effects from procreation and immigration. The old-age dependency ratio is simply the ratio of the number of working Singaporeans (from 15 to 64 years old) to the number of older Singaporeans aged 65 and above. For this conceptualisation of old-age dependency to be meaningful, it has to be assumed that it is appropriate to separate Singaporeans into two groups with those below the age of 65 having to economically support those above it. But the validity of this assumption is questionable on both economic and social grounds. It incorrectly assumes that upon reaching 65 years of age, Singaporeans are no longer able to contribute to society at large and will suddenly and automatically become a burden and dependent on those who are younger.

The age of 65 years is one of many arbitrary cut-offs that could be selected to indicate economic contribution and dependency. The official retirement age is a function of national and organisational employment policies, which can be changed and is likely to be changed over time. In addition, actual permanent retirement from any employment and economically productive activity is partly dependent on the individual's choice and circumstances, some of which may be influenced by the prevailing social norms and policies. Currently, there are many Singaporeans aged 65 and above who are economically active and contribute either directly or indirectly, as well as significantly, to the vibrancy of Singapore's economy. This number is likely to increase in future as medical advances delay the onset of chronic health problems and people become healthier and live longer. On the other hand, many aged 25 years or younger persons are still in the schooling phase of life and they are not in a position to provide financial support to family members.

In the Population White Paper, the same age cut-off of 65 years old is used to operationalise old-age dependency that forms part of the basis for the population projections into 2030. But nearer to 2030, the older Singaporeans will be more highly educated and have longer life expectancy than today's older Singaporeans. Together with advances in technology and medical science, adoption of healthy lifestyles, and redesign of work, it is highly likely that post-65-year-olds will be in sufficiently good health for a longer period of time, thereby allowing older Singaporeans to make productive and significant contributions, both economically and socially.

Older Singaporeans have opportunities to stay well-integrated into both the workplace, at their pace, and in their chosen area of work. They also have opportunities to integrate well in society through various non-work activities such as voluntary endeavours. Each generation of older Singaporeans will possess not only economic capital but also important social knowledge and skills related to history, culture and practical experiences that can be transferred to younger generations. These resources are valuable assets to society and contribute positively to social capital. When older Singaporeans are cast in more positive light, or have built strong family ties, intergenerational relations are enhanced and positive intergenerational transfers are more likely to occur, which in turn contributes to the development of social capital.

In short, population policy formulation and public discussion need to move away from a fixation on reducing the old-age dependency ratio and the conjecture that a high ratio will produce adverse consequences. In addition, there is a need to question and remove many of the current assumptions upon which the conceptualisation of old-age dependency rests. These assumptions perpetuate a counterproductive stereotype that ageing is inherently negative and incorrectly cast older Singaporeans in a negative light. This is counterproductive to addressing population challenges, and likely to harm intergenerational relations and negatively affect social capital.

The concept of old-age dependency ratio is framed negatively as dependency and the underlying notion treats ageing as a liability. In contrast, the view of older Singaporeans as an asset and valuable resource will lead to a different orientation towards social expenditure on the elderly. Social expenditure on the elderly should not be construed as a zero-sum cost or as the depletion of resources. This erroneous construal will lead to misallocation of resources and funds. Instead, it should be construed as a continuous investment in human resources, with efforts to enhance health, work, community development and other elderly-focused initiatives regarded as strategic, goal-directed investment to enhance citizen well-being, and developing intergenerational relations. This investment will have a positive multiplier effect that broadens and builds social capital (Chan, 2013a).

If ageing should be understood as a potential asset and not just a liability, what are some concrete ways to address population challenges related to ageing? My colleagues and I have proposed at least three specific pathways (Chan, 2013a; Chan *et al.*, 2014).

The first pathway to address ageing is implementing mixed-use infrastructure and facilities. Facilities that are built to cater to the needs of the elderly and increase their well-being, such as senior activity and wellness centres, should be located within residential areas. This is consistent with "ageing-in-place" and it prevents social exclusion and increases social connectivity between elderly people and the rest of the population. However, wherever practically feasible, these facilities should be developed as part of a mixed-use infrastructure and facilities cluster as opposed to exclusively for elderly care. This will help prevent stigmatisation and isolation of the elderly and conflicts over land use in residential areas. The mixed-use and facility cluster should serve a complementary range of activities and services (e.g., childcare, senior activities, libraries, social enterprises, etc.) and enable accessibility to and foster interactions of different generations. These facilities could also be tailored to the specific needs of communities based on grassroots feedback, so as to create a sense of community ownership and belonging. In mixed-use facilities, elderly persons could take up work such as childcare duties and library services which may be employment or volunteer work.

The second pathway to address ageing is promoting social interactions through intensification of land use and integrated living. With increasing population density, there should be more efficient intensive use of land, combined with the provision of efficient infrastructure and quality mix-use amenities that are well-integrated, accessible and affordable. This will provide a highly effective physical environment that is conducive for high-quality living that promotes social interactions and therefore social capital. For example, well-integrated planning for mix-use facilities and public and recreational spaces with equitable access for all groups will encourage social interactions among elderly and younger persons as well as among people of different ethnicities, nationalities and social backgrounds. Integrated living will also involve creating suitable employment opportunities in residential areas that are close to home. This work-home proximity will contribute to social interactions involving different generations and diverse groups, together with other integrative functions made possible by the work-home proximity. These functions include enhancing part-time work, flexible work hours and work-life balance; reducing commuting time and easing the strain on the public transport system; encouraging the elderly to remain economically and socially active; enhancing general and asset-based volunteerism in the work-home vicinity, which contributes to the sense of community in the neighbourhood; encouraging entrepreneurship and innovation in business; and creating value-added jobs for various segments of the population.

The attractiveness of quality living in integrated mix-use facility clusters will increase the housing and rental prices in and near these areas. It may be useful to consider implementing equitable policies that lower the cost for residents taking up job opportunities in their neighbourhood. Given the multitude of social capital implications, we need to explicitly incorporate social and behavioural sciences in land use and infrastructure planning, so that the resulting physical environment will positively influence social interactions and behaviours and not create unintended negative social consequences.

The third pathway to address ageing is ensuring early and targeted health screening and promoting health. Research has shown that individuals with poor health are more likely to have poor social relations and low social well-being. Many activities for developing social interactions and relationships, especially those involving older persons, presuppose a basic level of health among the individuals involved. Healthy functioning is a fundamental pillar for enhancing well-being and developing social capital. Although the life expectancy of Singaporeans has increased, this index of human development does not measure health conditions such as long-term chronic illness or ailments that Singaporeans may face as they grow older. The government should work with the private and people sectors to institute a comprehensive and targeted national health screening programme over the individual's lifespan beginning from a young age. The early screenings will enable the early detection of health risks and more effective prevention and management of health problems for an ageing population. This in turn delays the onset of old-age health problems, promotes health and prolongs the period of active lifestyle.

The conceptualisation of ageing is of fundamental importance to the population discussion. If ageing is not adequately conceptualised, it will lead to inadequate inferences about what really matters in ageing issues and the related population matters. This in turn will lead to inadequate policies or programmes designed to address the purported problems of an ageing population. Thus, the facts and perceptions of ageing are practically important because they create both constraints and opportunities for the effectiveness of age-related public policies in virtually all domain areas.

It is true that an ageing population presents policy challenges. It can be a significant economic and social liability if there are no mitigation effects from procreation and immigration. But it is equally true that an ageing population also presents policy opportunities. It can be an asset that contributes to building a vibrant economy and strong society. In terms of revision of policy content, it is important to address the imbalance towards a pessimistic view of ageing and start construing ageing as an asset and not just a liability, with seniors able and willing to contribute economically and socially well beyond the arbitrary cut-off age of 65 years old.

More fundamentally, for Singapore to progress, we should not construe ageing as simply a population policy problem to be fixed. Instead, we need to approach ageing as a natural process that individuals, communities and the government should and can adapt to in order to enhance citizen well-being by developing economic and social capital. People need to adapt to the environment as they age. But jobs, organisations, urban planning, and policies also need to adapt to seniors and the changing population profile. When there is two-way adaptation to changes, ageing can paradoxically contribute to economic capital and social capital. That is, ageing is part of demographic challenges, but also part of demographic opportunities. The first step in improving policy content is to replace the term "ageing problem" with the term "ageing issues".

Moving forward: Population challenges and opportunities

The government has always recognised the importance and urgency to address the population issues, but what is becoming clear now is that the population challenges cannot be addressed in a top-down manner and by the government alone, and that what is needed is a "whole-of-society" approach. The first constructive step towards the population discussion is not to see it as a mere public communications exercise, even though more attention needs to be given to strategic communications. Policy content needs to be addressed dispassionately and in an evidence-based manner. This requires gathering relevant data from existing sources or well-designed studies. To understand and address social issues in population matters, relevant experts from the social and behavioural sciences need to be involved in designing and conducting research studies and given access to relevant data for adequate analysis. But these experts also need to strive for objectivity and professionalism, guard against the confirmatory bias that seeks out only information that will confirm as opposed to contradict their prior positions and personal preferences, and possess the intellectual honesty to present arguments based on facts and the political courage to revise their position in the light of clear and contrary evidence.

A whole-of-society approach will necessarily involve the public in policy discussions. But the debates and dialogues cannot be feel-good chit chats or griping sessions among converts only, either seeing only all the positives or seeing only all the negatives. Nor can it be simply an exercise in which the goal is for one side to convince why the other side is wrong. Whatever the population targets, projections or planning parameters might be, they need to be evaluated in terms of sustainability in relation to citizen well-being and quality of life. The same evaluation criteria could be applied to discussions on openness to foreigners, economic restructuring and even values and the kind of society that we want Singapore to be as a country.

The population discussion is an important national dialogue. It is a necessary and critical part of the actual problem-solving process towards enhancing citizen well-being and Singapore's national interests. Public discussion will also need to take into consideration public expectations and beliefs, which are influenced by the extent to which relevant information is publicly available. When relevant information is not available, people have a limited perspective. They may form unrealistic expectations about an issue, but understandably so. Information is not restricted to statistical data not released to the public. It can be information about the resources needed for sustaining a social policy, or effects that decisions on a manpower policy have on policies in other domains. Releasing relevant information will not always lead to agreement of viewpoints. But it is likely to engender more realistic and well-informed public expectations and beliefs (Chan, 2014b).

In the parliamentary debate in February 2013, Prime Minister Lee Hsien Loong indicated that the Population White Paper will be reviewed nearer to 2020 as it was not possible to see too far ahead beyond 2020. But this means there are only a few years left to conduct studies or implement and evaluate initiatives to inform the review, as well as to engage the public.

The review of the White Paper is critical because population policies have many consequences. Politically, the population discussion and the resulting policies will form a large part of the basis of how people perceive and respond to the government, not only during elections but throughout the term of the government. But more importantly, major changes to population policies will have wide-ranging effects on people and society, including future generations of Singaporeans. The impact could be positive or negative, depending on the effectiveness of the changes. Therefore, what is really at stake for Singapore is not the future of any political party but the well-being of citizens and national interests of the country. That is why the review of the Population White Paper needs to be honest and genuine, taken seriously, and proceed constructively.

The contentious population debate that occurred after the release of the White Paper in January 2013 provides important lessons for future debates. The debate, like much public discussion on sensitive issues, was often polarised into false dichotomies. For example, it was counterproductive when the population problem was framed as a contest between population increase and decrease, or pro- and anti-foreigner intake. The fact is no one was seriously saying that Singapore does not need foreigners or that Singapore needs anyone and everyone. Most Singaporeans recognise the need to have foreigners augment the core local workforce in order to have a vibrant economy. Policy-makers also understand the limits on population growth imposed by infrastructure and understand the importance of maintaining social harmony, and the challenges to integration and resilience from a huge influx of foreigners.

So no one is really arguing for the extremes. Criticising or admonishing the other side as such, and doing so at a regular and default response whenever alternative views are presented, is a sure conversation stopper. Moreover, it will likely create reactions of disappointment, anger and distrust which only serve to increase confirmatory bias thinking on both sides.

The real issue is how many foreigners, and which groups, does Singapore really need and how many can Singapore take in to be sustainable. Sustainability is about a strong and resilient economy, but it is also about liveability and quality of life. Singapore needs to address policy issues on efficient and effective land use, quality of infrastructure, work-life balance, active ageing, distribution of wealth generated through foreigner inflow, opportunities for citizens, and fair treatment of locals and foreigners whether they are low-wage workers or high-salaried professionals.

With more effective population, economic and social policies working in an integrative manner, and with more engaged communities, it is possible to move away from the unhealthy heavy reliance on large foreigner inflows. If the fundamentals are right, it should be possible to reduce foreigner inflow but increase its quality, and address issues of an ageing population and shrinking workforce.

Singapore's population policies are not inherently flawed. Many economic and social fundamentals in population matters have been taken care of. But policies can certainly be improved to yield more good. If a whole-of-society approach is adopted, Singaporeans can be confident that population challenges can be tackled. They will have hope that their goals and aspirations can be achieved, and be optimistic that the future will be better. Resilience develops when they recover from adversity and adapt to changes. This positivity mindset among Singaporeans, consisting of efficacy beliefs, hope, optimism and resilience, will build psychological capital in Singapore.

When the Population White Paper is reviewed, the debate should not be déjà vu for Singaporeans. It need not be driven by political correctness or populist concerns. Everyone gains from paying attention to policy content, public communication and psychological capital.

However, good intentions to enhance policy content, public communications and psychological capital do not necessarily translate into the desired outcomes. In fact, when one is convicted of a clear end goal and committed to a means to achieving it but the means is ineffective or maladaptive, effort and perseverance will lead to unintended negative outcomes. Hence, it is important for the policy-maker or social scientist to be well-equipped with an adaptive conceptual toolbox for analysing social issues. I propose such a toolbox. It contains a strategic focus and principled approach as well as contextualised modes of thinking. These conceptual tools could potentially facilitate the analyst to obtain good understanding of social issues and effective ways of addressing them.

A multifaceted strategic focus and principled approach

I first proposed the strategic focus and principled approach in the context of examining emergent group differences associated with changing population demographics (Chan, 2015b). The approach, however, is applicable to various social issues and it is not confined to population matters. There are five aspects in this multifaceted approach.

First, we need to think about the social issue in terms of its strategic social futures by specifying the new dimensions of the issue that could exist in the future. For example, if the social issue is about differences among various distinct nationality groups within the existing foreigner population in Singapore, then a possible strategic social future would be the new group differences that could emerge in the future foreigner population in Singapore and possible social divides that could occur. There is much to learn from the strategic futures thinking that the government has adopted for the country's water supply. The government thought about various scenarios concerning water supply and made plans well ahead into the future. This has led to very positive outcomes for Singapore's current and future state of affairs with regard to water supply. The scenario and strategic futures thinking involve both prevention and promotion approaches, where we thought about and planned for various negative consequences that could occur and also various positive outcomes to aspire to. The complexity and interdependency of social issues make it all the more important for the social analyst (i.e., social scientist or policy-maker) to adopt a strategic social futures thinking on how various population profiles and dynamics could impact group differences and social cohesion in Singapore in different ways.

In almost all social issues, it involves individuals as members of one or more groups and intergroup relations. A second aspect of strategic focus is to move beyond thinking of an individual as a member of a single group (e.g., race) and to think in terms of the individual's multiple social identities in a dynamic way. This is based on social and behavioural research which requires some elaboration.

Social identity is the part of an individual's self-concept derived from perceived membership in a social group (Tajfel & Turner, 1986). People possess multiple social identities corresponding to their social group memberships (e.g., nationality, ethnicity and religion), and these identities may vary in strength. Different identities can be activated in different situations. Individuals from different groups may differ in the weights and priority which they assign to their different social identities. Since social identities influence the way an individual thinks, feels and acts, they are primary drivers of behavioural manifestations of group differences. Social identities can be potentially unifying or divisive forces through their direct impact on cognition and emotion, which in turn influence individual and intergroup behaviours.

Research has shown that different social identities in an individual can be activated in different situations. Therefore, it is important to think about the coexistence of multiple social identities in an individual (e.g., race, religion and nationality) in terms of activation-in-context rather than in terms of competition between different identities leading to dilution in each identity. In managing intergroup relations and designing policy interventions, it is useful to examine how different social identities can be activated by various contexts to prevent intergroup conflict and enhance intergroup understanding and cooperation through commonalities or complementarity of social identities. This dynamic way of construing multiple identities is more productive than the traditional static way of categorising individuals according to fixed group membership. For example, a Singaporean and a foreigner in Singapore each has multiple social identities, some of which are common while others are different between the two individuals. Depending on which social identities are activated for each and both of them, they may experience and exhibit commonalities, complementary differences or contradicting differences.

This leads to the third aspect of my proposed strategic approach. I propose that when tackling social issues in Singapore, especially those involving interpersonal or intergroup relations, we use the concept of what I called "home-in-community" as a building block of Singapore society. This concept will facilitate discussions on commitment, social cohesion and local–foreigner relations. It could also help integrate Singapore's goal to be a global city and the goal to maintain and enhance national cohesion, so that Singapore remains vibrant and cohesive as a "city-in-a-country" (Chan, 2014c).

The concept of "home-in-community" applies to all people in Singapore. For example, a whole-of-society approach involving not just the government, but also the people and private sectors, should be used to enhance integration and community development through social interaction, mutual help and volunteerism. In this way, Singaporeans can feel a strong sense of belonging, national identity and rootedness to the country. Permanent residents can see the community as their current second home, with the potential and prospect of making Singapore their first home by becoming citizens. Non-resident foreigners can see the community as a good transient home away from home — one that is attractive to work and play in but also worthy enough for them to contribute to.

The fourth aspect of my proposed approach to social issues is about the need to be rooted in shared values and core principles that people can all agree to adopt as a country and society (Chan, 2013g). Values are convictions of what is important and beliefs of what ought to be. For example, if people agree on the core values of integrity, fairness and social harmony, they will have a common basis and guiding goals for discussing issues, negotiating differences and resolving conflicts between groups. To translate these abstract values into concrete policy and public actions, the people will need to agree on core guiding principles such as rule of law, accountability and "people-centricity".

The final aspect of the strategic focus and principled approach is that it must be evidence-based. This requires the social analyst to be more scientifically defensible and well-informed when conducting research and interpreting results reported from empirical studies. I will illustrate with two examples of simplistic treatment of group differences — one on the use of singular grouping of individuals and the other on the use of group mean scores.

In Singapore, the CMIO model — which distinguishes Singaporeans into Chinese, Malay, Indian and Others — is used to group individuals based on ethnicity for many social-political purposes. For example, the CMIO model is used to determine which language constitutes the mother tongue of a student in school. It is used to set racial quota for residency in public housing to prevent formation of racial enclaves and promote integration. The model is also used to specify a necessary criterion that at least one individual in the group of potential candidates contesting an election in a Group Representation Constituency (GRC) must be of Malay, Indian or another non-Chinese race, which enshrines racial minority representation in parliament.

However, the CMIO model does not adequately reflect the complex realities of how people perceive themselves and one another, especially with regard to local–foreigner perceptions. For example, based on the CMIO model, both PRC Chinese foreigners (i.e., ethnic Chinese who are citizens of the People's Republic of China) and new Singapore citizens who were PRC Chinese nationals are classified in the same Chinese ethnic category as Chinese Singaporeans who have grown up in Singapore or lived here for many years. While belonging to the same ethnic category according to CMIO classification, Chinese Singaporeans are clearly distinguishable from PRC Chinese foreigners and naturalised citizens in terms of some cultural beliefs, values, attitudes, norms, habits and perceptions. Moreover, PRC Chinese themselves are not a homogeneous group given the immense cultural diversity across different regions of origin in China. Such "within-PRC Chinese" differences create new layers of complexity.

The cultural differences among the various groups within the same ethnic classification are likely to result in important group differences in how they behave and react to the same situation. When not adequately managed, these practical group differences could lead to violations of expectations, misunderstanding and conflicts, which in turn threaten intergroup relations and social cohesion. Using the same ethnic category (e.g., Chinese) as a basis for policies (e.g., ethnic-based self-help groups) and predictions of behaviour is unlikely to achieve the desired goal. Instead, it is likely to lead to negative unintended consequences because important actual group differences are masked when individuals from these different groups are classified together into the same ethnic category.

Challenges similar to the issues on ethnicity also apply to the classification of individuals into religious groups. Religious customs and practices differ between distinct communities which could occur even within the same religion. These differences can sometimes alienate people or lead to conflicts between people who possess differing beliefs or between locals and foreigners who are unfamiliar with the religious landscape in Singapore. As with the CMIO model, the current classification of the major religions in Singapore does not capture the complexities and heterogeneity within the same religion. Failing to adequately manage differences that are rooted in religious group identities will threaten intergroup relations and social cohesion.

The second example of simplistic treatment of group differences is the use of group mean scores. Policy deliberations and public discourse on survey findings have focused almost exclusively on the comparison of mean scores between groups. Two groups can have an identical mean score but differ greatly in their patterns of within-group dispersion of scores. It is the pattern of dispersion (or within-group variance) that provides information on the dynamics of within-group differences such as whether there is high agreement, high disagreement or polarisation of attitudes within the group. It is possible for three groups to differ substantively, with each uniquely exhibiting one of these three within-group patterns and yet all three groups having an identical group mean score. The exclusive focus on mean scores and failure to consider between-group differences in within-group variances will miss important group differences and result in misleading inferences from the data (Chan, 1998a).

In conclusion, using the example of issues involving group differences in Singapore, there is much more about a social issue than the traditional social analysis approach (e.g., directly comparing the difference between two groups on a variable) can describe and explain. There are many layers of complexity that the social analyst needs to understand and address. Given the complexity, uncertainty and rapid changes associated with many social issues in Singapore such as those related to population challenges, as well as the criticality of the consequences of policy and public actions in these issues, the policy-maker and social scientist need to adopt a strategic focus and principled approach for examining the issues in research, policy and practice contexts.

Contextualised modes of thinking

Modes of thinking refer to the different conceptual ways of representing or construing social issues in terms of the nature of the interrelationships linking the issues or variables involved. These conceptual differences are important because it implies different understandings which in turn drive the way one interprets, argues or acts with regard to the social issues. In my proposed toolbox, there are three contextualised modes of thinking which are characterised by different types of context sensitivities. They are distinguished from the conventional modes of thinking about social issues which do not focus on the specific contexts. The three modes of thinking are 1) criticality thinking that focuses on the practical context, 2) paradoxical thinking that focuses on the integrative context and 3) dynamic thinking that focuses on the temporal context.

Criticality thinking is a mode of thinking that represents and solves problems in social issues by understanding and addressing the matter in its practical context. I have previously discussed this by making the distinction between complexity and what I called "criticality" (Chan, 2015c). When the government interfaces with people on complex issues such as demographic challenges, economic restructuring or local–foreigner relations, it is important to understand what is really critical in the particular context and address what really matters to the people.

Take, for example, the public communication on matters relating to economic growth and foreign manpower. Most people can grasp the idea that Singapore needs to increase the economic pie, and the idea that Singapore's limited local workforce means we have to be open to foreign labour. Therefore, the key communication problem is *not* about failing to explain the need for economic growth and foreign manpower in a way that the public can understand. Instead, the critical question is what matters to Singaporeans in these issues. For example, many Singaporeans may want to know how an enlarged economic pie will be equitably distributed and how it gets translated into actual benefits for citizens. Probably many more are concerned with the quantity or quality of the foreigner inflow.

A public communication or debate on population policy and foreign manpower that delves into the complexities of the economic issues could upset many Singaporeans. This is because they may feel the government is focused on defending its policies and does not understand their needs and problems. Consistent with the variety of psychological research literature showing the power that ego-involved issues have on human cognitive processing or emotional experiences (e.g., Tesser, 1988), Singaporeans are less interested in the complexity of the issue, and care more for what is critical to them. So, in the population debate involving issues on economic growth and foreigners, what matter to Singaporeans are answers to questions on how their life would improve with growth and how having more foreigners would affect them in terms of their job, housing, use of public spaces and facilities, and also the opportunities and quality of life for their children.

If people care most for what is critical to their lives, and less for the big-picture complexity of an issue, then the government has to adapt the way it relates to and communicates with the people. The focus has to be on understanding and addressing the people's concerns and aspirations. Therefore, it is important to have empathy and show it, as opposed to focus on presenting the same or even more complex arguments. Research in the behavioural sciences has shown that people may believe in the leader or be more willing to accept a difficult change if they think the leader understands and empathises with their situation. In addition, empathy can help repair a trust violation or address unfairness, whether it is actual or perceived.

Paradoxical thinking is a mode of thinking that endorses two seemingly contradictory views at the same time, but nonetheless produces a solution that is aligned with both views (Chan, 2014e). Its conventional counterpart is dichotomous thinking, which is a qualitatively different way of representing and approaching problems.

When there are two seemingly opposing positions or dimensions, it is common for people to see conflict. However, in many situations, the conflict can be resolved by adopting a paradoxical approach that embraces the two seemingly opposing dimensions. This can produce an outcome that is better than choosing one over the other. When the policy-maker or social scientist does so, he or she can unlock creativity in social analysis or produce policy innovation.

The paradoxical approach is helpful in looking at policies that aim to encourage certain behaviours. Take, for example, the Ministry of Education (MOE) Edusave Character Award which gives cash awards to students with good character and values. When it was announced in 2012, it attracted a lot of negative attention. Many people construed the award as one that gives "cash for values". By giving a financial incentive for good behaviour, the argument goes, the award is robbing students of intrinsic motivation to do good. This is a very common dichotomy, in which people distinguish between incentives and intrinsic motivation to foster desirable behaviour.

Incentive-based policies originate from a dependence on financial incentives to influence behaviours. Financial incentives for parenthood and tax rebates for donation to charities are clear examples. When applied appropriately, financial incentives can have powerful desired effects. But scientific research has shown that an over-reliance on financial incentives to influence a behaviour or decision to engage in an activity will lead to unintended negative effects. For example, giving money or an external reward for engaging in an independently enjoyable activity can reduce the intrinsic motivation and interest in the activity. It can also cast doubt on the intentions for altruistic behaviours because the financial incentive can now be associated with the motivation to act. Most people believe that altruism should be based on non-monetary motivations and values such as compassion and justice. That was why there was a public outcry over the Edusave Character Award. The public focus was on the issue of motivation. But in fact, MOE had introduced the award to signal that non-academic excellence in the areas of student leadership, character and values is of equal importance as academic excellence. The Edusave Character Award was meant to complement the Edusave Scholarship, which also gives cash awards — but for good academic performance. MOE's reasoning was: If cash awards are given to reward students for academic performance, why should not cash awards also be given to recognise good behaviour and character? Unfortunately, that point was lost on many, who view the issue as one of motivation and objected to the use of a financial incentive.

A paradoxical approach would integrate the seemingly opposing views of giving incentives and fostering intrinsic motivation. MOE could stipulate that the cash award for good character and values is given to the student as a form of recognition. It could then let the student independently decide what charitable causes or types of leadership development activities he or she wishes to spend the money on. This retains the signalling and recognition functions of the award, without turning the incentive into a pure monetary reward that is seen as an external driver of behaviour. At the same time, it focuses on the dimension of the student's intrinsic motivation and creates more opportunities for the student to engage in altruistic activities and develop leadership skills. These benefit the community and can have positive multiplier effects. This lets the financial incentive (the cash award) reinforce intrinsic motivation.

In recent years, there have been serious attempts from policy-makers in Singapore to better understand public sentiments and citizen needs. Also, there has been much effort devoted to encourage positive behaviours. But the different dimensions of needs and motivations that have emerged often create tensions. When tensions occur, it is important to recognise that not all difficult policy decisions involve zero-sum trade-offs. When a policy can embrace opposing views, the outcome can be more effective than a policy that chooses one view over another.

As a mode of thinking, the paradoxical approach is a potentially powerful conceptual tool for reconciling many long-standing conflicts from apparent contradictions. For example, I have applied paradoxical thinking to the analysis of social issues involving the development of positivity among Singaporeans. One way to foster positive attitudes is to involve people in identifying problems and generating solutions. This means giving people a real voice to express comments and ideas. A real voice means there must be genuine listening and openness to the possibility of change on the part of the listeners. An effective leader regards such views as important inputs when diagnosing problems and generating solutions. They are not regarded as mere noise or hurdles that must be cleared in decision-making. Of course, people should also be accountable for what they say, and put forward their views responsibly and reasonably.

If people do not have a voice or they conclude that their voices are not being heard, it produces angst and leads to a polarisation of attitudes. Negative attitudes will therefore develop. But when active participants have a voice, and the issues are discussed openly, constructive action follows.

Thus, paradoxically, voices and actions do not have to contradict. A paradoxical approach will treat voices and actions not only as compatible, but as complementing and reinforcing one another. For example, experiences from helping others motivate people to speak up, and having a real voice can lead them to take action to improve society.

When a paradoxical mode of thinking is applied to actions and voices, it contributes to the discussion of the evolving democracy in Singapore. Recently, Minister for Culture, Community and Youth, Lawrence Wong, highlighted the importance of Singapore being a "problem-solving democracy" and how it should be — in the words of late Mr S. Rajaratnam, one of the nation's pioneer leaders — a "democracy of deeds, and not words" (Wong, 2014). Deeds are actions to improve society. But voices are not merely words that speak softer than actions. Together, voices and actions solve problems. So, to me, to be a problem-solving democracy, Singapore should be a "democracy of deeds and voices". The combination of deeds and voices will lead to real improvements in society and people's quality of life — not just for people who are helped but also for those who step forward to give voice and take action. This will help build goodwill and trust between all the parties involved.

As involvement in deeds and voices expands, democracy in Singapore will mature when people are able to make decisions in more areas of their lives and then implement those decisions. In this way, people will take ownership of the decisions. They will feel responsible for seeing those decisions implemented, and will be more willing to help solve any problems that might arise. People will move away from a "blame mentality" to a problem-solving mindset. They will appreciate that while things cannot be perfect, they can be improved. They will effect positive change. Over time, people-centric involvement in deeds and voices will help foster a positivity mindset. As explained earlier in the chapter, a Singaporean mindset comprising efficacy beliefs, hope, optimism and resilience will build psychological capital in Singapore.

The final tool in my proposed adaptive conceptual toolbox is dynamic thinking, which focuses on the temporal context of the social issues and how the issue or its associated variables may change over time. This can be examined at the macro- or micro-level of analysis.

At the macro-level, dynamic thinking refers to the need to adopt a temporal perspective when approaching social issues. When we fail to recognise the situation as a snapshot in a process of changes over time in the Singapore society, we will be more likely to misread the situation and make decisions that are maladaptive — and this applies to the individual, the community and the government.

At the micro-level of analysis, dynamic thinking is more complicated and requires some elaboration. Take, for example, a social issue variable such as trust or fairness perception. A linear increase or decrease in the variable is only one of multiple distinct ways in which the variable can change over time. For example, changes over time may be non-linear representing reversibility in the direction of change. Alternatively, the change over time may be qualitative in nature such that the underlying construct is no longer comparable from one time point to another.

Qualitative changes over time are important but often neglected in social analysis such as longitudinal assessment of changes in social attitudes. Take, for example, Singaporeans' attitudes towards three specific foreign nationality groups. Instead of simply tracking the attitudes towards each group over time, one could hypothesise a specific pattern of qualitative change where Singaporeans' attitudes towards the three foreign nationality groups undergo changes in the nature of the attitudinal structure. The attitudes may begin as three differentiated and uncorrelated perceptions corresponding to the three distinct nationality groups. Over time, due to specific systematic changes in circumstances, the distinct perceptions may become increasingly correlated and eventually they integrated into a single perception representing a global attitude towards foreigners that are undifferentiated by the three specific nationalities. In other words, while the term "foreigner" may not be initially meaningful to the Singaporean without specifying the nationality, the term "foreigner" has, over time, acquired a meaning on its own. This type of qualitative changes over time can be used to conceptualise and assess the dynamics of intergroup perceptions and relations associated with socialisation or stereotyping processes.

It is beyond the scope of this chapter to discuss technical details of the conceptual and assessment issues involving different types of changes over time, which are available in Chan (1998b). It would suffice here to emphasise that policy-makers and social scientists need to pay more attention to the multifaceted nature of changes over time when they measure and interpret longitudinal studies that track social cognition, attitudes or behaviours over time. Failing to do so will lead to misleading inferences and recommendations that run counter to empirical facts. On the other hand, with an appropriate dynamic mode of thinking that explicitly incorporates the temporal context of the study variables, various types of changes in social issues can be more adequately described, interpreted and applied in practical use of the longitudinal findings.

Concluding remarks

On many social issues, the dynamics of changes over time are likely to get more complex but more important as Singapore undergoes rapid transformation in the next few decades. These changes would also need to be examined in their practical contexts of what is critical and matters most or more to Singaporeans. New conflicts and trade-offs are likely to occur more often but some apparent contradictions may be turned into commonalities and complementarities using paradoxical modes of thinking and problem-solving.

As Singapore moves forward to tackle new challenges and achieve new aspirations, it becomes more important to better understand and address various social issues. This, I believe, requires new modes of thinking on the part of social scientists and policy-makers, accompanied by the adoption of a strategic focus and principled approach. The need is particularly relevant and urgent for tackling social and behavioural issues that will arise with the dramatic changes to way of life that could occur as Singapore transforms into a "Smart Nation" that harnesses the advantages of technology and big data to enhance quality of life. Social issues must be adequately understood and addressed, so that the impending transformation will significantly impact the ways people live, work, play and learn in a positive way. To build Singapore's adaptive capabilities in handling rapid and novel changes in social issues, it will require much more than acquiring technical computing skills for big data analytics. I believe that one of the capability-building strategies should involve equipping social scientists and policy-makers with an adaptive conceptual toolbox for social analysis and policy action.

I will conclude on a personal note. As I was completing the final page of this chapter in the early morning hours on Monday, 23 March 2015, the Prime Minister's Office announced on its website that Singapore's Former Prime Minister Mr Lee Kuan Yew had passed away peacefully at 3.18 am at the Singapore General Hospital. As Singapore mourns the death of Mr Lee Kuan Yew, our grief is accompanied by deep gratitude to a great man who has devoted his adult life to the service of our nation. It is because of Mr Lee and his pioneer team that today, we share the core values of meritocracy, multiracialism, incorruptibility and self-reliance. As some grapple with the thought of what Singapore would be like without Mr Lee, we can be optimistic about the country's future. This is because he put in place institutions and values to ensure that Singapore continues to thrive without depending on any one individual. Our best tribute to him is to build a democracy of deeds and voices — to do what is right and to speak up for what we believe in.

References

Chan, D. (1998a). Functional Relations among Constructs in the Same Content Domain at Different Levels of Analysis: A Typology of Composition Models. *Journal of Applied Psychology*, 83(2), 234–246.

Chan, D. (1998b). The Conceptualization of Change over Time: An Integrative Approach Incorporating Longitudinal Means and Covariance Structures Analysis (LMACS) and Multiple Indicator Latent Growth Modeling (MLGM). *Organizational Research Methods*, 1(4), 421–483.

Chan, D. (2011a, October 27). Drill into What Makes Singaporeans Happy. *The Straits Times*, p. A25.

Chan, D. (2011b, November 9). Fairness: Processes as Important as Outcomes. *The Straits Times*, p. A30.

Chan, D. (2012a, May 10). The Heart of the Immigration Debate. *The Straits Times*, p. A31.

Chan, D. (2012b, June 15). The 5C Challenges of Cohesion. *The Straits Times*, p. A28.

Chan, D. (2012c, June 16). Five Cs to Manage Integration. *The Straits Times*, p. A40–41.

Chan, D. (2012d, August 28). The Goals Matter, So Does the Journey. *The Straits Times*, p. A22.

Chan, D. (2012e, November 28). Singaporeans' Well-being: It's Not Just About Emotions. *The Straits Times*, p. A24.

Chan, D. (2013a, February 4). Population Priorities and Perceptions. *The Straits Times*, p. A21.

Chan, D. (2013b, June 26). Break the Negative Spiral over the Haze. *The Straits Times*, p. A23.

Chan, D. (2013c, August 14). Taking Steps to Raise Social Mobility in S'pore. *The Straits Times*, p. A26.

Chan, D. (2013d, August 20). Sustainability Is Key. *The Straits Times*, p. A21.

Chan, D. (2013e, September 28). Trust Is a Many-Splendoured Thing. *The Straits Times*, p. A38.

Chan, D. (2013f, November 16). The Art of Disagreeing — It Can Yield Some Good. *The Straits Times*, p. A40.

Chan, D. (2013g, December 28). From Emotions to Shared Values. *The Straits Times*, p. A26.

Chan, D. (2014a). Emerging Themes in Adaptability Research. In D. Chan (ed.), *Individual Adaptability to Changes at Work: New Directions in Research* (pp. 177–192). NY: Routledge.

Chan, D. (2014b, February 19). Moving Forward with Great Expectations. *The Straits Times*, p. A20.

Chan, D. (2014c, April 5). Strike the Right Balance to Make Singapore a "City in a Country". *The Straits Times*, p. A40.

Chan, D. (2014d, June 7). Democracy of Deeds and Voices. *The Straits Times*, p. A42.

Chan, D. (2014e, August 23). A Paradoxical Approach to Policymaking. *The Straits Times*, p. A38.

Chan, D. (2014f, October 18). Why Bronze Medallists Are Happier than Silver Winners. *The Straits Times*, p. A42.

Chan, D. (2014g, December 6). Values, Outrage and the Good Society in 2014. *The Straits Times*, p. A40.

Chan, D. (2015a). *People Matter: Essays from David Chan*. Singapore: World Scientific.

Chan, D. (2015b). Approaches to Emergent Group Differences. In M. Mathew, C. Gee & W. F. Chiang (eds.), *Singapore Perspectives 2014: Differences* (pp. 41–50). Singapore: World Scientific.

Chan, D. (2015c, January 24). It Takes Two to Tango, and Progress. *The Straits Times*, p. A42.

Chan, D., Elliott, J., Koh, G., Kong, L., Nair, S., Tan, E. S., Wee, A. & Yeoh, B. (2014). Social Capital and Development. In M. Yap & C. Gee (eds.), *Population Outcomes: Singapore 2050*. IPS Exchange Series, 1 May 2014.

Heng, S. K. (2014). Dialogue with the Minister for Education, Heng Swee Keat. In M. Mathew, C. Gee & W. F. Chiang (eds.), *Singapore Perspectives 2014: Differences* (pp. 79–103). Singapore: World Scientific.

Lee, H. L. (2012, June 16). Comments on the 5C Challenges of Cohesion and Five Cs to Manage Integration. Retrieved 24 March 2015, from https://www.facebook.com/leehsienloong.

Ministry of National Development (MND) (2013). *A High Quality Living Environment for All Singaporeans: Land Use Plan to Support Singapore's Future Population*. Singapore.

National Population and Talent Division (NPTD) (2013). *Population White Paper: A Sustainable Population for a Dynamic Singapore*. Prime Minister's Office, Singapore.

Singapore Parliament Reports (2013, February 8). *Speech by Prime Minister Lee Hsien Loong*. Parliament no. 12, Session no. 1, Volume 90, Sitting no. 6. Motion: A Sustainable Population for a Dynamic Singapore.

Tajfel, H. & Turner, J. C. (1986). The Social Identity Theory of Inter-group Behaviour. In S. Worchel & L. W. Austin (eds.), *Psychology of Intergroup Relations*. Chicago: Nelson-Hall.

Tesser, A. (1988). Toward a Self-evaluation Maintenance Model of Social Behavior. In L. Berkowitz (ed.), *Advances in Experimental Social Psychology, 21: Social Psychological Studies of the Self: Perspectives and Programs* (pp. 181–227). San Diego, CA, US: Academic Press.

Wong, L. (2014, June 3). Towards a "Problem-solving Democracy". *The Straits Times*. Retrieved 24 March 2015, from http://news.asiaone.com/news/singapore/towards-%E2%80%98problem-solving-democracy%E2%80%99.

World Scientific Series on Singapore's 50 Years of Nation-Building

Forthcoming (continued from page ii)

50 Years of Malay-Muslim Community
edited by Zainul Abidin Rasheed (Former President, Singapore Islamic Religious Council, Singapore)

50 Years of Materials Science
edited by Freddy Boey (Nanyang Technological University, Singapore), Subramanian Venkatraman (Nanyang Technological University, Singapore) and B.V.R. Chowdari (National University of Singapore, Singapore)

The Singapore Research Story
edited by Hang Chang Chieh (National University of Singapore, Singapore) and Low Teck Seng (National Research Foundation, Singapore)

50 Years of Science
edited by Lim Hock (National University of Singapore, Singapore), Bernard Tan (National University of Singapore, Singapore) and K.K. Phua (World Scientific Publishing Company, Singapore, and Imperial College Press, London)

Perspectives on the Security of Singapore: The First 50 Years
edited by Barry Desker and Ang Cheng Guan (S. Rajaratnam School of International Studies, Nanyang Technological University, Singapore)

50 Years of Singapore–China Relations
edited by Zheng Yongnian and John Wong (National University of Singapore, Singapore)

50 Years of Singapore–Europe Relations
edited by Yeo Lay Hwee (European Union Centre, Singapore)

50 Years of Singapore and the United Nations
edited by Tommy Koh (Ministry of Foreign Affairs, Singapore)

50 Years of Technical Education
edited by N. Varaprasad (Institute of Applied Technology, Abu Dhabi, United Arab Emirates)

50 Years of Transportation
edited by Fwa Tien Fang (National University of Singapore, Singapore)

50 Years of Urban Planning
edited by Heng Chye Kiang (National University of Singapore, Singapore)